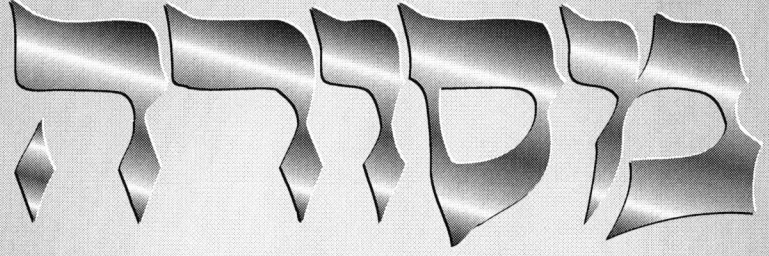

ArtScroll® Series

Rabbi Nosson Scherman / Rabbi Meir Zlotowitz
General Editors

Joseph H. Weiss Family Edition

MARAN HARAV OVADIA

*The Revered Gaon and Posek
Who Restored the Crown of Sephardic Jewry*

BY
RABBI YEHUDA HEIMOWITZ

Published by
ArtScroll®
Mesorah Publications, ltd

FIRST EDITION
First Impression ... May 2014

Published and Distributed by
MESORAH PUBLICATIONS, LTD.
4401 Second Avenue / Brooklyn, N.Y 11232

Distributed in Europe by
LEHMANNS
Unit E, Viking Business Park
Rolling Mill Road
Jarow, Tyne & Wear, NE32 3DP
England

Distributed in Australia and New Zealand
by **GOLDS WORLDS OF JUDAICA**
3-13 William Street
Balaclava, Melbourne 3183
Victoria, Australia

Distributed in Israel by
SIFRIATI / A. GITLER — BOOKS
Moshav Magshimim
Israel

Distributed in South Africa by
KOLLEL BOOKSHOP
Northfield Centre, 17 Northfield Avenue
Glenhazel 2192, Johannesburg, South Africa

**ARTSCROLL® SERIES
MARAN HARAV OVADIA**
© Copyright 2014, by MESORAH PUBLICATIONS, Ltd.
4401 Second Avenue / Brooklyn, N.Y. 11232 / (718) 921-9000 / www.artscroll.com

---

ALL RIGHTS RESERVED
The text, prefatory and associated textual contents and introductions
— including the typographic layout, cover artwork and ornamental graphics —
have been designed, edited and revised as to content, form and style.

No part of this book may be reproduced
IN ANY FORM, PHOTOCOPYING, OR COMPUTER RETRIEVAL SYSTEMS
— **even for personal use without written permission from
the copyright holder, Mesorah Publications Ltd.**
except by a reviewer who wishes to quote brief passages
in connection with a review written for inclusion in magazines or newspapers.

THE RIGHTS OF THE COPYRIGHT HOLDER WILL BE STRICTLY ENFORCED.

ISBN 10: 1-4226-1496-4 / ISBN 13: 978-1-4226-1496-9

Typography by CompuScribe at ArtScroll Studios, Ltd.
Printed in the United States of America.
Bound by Sefercraft, Quality Bookbinders, Ltd., Brooklyn N.Y. 11232

*I*t is a privilege to dedicate this biography of one of the greatest Gedolei Hador of our era in honor of our beloved children

Mendel and Tamar Zaks **Avi and Aviva Pifko**
Mendy and Michal Rovner **Chaim and Rivky Weiss**
David and Esther Weiss **Daniel Weiss**

*M*aran Harav Ovadia Yosef זצ״ל embodied an incredible multitude of virtues. Though he knew *kol haTorah kulah*, his thirst for learning remained unquenchable. Especially meaningful to us was his love for all segments of Klal Yisrael.

He dedicated himself to spreading the word of Hashem and unifying all Jews under the banner of Torah. Our children live with this ideal. We are proud that the Torah is their road map and that they respect the holiness of all our brethren, whatever their origin or *nusach*.

There are no second-class Jews.
כל ישראל בני מלכים הם

May this magnificent volume inspire multitudes to follow the ways of Maran, and may it be a *z'chut* for us, our children, and grandchildren.

Joseph H. and Miriam F. Weiss

מכתב ברכה • Approbation

Yitzchak Yosef
Rishon Lezion Chief Rabbi Of Israel
President of the Great Rabbinical Court

יצחק יוסף
ראשון לציון הרב הראשי לישראל
נשיא בית הדין הרבני הגדול

בס"ד י"א אייר תשע"ג

ב"ה

הנה לפנינו דפי גלנות הספר "עין הרע ומידה", אודות הנפלאות של עין
הרע ועל פתרון מהו עדדיו יכול לצבי הלב, ונהפך הנעטת להטב, ודבר
בעתו מה טוב "והמבין ויאמין" כי כל האמת המוחר ספרים של ספרי אמוני,
מדקדקים ככל ברמיו עלום להתקרב את אלושים ופעולותיו מן ולב.

הלוא ונעים טובה לגולה, "אנציקלופדיה-מטודה", שאחד על כמה קטלוגי
אילו ספר גם רגילים, וילון על דרכי הדר ב' מאיר הכהן, והד' נח שולדן
פישר, שכתב הדרך התיר דיקא רכוילת ספרי רמ"ח ותריצ"ו, ערוכה ואמור
כדי להבין את הדרך, את חדו אל, אישר הפל לעליונו.

וכהדר לכוונת מבטאי של רבא יאתא, כי התאמת לשחמת לעולם דוייון,
דחזקיהו שיוד תלי"ו, וסבי חדש למטרה יעיל הגולה לכיל מחינות ראינו
וצשו, ועוד למחות סיפורי מופסיק, וזל ויבי ה"ו וחניותו שלא נשכנו, כי אל
עלינו למחומר דקא עלות אם מעשרים שלומו חכ"ם זילוי לוצור הנחמה, ואל הטוב
יבין, והאמינו ואני להכחות אלוקי פעל הקורא ועפולתיה, ולא כסנונו של מן שלומנו
בצבקן. וכבר האלוננו רגא רפסי, "בלוא לך תודה" והגדרון אלה מחפלותיו כפי אפן.

ויהיה נה לעילוי הדרין.

אחתי לעוסקים וקדמים, שקיו לפעות עם הרו"ת,
ויכולן לעיתות התורה ותלמידה בקין, ועתדרה חנילי לתורה

לחתמה, מתוך נחת ואונה, לשלוה ויטיב ויוצר חיים.

ברכת התורה והחיים

מכתב ברכה • Approbation

הרב דוד יוסף
ראש בית המדרש "יחוה דעת" וחבר מועצת חכמי התורה

ב"ה ירושלים, כ"א אייר, ל"ו לעומר למטמונים תשע"ד

אגרת ברכה

לכבוד הרבנים היקרים והחשובים, מזכי הרבים ומקימי עולה של תורה, העומדים בראש הארגון הגדול להפצת התורה **"ארטסקרול — מסורה"**, הרב **מאיר זלוטוביץ** שליט"א והרב **נתן שערמאן** שליט"א, שלום וישע רב.

הנני בא בשורות אלו להביע את הערכתי הגדולה אל מפעלכם הכביר וזכות הרבים הגדולה התלויה בכם בהפצת התורה בכל רחבי תבל, על ידי תרגום כל הש"ס בכמה שפות, ובלשון ברורה וביותר ובהסברה נכונה וישרה של כל פרט ופרט שבתלמוד ומפרשיו, ועל ידם זוכים רבים מאחב"י ללמוד בעיון את סוגיות הש"ס, ורבים זכו להתקרב ללימוד התורה ולאהבת התורה ע"י ספרים אלו, וזכות לימודם של אלפים ורבבות מאחבי"י תלויה בכם, ובנוסף על כך זכה **"ארטסקרול — מסורה"** להוציא לאור עוד ספרים רבים בכל מקצועות התורה, תורה נביאים וכתובים עם מפרשים, הנלמדים ע"י רבים מלומדי התורה, וע"י התלמידים והתלמידות במוסדות החינוך התורניים בארה"ב, ומזה כארבעים שנה שספרים אלו חדרו ללבות רבבות אלפי ישראל, ועוד ידכם נטויה להמשיך במפעל הגדול בהוצאה לאור של התלמוד הירושלמי, ושל המשניות, בכמה שפות, ועוד ועוד, יישר חילכם לאורייתא.

והנה בנוסף על כל הנ"ל נתתם אל לבכם להוציא לאור סדרת ספרים על תולדות חייהם של גדולי ישראל זצוק"ל, אשר כל הקורא אותם מתחזק באהבת התורה ובאהבת תלמידי חכמים, וספרים אלו מחדירים אמונת חכמים אמיתית, והוראת דרך חיים תוכחות מוסר, ושאיפה גדולה ועמוקה ללכת לאורם ולהיות עוסקים בתורה ועובדי השי"ת בכל לב.

והן עתה הנכם עומדים להוציא לאור ספר גדול על מסכת חייו ופעלו של אאמו"ר אביר הרועים, עטרת תפארת ישראל מרן הגאון רבי **עובדיה יוסף** זצוק"ל, אשר נכתב ע"י ידידי הדגול זך השכל והרעיון, מורנו חריף בעל פיפיות, משכיל נבון וחכם, הרב **יהודה הייממוביץ** שליט"א, אשר ליקט ואסף ובירר ביסודיות רבה פרטים ועובדות על גדלותו העצומה בתורה ושיטתו בפסק ההלכה, ועל מסירות נפשו למען הכלל והפרט, הן באלפי פסקיו בהלכה, ובמיוחד בחידוש ענינים שבספריו שו"ת **יביע אומר**, אשר לאורם הולכים רבים מהדיינים בכל רחבי תבל, ובהרבצת התורה בקרב אחב"י, ובמיוחד במפעלו הכביר בחייתו קבלת הוראות מרן הבית יוסף בקרב הספרדים ובני עדות המזרח בכל רחבי תבל, ולהחזיר עטרת תפארת יהדות ספרד ליושנה, ובקירוב כל אחד ואחד מישראל באהבה רבה, וזכה על ידי כך לקרב אלפים ורבבות לשמירת המצוות וללימוד התורה.

והנני מעיד בזה נאמנה כי מאחר שלדעתי ישנה תועלת מרובה וחיזוק גדול בתורה ויראת שמים לכלל ולפרט בידיעת ארחות חייו של מרן אאמו"ר זצוק"ל, הסכמתי לסייע בכל האפשר בעריכת הספר, למען ילמדו הקוראים דרך חיים תוכחות מוסר, וישבתי שעות ארוכות עם עורך הספר הנ"ל, ומסרתי אישית בידו הרבה עובדות והנהגות ממסכת חייו של מרן אאמו"ר זצוק"ל, אשר בחלקם הגדול היית"י עד להם באופן אישי, וחלקם שמעתי מכלי ראשון מפי מרן אאמו"ר זצוק"ל בעצמו, וזאת לאור השנים הרבות שזכיתי לעסוק בתורה"ק ביחד עמו, ולראות את דרכי הנהגתו בעבודת השי"ת.

והנני מתכבד לברך מקרב לב את כל העוזרים והמסייעים בהוצאת ספר זה לאור עולם, שהפץ ה' בידכם יצלח להוציא לאור עוד ספרים רבים בכל מקצועות התורה, מתוך בריאות איתנה ונהורא מעליא, ואורך ימים ושנות חיים ושובע שמחות וכל טוב סלה אמן.

בברכת התורה
ובידידות נאמנה

דוד יוסף

TABLE OF CONTENTS

Publisher's Preface   17
Author's Introduction and Acknowledgments   21

SECTION I: A CHARMING SON

1   Hashem's General   27
Fight for Life / Positivity, Nonetheless

2   A Blossom Emerges   39
A Turning Point in Baghdad / Parents of Royalty / What's in a Name? / Moving to Eretz Yisrael / Bnei Zion / A Tale of Two "Meetings" / The First Taste of Gemara / Rav Shlomo Abo / The Fateful Trip to Baghdad

3   Ben Porat Yosef   59
Short-Lived Enrollment / The Sole Sephardi Yeshiva / Meeting His Mentor / Like a Rishon / Late-Night Learning / Hacham Ezra's Offer / A Mother's Sacrifice / Bar Mitzva / His "Friend" / The Works of a Sixteen-Year-Old / The Talmud at His Fingertips

4   The Public Takes Note   83
Knowing His Place / First Shiurim / Many Mentors / "The Meishiv of the Next Generation" / Controlling the Spirit / Rheumatism: Not From the Mezuzah / Close-Knit Friends / New Friends in Hevron / Locked In / Building Ahavat HaTorah / The Audience Grows

5 Finding His Gem   111

The Fattal Family / What Did You Say? / "I Promise You Olam Haba" / A Wedding Under Curfew / Poor in Possessions; Rich in Torah / First Dayanut Position / New Skills / Tending to the Tefillin / Begging for Teshuva / The Family Begins to Grow

❧ SECTION 2: VICEROY IN EGYPT

6 Down to Egypt   129

A Crumbling Community / Convincing the Family / A Complex Community / Ahava V'Ahva / Under Constant Threat / The Suspicions Mount / The Next Frontier

7 A Dangerous Battle   149

The Battle Over the Microphone / No to the Church / Reforming Shehita / For the Love of Money / Unchecked Knives / The Saga of Shimon A. / A Course of Action / Catching Up

8 Exodus From Egypt   167

Retraction Under Threat / The Resignation Letter / Plagued With Doubt / Last-Ditch Efforts / In Limbo / The Basis for Teshuvot / The Vote / The Final Insult / Leaving Egypt / A Changed Man

❧ SECTION 3: A RISING STAR

9 Back Home   187

Where to Enroll? / Lifelong Friendships / The Rejected Position / Anything But Milah / An Official Dayan / The Four-Month Sefer / Halacha vs. Kabbala / Hizzuk From Rav Ezra / Disputing the Ben Ish Hai / Respect for the Ben Ish Hai / No Spot in Yerushalayim / Rav Rosenthal to the Rescue

10 Restoring the Crown   207

The Need for Unity / The Yibbum That Wasn't / Unifying Sephardic Jewry Under Maran / The Mara D'Atra / Restoring the Halachic Crown / What's in a Name? / Just One Element

11 Leader of a Renaissance   225

Sephardic Aliya / Filling the Void / "We Want a Story!" / Beginning of a Revolution / The Nightly Shiur / Yeshivat Ohr Torah / Unpaid Positions / No Shiur Too Small / No Kids, No Goats

12 For the Future of Klal Yisrael   247

Four Streams / The "Status Quo" / Exemption for Talmud Torahs / The Chinuch Atzmai System / The Battle for the Country's Future The Threat / For One Jewish Soul / The Visit Does the Trick / The Adopted Street Youth

13 The Home Front — 263
Seventeen Years in the Making / Yabia Omer / Wall-to-Wall Approbations / "I Couldn't Sleep All Night" / Spiritual Highs, Financial Lows / The Fire / Tragedy Strikes / Double Consolation / A Lifeline

14 In the Eim HaMoshavot — 277
A New Experience / "He Can't Help But Spread Torah" / Convinced by a Snake / Long-Term Investments / Secularization Becomes a Factor / Torah Law or Rabbinic Law? / Soft Skills / A Sudden Loss / Forgoing the Promotion

15 Return to My Father's Home — 289
My Friend, My Brother / Always Awake / Hundreds Come Streaming / The Rav on the Radio / The Beit Din HaGadol Calls / Appeals in Beit Din? / The Neighborhood Hessed Hub / Expansion on Two Levels

16 A Unique Relationship — 307
Respecting the Differences / Two Matmidim / The Timely Theft / Respecting Hacham Ovadia's Five Minutes / Who Took the Child for Stitches? / "I Was Afraid to Live Above Him!" / Learning Amid the Bombs / Mutual Love and Respect / The Longest Teshuva

⊰ SECTION 4: LEADER OF THE LAND

17 On the Big Stage — 325
Private Coronation / The Void in Tel Aviv / More Delays / "His Honor, the Chief Rabbi" / A Servant, Not a Master / Kashrut First / At the Helm of the Batei Din / Shiurim, Shiurim, Shiurim / Restoring Sephardic Psak / Sharing the Duties

18 Jewish Law vs. Jewish State — 345
The "Brother and Sister" Saga / Political Machinations / The "Heter" Is Revealed / Pledges and Expectations / Harav Ovadia Called to Arms / The Quandary

19 A Stunning Victory — 359
The Baba Sali's Blessing / The Candidate Sits Out the Campaign / The Outcome / "Halacha Is Not Determined at Dizengoff" / The Fallout / Taking It to the Courts / Halacha Is Not Plastic

20 The Father of Agunot — 371
Yom Kippur War Agunot / Nightly Sessions / The ID-Tag Heter / Other Forms of Evidence / Feeling the Pain of the Agunot / The World Trade Center Case / When HaKablan Closed Down / The "Other" Agunot / The Erev Yom Kippur Get / Heter Aguna Before Surgery / No Returns

21 At the Summit — 389
Strengthening the Rabbanut / Rav Zolty and Rav Mashash / Group Decisions / The Carmel-Mizrahi Question / Chicken Inoculations / Unwitting Consumers Take Precedence Over Flagrant Sinners / Entebbe in Halacha / Positivity Wins / Taking It to the Top / No Changes / Spiritual State of the State / Say No to TV / Slow Down! Under Fire / Term Extension and Term Limits

22 Shas: Actualizing a Dream — 415
Diverting the Vigor / A Shocking Victory / The True Purpose / The Numbers / Maayan HaHinuch HaTorani / El HaMaayan / Adult Education / Kiruv Infrastructure / Atzarot Teshuva / Devotion to the Masses / Back to Learning

SECTION 5: BELOVED BY HIS PEOPLE

23 Channeling the Gifts — 433
No Distractions / No Cutting Corners / The Ultimate Matmid / Pining for Each Word / Forcing Him to Eat / The Two-Minute Pictures / Torah on the Road / Making the Most of Shabbat / "I've Never Seen Anything Like It" / Deeply Engrossed / Rav Elyashiv's Long Visit / "Stop, Coward" / The Best Anesthetic / The Prime Minister Watches

24 One for the Books — 457
All Torah, Any Torah / High Ceilings, Not Location, Location, Location / Nothing Too Minor / "He Forgot Yosef" / Shocking Discoveries / Nothing Escapes a Halachic Worldview

25 A Memorable Memory — 469
Building the Database / From Memory for Months / Fourteen Sources at His Fingertips / Minute Details / 100 Percent Accuracy / Not Relying on Memory / "I'm Learning It Anew"

26 A Walking Miracle — 483
In the Merit of Torah / "It's on My Shoulders" / Ready for the Brit / The Scent of Gan Eden / The Walking Miracle

27 The Power of a Posek — 493
Koha D'Heteira / Knowledgeable, Not Flippant / No "Rabbinic Will, Rabbinic Way" / Hawk or Dove? / The "Minor" Matters / Kulot for Others, Humrot for Himself / No Visitors Allowed

28 A Visit With Maran — 505
Never Too Young / Investing in the Future / Feeling the Pain / One Life Leads to Another / Family Time / A Package From Home / Trips Abroad / Sweeping Success

29 Harav Ovadia Goes Abroad   **521**
The First Visit to America / According to the Audience / With President Reagan / The Rav Renders Honor / Shabbat in a Closet / Visits to Deal / Funding in Israel

30 A Legacy for the Ages   **531**
Teeming With Torah / Taking Responsibility / The Written Word / Halacha and Kashrut / A Living Torah / Exulting in Torah

31 Sunset   **543**
The Home of a Gadol / An Exhausting Schedule / Always Gracious / Losing a Son / Uniting Klal Yisrael Once More / Last Rays / Last Shabbat at Home / One Final Hope / Petira

Epilogue   **563**

Glossary   **565**

Photo Credits:

Rav Yitzchak Yosef
Yaakov Sasson/ Abir HaRo'im
Tzvi Jacobson
Rabbi Yitzchak Dwek
Eli Cobin/ Mishpacha Magazine
Mr. Avraham Elbaz

Abby Sanfield
Author of HaShakdan
Wikipedia
Israel Government Press office (231)
מרכז תיעוד הגליל העליון (318)

A Note on Transliteration
The transliteration in this volume generally follows the typical Sephardic pronunciation.

PUBLISHER'S PREFACE

IT IS A GREAT PRIVILEGE FOR US TO PUBLISH THIS biography of one of the greatest Torah scholars and leaders of our time. Maran Harav Ovadia Yosef זצ"ל revolutionized his era like few others. He devoted his life to Torah study, to teaching scholars and laymen alike, to writing his scores of Torah works, and to restoring the crown of Sephardic Jewry to its historic glory. In all these areas, he succeeded to a phenomenal degree.

There is no need for us to speak of his greatness. More than we can ever say is found in this splendid biography and in the human legacy he left behind. Nearly a million people flocked to Jerusalem on only a few hours' notice to escort him to his final rest — Sephardim and Ashkenazim, Hassidim and Mitnagdim, yeshiva students and laborers, men and women, young and old, observant and secular — all felt touched by "Maran." And they were — because he changed the world.

In researching and writing this magnificent work, RABBI YEHUDA HEIMOWITZ interviewed many members of the Rav's family and many people who were close to him. We are grateful to them all for their cooperation, especially to his sons the RISHON LEZION HAGAON HARAV YITZCHAK YOSEF שליט"א and HAGAON HARAV DAVID YOSEF שליט"א, who perpetuate their father's teachings through their own kollelim and their prolific Torah writings. Rabbi Heimowitz read virtually everything written about Maran Ovadia and listened to any number of eulogies and first-person reminiscences about him. Diligently and masterfully he verified, compiled, and blended everything into this work. We are confident that it will be regarded as the definitive story of Harav Ovadia.

This volume is dedicated by our dear friends MR. AND MRS. JOSEPH H. WEISS AND FAMILY. Mr. Weiss is a noted *talmid chacham* and leading attorney, and the scion of a distinguished pre-War family. He recognizes the importance of this work and the greatness of its subject. Mrs. Weiss is a great-granddaughter of the Kaf HaHaim, the great Sephardi *posek*, so it is especially appropriate that the Weisses should dedicate this biography of the preeminent *posek* of his time. Mr. Weiss has dedicated volumes of the ArtScroll Talmud Yerushalmi, and has offered important comments on their manuscripts. Quietly and usually anonymously, he contributes his expertise and support to numerous institutions and individuals. The Weiss family, parents and children, embody the great traditions of Ashkenazi and Sephardi Jewry. May the dedication of this biography be a *z'chut* for Mr. and Mrs. Weiss and their children and grandchildren.

We are grateful to RABBI DAVID OZEIREY, whose guidance and help have been indispensable to the success of this project. The list of causes and individuals helped by him is endless; the extent of his *hessed* is legendary. We are indeed fortunate that he makes himself available to us whenever called upon. RABBI DAVID SUTTON, a respected rav and educator in the Sephardic community, has always been a major source of advice and guidance on this and other projects.

RABBI AVROHOM BIDERMAN was involved in all aspects of the project, from liaison with the author to reviewing the text and photos. He reviewed every word of the manuscript, and his perception, knowledge, and judgment contributed to its excellence. MENDY HERZBERG has overseen and expedited the production. His cheerful efficiency makes it a pleasure to work with him.

ELI KROEN designed the beautiful cover. The book was paginated and the pictures were laid out by DEVORAH BLOCH and

RIVKY PLITTMAN. MRS. MALKY HEIMOWITZ assisted her husband in the writing and editing. The book was proofread by MRS. MINDY STERN and MRS. FRIMY EISNER with their customary efficiency.

We are grateful to them all and to everyone else who assisted in the production.

Finally, we are grateful to Hashem Yitbarach for enabling us and our colleagues to bring His word to His people, and for enabling us to present this portrait of one of the greatest Jews of our era.

Rabbi Meir Zlotowitz / Rabbi Nosson Scherman

Iyar 5774 / May 20014

AUTHOR'S INTRODUCTION AND ACKNOWLEDGMENTS

On 3 Heshvan 5774, at approximately 1:30 p.m., I found myself in a diner in the Geula neighborhood purchasing a bottle of water. Suddenly, after a day of conflicting reports as to whether his condition was improving or deteriorating, the news came over a radio blaring behind the counter: Maran Ovadia Yosef had passed away.

Though my own vision was blurred by tears I hadn't realized I would shed, I saw diners in the store stop in mid-chew. It was as though someone had frozen the frame on that moment, when many Jews suddenly felt a closeness to Harav Ovadia Yosef in his absence that they hadn't felt during his lifetime.

Later that day, still numb from the news, I found myself squeezed between every stripe of Israel's Jewry: Sephardi and Ashkenazi, religious and secular, old and young — all turning out to pay their respects to a figure that had towered above us for 93 years. In the days that followed, I heard countless anecdotes and bits of information about this great giant, and the decision to undertake this monumental project was not long in coming.

People love to ask, "Do you start your books before a *gadol* is *niftar*?" The answer is a resounding no. Though the eight months since Harav Ovadia passed away were certainly one long blur of sleep deprivation, I have found that it's the raw emotion that follows the *petira* of a *gadol* — and perhaps his *neshama* praying that its spiritual achievements will leave a lasting impact on the world — that brings out the most powerful thoughts and memories from those delivering *hespedim* and subsequent interviews.

Understandably, then, a project undertaken under a tight deadline must be the sum total of many people's efforts, and it is an honor to mention those who have made this dream into a reality.

First, to Harav Ovadia's family members who were involved in this project from its inception:

The Rishon LeZion, RAV YITZCHAK YOSEF, welcomed me into his home and graciously shared both historic information and many important documents about his father's life. A special thank-you to R' YOSEF ETTLINGER for coordinating this effort.

HAGAON RAV DAVID YOSEF, rav of Har Nof and a member of the *Moetzet Hachmei HaTorah*, was extremely generous with his time despite his numerous obligations, granting me four lengthy sessions in which he shared his personal memories of his father.

RABBANIT YEHUDIT YOSEF, wife of RAV MOSHE YOSEF, who cared for Maran during his last twenty years, shared precious personal memories of her illustrious father-in-law. I appreciate RABBI DAVID SHELBY'S efforts to set up that meeting and his invaluable assistance in other areas during the early stages of this project.

R' YAAKOV SASSON, a grandson of Harav Ovadia and author of the Hebrew *Abir Haro'im*, a biographical sketch of the first thirty years of his grandfather's life, helped pick apart fact from fancy during these months. I appreciate his willingness to help, and his unflagging good humor. R' YAAKOV has also granted us the use of many photos from his work, which now grace the pages of this book.

May Hashem grant all of them success in perpetuating the legacy of Harav Ovadia.

I woud also like to thank all those who took the time to share their memories of Harav Ovadia, and specifically RABBI YITZCHAK DWEK, MR. AVRAHAM ELBAZ, and R' AMI COHEN.

וְהַחוּט הַמְשֻׁלָּשׁ לֹא בִמְהֵרָה יִנָּתֵק. In the last three years, the Ribbono shel Olam has granted me the *z'chut* to publish three biographies with ArtScroll/Mesorah. Though there is no shortcut to success, having such a talented and dedicated team to work with is what makes a project like this possible.

RABBI MEIR ZLOTOWITZ and RABBI NOSSON SCHERMAN have reviewed every word of this manuscript and have invested untold hours into ensuring that this book will be accurate, honest, and inspiring. May Hashem bless them with further success in bringing His word to His people.

RABBI AVROHOM BIDERMAN, a true friend and kindred spirit, also reviewed the entire manuscript. Aside from his insightful comments that are an absolute necessity as we piece together a *gadol*'s lifetime, his good humor is always an added bonus.

SHMUEL BLITZ is the secret force behind many ArtScroll works. It is thanks to his gentle prodding and encouragement that a project of this magnitude can be moved along in so short a time frame.

MENDY HERZBERG is an island of serenity no matter how turbulent projects get — and they do get turbulent. It is only through his calm perseverance that these works come out as beautiful and professional as they do.

MRS. FRIMY EISNER and MRS. MINDY STERN proofread every word of this manuscript under a very tight deadline. I appreciate the long hours they put into this book and all my other ArtScroll works.

ELI KROEN and his graphics team of DEVORAH BLOCH and RIVKY PLITTMAN ensured that this biography is not only comprehensive but beautiful as well. A special thank-you for the extra effort that went into working with all the old historical photos in this book.

I have been blessed with talented colleagues in many venues, and although they are too numerous to mention, I would like to thank some of them for specific contributions to this book.

RABBI YONOSON ROSENBLUM is humble enough to call me a friend, even as I call him a mentor. His insight and good sense are reliable assets as I undertake any project; this book was no different.

To my friend R' YISROEL BESSER — thanks for being there, always. To the rest of my colleagues at *Mishpacha*, thank you for your assistance.

Since the release of my last biography, I have been fortunate to begin teaching in two seminaries in Yerushalayim. A special thank you to RABBI and MRS. ZECHARYA GREENWALD and MRS. BRACHA ROSENBLUM for granting me the opportunity to share the joy and love of a life of *avodat Hashem* with their students.

וּמִתַּלְמִידוֹתַי יוֹתֵר מִכֻּלָּם — or more accurately, וּמִתַּלְמִידַי יוֹתֵר מִכֻּלָּם. Many stories and facts in this book have been shared with the 240 students I taught this year in Meohr Beis Yaakov and Bais Yaakov Machon Raaya. Their reactions and questions helped shape my own understanding and appreciation of the life of Harav Ovadia.

This book is a product not only of long hours and effort, but of the love and support of a family behind me.

Thanking my wife MALKY for her help seems almost ludicrous, considering that her input on every word of this book makes this nearly a joint project. May we be *zocheh* to continue disseminating the *dvar Hashem* and to see His steady guidance in our lives as we have until now.

My parents, R' MEIR ZEV and MRS. DINA HEIMOWITZ, and my in-laws, R' TZVI and MRS. ESTHER GERSTEL, are always behind us in everything we do. Thank you for your love and moral support that bridges the 6,000 miles from North America to Yerushalayim.

Appreciation is due to all of our siblings as well, and especially to my brother-in-law MOSHE SHINDLER, who made some key connections at the outset of this project and was responsible for some beautiful photos that complete this work.

On 20 Shevat of this year, while I was working on this volume, we mourned the loss of my grandmother, MRS. CHAYA WACHSMAN. May this book be a *z'chut* for the *neshama* of חיה בת ר' מרדכי ע"ה.

To my children, who were always there to help at home so that I could free more hours for this project — thank you!

On a final note: to the hundreds who have been asking me in the last few months, "So when will the book be out?" You're holding it, at long last.

Rabbi Yehuda Heimowitz

Iyar 5774

SECTION ONE

A CHARMING SON

בֵּן פֹּרָת יוֹסֵף

A charming son is Yosef

(Bereishit 49:22)

CHAPTER ONE
HASHEM'S GENERAL

THE YOUNG CHILD WATCHES, WIDE-eyed, as his older brother dresses quietly.

These are exciting — and dangerous — times in Eretz Yisrael. As the British maintain a stranglehold over the land, idealistic youngsters join a group called Irgun Tzva'i Leumi (a.k.a. Etzel or the Irgun) to try to wrest control of the homeland of their forefathers from the British Empire. Countless religious young men and women are drawn to this cause, and sneak about in the darkness of night to plan attacks against British strongholds.

But no, the 10-year-old boy dressing quietly in the darkness is not sneaking out to reconnoiter with counterparts in the Irgun; on the contrary, when his younger brother eventually does join the group, he tries to discourage such involvement.

This 10-year-old is heading to a local beit midrash, where in the silence of the night — and in utter darkness save for the light of a small candle — he will learn Torah for a few hours before returning home.

The young boy, Avraham, is not sure whether he should inform his parents of his older brother, Ovadia Yosef's, nocturnal activities. On the one hand, when his parents find out that Ovadia is sneaking out, they may grow angry. On the other hand, he isn't out doing anything dangerous...

Generally speaking, if one were to describe a specific individual as having singlehandedly changed the course of history, that statement would be a gross exaggeration, if not an outright lie.

In regard to Maran Ovadia Yosef *zt"l*, it might be an understatement.

Born into a world in which Sephardic Jewry was at a nadir, he would eventually lead a rebirth of a glorious populace that had survived expulsions, persecution, and pogroms — only to nearly be decimated by their own brethren seeking to create a "new Jew" in the nascent Jewish state. When he came of age and began his lifelong goal of "restoring the crown to its ancient glory," there were

No matter how busy life got, Harav Ovadia's main focus remained the same: Torah, and more Torah.

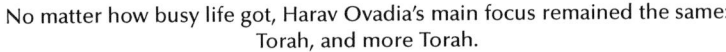

few Sephardic Jews in the world who considered themselves *"bnei Torah"* — people who not only study Torah, but consider upholding the Torah their mission in life.

To quote R' Aryeh Deri, one of the primary lay leaders Harav Ovadia relied on in the last few decades of his life, "When Maran started, there were a few hundred Sephardi *bnei Torah*. Now there are hundreds of thousands."

Along the way, Harav Ovadia created and dissolved governments in Israel, and met — and impressed — world leaders, but every meeting and every effort in his life was undertaken for one purpose: to create more and more *bnei Torah*.

> *Harav Ovadia kept a diary in which he chronicled his days, often in great detail. On 20 Kislev 5760 (November 29, 1999), Harav Ovadia tells the story of a small slice of his day on a trip to England:*
>
> *... We went to the palace of the Prime Minister, Mr. Tony Blair, at 2:30. He welcomed us warmly and with great joy, and he told us that he feels fortunate that we visited him, and that it is a great honor for him.*
>
> *We spoke to him about the peace process in Eretz Yisrael, and asked him to support Prime Minister Ehud Barak and ensure that the peace is bilateral, that the other side will fulfill its obligations toward making peace, and to ensure the security of Israel.*
>
> *He answered that that's what he is already doing, and that he will invest even greater efforts to this end.*
>
> *He told us that he reads history and the story of how Moshe Rabbeinu took Bnei Yisrael out of Egypt, and although they were originally twelve tribes, he made them into one nation and led them through the desert for forty years, and gave them the Torah, which is the "Light unto the Nations." He said that he admires Shas's[1] efforts to strengthen the Jewish nation to study Torah according to the principles of Moshe Rabbeinu.*

---

1. Shas is the political party Harav Ovadia began to lead in 1983; see Chapter 22.

Harav Ovadia traveled abroad only if his presence would help build more Torah or encourage mitzva observance.

We also spoke at length about peace and its importance to the Middle East. I asked him to influence the Syrian president to come toward Israel in an effort to create true peace. I also asked [him] to try to push the Iranian government to free thirteen Jews who were being held on espionage charges which we know are false.... He promised us that he is trying to urge them to do so, because he is also certain that [the imprisoned Jews] are innocent.

I then blessed him and his wife — who is in an advanced stage of pregnancy — that they should have a healthy child who would be as wise as he (his wife is 45 and the doctors are concerned for the welfare of the fetus). When we left, he escorted us outside and told us that he already feels a lightness of heart and joy from our blessing. He walked us all the way to the street and waved as our car pulled away.

Was this trip undertaken to meet the British Prime Minister and secure these assurances from him? No. It's quite obvious from earlier and subsequent entries in the diary that Maran Ovadia would not have embarked on his journey if not for the dire need for funds to maintain his school system, Maayan HaHinuch HaTorani. He only visited Mr. Blair — and French President Jacques Chirac a day later — as brief stops on a trip he undertook to ensure that the tens of thousands of children enrolled in his school system would continue to receive a Torah education.

Fight for Life

CONSIDERING ALL THAT MARAN OVADIA YOSEF ACCOMplished, one might assume that his path in life was paved in gold — born into a family of great scholarly lineage, encouraged from his youth to grow in Torah, facing little opposition as he progressed from scholar to *dayan*, from a young revolutionary turning the tide of Sephardic Jewry to the *gadol hador* — but the opposite is true. His was a life of constant battles from day one.

Although Harav Ovadia's father, R' Yaakov, was a God-fearing, righteous man, the family's early years in Israel during the 1920s were beset by severe financial difficulties in an era in which Jews were — quite literally — starving. We will encounter a young Ovadia fighting for the right to study in yeshiva, even "sneaking out" behind the backs of his concerned parents to learn Torah until the wee hours of the morning in a local shul.

As a teenager, he was fired from his first position teaching Torah because of his staunch belief that Sephardic Jewry — and especially those living in Eretz Yisrael — should be following the rulings of the *Beit Yosef*. When he married and was sent by Chief Rabbi Benzion Meir Hai Uziel to Egypt to serve as *Av Beit Din* and lead the community in all halachic matters, his life was in constant danger both from the Egyptian authorities, who suspected him of spying for Israel, and the secular Jewish community leaders, who wanted to depose him and send him back to Israel.

Once back in Israel, his first *sefer*, *Hazon Ovadia* on *Hilchot Pesah*, was banned and even burned for a perceived slight of the Ben Ish

Even after reaching the apex of the Rabbanut as Rishon LeZion, Harav Ovadia continued to strive for more.

Hai.[2] He then undertook to convince parents to enroll their children in Torah schools — and incurred the wrath of leaders of the National Religious movement, whose schools those children were abandoning, who threatened to prevent him from advancing in the Israeli Rabbanut.

His rise to the apex of the Rabbanut, the position of Rishon LeZion,[3] was also plagued by controversy, but he prevailed and could have remained Rishon LeZion for life — if not for a bill passed in the Knesset specifically aimed at preventing him from continuing on in that position.

But that law ultimately freed him to found the Shas party and realize his lifelong vision of creating a vast empire of Sephardi

---

2. For whom Harav Ovadia had the deepest respect; see page 203.
3. Lit., "The First of Zion," this position is also referred to as Rav HaRashi HaSepharadi — Chief Sephardic Rabbi.

Torah schools — although every step of this goal, too, would be a battle.

But even as a political leader, he rarely diverted his attention from his first love: studying Torah.

> *In 1984, Shas ran its first campaign for national office. The leaders of the party, including a very young Aryeh Deri, had no experience, no funds, and no guarantee that they would even pass the ahuz hahasima, the minimum number of votes necessary to receive a seat in the Knesset. Harav Ovadia had invested so much into those elections, traveling from city to city throughout Israel to encourage people to vote for Shas, yet he was the only one unfazed as the results were being tallied. "The night of the elections," recalls R' Deri, "we sat in the Rav's house on Rehov Jabotinsky. We were afraid to be seen in public; had we not received that minimum number of votes, it would have been too embarrassing. We were all sitting and waiting for the results to be announced, except the Rav, who was sitting and learning, oblivious to his surroundings.*
>
> *"When the radio announcer declared that Shas had garnered four seats (two above the necessary minimum), I cried out in delight, louder than I've ever shouted before. Harav Ovadia didn't even look up from his sefer; he apparently had not even heard my shout. So his son Rav David went over to him and said, 'Abba, we got four seats!'*
>
> *"Harav Ovadia lifted his head and said, 'Ah, yofi (oh, that's nice),' and went right back to learning.*
>
> *"After all that work we put in, I thought he would dance with us, maybe drink a l'hayim, but his attitude was, 'we already spent all that time to win the election, now let's get back to learning.'"*

From that fateful election on, Harav Ovadia spent the last three decades of his life guiding rabbinical and lay leaders on founding and funding Torah schools, often coming under personal and political attack for his efforts.

"It pains me more than the loss of my son."
Harav Ovadia at the *shiva* for his son Yaakov, pleading with Israel's Prime Minister Netanyahu not to harm the Torah world.

And like all good generals, Maran Ovadia would move on to the Next World with his proverbial boots on.

> Several months before Harav Ovadia's passing, his oldest son, Rav Yaakov Hai Yosef, predeceased him. This was a time of turmoil for the Torah community in Israel, with most parties in the government mobilizing to undermine the Torah empire that had been built in Israel in the 65 years of its statehood. When Prime Minister Binyamin Netanyahu came to be menahem avel (console the mourners), Harav Ovadia pounced immediately. "How can you be party to the destruction of the Torah world?" he demanded.
>
> "Honored Rav," Mr. Netanyahu replied, "I came to console you, not to discuss this issue."
>
> "You came to console me on the loss of my son?" Harav Ovadia retorted. "Believe me, the dismantling of the Torah world pains me much more than the loss of my own son."

In the end, the heart that beat only for the advancement of Torah couldn't hold out against the constant attacks on all that he treasured. In the words of his son, current Rishon LeZion Rav Yitzchak Yosef, "Just as the Hazon Ish despaired of battling *giyus habanot*[4] in This World and took the battle On High, so did Abba eventually feel that his efforts to preserve the Torah community were fruitless, and he took his battle to the Next World."

Positivity, Nonetheless

PEOPLE WHO FACE CONSTANT BATTLES IN LIFE TEND TO become crusty and combative, poised to mount a counterattack on those seeking to destroy them. Certainly someone as embattled as Harav Ovadia could easily have grown antagonistic and aggressive, constantly seeking to sink his attackers.

Yet few people in the world were as positive and loved every fellow Jew — even his detractors — as Harav Ovadia.

In countless video clips of the Rav meeting the everyman, one detects palpable affection as he smiles and delivers his trademark love slaps to his visitor. He detested losing time from learning, but he recognized how important a personal encounter could be to a visitor.

> *Rav Yitzhak Toledano, a grandson of Harav Ovadia, related that after his grandfather's passing, a fellow told him the following story:*
>
> *"I was married for five years without children, and all the treatments we had tried had failed. I went to Maran for a blessing, expecting him to give me just a few seconds of his time and send me on my way. I was shocked when he asked for all the details of my story — what the doctors said, what treatments we had tried — and only after hearing the full story did he issue his beracha."*
>
> *"Saba understood that a few minutes of his attention meant so much to people," concluded Rav Toledano, "so he gave gladly of his precious time to lift a load off the heavy heart of a supplicant."*

---
4. Mandatory conscription of women into the Israeli Army.

He loved every Jew: Harav Ovadia in a Torah discussion with Mr. Joe Weiss.

"As water reflects a face, so is the heart of a man to his fellow man" (*Mishlei* 27:19).

The public recognized Maran's love for them, and returned it in great measure in his final weeks, gathering to pray for him when he took ill, rejoicing upon hearing indications that he was recovering, and finally, when his frail body returned its soul to its Maker on 3 Heshvan 5774, escorting him to his burial in numbers unheard of in the last two millennia. An estimated 850,000 people took part in the actual funeral — held on only four hours' notice — and that does not include the droves who had traveled from the farther reaches of the country and were stranded on highways near Yerushalayim, unable to reach the capital because the city had closed down.

Perhaps most impressive was the diversity of the crowd: Sephardic Jews stood alongside Ashkenazim, ultra-religious with the not-yet-religious, young and old, men and women — for everyone realized that this was a man who represented truth, love of Torah, and love of his fellow Jew.

HOW DOES A CHILD BORN INTO AN ORDINARY FAMILY GO ON to lead his entire populace out of the scorn heaped upon them, to make them proud of their heritage — while simultaneously becoming an undisputed authority in many areas of halacha and spending upwards of 18 hours a day studying Torah?

Let's trace the path from his birthplace in Baghdad to his childhood home in the Beit Yisrael section of Yerushalayim, where he dressed quietly to sneak off to learn in a lonely *beit midrash*; accompany him through eight decades of constant toil to learn and build Torah; and finally, escort him along the path lined by the 850,000 strong who joined to pay homage to the giant whose leadership and love are sorely missed.

CHAPTER TWO
A BLOSSOM EMERGES

ON THE 12TH OF TISHREI 5761/1920, THE ELDEST SON OF an Iraqi goldsmith was born. Named Ovadia Yosef after his paternal grandfather,[1] his name was also chosen to commemorate two recently departed *hachamim* who were among the greatest *gedolim* of Iraq: Rav Ovadia Someich, author of *Zivhei Tzedek*,[2] and the Ben Ish Hai, whose name was Rav Yosef Haim.

Destined for greatness: Ovadia Yosef carried the names of two of Iraq's greatest scholars of the last few centuries, Rav Ovadia Someich (L) and Rav Yosef Haim of Baghdad, the Ben Ish Hai (R).

---

1. See page 44 below, where we explain that his grandfather's given name may actually have been Ovadia only.
2. Harav Ovadia Someich was actually called Rav Abdullah Someich (Abdullah is the Arabic equivalent of Ovadia; Abd is the Muslim version of עובד, and Allah is equivalent to the *yud* and *hei* of עובדי-ה, which is Hashem's Name). Several months after Rav Abdullah Someich's *petira*, there was a need to move his body from one cemetery to another. The Arab diggers expected to find a bare skeleton in the grave, but to their shock, Rav Abdullah's body was completely intact. One of the Arabs was so stunned that he converted to Judaism and moved to Eretz Yisrael, where his grandchildren continue to live until today.

The grandfather he was named after was a successful merchant whose primary business interests were in Baghdad.

A Turning Point in Baghdad

BY THAT POINT, JEWS HAD LIVED IN IRAQ (KNOWN IN HEBREW as Bavel) for close to 25 centuries, having originally arrived there upon the destruction of the first *Beit HaMikdash*. In the second half of the 1800s, the country was at a turning point. Until then, Jews had lived under relatively peaceful conditions; the Arab rulers of the country and the governing officials of the cities generally treated their Jewish citizens fairly. From approximately 1850, however, the atmosphere began to change. Jews were often attacked in the streets by Arab civilians, and although the authorities officially opposed such assaults — and even punished the aggressors in some cases — they frequently turned a blind eye to the attacks.

Interestingly, the attacks coincided with an era of prosperity for the Iraqi community, prompting at least one leading scholar, R' Avraham Haim Someich,[3] to see a direct correlation between the two. In an essay in *Hatzefirah*[4] he writes that there were two general reasons why the Muslims were attacking their Jewish neighbors: out of hatred, as fanaticism began to gain ground in Baghdad, and out of jealousy. He describes the luxury and modernity that had become commonplace among Baghdad's Jews, many of whom were living beyond their means. As an example, he writes, "If you walk in our streets on Shabbos, dear reader, you'll see people dressed in [princely robes]. You will be surprised and surmise that out of ten portions of wealth that came down to earth, nine of them must have gone to the Jews of Baghdad. But then you'll come back the next day to find

The Jewish neighborhood on the banks of the *Hidekel* (Tigris) River, where Harav Ovadia was born

---

3. A distant relative of Rav Abdullah Someich.
4. Year 16, Issue 109, dated 28 Iyar 5649/1889. *Hatzefirah* was a periodical published in Warsaw during in the late 1800s.

out what trade these people engage in, and you'll be shocked to find out that one is a greengrocer, the second dyes shoes, a third sells firewood, and so on... And the 'princesses' you saw walking around yesterday are in similar industries (or suffering from the same poverty) as the men."

Another factor that led to the Arabs' loss of respect for their Jewish neighbors was the spread of assimilation. Until the mid-1800s, most of the Eastern lands where Sephardic Jews resided escaped the scourge of the *Haskala* (Enlightenment), and the Jews in those countries remained religious even as many of their brethren in Europe began to stray.[5] But the Alliance schools — the educational wing of a movement that began in France under the name *Kol Yisrael Haveirim*[6] and expanded rapidly through Europe — eventually spread their wings through the Eastern world,[7] leading many youth astray. The first Alliance school in Baghdad opened in 5625/1864,[8] and caused a rapid deterioration in the commitment to Judaism that had been the crowning glory of Iraq's Jews for many centuries. Rather than find respect in the eyes of their Arab neighbors, the "enlightened" Jews triggered even more anti-Semitic attacks.

"Our city also [suffers] from the enlightened youth groups," writes R' Avraham Haim Someich, "whose first objective is to shuck the yoke of *emuna* and our holy customs. [Enlightened Jews] do not find favor in the eyes of the Muslims... the Muslims respect a genuine Jew far more than they respect an assimilated Jew."[9]

---

5. *Be'er Ro'i*, Rafael Eliyahu Yitzhak Katzenellenberg, p. 108.
6. Often referred to in literature from that era as חברת כי״ח, an acronym for כָּל יִשְׂרָאֵל חֲבֵרִים. The movement was also referred to as Alliance Israelita.
7. The movement reached Eretz Yisrael in approximately 1870, eventually causing many children from traditional families, to go astray. Sadly, these parents failed to perceive the danger of sending their children to these schools, whose official platform was merely to teach secular knowledge to their students, not to encourage them to drop religion.
8. *Otzar HaShirim, Haderashot, Vehahiburim shel Harav Yosef Haim*, Avraham ben Yaakov, p. 267.
9. Just how much the Muslims respected authentic Jews is evident in a story told by author and poet Reuven Haim Bar Amon, who grew up in Iraq in the early 1900s and later lived in Haifa.
He writes that the home of Rav Yosef Haim, the Ben Ish Hai, was considered holy by Baghdad's Jews, Muslims, and Christians alike, all of whom referred to it as Beit Elhacham. Once, when he was 10 years old, he passed Beit Elhacham on his way home from the Alliance school he attended, and he saw a Muslim woman dressed in a black robe that came to her ankles carrying ten platters of leben on her head, apparently on the way to sell them in the local marketplace. She set the platters down at the doorstep of Rav Yosef Haim's house, stood up, raised her hand to the

With the turn of the 20th century, the attacks on Jews grew in intensity and frequency. In 5634/1876, a Jew was burned alive at a central intersection in Baghdad as a "warning" to the community. By 5678/1917, government complicity in assaults on the Jewish community became more common. The governor, Turkish military commander,[10] and police chief of Baghdad banded together to accuse the city's Jews of engaging in illegal commerce that led to a devaluation of the Turkish currency during the recently ended World War I. Seventeen community leaders, many of whom had lent significant sums to influential Muslims, were arrested by Turkish authorities, beaten, and then dismembered and thrown into the *Hidekel* (Tigris) River.

AMONG THOSE KILLED IN ONE SUCH UPRISING SHORTLY after the turn of the 20th century was R' Abdullah Yosef, the grandfather for whom Harav Ovadia was named. His son Yaakov was just six years old at the time, and his wife Hatoun needed the help of her sister and brother-in-law, Sala and Zahla Shabo, who also resided in Baghdad, in raising her young children. The couple "adopted" and raised

Parents of Royalty

---

mezuza and said, "*Basem Allah El Rahman* — in the Name of God, the Merciful God, please, may the holy *hacham* beg for mercy for my son, Hassan, who is lying on his sickbed. May he be healed, amen. Please, O righteous and great *hacham*, ask for mercy for me, your maidservant, beg for mercy before your God; since you are holy and good, I am certain He will listen to you. And if my requests will be fulfilled, just as you answered the requests of my neighbor, Zahara bat Salah, I vow that if my son Hassan is healed from his illness, I will send a lunch meal of kosher slaughtered meat to all the students in the *beit midrash* of the Talmud Torah. I know they are orphans; they will eat and bless and ask for mercy for us."

She then kissed the *mezuza* many times and said "Amen," then bowed at her knees and kissed the doorstep. Finally, she took earth from the doorstep and spread it on her face and other parts of her body.

"When she saw me staring at her in wonderment," writes Bar Amon, "she hugged me and said, 'Place your hands on this *mezuza* and kiss it, for it is the source of healing and a wellspring of goodness. It is in the blessed house of the greatest of the Jewish rabbis. Ask for anything you want, and he will give it to you.'

"I did as she told me. As she placed her platters back onto her head, she said, 'Remember, son, and do not forget: each time you pass by this house, place your hand on the "Torah" and kiss it, and ask God to watch over you from all evil.' Even as she wished me farewell and turned to leave, she kept turning back to Beit Elhacham, reaching with her hand toward it and kissing the tips of her fingers.

"I was so astonished at what I had witnessed that I ran home to tell my parents what had transpired" (*Harav Yosef Haim M'Baghdad*, Avraham Ben Yaakov, p. 137).

10. At that point, Iraq was part of the Ottoman Empire and controlled by the Turks.

Yaakov along with their own children, among whom was their daughter Georgia. Like most children of simple, non-aristocratic families in Baghdad at the time, Yaakov attended a Talmud Torah for a number of years, but then had to put his studies aside and learn a trade. He chose to apprentice with a goldsmith, and became an expert in the craft.

When Yaakov and Georgia turned 18, they married. Although his Jewish education was limited, Yaakov was famous for his love of Torah. He was nicknamed "Gali" because each year on Simhat Torah he would sing and dance in the honor of the Torah for many consecutive hours, and his favorite *piyut*, which he would sing over and over, was "*Gali Gali Ziv Hodi* (reveal the shine of my glory)."

R' Yaakov Ovadia, Harav Ovadia Yosef's father, as a young man

The Torah would indeed reveal its glory through R' Yaakov, with the birth of his son Ovadia Yosef.

BEFORE PROCEEDING ANY FURTHER, WE SHOULD CLARIFY A point regarding Harav Ovadia Yosef's family name. His father, R'

What's in a Name?

Yaakov, was actually called R' Yaakov Ovadia; his family name in Iraq was Ovadia, and the family continued to use that name when they moved to Eretz Yisrael. All of Harav Ovadia Yosef's brothers used the Ovadia family name throughout their lives; only he used the surname Yosef.

The simplest and most obvious reason for his name change was that since he was called only by his first given name, Ovadia, were he to have kept the family name Ovadia he would have been known

Chapter Two: A Blossom Emerges ☐ 43

as Ovadia Ovadia, which would have been confusing. He therefore adopted his other given name, Yosef, as a family name,[11] and his children continued to use that as their surname.

In *Abir Haro'im*, Harav Ovadia's grandson and biographer R' Yaakov Sasson sheds light on the deeper, more intricate — and historically fascinating — background for this name change:

It seems that most people in Iraq did not use a typical surname, but rather identified themselves with their given name, followed by their father's given name. Harav Ovadia's father was known as Yaakov Ovadia, for instance, because *his* father (for whom Harav Ovadia was named) was named Ovadia. Harav Ovadia's grandfather, in turn, was known as Ovadia Yosef because *his* father was Yosef.[12]

In theory, Harav Ovadia and all of his siblings should have used the family name Yaakov, adopting their father's name as their family name. Families that moved to Eretz Yisrael, however, generally stuck with the last family name they used in Iraq, so his brothers retained the name Ovadia.

In his early years in Eretz Yisrael, Harav Ovadia began to identify himself as Ovadia Yosef Yaakov, and, in fact, he would initial his notebooks from that period ע.י.י., sometimes adding the words:

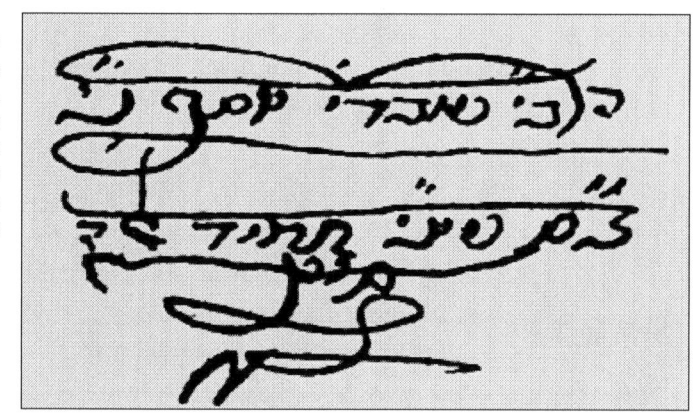

Rav Ovadia's signature as a young child, with the words ב״ס (בא סימן) עיני״י תמיד אל ה׳ under the signature

---

11. Technically, then, his full name should have been Ovadia Yosef Yosef.
12. According to this explanation, Harav Ovadia Yosef was actually named for both his grandfather and great-grandfather.

בא סימן ע.י.נ.י,¹³ with the letters ע.י.נ.י. serving as an acronym for: עובדיה יוסף נ׳ יעקב – Ovadia Yosef, son of Yaakov.¹⁴

Later in life, when the rest of his family decided to retain the family name Ovadia, he realized that this would mean that he would be identified as Ovadia Ovadia, so he kept his second given name as his family name.

Moving to Eretz Yisrael

LITTLE IS KNOWN ABOUT YOUNG OVADIA'S FIRST FEW YEARS. In fact, only one story — albeit a remarkable one — is told about his years in Baghdad. When Ovadia was an infant, his mother Georgia would place his bassinet out in the courtyard during the blazing summer months so he could get fresh air. Once, a venomous snake made its way into the bassinet while she was tending to some housework. An Arab neighbor¹⁵ walked into the courtyard just as the snake was about to attack baby Ovadia, and she ran over and lifted him out of his bassinet — saving his life.

When Ovadia was four years old, the family immigrated to Eretz Yisrael. By that point, R' Yaakov and his wife had already been blessed with two more children: Na'im, who was two years younger than Ovadia, and Shoshana. They made the 560-mile (900-kilometer) trek on camelback, together with other families moving to the Holy Land.

Bnei Zion

UPON REACHING ERETZ YISRAEL IN 5685/1924, R' YAAKOV SETtled his family in the Beit Yisrael section of Jerusalem. Originally built to accommodate the exponential growth of families residing in the overpopulated Old City, Beit Yisrael eventually became a magnet for new *olim*, many of whom couldn't afford anything more spacious than the small apartments of this neighborhood. The family moved onto Rehov Shmuel HaNavi, and after losing the considerable fortune he had brought

---

13. I.e., already as a child of about 10, he found an allusion to his name in the verse: עֵינַי תָּמִיד אֶל ה׳, *My eyes are constantly to Hashem*.
14. The letter נ is often used — especially among early Sephardic scholars — as a shorthand for *ben* (son of).
15. Another version of this story is that Ovadia's parents employed an Arab maidservant to help with the household chores, and she was the one who saved his life.

R' Yaakov and Georgia Ovadia, with their children. The precocious Ovadia is at left (standing).

with him from Iraq in a business deal that soured, R' Yaakov opened a *makolet* (grocery store) within the confines of his small home to support his family. Eventually he was able to build up his business and rent a storefront, and he supported his family from his *makolet* for the next 40 years.

> *In his later years, people would throng to Harav Ovadia for advice on a host of matters, including business advice. Once, a fellow came to ask whether to enter a partnership with a certain person. Harav Ovadia wouldn't give him a definitive answer. He kept saying, "You have to look into the person very well to make sure he's honest."*
>
> *No matter how many times the fellow asked whether he should accept the offer, Harav Ovadia refused to answer directly.*

> When the man left, Harav Ovadia turned to his havruta, R' Eliyahu Shitrit, and explained why he was hesitant to answer the question. "When we arrived in Eretz Yisrael from Iraq, my father entered a partnership with a fellow who was dishonest, and he lost all his money.
>
> "It took many years for my father to stabilize our family's finances, and we lived in extreme poverty in the interim."[16]
>
> Because of his own family's experience, Harav Ovadia was loath to advise anyone to enter business partnerships unless they were absolutely sure that the would-be partner was honest.

In those years, the Alliance schools were making inroads in Eretz Yisrael, and while Ashkenazi rabbanim fought the threat openly, Sephardic Jewry did not have anyone to lead the fight, and many Sephardim enrolled their children in Alliance schools. Rav Yosef Haim Sonnenfeld, who would eventually become the rav of Yerushalayim, was one of the leading figures in battling Alliance's advance into Eretz Yisrael. On Hol HaMoed Pesah 5679/1919, he summoned the recently widowed R' Moshe Porush and asked him to found a Talmud Torah for Sephardic children whose parents might otherwise send their children to an Alliance school.

Putting aside his sorrow at the sudden passing of his young wife, R' Moshe opened Talmud Torah Bnei Zion in the Bucharim neighborhood while somehow caring for his two young children on his own. Some of the greatest *gedolim* of Sephardic Jewry emerged from this Talmud Torah — including Harav Ovadia, Rav Ben Zion Abba Shaul, and Rav Yehuda Tzadka, all of whom had the deepest respect for Rav Moshe, referring to him as *"Moreinu VeRabbeinu"* at his funeral. In his eulogy, Harav Ovadia also described the devotion of the rebbeim at Bnei Zion:

> The teaching staff made their nights like days, never worrying about the amount of time they were investing into us, never glancing at the clock. Their objective was to teach, teach, and teach some more — even on Shabbat

---
16. See p. 111.

— with the encouragement of R' Moshe Porush. Some students went on to become *dayanim*, others are rabbanim who serve in positions both in Eretz Yisrael and abroad ... *if not for R' Moshe Porush, Torah would have been forgotten from Sephardic Jewry.*[17]

From the start, Ovadia's rebbeim and classmates at Bnei Zion could tell that this child was cut from different cloth. While all the other children ran outside to play during breaks, the young Ovadia had no interest in playing. He would sit in the room and review what they had learned.

Harav Ovadia as a young child of approximately seven, when he was a student in Talmud Torah Bnei Zion

In his first few years in the Talmud Torah, Ovadia studied under Rav Yaakov Meir Schechter, who taught the children not only read-

Rav Yaakov Meir Schechter taught Ovadia not only to read *Humash* and write, but also mathematical and scientific skills that would help him master complex *sugyot* in the Talmud.

---

17. Emphasis added. A transcript of Harav Ovadia's eulogy is printed in *Sharsheret Hadorot Betkufot Haso'arot* (V. 6, p. 35), published by R' Moshe's son, longtime Agudah MK Rabbi Menachem Porush *z"l*.

ing, writing, and *Humash*, but also math, science, and language. Ovadia, who was extremely gifted as an artist aside from his brilliance, picked up these secular subjects quickly, and they would eventually help him in his quest to understand *sugyot* in *Shas* for which mathematical equations are necessary, such as *Eruvin*, *Kiddush HaHodesh*, and the like.[18]

A Tale of Two "Meetings"

ALREADY AT THAT TENDER AGE, when other children would go home after school, Ovadia would head to a local *beit midrash* called Shoshanim L'David, and learn from a *Torah Temimah Humash*, writing summaries of what he learned. This *beit midrash* was the building in which Rav Yaakov Haim Sofer secluded himself in the *ezrat nashim* (women's section) on the third floor, where there was a large *sefarim* library,[19] learning and writing his halachic compendium *Kaf HaHaim*.

Rav Yaakov Haim Sofer, author of *Kaf HaHaim*, couldn't know that the six-year-old he saved would eventually complete his *sefer* after his passing.

> Shortly after 3 p.m. on 11 Tammuz 5687 (July 11, 1927), an earthquake registering 6.2 on the Richter scale shook the entire area around Yam HaMelah (the Dead Sea), including Jerusalem and its environs.[20] Approximately

---

18. His son R' David relates that his father could multiply four digits by four digits in mere seconds.
19. This library was compiled primarily through donations of *sefarim* that had belonged to scholars who passed away. In those days, *sefarim* were rare, and beyond the primary works such as Talmud Bavli and *Shulhan Aruch*, few could afford to have *sefarim* in their homes. This library would soon become one of Harav Ovadia's favorite places to learn, as he aimed to master many texts from the *Rishonim* and *Aharonim* that were not available elsewhere; see pp. 104 and 107
20. See *Kaf HaHaim* 576:26, where Rav Sofer cites from *Pri Ha'adamah* that there is a halachic difference between Yerushalayim and all other areas regarding disasters that strike. Whereas in other locations, *beit din* would proclaim a public fast day following certain calamities, such as an earthquake or a building collapse, in Yerushalayim fasts are not proclaimed due to such events, because "these events do not cause death in Yerushalayim." Rav Sofer then describes the

300 buildings in the city suffered severe damage, including Shoshanim L'David. When the tremors stopped, Rav Sofer slowly made his way down from the ezrat nashim to the main beit knesset on the second floor, where he found the young Ovadia Yosef quaking in fear. He calmed the child, then took him by the hand and said, "Come, let's leave the building." They went to the door and were about to step outside, when they realized that the steps leading to the sidewalk had completely collapsed. Rav Yaakov Haim Sofer called out to passersby, and someone fetched a ladder to rescue the 57-year-old gadol and the six-year-old child. Rav Sofer wanted to escort Ovadia home, certain that his parents were worried as to his whereabouts, but a neighbor who recognized the child offered to take him home.

Twelve years later, the Kaf HaHaim passed away, and his son, R' Moshe Sofer, took upon himself to publish his father's manuscript. He spent seven years preparing it for publication, but he had a problem: his father had passed away just short of finishing the second volume of Yoreh Dei'ah, stopping in the middle of Siman 117. Who could go through all the Rishonim, Aharonim, and Poskim and issue rulings on the remaining two simanim in that volume? There was one person who came highly recommended: a 26-year-old dayan serving on the Sephardic Beit Din in Yerushalayim, by the name of... Harav Ovadia Yosef.[21]

The First Taste of Gemara

IN 5687/1927 OVADIA BEGAN TO STUDY UNDER RAV NATAN Salam. One day, Rav Salam was absent from Bnei Zion, and all the children in his class went out to play. Harav Ovadia wandered off in search of a class in progress, and chanced upon the highest class, which was learning Gemara. He slipped into the room and surreptitiously began listening to the *shiur*. Although the discussion was

---

earthquake that took place in 5687, and writes that miraculously, not one Jew in Yerushalayim was harmed by it.

21. R' Ehud Shraga, with details verified from other sources. Harav Ovadia dedicated his work on the last two-and-a-half *simanim* in memory of his mother, who had just passed away.

beyond his grasp, he was immediately transfixed. From then on, each day after school he would find a *beit midrash* in which there was a Gemara *shiur*, and he would sit and listen to the men learning.

Rav Natan Salam, Ovadia's rebbi who acceded to his 6½-year-old student's request that he teach him Gemara

Already as a 6½-year-old, Ovadia developed such a thirst to learn Gemara that he approached his rebbi, Rav Natan Salam, and requested that he teach him Gemara. Rav Salam readily agreed, and the two started learning together in the afternoon when regular classes at Bnei Zion were over.

Harav Ovadia related that after he finished his sessions with Rav Salam, he would spend hours upon hours toiling over new pages of Gemara to try to understand them himself — sometimes staying out until midnight in a beit knesset across from their home. His pious mother would wait up to serve him dinner when he finally came home, and she would give him a piece of chocolate — a great luxury in those days — to reward him for learning Torah.

"Didn't you want to go play with the other children?" his son Rav David once asked him.

"From the day I started to learn Gemara," replied Harav Ovadia, "I lost all interest in playing."

BY THE END OF 5687, THE ADMINISTRATION OF BNEI ZION realized that the young Ovadia was ready to move up to the highest level in the Talmud Torah, and they placed him into the class of Rav Shlomo Abo, who would be his rebbi for the next three years.

Rav Shlomo Abo

Throughout his life, Harav Ovadia would talk about Rav Shlomo

Chapter Two: A Blossom Emerges ☐ 51

The staff of Talmud Torah Bnei Zion
The first row includes founder and principal Rav Moshe Porush (L) and Ovadia's two primary rebbeim, Rav Natan Salam (seated next to R' Porush) and Rav Shlomo Abo (R).

with great love and respect, comparing him to Rav Shmuel bar Shilas, whom the Gemara (*Bava Basra* 8b) deems the quintessential *melamed tinokot* (teacher of young children). Rav Shlomo succeeded not only in teaching his charges *how* to learn, but also to *love* learning and to be willing to sacrifice for it.

Harav Ovadia related that the childless Rav Abo made his students' success in learning his life's goal. He would gather them around him each Friday and ask each one to recite a full *daf* of Gemara by heart. He would encourage them by buying platters of treats, allowing each child who succeeded in memorizing the Gemara to take a few candies or nuts.[22] He also taught them to read the *parasha* with the *ta'amim* (cantillation).[23]

Ovadia quickly mastered everything Rav Shlomo taught, becoming a source of a great pride to his rebbi. The *mussar* volume *Reishit Hochma* in Harav Ovadia's library contained an inscription, dated 15 Menahem Av, 5691/1931, on the title page: "When I was

---

22. *Abir Haro'im*, R' Yaakov Sasson, pp. 37-38. That a rebbi would spend part of his own salary on such delicacies during those years of utter privation is truly remarkable.
23. *Hazon Ovadia, Hilchot Shabbat*, V. 1, p. 307.

Harav Ovadia's copy of *Reishit Hochma*, with his inscription explaining why he was awarded the volume

eight or nine years old, I recited to [my great master] Rav Shlomo Abo the Mishnayot of tractates *Shabbat, Pesahim, Avot, Succa,* and *Yoma,* and the Gemara of *perakim Shnayim Ohazin, Eilu Metziot, Hamafkid,* and *Hazahav* by heart. Some of them were recited before Rav Amram Blau [son of Rav Moshe Blau], and they therefore gave me this *sefer* as a present, to learn from it. I, the impoverished one,[24] have commented on it as I could muster."[25]

The Fateful Trip to Baghdad

BY THE TIME OVADIA TURNED 10, HE HAD COMPLETED THE entire curriculum of Talmud Torah Bnei Zion. Many students his age sufficed with that level of Torah education and started to apprentice in some field or another, and it was far from clear how Ovadia would spend his next years. Yeshiva Porat Yosef would have seemed the logical choice, but the youngest students there were over bar mitzva. The family was in a quandary as to where he would continue his studies — until R' Yaakov decided to take his son along on a six-month business trip to Iraq.

Since there were no yeshivot in Baghdad for children his age — by that point, all the Jewish schools there were Alliance schools — Ovadia asked his father if he could sit and learn in the famous yeshiva Midrash Beit Zilcha, led by Rav Salman Hugi Aboudi.[26] Despite its being largely assimilated, the Baghdad community retained an ancient tradition and supported ten men whose Job" it was to learn full time in Midrash Beit Zilcha. R' Yaakov gladly agreed, and he left his 10-year-old son in the *beit midrash* and went on his way.

When the men in Midrash Beit Zilcha saw this young boy sit down at their table with a volume of Talmud, they couldn't believe

---

24. Already at this age, Harav Ovadia's humility shone through in every word he wrote. Although his annotations were worthy of a scholar well beyond his 10 years, he writes, "*V'anochi hadal...*"
25. Cited in many works, including *Posek HaDor*.
26. Founded by Rav Abdullah Someich, Midrash Beit Zilcha was led by the young Rav Salman Hugi Aboudi, who became the Rosh Yeshiva and *Av Beit Din* of Baghdad in 5688/1928, at the age of 34. Rav Aboudi was a Torah giant renowned for his encyclopedic knowledge of all areas of Torah, including Kabbala. He moved to Eretz Yisrael in 5711/1951 and was appointed *dayan* in Petah Tikva. In 5725/1965 he moved to Jerusalem and was appointed to the Beit Din HaGadol (along with Harav Ovadia), where he served until his passing in 5733/1973.

their eyes. In Baghdad at that time, no one began to study Talmud before the age of 15. The boy listened quietly while the group learned a Gemara in *Shabbat*, but after half an hour, he told them that they had misunderstood a *Tosafot*. "Quiet, *hatzuf* (insolent one)!" one man chastised him.[27]

"Why are you calling him *hatzuf*?" another man retorted. "Let's hear what he has to say. Why do you think we misunderstood the *Tosafot*?"

The men sat, mouths agape, as Harav Ovadia proceeded to explain the entire *sugya* (topic) to them from the basics, eventually expounding the *Tosafot* in line with the rest of his explanation. They ran to Rav Aboudi and, paraphrasing the Talmud, they said, "*Ari allah leBavel* — a lion came up *to* Bavel!"[28]

After Rav Aboudi heard what had transpired, he asked Ovadia, "What have you learned so far?"

Even at the age of 10, Ovadia was quick-witted enough to remember the Talmud's statement (*Bava Metzia* 23a) that one may mislead someone by implying that he hasn't learned something he actually *has* learned. "I learned some Mishnayot," he answered.

"Which *Masechtot*?"

"*Masechet Shabbat*."

"What else?" Rav Aboudi pressed.

"*Masechet Eruvin*."

"What else?"

"*Masechet Pesahim*."

"Tell me the truth — what else?"

Finally, Ovadia realized that he wouldn't get away with this line of answering, so he said, "All of *Seder Mo'ed*."

"What else?"

"*Seder Nashim*."

"And?"

"*Seder Nezikin*."

"Can I test you on it?"

---

27. Rav David Yosef, with details filled in from other sources.
28. The Talmud (*Bava Kamma* 117a) uses this phrase in the reverse regarding Rav Kahana, who went from Bavel to Eretz Yisrael. Upon Rav Kahana's arrival, Reish Lakish told Rav Yohanan, "*Ari allah miBavel*."

Thirty years after they first met in Iraq, Harav Ovadia (R) and Rav Salman Hugi Aboudi (next to Harav Ovadia) sat together on the Beit Din HaGadol.
Also pictured are Rav Betzalel Zolty; Chief Rabbi Yitzchak Nissim (standing); Rav Yosef Shalom Elyashiv, Rav Eliezer Goldschmidt, and Rav Shaul Yisraeli.

"Yes," the young Ovadia answered.

"Wait one second," Rav Aboudi persisted. "The rabbanim told me that you explained a *Tosafot* to them. How much Gemara did you learn?"

"Only a little," Ovadia replied.

"Tell me exactly what you learned."

Ovadia eventually admitted to having learned three *perakim* in *Bava Kamma* and two in *Bava Metzia*.

Rav Aboudi took out a Gemara and turned to *Perek Hamafkid*,[29] which Ovadia had learned at the age of seven, and tested him on it.

Thirty years later, when the two sat together on the Beit Din HaGadol, Rav Aboudi related that on that memorable day, he had asked the young Ovadia a question on a *Tosafot* in *Hamafkid*, and Ovadia had recited the entire *Tosafot* word-for-word from memory.

After this initial meeting, Rav Aboudi sent Ovadia back to Midrash Beit Zilcha to study with the accomplished scholars — some of whom considered him their *"maggid shiur"* for the six months he was there.

---

29. The third *perek* in *Bava Metzia*, which is commonly learned with students no younger than 10 or 11.

Before they returned to Eretz Yisrael, Rav Aboudi summoned R' Yaakov and cautioned him to guard his son carefully and be sure to invest in his Torah studies, predicting that Ovadia would go on to light up the world with his Torah.

Heeding Rav Aboudi's instructions, R' Yaakov tried to send Ovadia back to Rav Shlomo Abo's classroom when they returned to Eretz Yisrael after Purim 5691/1931, but the staff of Bnei Zion informed him that there was no way for his son to continue learning in the school. "He's far too advanced for his fellow students," they explained, advising R' Yaakov to try to enroll him in Porat Yosef, despite his being several years younger than the youngest student enrolled there at the time.

CHAPTER THREE
BEN PORAT YOSEF

YOUNG OVADIA'S FIRST STINT IN YESHIVAT PORAT Yosef, at the age of 10, was short-lived, due to the precarious security situation in Yerushalayim.

The early 1930s were a tumultuous time in Eretz Yisrael. As it became clearer to the Arab residents of Yerushalayim that the British who held a Mandate to govern the land[1] were going to

---

1. Although a detailed history of the British Mandate is beyond the scope of this work, some background information is necessary to set the scene for the life story of Harav Ovadia.
   During World War I, British General Edmund Allenby led a force through parts of the Middle East, promising the native Arabs independence if they would rebel against the Turkish Ottoman Empire that had controlled the Middle East for several centuries, and thereby help the British take control of the territory. Ultimately, the British reneged on the promise and set up a military administration named the Occupied Enemy Territory Administration in the captured territory. They legitimized their control of the region by obtaining a mandate, called the British Mandate for Palestine, from the League of Nations (the precursor to the United Nations) in 1923. The area they controlled included modern-day Israel, as well as areas that are now under Palestinian or Jordanian control.
   Already before World War I, however, the British had issued the Balfour Declaration, which committed the empire to furthering the rights of the Jews to set up a Jewish homeland in what was then known as Palestine. The Zionist movement took that declaration to mean that they would eventually receive a state in the area, while the British may have meant merely that they would facilitate Jewish return to the Land, without granting the Jews rights to a self-governing state. At first, the Zionists began to set up semi-governmental bodies, such as the Jewish Agency, waiting for the day when the British would end their rule and relinquish control of the land to them. When the Zionists realized that the British had no intentions of doing so, however, they splintered into a few groups. The main group, the Haganah (led by David Ben-Gurion, who would eventually serve as Israel's first prime minister), continued to try to achieve independence primarily through diplomatic channels. Other groups, such as the Irgun Z'vai Leumi

Short-Lived Enrollment

allow the Jews to establish a state — and not merely a homeland — they erupted in violent protests. These pre-State protests hit their peak in 1936-1939, but already in 1930 a group of peasants, trained and led by Sheikh Izz ad-Din al-Qassam,[2] organized a militia called the Black Hand, wreaking terror on both the Jewish residents of Eretz Yisrael and the British forces.

The Porat Yosef building in the Old City of Yerushalayim, where the budding Torah giant Ovadia Yosef thrived

---

(or simply "The Irgun," led by Menahem Begin) and Lehi (an acronym for לוחמי חירות ישראל, Fighters for Israel's Independence, also known as the Stern Gang for its leader Avraham "Yair" Stern), tried to force the British to relinquish control of Eretz Yisrael by regularly attacking their strongholds, rebelling against their curfews, and generally making life miserable for the British occupying forces.

The Arabs were equally determined to self-rule, and they tried, unsuccessfully, to drive both the British and the Jews out of the land through terrorism during the 1930s. Eventually, the Jewish attacks became unbearable to the British, and they ended their Mandate on May 14, 1948. A day later, Israel declared independence, which prompted an immediate attack by seven Arab armies. With much *siyata d'Shmaya*, Israel eventually vanquished these enemies in the War of Independence.

2. This Syrian-born sheik is regarded as the forefather of the anti-Israel movements; Hamas's military wing is named after him.

Ovadia's father, R' Yaakov Ovadia, was concerned that his son would be attacked as he passed through Arab neighborhoods in the Old City en route to Porat Yosef, which was situated right near the Kotel. At the end of 5691/1931, after Ovadia had been in Porat Yosef for just three months, R' Yaakov decided to reenroll him in Bnei Zion for the 5692 school year. But his level of learning proved too much for his fellow students in Bnei Zion, and during the winter of 5692 R' Yaakov sent him back to Porat Yosef, which would become his second home — or some say his primary home — for the next 15 years, until the end of 5707/1947.

YESHIVAT PORAT YOSEF WAS THE BRAINCHILD OF RAV YOSEF Haim of Baghdad, the Ben Ish Hai. Shortly before he passed away in 1909, he asked R' Yosef Avraham Shalom, a student of his who had moved to Calcutta, India and had built a considerable fortune there, to donate money to build a yeshiva in Eretz Yisrael that would enable Sephardic *talmidei hachamim* to sit and learn comfortably.

The Sole Sephardi Yeshiva

There were few yeshivot in Yerushalayim at that point. For Ashkenazim there was Eitz Haim, and for Sephardim there was Ohel Moed, a small yeshiva led by Rav Shlomo Laniado.[3] Rav Yosef Haim wanted to create one large yeshiva that would absorb Ohel Moed and the few Sephardi kollelim — including Kabbala kollelim — that existed in those years.[4] The plan was to build twenty apartments in which married scholars could live, so that they could pursue their Torah study without having to worry about their finances.

---

3. Born in 5636/1876 in Aleppo, Syria, R' Rafael Shlomo was the 14th generation in the Laniado family to serve as a rav.

He was known in Syria not only for his Torah scholarship, but also for his great *hessed* on behalf of his community. Aside from founding an organization called Tzedaka U'Marpeh to aid the ill and indigent, R' Rafael Shlomo was constantly working to bring peace among feuding family members and different factions in the community.

R' Rafael Shlomo moved to Eretz Yisrael in approximately 5660/1900. In 5667/1907, the *mekubal* R' Ezra Harari-Raful established Yeshiva Ohel Moed, and he asked R' Laniado to serve as Rosh Yeshiva. When Porat Yosef opened in 5683 (1922-1923), Yeshiva Ohel Moed moved into its new building, and R' Rafael Shlomo became Rosh Yeshiva of the new yeshiva.

On 14 Shevat, 5685/1925, R' Laniado suddenly fell ill, and he passed away the very next day.

4. Rav Benzion Mutzafi's introduction to *Tiferet Zion*.

Rav Ovadia's mentors in Porat Yosef included such great *geonim* and *mekubalim* as Hacham Ephraim Cohen (R) and Rosh Yeshiva Rav Ezra Attia and Rav Yaakov Ades (first two on the left).

Construction on the Porat Yosef building in the Old City of Yerushalayim began in 1914, but it was delayed several times, due in part to the passing of R' Shalom, its sponsor. The building was completed in 5683/1923, and the yeshiva began to function then with Rav Shlomo Laniado and Harav Ovadia Hadaya[5] at its helm. Aside from the regular program of *Torat Hanigleh*,[6] there was a section of the yeshiva, housed in a separate area, in which elderly *mekubalim* would study Kabbala. The young Ovadia didn't spend much time in that area of the yeshiva, but he nevertheless caught the eye of the *mekubal* who led the group, Rav Ephraim Cohen.[7] Rav Cohen would become one of Ovadia's key mentors in his early years, despite the relatively minimal contact the two had in the yeshiva.

When Ovadia arrived in Porat Yosef, Rav Ezra Attia was already serving as Rosh Yeshiva, a position he would hold for nearly fifty years.

---

5. Rav Ovadia Hadaya was born in Aleppo, Syria, in 5650/1890, and his family moved to Eretz Yisrael when he was a young boy. His father, Rav Shalom Hadaya, was considered one of the greatest *mekubalim* of the time, and when he saw his son succeeding in learning, he invested every effort into finding suitable teachers to guide him. Rav Hadaya would go on to become one of the leading Sephardic sages of his time, moving in 5699/1939 from his position as one of the Roshei Yeshiva of Porat Yosef to serve as the Sephardic Chief Rabbi of Petah Tikva, and eventually moving back to Yerushalayim when he was appointed to the Beit Din HaGadol in 5711/1951. He passed away at the time of *Seudah Shlishit* on Shabbat, 20 Shevat 5729/1969.

6. *Torat Hanigleh* refers to the "revealed" parts of Torah — i.e., the study of the Talmud, halachic works, and ethical works, as compared to *Torat Hanistar*, the "hidden" parts of Torah, which refers to the study of mystical or esoteric subjects, commonly referred to as Kabbala.

7. In the 1950s, Rav Ephraim Cohen's son, Rav Shalom Cohen, would join a night kollel founded by Harav Ovadia, and much later, when Harav Ovadia began to lead the Shas party, Rav Shalom Cohen became one of only four members of the Moetzet Hachmei HaTorah. Approximately half a year after Harav Ovadia's passing, Rav Shalom was declared as his successor as the leader of the Moetzet.

Meeting His Mentor

NO WORK ON HARAV OVADIA YOSEF — AND, FOR THAT MATter, no work on almost any Sephardi leader of the last few generations — would be complete without an appreciation of Hacham Ezra Attia, the *moreh derech* of nearly every major Sephardi Torah leader throughout the world in the last fifty years. He was so influential, in fact, that after his passing, Harav Ovadia eulogized him by saying, "If not for him, the Torah would have been forgotten from Sephardic Jewry."

Born in Aleppo, Syria on 15 Shevat 5641/1881, the young Rav Ezra possessed an unusual love for learning, one that did not go unnoticed. By the time his parents, Rav Yitzhak and Leah Attia, decided to move to Eretz Yisrael in 5655/1895, the teenager had already become so proficient in learning that when his father passed away suddenly shortly after the family settled in Yerushalayim, Ezra would simply hide away in the Shoshanim L'David *beit midrash* in the Bucharim neighborhood and learn day and night, studying *masechet* after *masechet* diligently.

In order to support Ezra and her other son, Eliyahu, Mrs. Leah Attia would do housework in the homes of wealthier Jews, but her earnings were hardly enough to cover their expenses. "Hashem's kindness overwhelmed us," recalled Rav Ezra many decades later, as he reflected on the family's survival despite the dire poverty. "We usually had a full pita to split between us. Sometimes we even had an egg to split as well."

Yet young Ezra didn't allow hunger to deter him from learning. He would closet himself in Shoshanim L'David for days at time, bringing along some crusty bread to dip in salt, and lying down on the benches to sleep when he grew too tired to continue learning.

Although he did engage in Torah discussions from time to time with some of the Torah leaders of Yerushalayim, for the most part, Ezra spent those years developing his own approach to learning. Perhaps it was the years he spent learning in solitude that gave Hacham Ezra the unique ability to remain focused on finding a solution to a question long after others would have given up.

"Most people can work on a solution to a question for 12 hours, maybe 16 hours," said Rav Benzion Abba Shaul, who succeeded

Hacham Ezra as a Rosh Yeshiva of Porat Yosef.[8] "But who can work on a solution for a few weeks or months at a time?

"I remember one instance in which he mulled over a question for six months — and eventually came up with a novel approach to the *sugya* to resolve the difficulty. He wouldn't suffice with just any approach; it had to ring true. I remember him working for a long time on a comment of a Maharsha, for instance, until he was satisfied that he understood it fully."

Despite his own solitude as a youngster, as Rosh Yeshiva of Porat Yosef, Hacham Ezra was able to understand each individual *talmid* in the yeshiva and work with his unique traits, bringing out his greatest qualities and crafting many of the future leaders of Klal Yisrael. These *talmidim* included Harav Ovadia; Rav Benzion Abba Shaul and Rav Yehuda Tzadka, both of whom Hacham Ezra tapped to help him run Porat Yosef and who would go on to lead the yeshiva after his passing; Rav Baruch Ben-Haim (rav of Congregation Shaare Zion in New York); Rav Zion Levi, chief rabbi of Panama; and Rav Yosef Harari-Raful, Rav and Rosh Yeshiva of Ateret Torah.

Like a Rishon

HACHAM EZRA'S HUMILITY WAS LEGENDARY. EVEN IN HIS capacity as the leader of the greatest Sephardic Torah center in the world and the mentor of rabbanim throughout the world, he treated his students with the utmost respect, and tried to hide his greatness in Torah as much as possible.

> When the Hazon Ish visited Porat Yosef on his way back from the Kotel HaMaaravi, he wanted to converse with Hacham Ezra in learning, but the latter demurred, explaining that he was very tired. His humility couldn't obscure his greatness in this instance, however. The Hazon Ish spoke in learning with students in the yeshiva, and was extremely impressed when they told him some of the hiddushim their Rosh Yeshiva had said that day.

---

8. At a *hesped* delivered in Porat Yosef commemorating Hacham Ezra's 20th *hilula*.

Rav Baruch Ben-Haim[9] related that shortly after this incident, he traveled with a friend to Tel Aviv, and the two then went to learn for a few hours in a yeshiva where the Hazon Ish used to learn. The Hazon Ish walked over to them and asked, "Are you from Porat Yosef?" They answered in the affirmative. A few minutes later, a group of twenty students surrounded them, asking, "Who is your Rosh Yeshiva?"

"He is like one of the *Rishonim*."
Hacham Ezra Attia, Rosh Yeshivat Porat Yosef

"Why are you taking a sudden interest in us?" the boys from Porat Yosef asked in reply. "We've been studying here for a while and you haven't said a word to us."

"The Hazon Ish told us that your Rosh Yeshiva is like one of the Rishonim," they explained.

Late-Night Learning

OVADIA'S FIRST REBBEIM IN PORAT YOSEF WERE RAV YOSEF Shlush and Rav Moshe Ades,[10] and he would talk about both of them with great reverence throughout his life. They took a deep interest in the boy who not only had a lightning-quick mind and could master in minutes whatever they taught, but was also a *matmid* who spent every available moment learning.

---

9. Rav Baruch Ben-Haim was one of Harav Ovadia's lifelong friends, having learned with him for years in Porat Yosef. He eventually moved to America and served as the rabbi of Congregation Shaare Zion in Brooklyn for more than 50 years.

10. Rav Moshe Ades was one of the founding members of Porat Yosef in 1923, and he taught there for close to 35 years. In his later years, when the yeshiva was exiled to Beit Knesset Tzofayof after Jordan took control of the Old City, Harav Ovadia would occasionally substitute for Rav Ades, his former rebbi, who was ailing in his later years.

Rav Moshe Ades (above, delivering a *shiur*) and Rav Yosef Shlush (R) were delighted with the young boy whose lightning-quick mind was augmented by his diligence.

During those years, when his parents thought he was asleep for the night, he would sneak out and head to a local shul where he would learn for a few hours before slipping back into the house.[11]

> *One night, when he arrived home, he found that the door was locked. He knew that by that time, the entire family was asleep, so he opened one of his sefarim and learned by the light of the moon. When R' Yaakov opened the door in the wee hours of the morning, he was shocked to see his son sitting on the stoop, learning as though it were the middle of the day.*[12]

He was willing to go to great lengths so as not to cause his family to suffer because of his own learning.

> *His brother Na'im related that on one winter morning, Ovadia rose extremely early to go learn, and he couldn't find his shoes. Concerned that his search might awaken other members of the family, Ovadia slipped on several pairs of socks and walked out into the Yerushalayim morning chill.*

Those were years when many adolescents sneaked out of their homes at night, but most were doing so to join clandestine Irgun meetings and plan attacks on the British to try to force them out of Eretz Yisrael.[13] But Ovadia had no interest in the nationalistic visions that attracted so many of the youth of his day, including all of his younger brothers and several of his sisters. All of his dreams revolved around Torah study — and like his fellow youth who joined the various Jewish militias he, too, endangered himself, albeit for the sake of Torah.

> *Arab gangs often roamed the streets of Yerushalayim at night, trying to instill fear in the hearts of the city's Jewish residents and shake their nationalistic fervor. One night,*

---
11. See p. 27.
12. *Iggeret L'Ben Torah*, by Rav Yitzchak Yosef, p. 80.
13. See footnote 1 in this chapter.

Rav Shimshon Aharon Polansky, the Tepliker Rav (middle), rescued Harav Ovadia as a young child, then bestowed *semicha* upon him as an adult.

when he was 13 years old, Ovadia made his way from his home to the beit knesset on top of the "shtieblach" in Beit Yisrael, carrying a small candle by which to learn.

When residents of the neighborhood saw the flickering light coming from the window, they assumed that Arabs were in the midst of vandalizing the beit knesset. They ran to ask Rav Shimshon Aharon Polansky, the Tepliker Rav,[14] who was the official rav of the neighborhood, what to do. He decided to investigate for himself. When he entered the beit knesset, expecting to confront unruly Arabs, he was

---

14. Known as the Tepliker Rav for the city in Europe in which he had served as rav before immigrating to Eretz Yisrael, Rav Shimshon Aharon Polansky was a tremendous *talmid hacham* who trained numerous future rabbanim in practical halacha — especially in areas related to family purity.

Years after this incident, the Tepliker Rav would be the one to bestow *semicha* upon Harav Ovadia, investing him with the authority to rule on halachic matters — as he did for nearly every one of the leading *poskim* in Eretz Yisrael: Rav Shlomo Zalman Auerbach; Rav Yosef Shalom Elyashiv; Rav Yisrael Yaakov Fischer, *Raavad* of the Eida Haredit; and Rav Shmuel Wosner, author of *Shevet HaLevi*.

shocked to see a young man studying Torah, oblivious to the hullabaloo he had caused.

Rav Polansky laid his hand gently on Ovadia's shoulder and said, "Now is not the time to learn here, because the Arabs can spot where you are and attack you. Come with me, I'll walk you home."

When they reached Harav Ovadia's street, they saw his father R' Yaakov pacing nervously outside. Ovadia's parents had noticed his absence, and knowing that there were Arab mobs on the prowl, they were extremely concerned for his safety. When R' Yaakov saw Ovadia making his way home, he was about to reprimand him for his rash behavior, but Rav Polansky stopped him in his tracks. "Please leave the child alone," he said, predicting that with the great love of learning Ovadia was displaying at so young an age, he would go on to become a gadol.[15]

While Harav Ovadia's other rebbeim were influential in helping him develop his approach to learning, as we will see, it was Hacham Ezra Attia who charted Harav Ovadia's trajectory through life, helping him to advance from one level to another until he became the Rishon LeZion.

But before Hacham Ezra would guide his protégé in fighting political leaders who tried to stop Harav Ovadia from rising in the ranks of the Rabbanut, he had to help him fight a more mundane battle: surviving the rampant poverty in Yerushalayim that forced most of the boys his age into the working world.

EARNING ENOUGH TO SUPPORT A FAMILY WAS SO DIFFICULT in Yerushalayim of the early 1900s that most boys Ovadia's age were already apprenticed or working to help their families subsist. Yeshiva for those beyond the age of 10 or 11 was generally limited to children of great scholars or rabbanim. R' Yaakov, Ovadia's father, would have loved to allow his son to learn morning, noon, and

Hacham Ezra's Offer

---

15. *Iggeret L'Ben Torah*, p. 81.

night, but with a growing family to support, he needed his eldest son to help him stock shelves in his store and help customers carry home their groceries. He felt he had no choice but to take Ovadia out of yeshiva.

> It took a mere day or two for the heads of Porat Yosef to notice that their star pupil was missing. Hacham Ezra and Rav Ephraim Cohen then decided to pay a visit to the grocery store. When they asked R' Yaakov why Ovadia was no longer attending yeshiva, R' Yaakov explained that he needed his son to help in the store.
>
> "His future is in Torah," the two rabbanim explained, "not in the grocery business."
>
> R' Yaakov explained that it was too much for him to handle the burden of the store on his own, and he wouldn't commit to sending his son back to yeshiva. To his shock, Hacham Ezra immediately removed his rabbinic robe and donned a work apron.
>
> "Wh-what are you doing?" R' Yaakov stammered.
>
> "I'll work here for two hours a day instead of Ovadia," Hacham Ezra explained. "He's a genius, and it's vital that he spend his youth developing in learning."

Ovadia returned to Porat Yosef, but he was not entirely excused from the grocery. His day in yeshiva would start at around 9 in the morning, but by midafternoon, the yeshiva would empty out, because the streets became too dangerous to walk as night approached. When Ovadia would come home in the afternoon, R' Yaakov would press him into service at the grocery store. Ovadia would bring *sefarim* along with him, and when there were no customers, he would quickly open a *sefer* and snatch a few minutes of learning.

> Some crooks recognized this pattern and decided to exploit it. They would wait until Ovadia wasn't looking, then sneak into the store and steal expensive items, such as cigarettes. Ovadia would be so engrossed in his learning

that he wouldn't even notice them entering or leaving. His brother Na'im related decades later that when R' Yaakov realized how much merchandise he was losing because of this arrangement, he grew so frustrated that he told Ovadia, "A grocer you'll never be. Just go learn."

"I was always convinced that those were no ordinary thieves," Na'im surmised with a smile. "They were angels who dressed up as thieves to enable Ovadia to go back to learn."[16]

Some fifty-odd years later, when Harav Ovadia was the chief rabbi, he would visit prisons to offer hizzuk to the inmates and encourage them to mend their ways. During one such visit, a prisoner admitted that he had been one of the thieves who had taken advantage of Ovadia's diligence in learning to steal from the family's store. Harav Ovadia forgave him wholeheartedly and patiently explained how he should go about doing teshuva for the more significant sins he had committed since those days.[17]

Many decades later, a secular reporter once visited Harav Ovadia to discuss something he was writing, and he took the opportunity to ask him whether the story about Hacham Ezra and Rav Ephraim Cohen visiting his father in the grocery store was true.

Rav Ovadia acknowledged that it was.

"What would have happened," wondered the reporter, "had Rav Attia and Rav Cohen not succeeded in convincing your father to allow you to return to your studies?"

"*Be'ahavatah tishgeh tamid* — you will always be intoxicated with her love," Harav Ovadia answered simply, paraphrasing a verse in *Mishlei*.[18] Even in his youth, he was so enamored with Torah that he could never have given it up. Had it not worked out for him this way, he would still have found a way to continue learning.

---

16. Culled from a secular Israeli media program, *Panim Amitiyot with Amnon Levi*, whose inaugural broadcast was devoted to explaining to the Israeli public who Harav Ovadia really was. These two stories are quoted directly as they were told on *Panim Amitiyot* by Harav Ovadia's son Rav David Yosef and his brother Na'im Ovadia.
17. *Posek HaDor*.
18. 5:19.

"Be'ahavatah tishgeh tamid":
Rav Ovadia's famous inseparability from Torah began in his early youth,
and only grew through the decades.

A Mother's Sacrifice

EVEN BEFORE HE WAS OFFICIALLY REMOVED FROM HIS DUTIES in the family grocery, Ovadia's role was often filled by his mother, Mrs. Georgia Ovadia. Just as she had encouraged him to learn as a young child, she gladly offered to help in the store to free her son to learn. Harav Ovadia would always hail his mother's sacrifice in enabling him to learn, and when he donned his first rabbinic frock, he went to her house and put it on in her presence, in appreciation for her efforts to help him to grow into a *talmid hacham*.

And Harav Ovadia's mother was a presence in his life even after her sudden passing in 1957,[19] not only in the introductions to his many works that he dedicated to her memory, in appreciation for

---

19. See p. 287.

raising him to learn Torah, but in a much more tangible — and eerie — manner.

> Each day during the first month of mourning for Mrs. Georgia Ovadia, a dove would land on the windowsill beside where he learned. After the sheloshim, the dove disappeared, and Harav Ovadia thought nothing of it and never said a word about it to anyone.
>
> More than ten years later, when he was inaugurated as the chief rabbi of Tel Aviv, he addressed the large crowd gathered in the Great Synagogue. As he began his address, a dove flew into the beit knesset and landed on the teivah, sitting and "listening" to his address.
>
> After this incident, Harav Ovadia said that it seemed that this dove represented his mother's neshama, and had come to enjoy the nahat of seeing him rise to greatness.
>
> But that wasn't the dove's last visit.
>
> Nearly four decades later, toward the end of 5766/2006, Harav Ovadia underwent a stent operation to clear clogged cardiac arteries. The operation took place just before Rosh Hashana 5767, and he asked to be released from the hospital for Rosh Hashana.[20] On Erev Rosh Hashana, a dove flew into the private beit knesset that had been built for him under his home in Har Nof, Yerushalayim, and landed on his seat. The congregants shooed it away, but as soon as they sat down, it flew right back to his seat and landed once again. This process repeated itself several times, until someone decided to ask Harav Ovadia what to do about it. Rather than interrupt his learning immediately to behold this strange sight for himself, he learned until close to sundown, when it was time to go to the beit knesset for the tefillah.
>
> When he saw the dove sitting there, he walked over to it and stroked it a few times. Surprisingly, the dove just sat

---

20. His condition deteriorated after Rosh Hashana, and he returned to the hospital until after Yom Kippur.

there, allowing him to pat it. He recited a few verses of the piyut by Rav Yehuda HaLevi[21] that begins with the words: יוֹנָה מַה תֶּהְגִּי, O dove, why do you moan? He then recited the verse: וַיְשַׁלַּח אֶת הַיּוֹנָה וְלֹא יָסְפָה שׁוּב אֵלָיו עוֹד, And he sent away the dove, and it did not return to him again (Bereishit 8:12), and said to the dove, "You have completed your mission; go in peace. Amen, kein yehi ratzon (may it be [God's] will)."

The dove flew into the air, circled Harav Ovadia's head a number of times, and flew out the window. When his family members asked him to explain what they had just witnessed, he waved it off. "It was a dove like any other," he said simply.[22]

Bar Mitzva

OVADIA'S BAR MITZVA WAS CELEBRATED AT BEIT HAKNESSET Shimon HaTzaddik, situated at the grave of Shimon HaTzaddik in what is now considered East Jerusalem. So excited was he to don the *tefillin* his father had purchased for him from Rav Tzadka Huzin — a disciple of the Ben Ish Hai and an extremely pious vendor of *sifrei Torah*, *tefillin*, and *mezuzot* — that he wrote a long ode, in sophisticated poetry woven of scriptural phrases, to celebrate the mitzva that would now be his.[23]

He continued learning day and night, slowly but surely mastering large portions of Talmud Bavli. Already in his youth, his rebbeim took note of his ability to learn a topic through to its halachic conclusions. This ability sometimes yielded surprising results.

> One day, the entire Porat Yosef was in an uproar. A young man had claimed that he could prove that a particular halacha should not follow an explicit ruling of the Beit Yosef in Shulhan Aruch. Someone apprised Rav Ezra Attia of this audacious claim, whereupon Rav Ezra summoned

---

21. This *piyut*, written for the festival of Succot, is a hypothetical conversation between a *yonah* (dove), which represents the Jewish people, and Hashem.
22. Throughout his life, Harav Ovadia would try to dismiss or make light of any supernatural occurrences in his life — though they were many. See Chapter 26.
23. Published in its entirety in *Abir Haro'im*, p. 43.

the young man, Ovadia Yosef, to the front of the beit midrash and asked him to explain his position.

"We all know," said Harav Ovadia, "that Maran the Beit Yosef ruled according to the majority opinion of three Rishonim: the Rambam, the Rif, and the Rosh. In this instance, he rules a certain way because he did not have access to a work of one of these Rishonim. Since we do have access to it and we see that this Rishon agrees with one of the other two Rishonim, we have a majority opinion against the way Maran rules in Shulhan Aruch — but Maran himself would rule according to this majority."

Rather than rebuke the young man as others had expected, Hacham Ezra kissed him on his forehead and said, "He is correct."

Thus began a decades-long pattern in which Harav Ovadia would rule in a way that caused others to doubt or even condemn him, and Hacham Ezra would consistently support him and encourage him to continue issuing rulings despite opposition.

Perhaps Rav Ezra's own experience learning on his own as a teenager was what prompted him to support the young Ovadia on another front. A few years after arriving in Porat Yosef, Ovadia grew frustrated with the pace at which the yeshiva was learning. He felt that the yeshiva's approach — which was based primarily on probing the depths of each *sugya* at length, even at the cost of learning broader sections of Gemara — would limit the students' overall knowledge. He wrote about this problem in his own diaries even as a teenager, and later devoted the introductions of several volumes of his *Yabia Omer* to it. Although he did not succeed in changing the yeshiva's approach, he refused to go along with it himself. Rather, he would sit and learn on his own, without *havrutot*, pushing himself to cover at least two *dapim* a day. He did not gloss over the subject matter, however — he would learn all the *Rishonim* and glean the practical halacha from the *sugyot*.

Although many of his fellow students and even some rebbeim in the yeshiva disapproved of his solitary approach, Hacham Ezra encouraged him to ignore his detractors and continue learning in the way that he saw fit.

His "Friend"

OUR SAGES TEACH (*AVOT* 1:6), "*UKNEI LECHA HAVER* — ACQUIRE for yourself a friend." Some commentaries homiletically expound this to mean, "A pen should be your friend." (*Kaneh* is a writing instrument in Mishnaic terminology.)

In the absence of friends who could match his style of learning, Ovadia took to writing down what he learned, making his pen into a loyal friend. He wrote primarily in a classic Sephardi handwriting style called *hatzi-kulmus*. Toward the end of his life, he handed over to his children and grandchildren some of the multitudes of notebooks he had filled over the years. His sons Rav Yitzchak and Rav David both related that they were surprised to receive these notebooks, which contained his approaches to *sugyot* in the Talmud. They knew that their father had devoted almost all of his writing time to writing halachic responsa. When had he had the time to fill dozens of notebooks with notes on the Talmud?

They found the answer in the date written at the top of those notebooks and in the still-childlike handwriting: As a youth, from the ages of 11 through 15, he was already writing in a style on par with the great *Aharonim*, raising questions asked in earlier generations and answering them in a clear and concise manner. In his youthfulness, he was careful to label each notebook with a "*shaar*" (title page) that included his name, the title *Yabia Omer* (which contained an allusion to his own name),[24] and sometimes even a drawing of a rabbinic "stamp."

During these years, he also attended the *shiurim* of Rav Eliyahu Lofes, who would be one of the primary influences on his style of learning a *sugya*. Throughout his life, he would quote Rav Eliyahu on certain halachic matters, and he would forever appreciate all the efforts his rebbi invested into him.

The Works of a Sixteen-Year-Old

AT THE AGE OF 16, OVADIA WAS ALREADY HONING ANOTHER skill: how to teach Torah to an audience. He actually combined those two skills with his writing, as is apparent from an introduction to a notebook he wrote in at a time when others were enjoying a break from yeshiva:

---

24. See p. 87.

Rav Ovadia's *Humash* notes, written when he was 13. His "stamp" (R) is seen on top of the page.

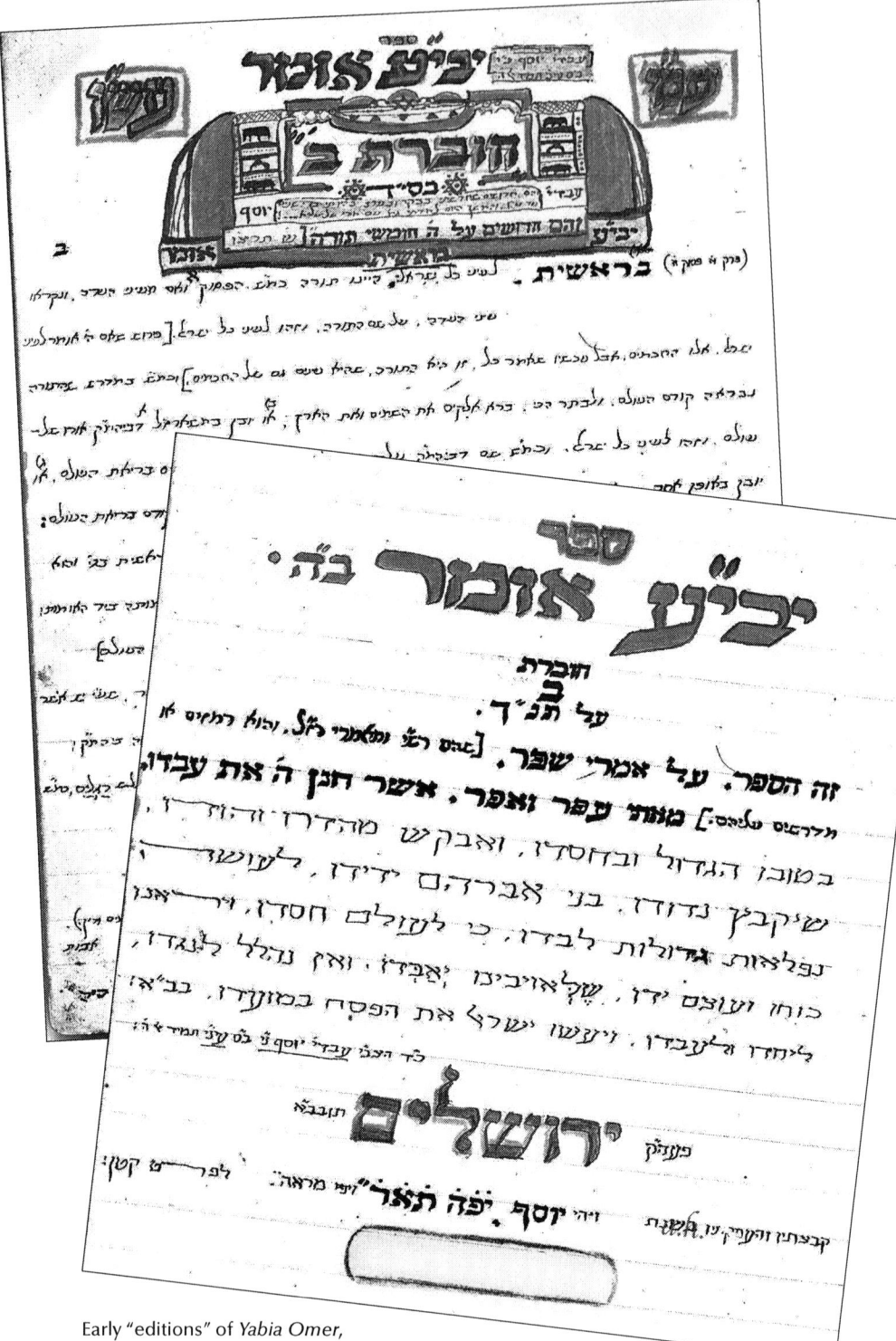

Early "editions" of *Yabia Omer*,
when that title was drawn carefully onto each of Harav Ovadia's notebooks

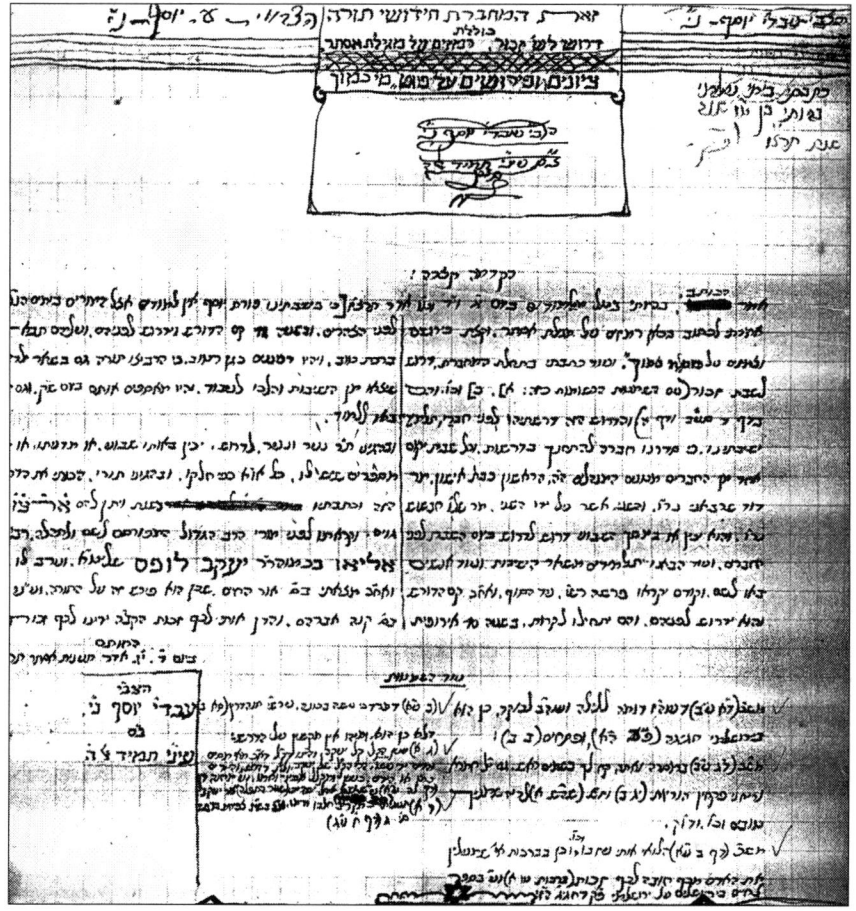

Rav Ovadia's commentary on the *piyut Mi Kamocha*, written at age 16

When we were off from learning on 13, 14, and 15 Adar 5697 (for in our yeshiva, Porat Yosef, the teachers do not teach on those days), I decided to record some *remazim* [allusions] on *Megillat Esther*, and some commentaries and *remazim* on the *piyut*, "Mi Kamocha."[25] I also included, at the beginning of the notebook, a discourse on *Parashat Zachor*. I delivered this discourse before my fellow students in the yeshiva, for we have organized a group to train ourselves to speak. Each Shabbat, one of the members would be appointed by the principal Mar David Sharbani or his assistant Mar Shalom

---

25. Recited in some communities on Shabbat Zachor, the Shabbat before Purim.

Habshush, and that student prepares a discourse during the week that he delivers on Shabbat before all of the members. We also invite students from other yeshivot, and other outsiders join as well. At first the group reads the *parasha* with *Rashi* from beginning to end, and then the speaker rises and speaks before them....

When each person's turn to speak arrives, he prepares during that week either his own material or a compilation from existing *sefarim* — each speaker according to his ability. When my turn came, I prepared this discourse, and I wrote it...and read it to my teacher, the great and renowned rav, Rav Eliyahu ben Moreinu Rav Yaakov Lofes *shlit"a*, and he approved of it.

The Talmud at His Fingertips

DURING THAT YEAR, OVADIA ALSO BEGAN TO RECORD A handbook of *Klalei HaShas* for himself. Such compositions, usually authored by scholars who have been learning the Talmud for decades, offer general guidelines into the terminology and logic of the Talmud. They typically cite numerous sources to prove that the Talmud uses a term to denote that it is beginning to ask a question, pose a contradiction, or the like. While he was writing this handbook, which he titled *Hinuch HaNaar*, he came across a note in the *Klalei HaTalmud* written by the author of *Knesset HaGedola*, stating that the term *vehatanya*, which is generally used to denote that the Talmud is about to refute a point based on a contradiction from a *beraita*,[26] is sometimes used "*benihuta*" — i.e., to *prove* a point from a *beraita* rather than to refute it.

Ovadia took pen into hand and wrote, "These are many, and I will record some of them with the help of Hashem Yitbarach." He then recorded 51 occurrences in 27 *masechtot*, with exact sources for each!

---

26. The *beraitot* quote opinions of Tannaim that did not make it into the Mishnah for one reason or another, but a logical point made by an Amora (Talmudic sage) is generally considered to have been refuted if it contradicts a *beraita*. When an Amora suggested a point in the Talmud, another Amora often refuted it by citing a *beraita* that was transmitted to him by his teachers, beginning with the word *vehatanya*, which meant, "How can you suggest this point, if we learned in a *beraita* otherwise?"

As a teenager, Ovadia was already able to list 51 occurrences in 27 *masechtot* in which the Talmud uses a term in a specific way.

No wonder that by the time Ovadia turned 17, his rebbeim, Rav Eliyahu Lofes and Hacham Ezra Attia, were ready to "promote" him to the next level, encouraging him to publish his writings and begin disseminating Torah to the public.

CHAPTER FOUR
THE PUBLIC TAKES NOTE

WITHIN YESHIVAT PORAT YOSEF, OVADIA HAD already made quite a name for himself. At the same time, he was very wary of overstepping what was appropriate for his age — even if he dreamed in his mind of the day he would be able to publish many different works. At 15, he drew up a list of sixteen *sefarim* he planned to publish — including the titles he planned to use (explaining the allusion to his name in each title),[1] and a brief description of the subject matter he would cover in the *sefer*. Incredibly, he indeed followed through on this dream and published most of those works in the course of his life, though some under different titles from the ones he had planned at 15.

At that point, however, cognizant of the limitations on a young man his age, he kept these writings to himself.

At the age of 17, he finished all of Talmud Bavli for the first time, having learned it in great depth and having kept copious notes on each *masechet*. When his rebbi, Rav Eliyahu Lofes, then encouraged him to publish a manuscript he had written on *Masechet Horayot*, he acquiesced. Although money was tight, he knew that he would

---

1. See p. 87.

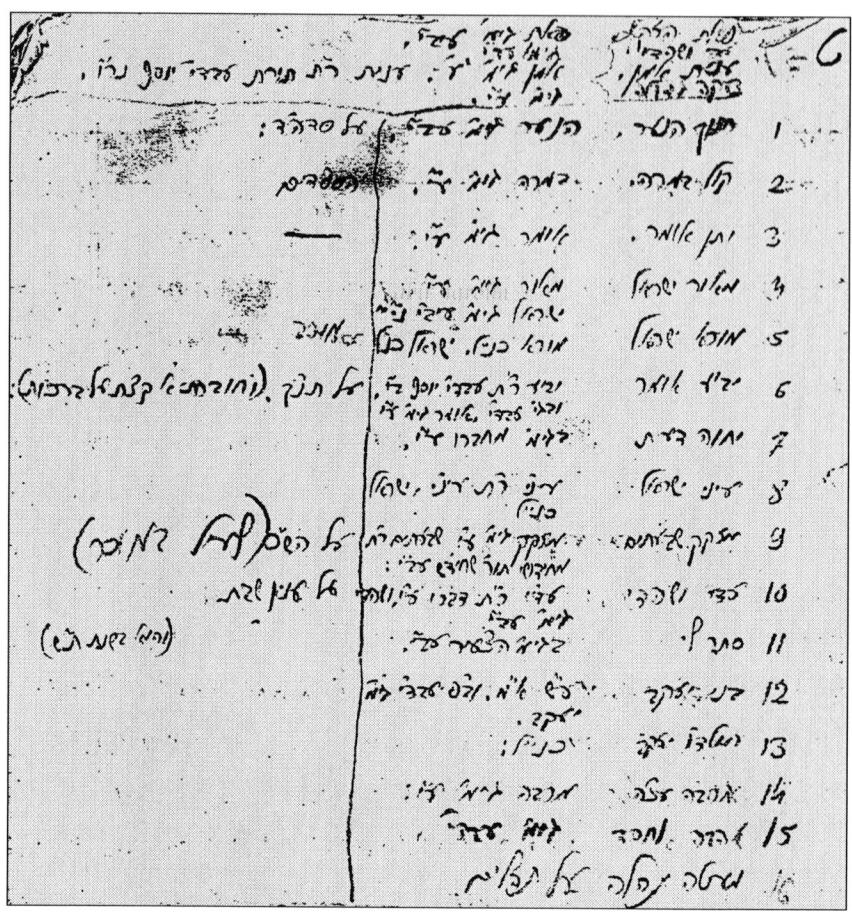

At 15, Ovadia wrote a list of sixteen works he planned to publish — many of which were indeed published, some in multi-volume sets.

be able to fund the publication, because he had been squirreling away money for this purpose for years.

> *One day, the Ovadia family heard a crash from Ovadia Yosef's room, followed by the sound of metal clinking on the floor. When they ran to his room, they found that the bottom of a desk drawer had collapsed, strewing small coins all over the room. They waited for Ovadia to come home to explain where the coins had come from.*
>
> *At first, Ovadia was concerned that his father, R' Yaakov, would be angry with him for having misappropriated money he had been given for transportation. "Don't be*

Rav Ovadia at 17, when he published his first work, *Yabia Omer* on *Horayot*

upset," he began. "You have been giving me money to take public transportation to and from yeshiva. I have been walking both ways, however, and saving up for when I would want to publish a sefer."

He looked at his father expectantly, waiting for him to admonish him. "I have only one problem with this," his father answered softly, much to Ovadia's surprise. "How can you go to a printer like a beggar, with this assortment of small coins? Give me the coins, and I'll give you respectable bills to take to the printer."

Rav Ovadia released the work on *Masechet Horayot*, in which he also included a portion of his compilation on the *Klalei HaShas*[2] and his notes on the *Seder HaDorot* of the Tannaim and Amora'im, in which he organizes the generations of the sages quoted in

---

2. See p. 80.

The prepublication notes for *Yabia Omer* on *Masechet Horayot*

Mishnayot and Gemara. (The *Seder HaDorot* was an important work in its own right, because scholars can often resolve difficulties in the Talmud just by knowing which sages preceded which.[3])

---

3. After Harav Ovadia's passing, his son, Rishon LeZion Rav Yitzchak Yosef, noted that his father's *teshuvot* — which often cite dozens of sources — are all sourced chronologically, with earlier sources quoted first and more recent ones later.

He chose the name *Yabia Omer* for this work, from the verse: יוֹם לְיוֹם יַבִּיעַ אֹמֶר וְלַיְלָה לְלַיְלָה יְחַוֶּה דָּעַת, *Day following day utters speech, and night following night declares knowledge* (*Tehillim* 19:3). He had already been applying this title to his notebooks long before he actually released his *sefer*, but he later decided to use it only for his *sefarim* of complex *teshuvot*,[4] which he considered his crowning achievement, and he released all of his other works under different titles.

The title *Yabia Omer* alludes to his name in several ways:[5] The word יביע is an acronym (when read backward) for עובדיה יוסף בן יעקב; אומר has the same numerical value as עבדיה יוסף; and יוֹם לְיוֹם יַבִּיעַ אֹמֶר has the same numerical value as עבדיה יוסף בן יעקב.

Rav Eliyahu Lofes wrote a *haskama* for the work, calling Ovadia a "*bahur* who excels in Torah and fear of Heaven," and stating, "I recognized as soon as he started learning under me that he would go on to achieve greatness in Torah." Rav Eliyahu helped him sell the small booklet as well, to try to help him raise funds to print his writings on other *masechtot*. Interestingly, although the work on *Horayot* was later reprinted in the sixth (and last) volume of *Yehaveh Daat*, Harav Ovadia published very few of his other writings on the Talmud during his lifetime,[6] preferring instead to focus on his halachic writings.

Rav Lofes also bought a set of Talmud and *Ein Yaakov* for his beloved pupil, so that he would have them on hand to learn during any free moment. The love between rebbi and talmid was so intense that when Rav Eliyahu Lofes suddenly fell ill a month after the publication of *Yabia Omer* and passed away two months later, Ovadia was distraught and inconsolable.

One night Rav Eliyahu Lofes came to him in a dream and said,

---

4. He used words from the second half of the verse: וְלַיְלָה לְלַיְלָה יְחַוֶּה דָּעַת, *and night following night declares knowledge*, as the title of his series of less complex *teshuvot* (see p. 297). Some saw a deeper message in the use of these two titles: During the day (יוֹם לְיוֹם), when people are able to focus and concentrate, they can learn the complex *Yabia Omer* series. At night (לַיְלָה לְלַיְלָה), when they need to learn something less complicated, they can learn *Yehaveh Daat*.
5. In the introduction to *Sh'eilot V'Teshuvot Yabia Omer*, Vol. 2, he cites several sources that state that one should allude to his own name in the title of a published work.
6. As of the publication of this work, his family and students have plans to publish more of his writings on the Talmud.

"Shalom," with a bright smile on his face. Then, he immediately disappeared. This visit brought Ovadia consolation.

On 4 Av 5698/1938, the day of Rav Lofes's sheloshim, Porat Yosef held a public hesped to commemorate the rebbi who had been loved and revered by so many talmidim. The heads of Porat Yosef spoke, as did several venerable rabbanim from outside the yeshiva — but Hacham Ezra Attia asked one more person to speak: 17-year-old Ovadia Yosef. The latter demurred, on the grounds that it wasn't appropriate for someone his age to speak alongside such advanced scholars, but Hacham Ezra would not take no for an answer. "Your rebbi loved you so much," he said. "Your souls were bound to each other."

In lieu of a eulogy, Harav Ovadia wrote and recited a 12-stanza kinna (elegy), each stanza of which begins with the word kol and ends with his rebbi's name, Eliyahu. Each two-to-five word set was taken from either a verse in Tanach or from the words of the Sages, and in total, Ovadia cited from 369 (!) sources.[7]

Rav Eliyahu Lofes, whose sudden passing left a young Harav Ovadia utterly disconsolate for weeks, until he appeared to his 17-year-old star pupil in a dream

Throughout his life, he would quote Rav Eliyahu Lofes with reverence, and would say that any trait that he managed to perfect was only because of his association with Rav Eliyahu Lofes.

---

7. The *kinnah* is printed in its entirety in *Abir Haro'im*, pp. 65-71, with all 369 sources annotated by Rav Gad Yazdi.

The first handwritten page of Harav Ovadia's *kinnah*, based on 369 sources, which he recited in Porat Yosef on Rav Lofes's *sheloshim*

Knowing His Place

WHILE OVADIA AGREED TO PUBLISH HIS WRITINGS ON *Horayot*, he recognized on his own that there were limits to what a person his age should release to the public. Just three weeks after publishing his first work, on 23 Nissan 5698, he wrote a *teshuva*[8] regarding the propriety of a person publishing a halachic work before he turns 40.[9] Although he concludes that it would be permissible to publish halachic writings at a young age, he kept the *teshuvot* he wrote during those years hidden from the public, only publishing them in the *Sh'eilot V'Teshuvot Yabia Omer* series that he began to release after his 30th birthday.

Nevertheless, Ovadia did correspond with the Torah leaders of his time, sending them lengthy letters examining their writings

Rav Ovadia with Rishon LeZion Rav Benzion Meir Hai Uziel, who published his correspondence with the teenaged Ovadia in his *Mishpetei Uziel*

---

8. He published an expanded version of this *teshuva* several decades later, in *Yabia Omer*, *Hoshen Mishpat* 1.

9. The question was based on a long-standing ban, first enacted by Rav Yehezkel Landau (author of *Noda B'Yehuda*) and other leaders of his generation, who had seen unworthy manuscripts published by authors who had not fully developed as scholars before they committed their opinions to writing.

and respectfully disagreeing with some of their opinions. Even in those years, Torah leaders recognized his greatness at that young age, publishing his letters in their own works. In 5707/1947, when the Rishon LeZion, Rav Benzion Meir Hai Uziel, published the third volume of his *Sh'eilot V'Teshuvot Mishpetei Uziel* (*Mahadura Tinyana*), he included two full-length *teshuvot* responding to letters Harav Ovadia had written to him as a teenager.[10]

The two developed a warm relationship, with Ovadia visiting Rav Uziel frequently and receiving guidance in learning from him. In fact, it was Rav Uziel who encouraged him not to suffice with learning *Tur*, *Beit Yosef*, and *Shulhan Aruch*, but rather to study every available work of the *Rishonim* and *Aharonim*. This became Harav Ovadia's practice for the rest of his life; every *teshuva* he writes is based not only on the primary sources, but on dozens of other sources, ranging from the greatest sages to authors decades younger than himself.[11]

First Shiurim

WHEN HARAV OVADIA WAS 17 YEARS OLD, RAV YITZHAK Kadouri, who would eventually become a famed *mekubal* but was then the *gabbai* of Beit Knesset Ohel Rahel on Rehov David Yellin in the Geula area, asked him to begin delivering *shiurim* at 7 p.m. Since the learning in Porat Yosef ended in the midafternoon, Harav Ovadia was available at that hour, but he wasn't sure whether it was appropriate for someone his age to deliver *shiurim*. He consulted with Hacham Ezra Attia, who immediately expressed his enthusiastic approval. "You should give the *shiurim*," he declared, "and I'm giving you the right to rule on halachic matters for Klal Yisrael."

Rav Ovadia began to deliver *shiurim* in Ohel Rahel, using the *sefer Ben Ish Hai* as his basic text. There were instances, however, in which the Ben Ish Hai disputed a ruling of the *Beit Yosef*, and after learning the *sugyot* well to ensure that his understanding was

---

10. See *Siman* 12 about whether one could recite *Kaddish* with his back to the *aron kodesh* (holy ark), and *Siman* 38 regarding reciting the blessing of *Borei Me'orei Ha'eish* to the light of an electric bulb.
11. See p. 439.

More than half a century before Rav Yitzhak Kadouri joined Harav Ovadia in Shas campaigns, he hired him to deliver a *shiur* to the *baalei batim* at Ohel Rahel.

correct, Harav Ovadia told the congregants, "In this halacha, since we [i.e., Sephardim] follow the rulings of Maran the Beit Yosef, we do not follow the opinion of the Ben Ish Hai."[12]

When Rav Kadouri heard about this, he confronted the 17-year-old and said, "How can you argue with the Ben Ish Hai? This *beit knesset* is for those of Iraqi descent, and we faithfully follow the rulings of the Ben Ish Hai [who lived in Iraq]."

Rav Ovadia explained that since he was citing the rulings of the Beit Yosef,[13] not arguing on the basis of his own reasoning, he was allowed to rule against the Ben Ish Hai. Rav Kadouri was adamantly opposed to this approach, however. "If you continue to issue rulings against the Ben Ish Hai," he warned, "I'm going to have to dismiss you."

Rav Ovadia, whose parents were still struggling financially, had grown accustomed to the meager salary he received for delivering

---

12. A classic example, which Harav Ovadia would reinforce frequently throughout his life, was the minimum amount of flour upon which one can separate *halla* with a *beracha*; see *Yehaveh Daat* 4:55.
13. Later in life, one of Harav Ovadia's primary objectives would be to restore the crown of Sephardi *psak halacha* to the Beit Yosef. See pp. 217-219.

these *shiurim*. On Rosh Hodesh of each month, as soon as he would receive his payment, he would run to the local bookstore to buy whatever *sefarim* he could afford.

Nevertheless, he refused to yield. "If the halacha is not like the Ben Ish Hai," he said, "how can I rule in accordance with him?"[14]

Rav Ezra Attia backed him on this approach, telling him that he was correct for ruling according to the way he understood the *sugya*.

Ultimately, he was fired by Ohel Rahel over this issue. He wouldn't be without a position for long, though. When the leaders of Beit Knesset Shaul Tzadka, whose members were of Persian (Iranian) descent, heard that he was available, they quickly approached him and asked him to deliver *shiurim* in their *beit knesset*. This was the beginning of a lifelong mutually beneficial connection with Persian Jewry, who would support him through thick and thin. In fact, Harav Ovadia's famous Motza'ei Shabbat *shiur*

A lifelong relationship: Harav Ovadia delivers a *shiur* to Persian Jews, many of whom accepted him as their rav at the age of 17 and remained loyal students throughout their lives.

---

14. See Chapter 8, pp. 200-201, for the culmination of this debate regarding the *piskei halacha* of the Ben Ish Hai.

— which would eventually draw the largest audience of any *shiur* in the world, via satellite broadcast — began in Beit HaKnesset Olei Mashhad in Bnei Brak, and then moved to Beit HaKnesset HaYazdim in Yerushalayim — both of which served Persian Jews.[15]

Already at this point, many attendees of Harav Ovadia's *shiur* viewed him as their rav for all matters, and turned to him with their *sh'eilot* and even for personal advice. He led them in every way, eventually serving as *mesader kiddushin* at their weddings and as *sandak* at many of their *britot*.

Rav Ovadia's relationship with the Persian community extended beyond the Persian Jews living in Eretz Yisrael. He spent time with Jewish Persian communities worldwide — in New York, Los Angeles, and other locations — and eventually visited their country of origin, Iran, in 1979. One of his stops was in Mashhad, Iran's second most populous city, where he expressed an opinion that community members consider a clear sign of his *ruah hakodesh*:

> *One of the most impressive achievements of the Mashhad Jewish community was the construction of Beit Knesset Anjoman, a magnificent synagogue and communal center. Aside from the beit knesset that seated several hundred congregants, the four-story building included a simha hall, a large kitchen, and rooms for youth activities, all designed and constructed with high-end materials. The total cost of the building was 3.6 million toman,[16] at a time when one could purchase a house with a lawn, a pool, and all other amenities for just 100,000 toman.*
>
> *When community leaders brought Harav Ovadia to visit this edifice, his reaction took them by surprise. "Why are you investing so much in the buildings, and not in developing learning programs for the youth?" he asked. "Do you realize that in Europe, all the money the Jews invested into buildings and the like went to waste during the Holocaust,*

---

15. Mashhad and Yazd are two cities in Persia (Iran).
16. A toman is a super-unit equaling 10 rial, the ordinary currency unit in which business is conducted in Iran. (The term toman is sometimes used to denote even greater multiples of rial, such as 10,000 or 10,000,000 rial.)

and only the money invested in education bore fruit for future generations?"

Communal leaders gently pointed out that their situation in Iran was extremely secure and favorable, unlike that of the Jews in Europe during the thousand years they lived there before the Holocaust. The leaders of Iran's Jewish community shared close ties with the Shah; with one phone

Rav Ovadia (top, middle) surrounded by some students — many of whom are far older than he — at the recitation of *Birkat HaHamah*, 23 Nissan 5715/1955.

call to his palace they would be granted an immediate audience with him, even though such a meeting took months for anyone else to schedule.

Rav Ovadia would not be deterred. "This could all go to waste in a matter of moments," he insisted.

At a hesped after his passing, Mr. Yaakov Avrahami, the secretary of the Mashhad community in Bnei Brak, recounted with wonder and sadness how these words had been proven all too true:

"A few months after his visit, the Islamic revolution began. The Shah was overthrown, and all the affluent Jewish leaders in the city had to run for their lives.

"Beit Knesset Anjoman now sits desolate during the week, and when it is open on Shabbat and the festivals, the Jews who participate in the tefillot are all newcomers; not

Rav Yaakov Ades (R) converses with Harav Ovadia at a family *simha*. Hacham Avraham Fattal, Harav Ovadia's father-in-law, is seated at his other side.

one person is left from the large community that built the beit knesset.

"This was all a direct sign of Maran's ruah hakodesh."

Many Mentors

AFTER HE STUDIED UNDER RAV LOFES, HARAV OVADIA began to attend Rav Yaakov Ades's *shiur* at Porat Yosef. Rav Ades was already a member of the Beit Din HaGadol at that point, and in addition to the material the *talmidim* studied in the *shiur* — which included *Masechet Gittin* and all of *Hilchot Issur V'Heter*[17] — Harav Ovadia also tapped into Rav Ades's knowledge of how to rule in practical halacha. The two shared an extremely warm relationship for the rest of Rav Ades's life, and Harav Ovadia so greatly appreciated Rav Ades's influence on his life that when the latter passed away

Rav Yehuda Ades (R) with Harav Ovadia at the inauguration of Yeshiva Kol Yaakov, named for Rav Yaakov Ades, with Rav Yosef Shalom Elyashiv (L) also in attendance

17. *Issur V'Heter* deals with the complex topics related to *kashrut*.

and his son Rav Yehuda wanted to open a yeshiva in his memory, Harav Ovadia committed to fundraise in order to start the yeshiva, called Kol Yaakov,[18] and he fundraised many times over the years to keep it running. He would also deliver *shiurim* at the yeshiva on occasion.

Ovadia sought the guidance of many other mentors from outside Yeshivat Porat Yosef as well. As a teenager, he developed relationships with many of the greatest *talmidei hachamim* and *tzaddikim* of Yerushalayim. Although detailing his relationships with all these great scholars could fill a volume of their own, some of those relationships were more noteworthy than others and bear mention.

"The Meishiv of the Next Generation"

WHEN HARAV OVADIA WAS 18 YEARS OLD, HE STARTED ATtending a weekly gathering of budding *talmidei hachamim* on Shabbat afternoon at the home of Rav Tzvi Pesach Frank, the rav of Yerushalayim. During these gatherings, Rav Frank or others would present *sh'eilot*, and then the group would try to answer the questions, with Rav Frank validating or refuting their suggestions and helping them understand how a rav applies his Torah knowledge to a halachic question.

Although a select group of Ovadia's friends from Porat Yosef attended these sessions — along with a larger contingent from Yeshivat Eitz Haim and other Ashkenazi yeshivot — most of the Porat Yosef students hung back and just listened to the exchanges. Ovadia had a great deal to say, however, and he quickly became one of the most active contributors to the discussions.

This young scholar's breadth of knowledge — and his ability to apply that knowledge — astounded the elderly Rav Frank, who began to spend much time talking to Harav Ovadia, even reserving

---

18. Kol Yaakov is unique in that it is non-denominational, with Sephardim and Ashkenazim learning alongside one another. It is said that when Rav Yaakov Kamenetsky visited Eretz Yisrael in his old age, he turned down many invitations to deliver *shiurim*, accepting only one: that of Rav Yehuda Ades, Rosh Yeshiva of Kol Yaakov. When someone asked him why he agreed to speak at that particular yeshiva, he explained that he wanted to see the yeshiva that didn't differentiate between sectors of the Jewish community and accepted any student who wanted to learn Torah. He added that Kol Yaakov would probably merit the first visit from Mashiah because of its *ahdut*.

The elderly Rav of Yerushalayim, Rav Tzvi Pesach Frank, who was so astounded by Harav Ovadia's breadth of knowledge that he would save him a seat at the weekly gathering at his home

a spot close to him for Ovadia if he arrived after the discussion had commenced.[19] Once, a fellow who was obviously jealous of Harav Ovadia's success, derisively asked Rav Frank, "Why do you spend so much time with that one young man?"

"That young man will be the *meishiv*[20] of the next generation," Rav Tzvi Pesach retorted. His prediction proved to be prescient.

> *A rav in the United States once received a difficult sh'eila regarding whether a woman whose husband had disappeared could remarry.[21] He posed the question to rabbanim in America, but no rav wanted to take responsibility for*

---

19. Rav Frank would be one of Harav Ovadia's primary mentors and supporters until his passing in 1961; see pp. 191 and 267.
20. I.e., he will respond to the challenging halachic questions posed by the public.
21. See p. 377.

Chapter Four: The Public Takes Note ☐ 99

Rav Ovadia and Rav Aharon Leib Shteinman greet one another warmly at a Torah gathering in Elad.

ruling; several rabbanim suggested that he take the sh'eila to one of the great poskim in Eretz Yisrael.

This rav had a relationship with Rav Aharon Leib Shteinman, so he visited him first. When Rav Shteinman heard the sh'eila, he said, "This question is not for me. You have to take this to Yerushalayim."

The rav secured an appointment with Rav Yosef Shalom Elyashiv, and told him that Rav Shteinman had advised him to take the sh'eila to Yerushalayim. "Rav Shteinman didn't mean me," Rav Elyashiv replied, to this rav's astonishment. "This sh'eila has to go to Rehov HaKablan [Rav Ovadia's address]."

The rav proceeded to visit Harav Ovadia, and told him the woman's story. "Leave us a number," Harav Ovadia replied simply, "and we'll call you when we have a response."

> This visit took place on a Sunday night, and the rav expected that it would take some time before he heard back from Harav Ovadia. To his surprise, on Tuesday morning he received a phone call to come pick up the teshuva — which turned out to be a full examination of the case, from every angle, researched and written in less than 36 hours.
>
> The rav took the teshuva back to Rav Elyashiv and then to Rav Shteinman, both of whom reviewed it and signed that they agreed with his ruling.[22]

Controlling the Spirit

ANOTHER INFLUENCE ON THE YOUNG OVADIA WAS THAT OF the elderly Rav Yehuda Petaya,[23] a phenomenal *talmid hacham* and renowned *mekubal* who authored *sefarim* on the hidden portions of the Torah. Rav Petaya was most popularly known for his ability to converse with spirits and remove a *dibbuk* that had entered a person's body, and some of his works reveal conversations that he had with those spirits.

> Although he admired and revered Rav Petaya greatly, Harav Ovadia did not consider removing a dibbuk to be a major accomplishment. He related that when a dibbuk had entered a person's body, R' Benzion Hazzan, the gabbai of Porat Yosef, took a minyan and followed a tikkun printed in a sefer, and the dibbuk left.
>
> He was also extremely pragmatic about dibbuk stories; grandson R' Yaakov Sasson relates that when a story was circulating about a woman who was possessed by a dibbuk, he asked Harav Ovadia whether there was still such a thing

---

22. Rav Yisrael Pinhasi, Rosh Kollel Ha'Ari in Bnei Brak.
23. Rav Yehuda Petaya was born on 2 Shevat, 5619/1859 in Baghdad, where he received *semicha* at the young age of 17 from Rav Abdullah Someich (one of the people for whom Harav Ovadia was named; see p. 39, fn. 3). Although he mastered all areas of Torah, he was particularly sought after to deal with spirits (*dibbukim*) that had entered other people's bodies. Upon moving to Yerushalayim in 5694/1934, he immediately impressed all of the leaders of the city, including Chief Rabbi Rav Tzvi Pesach Frank, who described him as "the great rav, a hidden expert and wondrous light." By the time Harav Ovadia made his acquaintance, Rav Petaya was approximately 80. He passed away on 27 Av 5702/1942, at the age of 84.

nowadays. "It's possible," Harav Ovadia replied, "but before doing anything else they should take her to doctors to see if there's a natural cure for what ails her."

Rav Petaya was also an expert in writing *kamei'ot* (amulets), and Harav Ovadia once took advantage of this expertise to help an acquaintance.

> *When Harav Ovadia began to deliver shiurim in Ohel Rahel,[24] one of his students, a fellow by the name of Moula, had a terrible problem. His wife was suffering from mania, and her case was so severe that no one could handle being in her presence. When Moula tearfully confided his problem to Harav Ovadia, the latter insisted that they visit Rav Yehuda Petaya together, in the hopes that he could heal her.*
>
> *After listening to details of the malady, Rav Petaya wrote an amulet and said, "You must be aware that after you hang this amulet around your wife's neck, her condition will deteriorate for several days. You must therefore tie her to her bed until she begins to improve, and afterward you'll be able to live together in good health for many long years."*
>
> *Moula followed Rav Petaya's instructions, and events subsequently unfolded exactly as he had predicted: For a few days, Moula's wife got much worse, but she then calmed down and returned to normal function.*
>
> *After two years, she lost the amulet, and she once again began to exhibit maniacal symptoms. Harav Ovadia once again took Moula to Rav Yehuda Petaya, but he told them sadly that due to his advanced age, he no longer had the power to write an amulet for the woman. He added, however, that he did have an amulet that he had once written for another person suffering from the same illness. He wasn't sure that it would work, since it had not been written for this woman, but he told them to try.*

---

24. See p. 91.

Rav Yehuda Petaya, who was able to help Harav Ovadia's student by writing an amulet for his wife

> Moula took the amulet and hung it around his wife's neck, and the process repeated itself: her condition deteriorated, but she then recovered completely. Several years later, however, after Rav Petaya had already passed away, she once again lost the amulet, and her mania returned with such a vengeance that she burned her entire apartment down to the ground, with herself inside it.

Despite having witnessed Rav Yehuda Petaya's powers firsthand, Harav Ovadia did not consider the focus on spirits to be a good use of time.

> Approximately two decades later, Harav Ovadia saw his 12-year-old daughter Malka reading Rav Petaya's work *Minhat Yehuda*, in which he describes discussions he had with spirits. Harav Ovadia took the sefer away from Malka, because he did not want his children to read about spirits — but he then bought her a four-volume biography of the Hafetz Haim to replace the "confiscated" work.

Rheumatism: Not From the Mezuzah

LATER IN LIFE, HARAV OVADIA WOULD FREQUENTLY CAUTION people not to be fooled by "Kabbalists" who claimed — or even proved — to possess supernatural knowledge and powers. He would repeatedly cite the Rashba's statement in his *teshuvot* that only a person who has toiled in Torah can possess the power to effect a salvation, and any predictions or instructions issued by someone who was not a Torah scholar but claimed to have hidden powers could be ignored.

As with everything else that he taught to the public, he practiced this teaching in his own life as well.

> *In his teenage years, Ovadia would spend long hours in the library of Beit HaKnesset Shoshanim L'David, taking advantage of its extensive library. But the roof of the beit knesset leaked terribly during the winter rains; Harav Ovadia related to his son Rav David that he wore the heaviest coat he could obtain, and tried to find a seat where water wasn't seeping in, but he could not escape the rain. He remarked that he had learned certain dapim of Masechet Yevamot under those conditions, and throughout his life, each time he reached those dapim he would shiver involuntarily, apparently jarred by the association from his teenage years.*
>
> *Half a century after those learning sessions in Shoshanim L'David, there was some sort of problem plaguing the Yosef household, and Rabbanit Margalit asked Harav Ovadia whether she could summon a certain mekubal who had a reputation for being able to look at the mezuzot in a house and determine the source of the family's problems. Although Harav Ovadia didn't place much faith in such Kabbalists, he told the rabbanit that if it would calm her, she could invite this mekubal to their home.*
>
> *The mekubal arrived and began to examine the mezuzot. After looking at a particular mezuza, he asked, "Who in the family has rheumatism?"*

"I do," Harav Ovadia replied.

"This mezuzah is full of moisture," the mekubal said. "That's causing the rheumatism."

The mekubal then asked, "Is there a cross somewhere in the house?" Harav Ovadia replied that when he had visited the king of Spain, the two had conversed at length, and the king had then given him a gold medallion bearing the royal coat of arms — part of which was a cross. The mekubal told him that he had to destroy the medallion.

"Suddenly," recalls Rav David, "Abba summoned me and asked me a Torah question. I told him what I thought would be the correct answer, and Abba then asked the mekubal for his opinion. Rather than agreeing with what I had said, or keeping silent, the mekubal offered his own answer, and we realized that he didn't know what he was talking about."

When the mekubal left, Harav Ovadia told his family members to place all the mezuzot back on the doorposts.

"What about the medallion?" Rav David asked.

"I have a teshuva[25] about this issue," Harav Ovadia replied. "Since the coat of arms is a symbol of honor, not a religious object, it's not forbidden to own it."

He then added that when the Rashba[26] was asked about a person who was able to predict the future and see hidden things, he replied that ruah hakodesh cannot rest on an am ha'aretz, and suggested that perhaps an impure spirit had entered the person's body.

"I asked you a Torah question," Harav Ovadia explained to Rav David, "and then I posed the same question to this mekubal to see if he knows how to learn. Since he doesn't, we don't have to heed anything he said."

"What about the mezuza?" Rav David asked.

"According to halacha," Harav Ovadia replied, "one is not allowed to bury a kosher mezuza. Not only is this mezuza kosher, it's *mehudar*. There's no reason to replace it.

---

25. *Yabia Omer* 3:65.
26. *Teshuvot HaRashba* 1:548.

"I know that I developed rheumatism as a result of learning in the freezing, wet Shoshanim L'David library," he continued. *"How can the rheumatism have anything to do with the moist mezuza if I have had it for decades as a result of learning under those conditions?"*

RAV OVADIA DIDN'T GROW ONLY THROUGH THE INFLUENCE of his mentors; he had close friends who contributed to his growth as well. He maintained those relationships throughout his life, remaining extremely loyal to the friends of his youth.

Close-Knit Friends

His closest friends from early childhood were Rav Baruch Ben-Haim, who would go on to lead the Syrian community in New York for many decades, and Rav Benzion Abba Shaul, who would eventually succeed Hacham Ezra Attia as Rosh Yeshiva of Porat Yosef.[27]

Each day during his years in Porat Yosef, Harav Ovadia would walk to and from the Beit Yisrael neighborhood with his friends — most frequently with Rav Benzion. On the way to yeshiva, he and Rav Benzion would review a *daf* with *Rashi* and *Tosafot* from memory, and on the way home they would review another *daf*. They would alternate, with one saying the Gemara and the other reciting the *Rashi* and *Tosafot* on the way to yeshiva and vice versa on the return.

Decades later, Hacham Benzion told his students about these sessions, and noted something unique about Harav Ovadia: There

Rav Ovadia (L) and Rav Benzion Abba Shaul in their youth, several years after they reviewed a *daf* each way to and from Porat Yosef

---

27. See Chapter 16 for the details of their unique relationship.

was a spot on the way into the Old City where hundreds of pigeons would congregate and coo very loudly. Every person who walked by that spot would be distracted by the sight and the noise — except for Harav Ovadia, who would just continue reciting his learning from memory even as he passed that area.

New Friends in Hevron

AS YOUNG TEENAGERS WHO WANTED TO MAXIMIZE THEIR learning time despite Yeshivat Porat Yosef having to close during the early afternoon due to security issues, Ovadia and Benzion sought a place to learn at night, and they chose the Hevron Yeshiva. The yeshiva had recently moved to the Geula neighborhood in Yerushalayim after being forced out of the city of Hevron by the infamous Arab massacre in 1929 in which dozens of students were killed and many others wounded.

When they began to learn in Hevron, someone called their attention to one of the boys in the yeshiva and said, "His name is Betzalel Zolty, and he has already learned most of *Shas b'iyun* (in depth)." Harav Ovadia was amazed that someone that age could have amassed so much knowledge, and he decided both to befriend Betzalel Zolty and to emulate him by attempting to finish *Shas b'iyun*.[28] This was indeed the beginning of a lifelong friendship that ended only when Rav Zolty passed away suddenly in 1982.

Locked In

DUE TO ITS PRECARIOUS FINANCIAL SITUATION, PORAT YOSEF was also closed on Friday and Shabbat. Needing somewhere to learn, Harav Ovadia chose one of his old favorite places: the third-floor library of Beit Knesset Shoshanim L'David.

> *After a few weeks, the gabbai approached him and said that he didn't allow him to learn there. When Ovadia asked why not, the gabbai explained that there were some very valuable sefarim in the library, and he was concerned that some volumes might go missing. Ovadia tried to convince him that*

---

28. Rav David Yosef.

he could be trusted not to remove volumes, but to no avail. Finally, the gabbai offered to lock him into the library each Friday morning and allow him to stay there until Minha. Ovadia immediately agreed; since his entire interest was to learn, it didn't bother him to be locked into the library.

After davening at sunrise each Friday, Ovadia would hurry home to get ready for Shabbat, and would then run to Shoshanim L'David to be sure to arrive before the gabbai left. He would learn until Minha, at which point the gabbai would come upstairs and let him out.

This arrangement continued for some time, until one week, the gabbai forgot to go upstairs and open the door to the library. Ovadia was so engrossed in his learning that he didn't even notice the voices from downstairs as the congregation prayed Minha, followed by Kabbalat Shabbat and Arvit. Suddenly, he looked up at a clock on the wall and noticed that it read 8 o'clock — and Shabbat had come in shortly after 4! Most people had long finished their seudat Shabbat, and his family would doubtlessly wonder where he was.

He was very disappointed with himself for missing the tefillot, so before he did anything else, he prayed Kabbalat Shabbat. Then he opened a window and tried to call for help, but the driving rain outside drowned out his voice. He started shouting, until someone who lived nearby and was already in bed for the night finally heard him, got dressed, and went to get the key from the gabbai.

A few days after Shabbat, Hacham Ezra Attia heard what had transpired, and was so upset that he went straight to the gabbai's house and instructed him to give a copy of the key to Ovadia and allow him to learn in the library in peace.

At some point in his teenage years, Ovadia devoted those Friday sessions to memorizing the *Sh'eilot V'Teshuvot* of the primary *Aharonim* — the Noda B'Yehuda, Hatam Sofer, etc.[29]

---

29. Rav David Yosef.

Building Ahavat HaTorah

WHILE DEVOTING NEARLY EVERY WAKING MOMENT TO learning, Harav Ovadia also found time to perfect his *middot* and draw inspiration to keep him motivated in his endless pursuit of Torah.

He would rise early each morning, an hour before Shaharit, and learn *Reishit Hochma* with his close friend R' Yaakov Dwek HaKohen. He also rose many nights to recite *Tikkun Hatzot*, a practice he maintained whenever he could throughout his life. In fact, he ruled, based on earlier authorities, that reciting *Tikkun Hatzot* takes precedence over reciting *Selihot* (for someone who cannot recite both).[30]

On wintry Friday nights, he would walk in the middle of the night to hear the *shirei habakashot* in Beit Knesset Ades in the Nahlaot neighborhood. These gatherings were attended by rabbanim and *mekubalim*, including the famed *mekubal* Rav Mordechai Sharabi, whose face would shine while he listened to the *shirei habakashot*. Ovadia became acknowledged among his peers as an expert in the *piyutim* and *bakashot* — many of which are extremely complex, with tunes that change cadence and tone frequently.

Decades later, in his old age, he still remembered the exact words and tunes of each of the shirei habakashot, and he

With the *mekubal* Rav Mordechai Sharabi. The two were among the attendees of the *shirei habakashot* at Beit Knesset Ades, held in the wee hours of Shabbat morning, during Harav Ovadia's teenage years.

---

30. *Yehaveh Daat* 3:44.

would be bothered if someone would veer off tune. Rav Moshe Hizkiyah, rav of Kiryat Herzog, explains that Harav Ovadia's quest for any knowledge even indirectly related to Torah was so intense, it even encompassed the tunes of the shirei habakashot.

Harav Ovadia related that as a young man, he drew *ahavat haTorah* and *ahavat Hashem* from these Friday night sessions at Beit Knesset Ades. Later in life as well, he would enjoy visits from Moshe Havusha, one of the most popular contemporary *paytanim*. Harav Ovadia mentioned to his family that he also enjoyed listening to recordings of Hazzan Yossele Rosenblatt.[31]

The Audience Grows

OVER THE NEXT FEW YEARS, AS HARAV OVADIA CONTINUED to grow in both his learning and his skillfulness as a teacher of Torah, his audiences grew as well. He began to deliver *shiurim* on Shabbat in addition to his nightly *shiur*, gladly giving of his time to any group that wanted to learn Torah. His emphasis was on halacha, although he often used his influence as a teacher to encourage his students — many of whom were years, if not decades, older than he — to send their children to Torah schools.

By the time he was in his early 20s, there were already well over 100 people who were avid attendees of his regular *derashot*. It was now time to face the next frontier: finding a wife and building a family.

---

31. *Abir Haro'im.*

CHAPTER FIVE
FINDING HIS GEM

IT WAS CLEAR TO HARAV OVADIA THAT FINDING A wife who would share his life's goals would be extremely difficult.[1] In those years, it was virtually unheard of among Sephardic Jews for someone to devote their entire lives to disseminating Torah.[2] The woman he was looking for had to be willing to forgo a life of ease and comfort in favor of spiritual reward.

His family's financial situation didn't make matters easier; Harav Ovadia related that his father would buy him clothing third- or fourth-hand from the ubiquitous "*Alte zachen*"[3] peddlers, and his mother would occasionally sew him shirts without collars to save money on the extra fabric.[4] Even when it came time for him to marry, his family couldn't afford the basic necessities for the wed-

---

1. The lion's share of information in this chapter is based on an interview with Rav David Yosef, with some facts and supporting information added from other sources.
2. A telling incident appears in *Abir Haro'im* (p. 177). When Harav Ovadia was 22, one of his close friends married an orphan, and he told Harav Ovadia that his wife, who was *tzanua* and came from a fine family, had a younger sister of *shidduch* age. He recommended that a mutual friend of the two families suggest the *shidduch*. When the mutual friend approached this young girl's brother to suggest it, the reply was: "My other sister just married his friend, and it's enough to have one *hacham* in the family. Now we're looking for an accomplished businessman for our younger sister." The younger sister ultimately married a simple electrician, garnering neither the Torah she could have had with Harav Ovadia nor the wealth her brother sought for her.
3. Yiddish for "old things."
4. R' Eliyahu Shitrit.

ding. Harav Ovadia saved up money that he was awarded in Porat Yosef for excelling on exams to buy himself a suit.

Furthermore, even girls who were willing to marry someone committed to a Torah life didn't necessarily want to live a Torah lifestyle themselves. During a meeting with one eligible young lady, Harav Ovadia was shocked when she related that she went to the theater with her friends. He felt that all his learning would be in vain if his home was tainted by the values his wife picked up in the theater.

Harav Ovadia at his eirusin (engagement)

For him, therefore, looking for a *shidduch* would be like mining for a rare gem — and indeed, it took him a few years to find his Margalit.[5]

The Fattal Family

MARGALIT FATTAL WAS BORN IN ALEPPO, SYRIA, IN 5686/1926, TO R' Avraham and Zakiya Fattal. R' Avraham was known as a fine *talmid hacham* even then, in his younger years, and Zakiya was one of the few women in her entire village who covered their hair.

Margalit was orphaned from her mother very suddenly. On Erev Pesah 5691/1931, when Margalit was five years old, Zakiya woke up feeling perfectly fine, and went about preparing for the Seder as she did every year. In midafternoon, when everything was ready for the Seder, she suddenly felt ill, and before anything could be done to help her, she died. Her family and friends hurried to bury her before Pesah, but the horror of that day never left Margalit. Later in life, she would recount to her children how the family sat down to

---

5. Hebrew for "gem."

the Seder that year, shell-shocked by the loss of their beloved wife and mother.

In her youth, Margalit had no choice but to attend the Alliance[6] school, because there was no Torah school for girls in Aleppo at the time. She was a very studious and talented girl, and she picked up three languages — Hebrew, Arabic, and French — on mother-tongue level, becoming proficient enough to read and write in all three.

When she turned 12, R' Avraham, who was raising his children on his own, realized that it was improper for the daughter of a *talmid hacham* to continue attending an Alliance school, so he decided to move to Eretz Yisrael. Upon his arrival in Yerushalayim, R' Avraham established a Talmud Torah in the Nahlaot neighborhood for the children of Syrian immigrants.

He could not find a school in which he felt comfortable enrolling Margalit, so she stayed home and learned how to sew and knit. By the time she turned 17, she had earned a reputation as an extremely talented, charming girl, and all of her friends and neighbors assumed that she would marry a wealthy young man with

Hacham Avraham Fattal was amazed by the positive reports about his future son-in-law.

---
6. See Chapter Two, p. 31.

great financial potential, which is what most girls of her caliber were seeking.

But R' Avraham wanted something other than a rich boy for his daughter. In an era in which a learning boy was considered an anomaly and most people looked askance at boys with no earning power, Margalit's father sought a *talmid hacham* for her. The first person to suggest the *shidduch* with Harav Ovadia was Rabbanit Mazal Laniado. Although Margalit was young, Rabbanit Laniado urged Hacham Avraham Fattal to grab Harav Ovadia from Porat Yosef before someone else would take him. Afterward, Harav Ovadia's uncle, R' Ovadia Shabo, worked hard to advance the *shidduch*.

When Hacham Avraham visited Porat Yosef, he was amazed by the positive reports he heard from Rav Ezra Attia and Rav Yaakov Ades, and he agreed to allow his daughter to meet with Harav Ovadia.

THE FIRST MEETING BETWEEN THE TWO ENDED IN SOMEWHAT of a disaster.

What Did You Say?

After talking in learning with Hacham Avraham for a while, Harav Ovadia and Margalit took a walk outside. The naturally vivacious Margalit was doing most of the talking, with Harav Ovadia nodding and smiling in response. At one point, after she expressed her opinion on a certain matter, she turned to her suitor and asked, "What do you think?"

Harav Ovadia turned to her abashedly and stammered, "I'm so sorry, I was learning a sugya before we came, and I got lost in thought about it while you were talking. What did you say?"

Margalit was upset. How could she marry a husband who didn't care about what she had to say? She decided that she would call the shidduch off after that one meeting.

Harav Ovadia sensed that Margalit Fattal would make a good wife, and he decided to pursue the match in an unusual manner.

The Shabbat after that first meeting, he walked over to the Fattal home in Nahlaot and asked Hacham Avraham if he could meet her again. The Hacham was overjoyed to see him, but he didn't think that he could convince his daughter to go out again. "She was very upset about what happened last time," he explained. "But we can talk in learning if you'd like!"

Harav Ovadia asked for a chance to talk to Margalit, and he apologized profusely for what had transpired during their previous meeting. "It won't happen again," he assured her. "Can we take another walk today?"

To his relief, Margalit agreed.

After the two walked and conversed for an hour, Harav Ovadia turned to her and said, "I have to go deliver a shiur in a beit knesset in Beit Yisrael now. If you'd like, I can walk you home, or you can accompany me to the shul and listen in from the ezrat nashim, and then we can continue talking afterward."

Margalit decided to join him. She found a seat in the ezrat nashim from which she could observe the proceedings in the men's section below. To her surprise, as her relatively young suitor entered the beit knesset, men decades his senior knelt to kiss his hand. She sat there transfixed as he delivered his shiur in his classic style, moving seamlessly from one concept to the next and captivating his audience with his rapid-fire delivery.

When the shiur was over, the two walked again for an hour. He then turned to her yet again and said, "I need to deliver another shiur. If you want you can come along...."

"Will it be on the same topic?" she asked.

"No, a different topic."

"Then I'll come."

This process repeated itself yet a third time. By the time the day was over, she had heard him deliver three hour-length shiurim, effortlessly segueing from one topic to the next. She knew that he had done this without preparing immediately beforehand, because he had spent the time between the shiurim talking to her.

By the time he dropped her off at home later that day, Margalit's impression of Harav Ovadia had completely turned around. She was absolutely taken by his brilliance in learning. From that day on, she never referred to him by his first name alone; even when speaking to him privately, she called him "Harav Ovadia."

Before they got engaged, Harav Ovadia made sure that she was ready for a life that would be spiritually rewarding, but physically strenuous: she would have to run the home and raise the children without much help from him. He also ensured that she was willing to cover her hair, which was extremely unusual among her peers in those days. After she agreed to these conditions, the two celebrated their engagement, during Chanukah of 5704/1944, with Rav Ezra Attia, Rav Yaakov Ades, and Rav Ephraim Cohen in attendance.

THE COUPLE'S ENGAGEMENT PERIOD DID NOT PROCEED ALTOgether smoothly.[7] Harav Ovadia would visit the Fattal home every so often, but he would spend the entire time in Torah conversation with Hacham Avraham.

"I Promise You Olam Haba"

Once, when he came to the home, Hacham Avraham greeted him with sadness. "You're welcome to talk to me in learning," he said, "but Margalit wants to call off the *shidduch.*"

"Why?" Harav Ovadia asked, shocked.

"Because she says that you come to talk to me, but you don't pay any attention to her. She can't handle being married to a husband who will ignore her."

Harav Ovadia asked to speak to his bride in private. By the time she walked out of the room, Margalit was all smiles, ready to go into marriage.

"What did he say?" her family asked.

"First he said that he felt it was halachically wrong for an engaged couple to spend too much time with each other. But then

---

7. From Rav Yitzchak Yosef, published in *Posek HaDor*.

he added that he was planning to disseminate Torah to the masses through his *shiurim* and his writings, and he pledged to share those merits with me equally."

A Wedding Under Curfew

THE YOSEFS MARRIED ON TUESDAY, 4 NISSAN 5704/1944, IN THE hall of the Spitzer school on Rehov Ezra, with the Rishon LeZion, Rav Benzion Meir Hai Uziel, officiating. The wedding took place at 3 o'clock in the afternoon, because the British, who were under constant attack from the Irgun and other Jewish militias, had

"He promised to share his merits with me equally."

Harav Ovadia and Rabbanit Margalit at their wedding

Chapter Five: Finding His Gem ☐ 117

Harav Ovadia and Rabbanit Margalit's wedding invitation.

imposed a curfew on the city after dark. Anyone caught outside after sundown could be imprisoned — or worse. The entire wedding lasted approximately two hours, and then all the guests ran home before nightfall.

But the curfew didn't deter the Irgun fighters, including Harav Ovadia's brother Na'im,[8] who took part in an attack on British troops on the day of the wedding. When Harav Ovadia later learned of his brother's activities, he was upset. "Even on the day of my wedding you can't take a break?" he lamented.

---

8. Na'im was one of the Irgun fighters who took part in the mission to blow up the King David Hotel, considered by many to be one of the primary attacks that shook the British resolve and made them end their Mandate over Eretz Yisrael. The southwest wing of the King David Hotel was, at that time, the British administrative headquarters in Palestine, where they housed their records and evidence against all Jewish militias. Irgun operatives blew up that wing of the building to destroy the records. Dressed as milkmen, they sneaked bombs hidden in metal milk canisters into the basement kitchen. They then called the switchboard at the hotel, as well as the Palestine Post, to warn that a bomb would go off in twenty minutes, but the warnings were ignored. They kept calling with the exact number of minutes until the bomb would detonate, but the hotel was not evacuated. Over 90 people were killed and the entire southwest wing of the hotel was destroyed in the blast.

Considering the excitement these militias generated, the fact that the young Harav Ovadia didn't get caught up in these activities — especially when his own siblings and closest friends were earning their stripes militarily — is a testimony to his commitment to Torah, which was then a far less popular pursuit.

Harav Ovadia with his brother Na'im, who was late to his wedding because he took part in an Irgun attack on British troops

THE COUPLE'S FIRST HOME WAS A ONE-ROOM APARTMENT ON Rehov Be'er Sheva in the Beit Yisrael neighborhood. The apartment was so small that it could fit only beds, a small table, and some lamps. Although there was electricity in Eretz Yisrael at the time, the Yosefs couldn't afford to pay an electric bill, so they used kerosene lamps. They shared their restroom and other facilities with their neighbors in a common area outside. Harav Ovadia related that rabbanim from Porat Yosef, and especially Rav Ephraim Cohen, would visit him on occasion, but he couldn't even invite them inside because there was no room. Even when the Rosh Yeshiva, Rav Ezra Attia, came to visit, there wasn't as much as a chair for him to sit on.[9] The only thing the couple had in abundance were the *sefarim* Harav Ovadia had purchased before his marriage.

Poor in Possessions; Rich in Torah

Although Hacham Avraham loved his son-in-law dearly, not everyone was so enamored with the *hattan*.

---
9. *Abir Haro'im*, p. 187.

> A few months after the wedding, one of Margalit's older sisters, who lived out of the country and had not been able to attend the wedding, came for a visit. When she saw the living conditions of her younger sister and her new brother-in-law, she flew into a rage. "You're a cruel father," she yelled at Hacham Avraham. "How could you do this to your daughter after she grew up as an orphan? What will she eat? His sefarim?"
>
> She was so angry that she took Margalit's head covering, threw it on the floor, and stepped on it.
>
> Harav Ovadia was sitting in the room during this outburst, and he didn't utter a word. Later, however, when his sister-in-law calmed down, he explained to her why he had chosen this lifestyle, and why Margalit agreed to go along with it. By the time she departed, this sister-in-law was so impressed with Harav Ovadia that she later sent her own children to yeshivot, and her descendants are bnei Torah.

First Dayanut Position

DESPITE HARAV OVADIA'S RELATIVELY YOUNG AGE — HE WAS 23 — immediately after his wedding, Rishon LeZion Rav Uziel asked him to become the third member of the Beit Din HaSephardim of Yerushalayim, joining Av Beit Din Rav Yehuda Shako and Porat Yosef's Rosh Yeshiva, Hacham Ezra Attia.[10] While sitting on the *beit din*, Harav Ovadia learned to apply his knowledge of the four sections of *Shulhan Aruch* — which he knew word-for-word — to an actual *din Torah*. He also absorbed many practices from the other two *dayanim* that he applied to cases he adjudicated later on in life, some of which he cites in *Yabia Omer*.

> Once, the three dayanim were preparing a get (halachic certificate of divorce), when the husband suddenly had a change of heart and said that he was unwilling to give the get, which meant that his wife would not be allowed

---

10. *Kol Sinai*, issue #72, 8 Shevat 5731, p. 3.

Rav Yehuda Shako, head of the Beit Din HaSephardim of Yerushalayim, which Harav Ovadia joined at the age of 23

to remarry. The dayanim managed to convince him to go through with the get, but now a problem arose: there is a dispute in halacha as to whether a husband's statement of refusal to give the get after it is drafted invalidates the get. Were the dayanim required to write a new get?

Rav Shako and Rav Attia proceeded with the original get, in accordance with the authorities who maintain that as long as the husband rescinds his refusal to give the get, the original document can be used.

When Harav Ovadia served as rav in Egypt, he was involved in a similar case, and he cites the above precedent-setting incident as one of his reasons for not writing a new get.[11]

Between deliberating on the cases that came to the *beit din*, Harav Ovadia would share his recent *hiddushim* with the two elder

---
11. *Yabia Omer*, Vol. 5, *Even Ha'ezer* 16.

dayanim, and they would engage in lively debates on his expositions, taking great joy in hearing the brilliant, novel insights he formulated to resolve their questions.[12]

New Skills

IN ADDITION TO CONTINUING HIS STUDIES IN PORAT YOSEF and serving as a *dayan*, Harav Ovadia continued to deliver *shiurim* in many venues, developing and polishing his oratorical skills.

After his marriage, he developed the speaking style that would remain his trademark for the rest of his life. He would choose a halachic topic and delve into it deeply, blending in stories and even jokes that kept the audience enraptured.[13] For the next 70 years, there was almost no *derasha* of his that didn't contain at least a few stories and some humor. In time, the audience came to expect him to enliven his *drashot* in his signature style.

> *Rav David Yosef relates that at one point in his father's later years, he asked the elderly Harav Ovadia why he continued to tell jokes and stories. "The audience has grown in their love of Torah," Rav David posited, "and they can handle a more serious shiur."*
>
> *"You think so?" Harav Ovadia asked. "Okay, we'll see."*
>
> *The next time he delivered a shiur with Rav David in attendance, he began to blaze through the topic, teaching the halachot without interspersing any stories or jokes. After a while, several heads began to bob, and drowsiness slowly overtook the audience.*
>
> *Suddenly, Harav Ovadia turned to Rav David and winked at him, indicating that he was about to shift course. He began to tell a story, and the heads that had*

---

12. *Le'oro Neileich*, p. 4.
13. Some maintain that Harav Ovadia adapted this approach from the Ben Ish Hai, whose *drashot* were often presented as stories. If, for instance, he would have to teach the halachot of *Netilat Yadayim* (washing one's hands upon arising in the morning), he would start by saying, "There was a man who had to go on a business trip, and he made a point of waking up early in the morning so he could depart on time. When he got up, he made sure to wash *netilat yadayim*, taking care to wash with a proper cup...." He would couch the halachot he was teaching in the guise of a story so that his constituents would continue to join his *shiur* and learn the halachot they needed to know.

Harav Ovadia delivering a *shiur* in the early years after his wedding. As his teaching style evolved, his audience — and the subjects he would discuss — grew more diverse.

become heavy shot up again. Sure enough, by the time he finished that story he once again had his audience's attention, and he finished the derasha without anyone falling asleep.

ASIDE FROM TEACHING BASIC HALACHOT, HARAV OVADIA also began to raise awareness regarding long-standing practices that had developed over centuries in the Diaspora but were not in accordance with halacha.

Tending to the Tefillin

In 5706/1946, for instance, he was asked whether *tefillin* imported from Iraq, which were extremely popular among Iraqi Jews who had immigrated to Eretz Yisrael, were reliable. It was clear, however, even to the naked eye, that the *batim* of these *tefillin* were not square, as required by halacha.

This was not the first time this issue had arisen with regard to

Chapter Five: Finding His Gem ☐ 123

Iraqi *tefillin*. Already in the 1800s, Rav Yosef Haim, the Ben Ish Hai, wrote[14] that when his grandfather, Rav Moshe Haim, was the rav of Baghdad, a Jew by the name of Rav Yehuda Ashkenazi had visited from Damascus and had pointed out that the *tefillin* in the city weren't square. He told Rav Moshe Haim that he could train the *batim* producers to square the *tefillin* properly, and after investigating the matter, Rav Moshe Haim announced that all the non-square *tefillin* in the city were *passul*, and should be donned without a *beracha* until new *tefillin* that were squared properly could be produced.

It seems that in the generations since the days of Rav Yehuda Ashkenazi, the *batim* producers had not followed the correct method of squaring the *tefillin*, and the *batim* being imported to Eretz Yisrael in Harav Ovadia's time weren't kosher.

It wasn't only the *batim* that were problematic. In a series of random checks he did on imported Iraqi *tefillin*, Harav Ovadia found that many of the *parashiyot* were invalid as well, and that they had obviously been written by ignorant *sofrim* who were not God-fearing.

It was particularly inappropriate for the Jews of Eretz Yisrael to be purchasing those *tefillin*, because the local *batim* producers and *sofrim*, who were God-fearing Jews, were making halachically valid *tefillin*. The importers, who often presented themselves as "*hachamim*" to market their products, were bringing in the *tefillin* from Iraq only to drive down the prices. This business tactic would have been legitimate had the *tefillin* been kosher — but they were not.

Harav Ovadia took it upon himself to correct this travesty. He would go around speaking about the problem and urging people not to buy the *tefillin*. He also begged the merchants who sold these *tefillin* to stop importing them.

He wrote[15] that after he was able to stir up a grassroots consumer boycott against the *tefillin*, several merchants decided to heed his words as well, and they stopped selling the invalid *tefillin*.

---

14. *Sheilot V'Teshuvot Rav Pe'alim*, Vol. 4, *Orach Haim* 2.
15. *Yabia Omer*, Vol. 9, *Orach Haim* 6.

HARAV OVADIA DIDN'T CONFINE HIS SPEECHES TO HALACHA. In those years, with World War II raging and reports of the Nazi atrocities reaching Eretz Yisrael, he would exhort his audience toward repentance, citing the *Nevi'im* who said repeatedly that sincere *teshuva* could prevent the forthcoming destruction. He emphasized that the entire nation — not only the Jews in Europe — must repent. He begged the people to be more careful in *shemirat Shabbat*, and openly suggested that secular people who were trying to bring about a mass desertion from the Torah were a primary spiritual cause for the atrocities in Europe.

Begging for Teshuva

DURING THE FIRST THREE YEARS AFTER THEIR MARRIAGE, Harav Ovadia and Margalit celebrated the births of their oldest daughter, Adina, and their oldest son, Yaakov.

The Family Begins to Grow

Living in these tiny quarters was becoming impossible. Adina slept in her mother's narrow bed, and Yaakov slept in a little crate that was used to deliver fruits and vegetables. Harav Ovadia was advancing in his learning and his teaching, and his fame as a speaker and halachic authority had spread throughout Yerushalayim. But Harav Ovadia needed a position that would provide for his family — and that first major rabbinic post was not long in coming.

Harav Ovadia with his oldest daughter, Adina. As the family began to grow, it was time to find a means of support.

Chapter Five: Finding His Gem □ 125

SECTION TWO

VICEROY IN EGYPT

וַיֵּצֵא יוֹסֵף עַל אֶרֶץ מִצְרָיִם

*Yosef emerged in charge
of the land of Egypt*

(Bereishit 41:45)

CHAPTER SIX
DOWN TO EGYPT

IN 5707/1947, A RABBI BY THE NAME OF RAV AHARON Shwekey[1] arrived in Eretz Yisrael with the goal of finding one rav who could serve as the deputy chief rabbi of Egypt; take control of the country's crumbling system of

---

1. The pronunciation and spelling of Shwekey follows the modern usage. The name was originally Choueka, spelled in Hebrew שוויכא. (In Hebrew, too, there are alternative spellings, but this is the spelling Rav Aharon used on his letterhead.)

Born in Aleppo, Syria in 5657/1897, Rav Aharon Shwekey was born into a family of rabbanim. His grandfather, for whom he was named, was the deputy to the Hacham Bashi (chief rabbi) of Aleppo. His grandfather passed away when his father, R' Menahem, was just eight years old. R' Menahem continued to study Torah after his father's passing and became a *Hacham*, but he never accepted a rabbinic position, preferring to earn a livelihood in business. In 1911, the family moved to Egypt, which would have a deciding influence on the then 14-year-old Aharon's path in life, for three years later, during World War I, Rav Ezra Attia was exiled to Egypt. Aharon became one of his prized students in Egypt, eventually carrying on his work there, teaching Torah to Cairo's Jewish youth after Rav Ezra moved back to Eretz Yisrael.

During the 1950s, several years after Harav Ovadia left Egypt, Rav Aharon's yeshiva came under suspicion for aiding and abetting Israel against Egypt. Many Jews in Egypt were arrested and some were even executed for collusion with an enemy. In 1955, a student at Ahava V'Ahva found out that Rav Aharon was going to be arrested, and in a dramatic rescue mission, his students procured a passport from a South American country and got him onto the first flight out that night. Several hours after his narrow escape, the secret police knocked at his door to arrest him.

From South America he traveled to New York, where he served as a rav in Magen David for two years. He then took a trip to bring *hizzuk* to Sephardic communities in South America. Although many communities begged him to remain there as their rav, he was determined to move to Eretz Yisrael, which he did in 1960. At first he lived in Yerushalayim, until he joined the Rabbanut of Tel Aviv-Yafo several years later. He also built new yeshivot in the mold of Ahava V'Ahva. He passed away on 4 Shevat, 5738/1978.

Rav Aharon Shwekey, founder of Yeshivat Ahava V'Ahva, recruited Harav Ovadia to lead his yeshiva and Cairo's Torah community.

batei din; lead Ahava V'Ahva, the yeshiva Rav Shwekey had founded; and reverse the trend of the Egyptian Jewish community drifting away from Torah and halacha.

The chief rabbi of Egypt at the time was aging and losing his eyesight, leaving somewhat of a rabbinic vacuum. In the absence of a powerful rav, the community was run primarily by a *vaad hakehilla* (community council) staffed by wealthy secular men, which had a devastating effect on the community's religious observance.[2] Rav Shwekey was one of the only people of influence in Cairo who cared about the religiosity of his community. He turned to Rishon LeZion Rav Benzion Meir Hai Uziel to determine who would be the most appropriate candidate for the position, and Rav Uziel consulted with Hacham Ezra Attia, Rosh Yeshivat Porat Yosef, who was able to answer without deliberation: His star pupil, Harav Ovadia Yosef, was more than ripe for a leadership position in Klal Yisrael. With his encyclopedic Torah knowledge, oratorical skills that could excite both the scholars of Ahava V'Ahva as well as the country's simple laymen, and youthful energy that would enable him to tackle all the facets of the job with vigor, he was the most likely to succeed at this post.

This recommendation was extremely important to Rav Shwekey, who had learned under Rav Ezra when the latter was exiled to Egypt during World War I, and had grown extremely close to him.

---

2. Rav David Yosef.

In fact, when Rav Ezra Attia left Egypt after the war, Rav Aharon Shwekey was one of a select group of his students who continued to teach Torah to Cairo's youth.

Rav Shwekey met with Harav Ovadia, who was more than two decades his junior, and an immediate rapport developed between them. This was the beginning of a friendly, mutually respectful relationship that would last more than thirty years, until Rav Shwekey's passing.[3]

A Crumbling Community

AT THAT JUNCTURE, THE JEWISH COMMUNITY OF EGYPT could accurately have been described as having a glorious past — and a dismal future.[4]

The community dated all the way back to the destruction of the first *Beit HaMikdash*, when exiles from Eretz Yisrael settled in the country, mostly in the port city of Alexandria. Although there was constantly a Karaite presence in Egypt that did not recognize the *mesora*,[5] the religious community maintained an unbroken commitment to Torah for 2,000 years. During those two millennia, the community had waxed and waned several times, growing to tens of thousands at times and dwindling to a few thousand at others.[6] Periods of persecution and even expulsion were interspersed with periods of great renaissance, when both the political leaders and the simple folk of Egypt allowed the Jews to take part in commerce and to practice their religion freely.[7]

---

3. Harav Ovadia addressed several *teshuvot* to Rav Shwekey, using extremely respectful appellations. After Rav Shwekey moved to Eretz Yisrael, Harav Ovadia would visit him every so often in appreciation for Rav Shwekey's efforts on his behalf in Egypt.
4. Most of the history of the Cairo community in this chapter is based on the book *Hachmei Yehudei Mitzrayim*, by Dr. Giora Pazalov.
5. Karaites believe only in the written Torah, but not in the transmission of the Oral Law (*Torah Shebe'al Peh*) and the requirement to follow halacha as determined by the *Hachamim* throughout the ages. They are deemed heretics in all matters of halacha.
6. For instance, famed traveler Binyamin of Tudela reported that in the 13th century, there were between 10,000 and 20,000 Jews in Egypt, but by 5248/1488, when Rav Ovadia of Bertinoro (the author of the basic commentary on Mishnayot) passed through Egypt en route to Eretz Yisrael, he found just 4,000 Jews in all of Egypt. Shortly thereafter, however, Jews expelled from Spain began to trickle into the country, and the numbers continued to swell until Israel declared independence in 1948, forcing a mass exodus.
7. Generally speaking, the Jews were treated relatively fairly under Muslim rule. Although they were often considered second-class citizens, they were entitled to religious autonomy and encouraged to take part in the economy. In contrast, when Christians ascended to major political posts in Alexandria in 4175 (415 C.E.), the Jews were expelled from the city.

Throughout the generations, a number of great Jewish leaders — including Rav Saadia Gaon, Rav Shmaryahu,[8] and, perhaps most famously, the Rambam — resided in Egypt.[9]

By the late 1800s, however, the arrival of Jews from emancipated parts of the world had taken its toll on the community's religious character, and most of the Jews in Alexandria and Cairo were no

Cairo's Tahrir Square in the 1940s, when Harav Ovadia became the deputy chief rabbi of Egypt and the head of the city's *beit din*

---

8. Rav Shmaryahu was one of the "Four Captives," a group of four great scholars traveling by boat in 4620/960 who were captured by pirates and ransomed by four major Jewish settlements. Only three of the Four Captives are known: Rav Moshe ben Hanoch, who was redeemed by the Jews of Cordova, Spain; Rav Hushiel, father of Rabbeinu Hananel, who was sold to the community of Kairouan, Tunisia (in Africa); and Rav Shmaryahu, who was redeemed by the Alexandrian community. All four opened yeshivot in their new homes, transmitting the *mesora* (Jewish heritage) to areas in which there had been very little Jewish education.
9. Rav Saadia Gaon was actually born and raised in Egypt.

longer observant. The community had grown in size — there were close to 600,000 Jews living in Egypt by then — but in terms of commitment to Torah, it was floundering. Pockets of strongly committed Jews remained, but as we will soon see, the communities were run primarily by secular leaders, who were some of the richest people in all of Egypt.

By 1919, the large-scale Jewish immigration reversed itself, and the community dwindled to approximately 60,000 people, most of whom were born in countries that were part of the Ottoman Empire.

Convincing the Family

WHEN RAV AHARON SHWEKEY, ALONG WITH RAV UZIEL AND Rav Attia, first approached Harav Ovadia to offer him the position of rav in Cairo, he immediately declined; he couldn't fathom leaving Eretz Yisrael, where he was growing in learning, for the unknown prospects of Egypt. When the three convinced him, however, that there was no other person who could fill the educational and rabbinical vacuum in Cairo as well as he could, he agreed to discuss the matter with his family.

Rabbanit Margalit was concerned that they would be isolated in Cairo and would not be able to travel back to Eretz Yisrael, and his father R' Yaakov and his father-in-law Hacham Avraham Fattal both begged the couple to turn down the offer. Their concerns were well-founded: By that point, the British had already announced their intentions to end their Mandate over Palestine, and Jew-hatred was mounting among the country's Arab neighbors. And when Israel declared its independence in May 1948, Cairo's Jewish areas were subjected to deadly riots, as well as a spate of bombings that killed 70 Jews and wounded almost 200.

Rav Avraham Fattal went as far as to take out loans to help the couple with their finances so they wouldn't have to move.[10]

Harav Ovadia himself was torn between his sense of duty to reignite Torah Judaism in Egypt on one hand, and his wife and family's safety concerns on the other.

---
10. *Abir Haro'im.*

הרבנות הראשית
במצרים

GRAND RABBINAT

קהיר ס׳ בניסן התש"ז
Le Caire, le 30 / 3 / 47
Tel. 45213

לכבוד
מעלת הארון הנכבד אליהו אלישר יצ"ו
נשיא ועד עדת הספרדים בירושלים ת"ו.

א. נ.

בתשובה למכתב כב' מיום כ"ח באדר ש"ז, החתום גם ע"י מעלת הר"הג ראל"צ שליט"א, הנני שמח להודיע כי ועד עדתנו חסכים והביר כבר ע"י מברק, באמצעות הבנק מוסירי לבנק אפ"ק בירושלים ועל שם עדתכם, סך חמישים לא"י לטובת עניי הספרדים בירושלים. והריני מאחל לכב' ולכל אחינו הספרדים צאן אשר בקהילתו, חג כשר ושמח. מי יתן ויוקל המשא הכבד הזה מעל שכמיכם, ומחה ח' דמעה מעל כל פנים וחרפה עמו יסיר מעל כל הארץ, ויגאל אותנו גאולה שלמה בביאת משיחנו בב"א.

זאת שנית, ידוע בודאי לכב' כי, מזמן, הרינו מחפשים ת"ח מובהקים לחתם על כסא הדין בקהיר, דרך מקרה, שמענו ונודע לנו כי נמצא בירושלים ת"ו ת"ח צעיר לימים שחונן בכשרונות גאוניים, הוא הר"ר עובדיה יוסף נ"י, מצוצא בבלי. ועל פי אמלצתו של הר"הג כמוהר"ר עזרה עטייה הי"ו ראש ישיבה פורת יוסף, כתבנו למעלת הר"הג ראל"צ שליט"א כדי לשאול את רעהו ולבקש ממנו להזמין אליו את הרב ר' עובדיה יוסף נ"י הנ"ל לפניו ולהודיע לו זה רצוננו למנותו דיין בקהיר.

והנה, באיחור רב, מסיבת המצב הצבאי ששרר בארץ, השיב לנו מעלת בקש"ה הר"הג ראל"צ כי הרב עובדיה יוסף, שהסכים באופן עקרוני לבוא, נמנע מסיבות משפחתיות. ואכן גודע לנו כי אשתו וחמיו מעכבים בעדו ועומדים על דעתם בכל תוקף.

הנני לבקש את כב' שינסה גם הוא להשפיע על הרב ר' עובדיה הנ"ל ועל משפחתו בכל הדרכים הנאותים העומדים ברשותו, היות וגנו זקוקים מאד מאד לדיין מוכשר, וחלינו תקוה רבה בת"ח צעיר זה שיבוא להרים את קרן התורה בקהילתנו ולעסוק במלאכת שמים.

ואם יצלית כב' לשכנע אותו, נא לכתוב לנו את המשכורת שהוא מבקש את מספר בני ביתו ושמותיהם, ואת גתינותו, ע"י זה אוכל לעשות את כל הצעדים הנחוצים מהר, חן בפני ועד הקהילה וחן בפני הממשלה המצרית כדי להשיג עבורו רשת כניסה למצרים.

הדו"ש וסחכה לתשועת ה' ולתשובתו חרמה אשר במהרה תצמת,

ראש הרבנים במלכות מצרים יע"א

*A letter from the chief rabbi of Egypt to R' Eliyahu Elyashar,
asking him to convince Harav Ovadia to move to Cairo*

While they deliberated, committed Torah Jews in Egypt were hearing glowing reports about him from Rav Shwekey, who had traveled back home in the interim, and they were anxiously awaiting his arrival. Upon hearing that Harav Ovadia was hesitating because of his family's concerns, they turned to their chief rabbi and asked him to intervene. The chief rabbi had received reports about Harav Ovadia from Rav Uziel and Rav Attia, and he, too, was excited to have Harav Ovadia serve as his deputy. In Nissan of 5707/1947, he wrote a letter to the president of the *Vaad Adat HaSephardim* (Sephardic Community Council), R' Eliyahu Elyashar, asking him to convince Harav Ovadia to take the position:

> … It is known to his honor that, for some time, we have been seeking a great *talmid hacham* to serve as *dayan* in Cairo. We found out that in Yerushalayim there is a young *talmid hacham* of Iraqi heritage, Harav Ovadia Yosef, who has been blessed with great genius. Upon receiving a recommendation from Harav Hagaon Rav Ezra Attia, Rosh Yeshivat Porat Yosef, we wrote to the Rishon LeZion,[11] seeking his opinion on the matter and asking him to invite Harav Ovadia Yosef to appear before him and inform him of our desire to appoint him as *dayan* in Cairo.
>
> After great delay due to the security situation in Eretz Yisrael, we received a response from the Rishon LeZion that Harav Ovadia Yosef has agreed, in principle, to come, but that he is refraining from actually making the trip due to family issues. Indeed, we have found out that his wife and father-in-law are insistent that they not make the move.
>
> I therefore request that his honor should also try to influence Harav Ovadia and his family to agree to come, because we are in desperate need of a qualified *dayan* and have great hopes that this young *talmid hacham* will come and uplift the glory of Torah and fulfill a Heavenly service.
>
> If his honor succeeds in convincing him, please write to inform us regarding the salary he requests, the number

---

11. According to most sources, Rav Aharon Shwekey went first to the Rishon LeZion, who sent him to Rav Ezra Attia.

of family members, their names, and their citizenships, so we can take the necessary steps, with both the community council and the Egyptian government, to secure entry rights into Egypt for them.

As this letter was being sent, Rav Uziel, who was personally familiar with the desperate leadership void in the Egyptian Jewish community, took it upon himself to convince Rabbanit Margalit to make the move. He promised her that this would be a temporary position; she would not be stuck in Egypt long term. He also pointed out that the family's dire financial situation would improve greatly in Egypt, because the community council would pay them

Close to half a century after the *sefarim* library in Beit Haknesset Ben Ezra in Cairo was a factor in Harav Ovadia's decision to move to Egypt, he perused its bookshelves once again during a visit in 1989.

a generous salary. After much deliberation and with great trepidation, she agreed to go.

Even after securing the Rabbanit's consent, Harav Ovadia continued to vacillate. In Eretz Yisrael, he was able to learn day and night. His contemporaries in Porat Yosef[12] describe how, having mastered *Shulhan Aruch* and its commentaries, Harav Ovadia turned his attention to the classic responsa works. Already at the age of 26, he was growing familiar enough with the *Sh'eilot V'Teshuvot* of both the *Rishonim* and primary *Aharonim* to quote from them at will. And so he was faced with a dilemma: Should he forgo his personal growth in Torah — and lose the opportunity to keep broadening his knowledge base by studying from all the *sefarim* available to him in Yerushalayim — in order to serve the Egyptian Jewish community?

In this case, *Hashgaha* (Divine intervention) was clearly at work, for Rav Ezra Attia was in a unique position to answer this question. "You know that I was a rav in Egypt long ago," he said, "and I can tell you that there's a library there [in Beit Haknesset Ben Ezra] that is better than anything you'll find in Eretz Yisrael."

Realizing that it was up to him to make the most of his time but that *sefarim* were available in Egypt, Harav Ovadia acquiesced to take the position.[13] Although a *seudat preida* (farewell banquet) was held on 16 Av, 5707/1947,[14] with both chief rabbis, Rav Uziel and Rav Herzog, joining Hacham Ezra Attia in sending him off with fervent hopes and prayers that he would succeed in his mission, the family moved only after the *hagim* of 5708 (October 1947).

A Complex Community

TO UNDERSTAND HOW COMPLEX A SITUATION HARAV OVADIA was stepping into, we must first examine the socioeconomic conditions of the Jews in Egypt at the time.

When the British Empire wrested control of Egypt from the Ottoman Empire in the mid-1800s, it integrated Egypt into the world economy, which led to a marked

---

12. Rav Shalom Cohen and others.
13. *Abir Haro'im*.
14. This was a joint *seudat preida* for Harav Ovadia and his close friend and *havruta* Hacham Baruch Ben-Haim, who departed for New York to serve as the rav of the Syrian Shaare Zion community for over half a century.

A warm farewell: Porat Yosef held a *seudat preida* for two of its great students who were being sent to fill rabbinic positions, Harav Ovadia and Hacham Baruch Ben-Haim. Pictured are (L-R): Rosh Yeshiva Hacham Ezra Attia, Hacham Baruch Ben-Haim, Harav Ovadia, and the two chief rabbis, Rav Benzion Meir Hai Uziel and Rav Yitchak Eizik Halevi Herzog.

Last time together: Some of Porat Yosef's greatest students of all time pose for a picture at the *seudat preida*, before going on to lead many of the largest Sephardi communities and yeshivot in the world.
Seated (R-L): Rav Ezra Shi'u, Rav Saadia Lofes, Hacham Baruch Ben-Haim, Harav Ovadia , Rav Shabtai Atoun, Rav Pinhas Vaaknin, and Rav Haim David Halevi.
Middle (r-l): Rav David Shlush, Rav Yosef Harari-Raful (of Israel), Rav Ezra Ades, Rav Avraham Sherim, Rav Rafael Ades, Rav Yosef Nadaf.
Top (R-L): Rav Aharon Aboud, Rav Yosef Ades, Rav Zion Levi (future chief rabbi of Panama), and Hachem Benzion Abba Shaul (future Rosh Yeshiva of Porat Yosef).

improvement in the economic and social conditions of its Jews. If Egypt's Jews had previously been employed in traditional Jewish occupations — such as small business, art, money-changing, and money-lending — the immigrants who arrived after the British takeover broke into a wide range of industries, including banking, journalism, construction, and government. At one point, 90 percent of the stock market traders in Cairo were Jewish.

Cairo and Alexandria were home to several Jewish communities, but the Sephardic community was the largest and most prominent among them. It was officially recognized by the Egyptian government and authorized to administer communal matters autonomously.

A branch of the largest retail chain in Egypt, owned by one of the lay leaders of Cairo's Jewish community. Many members of the community council were fabulously wealthy, but were not committed to Torah and mitzvot.

The community had established many vital institutions — including a hospital, orphanages, and charitable organizations — and ran them in model fashion. A secular council, composed of wealthy businesspeople and lawyers, controlled the community. Some of the council members were pillars of the Egyptian economy — one came from a family that built and controlled the train system, another owned the largest retail chain in Egypt, and a third owned several large banks — and they wielded tremendous influence over government officials.

But as these Jews gained wealth and prominence, they abandoned the Jewish quarter, forged contacts with wealthy gentiles, and often worked against the interests of their own less-privileged brethren. Tension developed between the general Jewish community and the council members, who distanced themselves from their coreligionists and sent their children to non-Jewish schools — either Christian schools or Egyptian public schools. By the turn of the 20th century, many of the city's middle- and upper-class Jews had been educated in French, Italian, or British schools, while the Jewish schools were populated mostly by students from lower-income families. Members of the upper class strayed from tradition in large numbers, and both the religious leadership and the secular community council were alarmed by the number of Jews who were converting to other religions.

In the 20th century, the community undertook efforts to rejuvenate Jewish life in Egypt. This campaign accelerated in the 1930s to fight the influence of missionaries. Jewish schools were established, as well as youth clubs and groups that studied Jewish history and the Hebrew language.

The wealthy members of the community council were, for the most part, very generous in supporting the various Jewish institutions in the city, but since they were far removed from Torah, they were unwilling to invest much money into Torah institutions. And while they recognized the importance of having a competent rabbi officiate at weddings and administer *gittin* (halachic divorces),[15]

---

15. If a couple is married according to Torah law and they decide to divorce, the husband must issue a *get* (halachic bill of divorce) to his wife. If she does not receive a *get* and subsequently

they did not want to be forced to take on any more religious observance than they felt comfortable with. They definitely did not want rabbis dictating policy for the entire community.

In the eyes of the community council, therefore, Harav Ovadia was brought in only to perform technical rabbinic functions and sit at the helm of Cairo's *beit din*, which was frozen for lack of a qualified halachic authority to lead it.

The religious community, however, had other reasons to rejoice when they heard that Harav Ovadia agreed to move to Cairo. Only a dynamic personality could tend to other areas of religious life that needed to be bolstered, and Yeshivat Ahava V'Ahva, led by Rav Aharon Shwekey, needed a superior *talmid hacham* to deliver high-level *shiurim*.

WHILE MUCH OF HARAV OVADIA'S STAY IN EGYPT WAS fraught with difficulty and hard-fought battles, the crowning triumph of his tenure were his accomplishments as Rosh Yeshiva of Ahava V'Ahva and through *shiurim* he delivered at Midrash Rashbi, another learning program in Cairo. He embraced those roles with vigor, quickly sweeping up the students with his infectious enthusiasm. Throughout his stay, in fact, no matter how contentious the relationship between the community council and the new rav grew, his core group of followers at Ahava V'Ahva and Midrash Rashbi remained loyal to him and did everything they could to fortify him against the council members.

Ahava V'Ahva

Ahava V'Ahva was founded in 1929 by Rav Aharon Shwekey, along with Rav Yaakov Dwek and the *gabbai*, Hacham Haim Suleman Mizrahi. The yeshiva had a tremendous influence not only on its students, but on the Cairo community in general. Its influence eventually spread to other Jewish communities as well, as its

---

has children with another man, those children are *mamzerim* (illegitimate) and may not marry a proper Jew.

Historically, even irreligious Jews often realized that the consequences of having marriages and divorces administered by incompetent rabbanim — or "rabbis" from streams of Judaism that do not follow halacha — could be devastating to their offspring, and they were willing to follow the laws of the Torah at least in these areas.

HaRav Ovadia delivering a *shiur* to his devoted students at Yeshiva Ahava V'Ahva

alumni established shuls, yeshivot, and Talmud Torahs by the same name throughout the world.

Rav Aharon established the yeshiva for the benefit of the community's youth and laymen, many of whom had been educated in non-Jewish institutions and had little knowledge of halacha.

The yeshiva was located on the ground floor of a four-story building at Dahar Square in Cairo, and contained about ten study rooms and spacious halls. Ahava V'Ahva began to buzz before sunrise with the *vatikin minyan*, and for the next three to four hours, it hummed with worshipers who organized *minyanim* for themselves as needed. After the early *minyanim*, people could stay to participate in a *shiur* in Hok L'Yisrael[16] or halacha. The crowds petered out by the end of the morning, when everyone had left to work or school, but by 4 in the afternoon the building was once again full, this time with elementary school children who had come to learn Torah after finishing their secular studies. Some of these students

---

16. *Hok L'Yisrael* is a set of *sefarim* in which the weekly *parasha* is split into daily portions, followed by selections from Tanach, Mishnah, Gemara, Zohar, halacha, and other portions of the Torah.

came from assimilated homes and learned in non-Jewish schools; their first class at Ahava V'Ahva was a four-to-six week course in how to read Hebrew. Afterward, they moved on to the prayer "class," where they learned the prayers and their meanings, and halachot such as *hilchot berachot*. These studies took place from Monday to Thursday, with up to 300 students participating consistently.

Most of Ahava V'Ahva's activities were run by young, tireless volunteers who invested much of their time and energy into these initiatives. Only one or two rabbanim actually earned a full salary from the yeshiva, and a few others received a small stipend for their efforts.

The youth volunteers who taught the younger classes developed a deep camaraderie with their students. Special committees of youths who were close in age to the students planned activities and contests to help students maintain their interest in Torah studies. Students who excelled in their studies received weekly prizes. There were *Melaveh Malka* clubs that included singing and trivia contests, and on Yom Tov and other occasions there were group trips.

By 7 in the evening, all the schoolchildren left, and the build-

HaRav Ovadia visits the pyramids in Egypt with his students and his family. Note that while in Eygpt, he wore a *tarbush*, a tall hat traditionally worn by *hachamim* in Egypt.

ing filled up once again with working youths and laymen. Harav Ovadia would spend three to four hours each night teaching Torah, splitting his time between Ahava V'Ahva and Midrash Rashbi. Harav Ovadia didn't limit himself to delivering *shiurim* at Ahava V'Ahva; he would participate in trips as well to help his students develop into *bnei Torah* and impart to them the Torah outlook on life. Rabbanit Margalit and the Yosef children often joined these trips as well, affording them the opportunity to visit famous sites in Egypt.

Considering the number of students that Ahava V'Ahva brought under the umbrella of Torah study, Rav Daniel Levy was not exaggerating when he said that "if not for Rav Aharon Shwekey, Torah would have been forgotten in Egypt."

Under Constant Threat

ALMOST FROM THE FIRST DAY HE ARRIVED IN CAIRO, RAV Ovadia was under surveillance from the Egyptian government, which suspected him of being a spy for the Zionists who were soon going to declare independence and establish a state. They followed him wherever he went, and hauled him in for questioning on numerous occasions. Once, a group of policemen barreled into his home late at night and started searching for the weapons cache they were convinced he was hiding. Without flinching, Harav Ovadia pointed to his *sefarim*. "These are the only weapons I have," he said with a smile.[17] The officer in charge of the unit believed him, and the policemen left.

During one interrogation, they asked him why he taught and lectured in Hebrew, "the language of the Zionists."

"I teach the Torah in the language in which it was given," he replied coolly.[18]

On at least one occasion, he was arrested while traveling to deliver a *shiur* in one of the outlying areas, and he was jailed overnight. He was released only when the chief rabbi intervened on his behalf.

And it wasn't only the government he had to contend with. He

---

17. *Encyclopedia Lehalutzei Hayishuv U'bonav*, V. 18, p. 5422.
18. Ibid.

In his later years, Harav Ovadia was able to fulfill the mitzvot of *succa* and *etrog* with ease; in Egypt, they nearly cost him a prison sentence.

was once traveling on the train, and a group of youths approached him for a donation. The cause? The Muslim Brotherhood. Harav Ovadia realized that the money they were raising would go toward the purchase of weapons for use in terror attacks against Jews, so he refused to donate. The youths started to rough him up, knocking off his hat and threatening that if he wouldn't give them money, they would take it from him forcibly. "I can't stop you from taking my money," he replied, "but I'm not giving it to you."

The youths then reached into his pocket and helped themselves to his money.

When Harav Ovadia told this story to R' Massoud Elbaz,[19] the latter asked why he didn't just give them a small coin and send them on their way. "That coin could be used to buy one bullet that could be used against a Jew," Harav Ovadia replied.[20]

The Suspicions Mount

IN MAY OF 1948, WHEN ISRAEL DECLARED INDEPENDENCE AND was attacked by Egypt and six other Arab countries, the Jews of Egypt were thrust into tremendous danger, because every member of the community was a suspected Zionist spy.

On Hol HaMoed Succos of 5709/1948, nearly a year after Harav Ovadia had arrived in Cairo and a few months after the War of Independence commenced, he was in the *succa* he had erected on the roof of his building, waving the *arba minim*, when a policeman crashed through the door and placed him under arrest. It was obvious to the policeman that the *succa* was meant to mark a target for Israeli fighter pilots, and that Harav Ovadia was waving his *lulav* toward the skies to get their attention.

Only with much effort did Harav Ovadia manage to convince a judge that both the *succa* and *lulav* were being used purely for religious observance; even then, the judge refused to allow him to leave the *succa* intact. Fortunately, however, he ordered him to dismantle the *succa* within seven days, not realizing that by then Harav Ovadia would no longer need it.[21]

---

19. See p. 159.
20. Mr. Avraham Elbaz, a grandson of R' Massoud.
21. *Posek HaDor*.

The Next Frontier

BY THE SUMMER OF 5708/1948, HARAV OVADIA HAD ALREADY grown into his role as a teacher of Torah in Egypt. Not only was he delivering *shiurim* at Ahava V'Ahva, he was also speaking on an alternating basis at *batei knesset* in the Jewish neighborhood and in outlying areas to ensure that every Jew in the city who wanted to learn Torah or halacha had access to a *shiur*.

He had also established himself as the *av beit din* of Cairo and the address for difficult halachic issues related to marriages and *gittin*. In just three years in Cairo, he would tend to close to 100 *gittin*, ensuring that they were written and delivered properly so the future generations of these families would be able to marry proper Jews.

Once Harav Ovadia settled into his primary roles in Egypt, he was able to turn his attention to the next frontier: shoring up the religious observance in the community's institutions — although not all of Cairo's Jews were quite ready for him to lead them in that direction.

CHAPTER SEVEN
A DANGEROUS BATTLE

WERE IT ONLY FOR THE SECURITY SITUATION in Egypt, Harav Ovadia might have lasted there much longer than he did. In the end, it wasn't fear of the anti-Israel Egyptian government that sent him back to Israel; it was fear of Heaven.

From his very first days in Egypt, there was a decided split in the way the community reacted to his presence. While the Ahava V'Ahva community welcomed him warmly and revered him, the secular Jewish communities in Egypt were not particularly pleased with his attempts to change societal norms that contravened halacha.

Rav Ovadia documents some of those attempts in *teshuvot* in *Yabia Omer*, although he omits the details of his heroic stands for the sake of halacha.

ONE RELATIVELY MINOR BATTLE HE FOUGHT REVOLVED around the use of microphones in the *batei knesset* on Shabbat and *hagim*. He writes[1] that when he arrived in Egypt, he was shocked to find that on Rosh Hashana and Yom Kippur, when many more congregants attended the *tefillot*, *hazzanim* in the large *batei*

The Battle Over the Microphone

---
1. *Yabia Omer*, Vol. 1, Orah Haim 19.

knesset in Cairo used microphones to enable the entire audience to hear the *tefillah* clearly, and even the chief rabbi delivered his sermon over the microphone. One of the rationalizations offered was that a Jew wasn't turning on the microphone, he was only talking or singing into it.

After examining whether the use of electricity on Shabbat constituted a Torah-level prohibition or a rabbinic one, Harav Ovadia ruled conclusively that one may not use a microphone even if it is turned on by a gentile. He explains, based on expert opinions from electricians, that when a person speaks into a microphone, the sound waves generated by his voice cause a flow of electricity that heats the wires of the microphone, and when he stops singing or talking, the wires cool down. This, he concludes, is prohibited under the *melachot* of *maavir* and *mechabeh* (lighting and extinguishing a fire). He writes that his ruling was accepted in Egypt.

In the course of this *teshuva*, Harav Ovadia proves his acumen — at the age of just 26 — in two significant areas.

The first is the ability to filter information. Since rabbanim often

One of Harav Ovadia's first efforts in Egypt was to put a stop to the use of microphones on Shabbat and *hagim* in the *batei knesset*, including the Great Synagogue in Cairo, which he revisited in 1989, more than forty years after he left Egypt.

need to rely on outside experts to explain technical or scientific information to them before they can issue a ruling, it is vital for them to have a sixth sense enabling them to discern when an expert is giving accurate information and when he is fudging or mistaken. In the *teshuva*, Harav Ovadia writes that the first electrician he spoke to claimed that the wires do not heat up when a person speaks into the microphone. He sensed, however, that this electrician wasn't being honest with him, so he sought additional expert opinions. After he spoke to an engineer who explained the scientific reality to him clearly, the first electrician admitted that his initial assessment was wrong.[2]

The second is his ability to cite from a plethora of sources, including esoteric ones. In dealing with the question of whether electricity activated by voice is considered a *melacha*, he cites from *Geza Yishai*, an obscure work that states that one would not be allowed to use the Divine Names found in *Sefer Yetzirah* to create a person or an animal on Shabbat. This ability to apply concepts culled from far-flung, apparently unrelated sources to an everyday *sh'eila* would become one of the trademarks of Harav Ovadia's written works.

ALTHOUGH HE WAS A YOUNGSTER COMPARED TO OTHER RABbinic figures in the country, Harav Ovadia was unflinchingly assertive when it came to defending halacha.

No to the Church

In 5709/1949, a gentile diplomat in Cairo died. The chief rabbi couldn't make it to his funeral, so he asked Harav Ovadia to represent him. Since the deceased was Christian, however, the ceremony was to take place in a church, and Harav Ovadia balked at the idea of attending a church service. The chief rabbi assured him that, historically, many rabbanim in the city attended such funerals, and it was necessary for *darkei shalom*, in order to maintain peace with the gentiles.[3] In the *teshuva* he wrote

---

2. Interestingly, Harav Ovadia writes that Rav Eliezer Waldenburg (author of *Tzitz Eliezer*), whose *beit din* he would eventually join a decade later, had the same experience — the initial opinions he sought regarding the use of a microphone in radio broadcasting didn't satisfy him, and he kept seeking additional input from experts until he felt that he had a good handle on the subject.
3. While there is a concept of *darkei shalom* in halacha, it is not a concept that can be applied broadly; each case must be examined individually by competent authorities.

on the subject,[4] Harav Ovadia pondered the following issues: (a) whether one is allowed to enter a house of idol worship; (b) whether a church is considered a house of idol worship; and (c) whether it would be a *hillul Hashem* (desecration of Hashem's Name) for a rav wearing official rabbinic vestments to appear in a church.

He ruled that it was absolutely forbidden for a rav to appear in a church for this purpose, adding that if this was the prevailing custom, it was vital that the custom be abolished, because it caused a *hillul Hashem*.[5]

Reforming Shehita

IN ADDITION TO THE MANY ISOLATED SKIRMISHES THAT Harav Ovadia fought in his quest to uphold halacha, there were two protracted battles that eventually led to his return to Eretz Yisrael.

One of these battles came as no surprise to him. Even before taking the position in Cairo, he heard from recent immigrants to Eretz Yisrael that the *shehita* in the city was questionable, and that many God-fearing residents weren't willing to eat meat or poultry slaughtered by the local *shohtim*.

Upon arriving in Cairo, he discovered that the local system of *shehita* was rife with corruption, which was an outgrowth of previous *batei din* being more concerned about protecting the rights of the individual *shohtim* than about the community's need for reliable *shehita*. He writes[6] that the local *shohtim* were wary of newcomers entering into their industry, and the *batei din* protected these *shohtim* when they brought a newcomer to a *din Torah* claiming he was infringing on their territory.[7] The result was that nobody bothered to learn *shehita*, because they knew they wouldn't be able to use that skill, even if individuals brought animals to their homes — let alone in an official slaughterhouse.

---

4. *Yabia Omer*, Vol. 2, *Yoreh Dei'ah* 11.
5. Using a play on words, he writes that they should abolish the מנהג (custom), which is written with the same letters as גהנם (purgatory).
6. *Yabia Omer*, Vol. 9, *Hoshen Mishpat* 2.
7. There is a halachic concept of *hasagat gvul* that prevents newcomers from entering certain occupations if it means that others already working in that industry will lose their livelihood, but in this case, since the veteran *shohtim* weren't reliable, the concept wouldn't have applied.

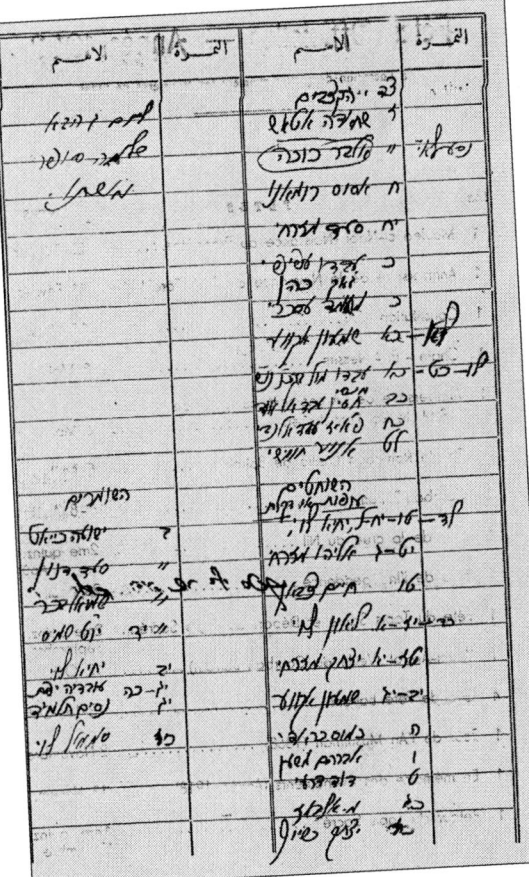

A list Harav Ovadia drew up to track the *shohtim* and butchers operating in Egypt upon his arrival

"They've made *shehita* into no more than a source of income," Harav Ovadia writes of the previous *batei din*, wondering why they never deposed older *shohtim* who no longer had the sensitivity in their fingers to check their knives properly, and why they allowed non-God-fearing *shohtim* to continue slaughtering, rather than bring in reliable *shohtim*.

In *teshuvot* penned mostly during his tenure in Cairo, some of which were updated and published over the course of several decades, Harav Ovadia describes the various problems that he discovered upon his inspection of the *shehita* practices in the city.

The main problem was that the *shohtim* felt that they, not the rabbanim, reigned supreme, and they felt comfortable threatening the rabbanim — or even resorting to violence — if they didn't get

Chapter Seven: A Dangerous Battle □ 153

their way. In addition, many of the *shohtim* were lacking in *yirat Shamayim*,⁸ which was reflected not only in their approach to *shehita*, but also in their generally lax approach to halacha.

IN HIS *TESHUVOT*, HARAV OVADIA DOCUMENTS SOME OF the battles he fought against *shohtim* who were violating halacha:

For the Love of Money *A shohet, Mr. L., was caught accepting money on Yom Tov for slaughtering animals. (Slaughtering for commercial benefit is prohibited on Yom Tov.) When Harav Ovadia heard about this blatant violation of halacha, he sent two valid witnesses to observe it in action. After the hag was over, he summoned Mr. L. and one of the witnesses to beit din, and had the witness testify before Mr. L. Not only did Mr. L. deny the claim, he actually swore, using the word "Hashem,"⁹ that it wasn't true.*

Rav Ovadia then summoned the other witness. As soon as Mr. L. realized that there were two valid witnesses, he backtracked from his initial denial, but the damage had already been done: not only had he been seen accepting money on a hag, he had exacerbated his transgression by swearing falsely.¹⁰

The beit din suspended Mr. L. from shehita until after Shavuot, stipulating that if he proved by then that he was keeping halacha properly, he would be reinstated as a shohet. If, however, he would violate the suspension, his shehita privileges would be terminated permanently.

There was a custom among Cairo's Jewish residents to slaughter ducks for Shavuot,¹¹ and when Harav Ovadia

---

8. There is a category of occupations known as *melechet Shamayim* (lit., the work of Heaven). *Yirat Shamayim* (fear of Heaven) is a prerequisite for any such occupation, because others are relying on the honesty and sincerity of the practitioner to ensure that they are keeping halacha properly. *Melechet Shamayim* includes all *kashrut*-related occupations, but it also includes other areas of halacha, such as *safrut*, because once *sifrei Torah, tefillin,* and *mezuzot* are completed, it is impossible to discern whether the *sofer* followed certain vital halachot when writing them.
9. Part of the *teshuva* deals with whether someone who swears using the term "Hashem," which is not an actual Name of God, is considered to have sworn in the Name of God.
10. *Yabia Omer,* Vol. 9, Hoshen Mishpat 2:1.
11. Rav Ovadia writes that this is akin to the custom of *kapparot* before Yom Kippur.

went to check the knives of the shohtim, he found Mr. L. in the slaughterhouse sporting a bloodstained shirt.

"Did you slaughter?" he asked.

"No," answered Mr. L.

"Tell me the truth," Harav Ovadia persisted. "Did you slaughter?"

"Yes," Mr. L. admitted, "I did."

Rav Ovadia instructed him to leave the slaughterhouse and to come to the beit din after the hag, at which point the dayanim would decide whether he would ever be reinstated as a shohet.

By the time Harav Ovadia returned home from the slaughterhouse, there was a "welcoming committee" awaiting him. Mr. L. and several of his Arab friends who helped butcher the meat after the *shehita* were loitering in front of his home, waiting to beat him for having taken a stand against Mr. L. Harav Ovadia writes that he was saved by some sort of miracle, though he doesn't explain exactly how he was spared.

He adds that one of Mr. L.'s neighbors later testified that he saw Mr. L. pay an Arab a significant sum to kill Harav Ovadia.

SOMETIMES, IT WASN'T OPEN DISREGARD FOR HALACHA THAT Harav Ovadia had to battle, but sheer ignorance.

Unchecked Knives Another shohet did not know how to sharpen and check his knife properly, as evidenced on many occasions.[12] Harav Ovadia suspended him several times from shehita and sent him to learn how to check his knife, but each time he "forgot" the proper technique after a short while. When Harav Ovadia would go to the slaughterhouse and check this shohet's knife, he would invariably find blemishes on the blade. Eventually, when he caught him in the act of slaughtering with a blemished knife, he dismissed him, telling him to find a new occupation.

---

12. The *shehita* knife must be perfectly smooth, without as much as a single blemish, for the *shehita* to be valid.

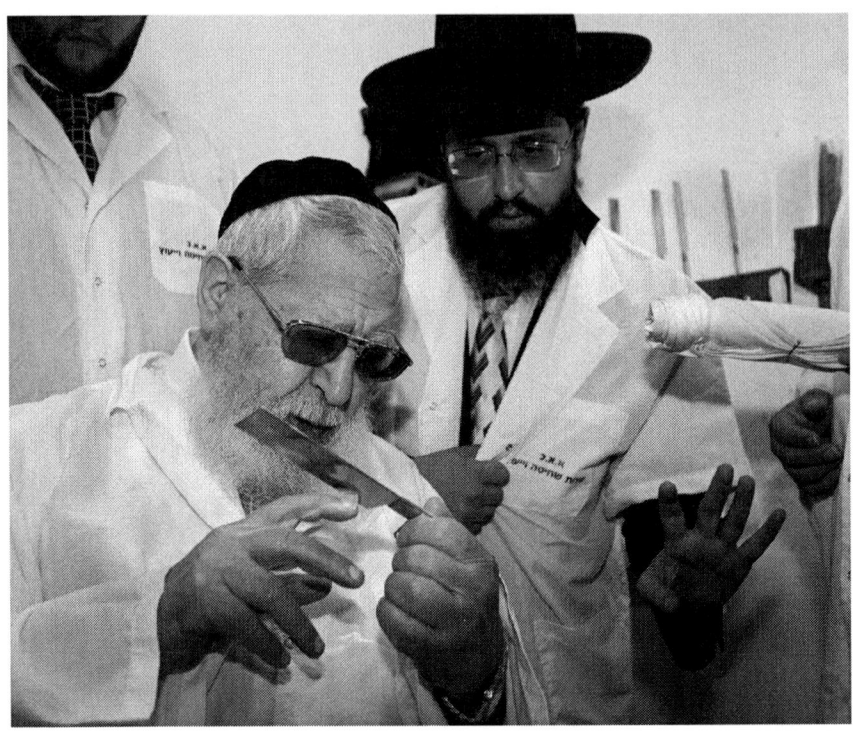

Decades after dismissing *shohtim* who slaughtered without checking their knives carefully, Harav Ovadia checks the knives of *shohtim* of the *hashgacha* he founded, Badatz Beit Yosef, as his youngest son Rav Moshe, who heads the Badatz, looks on.

> *This case, too, quickly turned dangerous, with the shohet threatening Harav Ovadia with bodily harm, and even hiring Arab goons to beat him.*

THE MOST DRAMATIC CASE INVOLVED A MR. SHIMON A., WHO held the official title of "chief of all the *shohtim*."

The Saga of Shimon A. For years, there were rumors that before checking the lungs of slaughtered animals for blemishes, Shimon allowed gentile workers to open the carcasses and remove certain parts that could invalidate the animal's *kashrut* status. The gentile employees at the slaughterhouse appreciated this privilege, since it ensured that the animal wouldn't be invalidated, causing a tremendous financial loss, and they even gave Shimon gifts for allowing them to do so. The rumors gained sufficient traction to stop many God-fearing Jews from eating any animal meat as long as Shimon was serving as a *shohet* and *bodek*.[13]

> In Tammuz of 5708/1948, less than a year after Harav Ovadia arrived, the allegations became much more serious. A *mashgiah*, Mr. Yihye Levi, reported that Shimon had commanded him to place a kosher stamp on meat from an animal slaughtered by a gentile. Shimon denied the charges, and there was no other witness to this specific case.
>
> There were many other witnesses, however, who could testify to Shimon's general laxity in halacha. He would take the electric tram on Shabbat, for instance, even paying for it as he would on an ordinary day.
>
> The problem was that aside from Yihye Levi, no other witnesses were willing to testify in Shimon's presence, because he was a violent man and they were afraid to confront him.

A Course of Action

THE WAY HARAV OVADIA DEALT WITH THE *SHOHTIM* IN Cairo established a prototype for the way he dealt with opposition when enforcing halacha during the nearly seven decades to follow.

His first step was to address each *shohet* politely and try to convince him to enter a different profession. Unfortunately, most of the *shohtim* would not hear of it. Harav Ovadia would then examine the case carefully, weighing the evidence of the *shohet's* indiscretions against any factors that might speak in his favor. If he ruled that the *shohet* had to be deposed, he subsequently saw to it that the ruling was enforced.

In the case of Shimon A., Harav Ovadia's defense of halacha nearly cost him his life.

During the *beit din* proceedings in that case, Harav Ovadia ruled

---

13. A *bodek* checks the animal after it is slaughtered to determine whether it had any blemishes that would render it nonkosher. A *shohet* often does both the slaughtering and the checking, and he is then known as a *shohet u'bodek* (or by the acronym שו״ב).

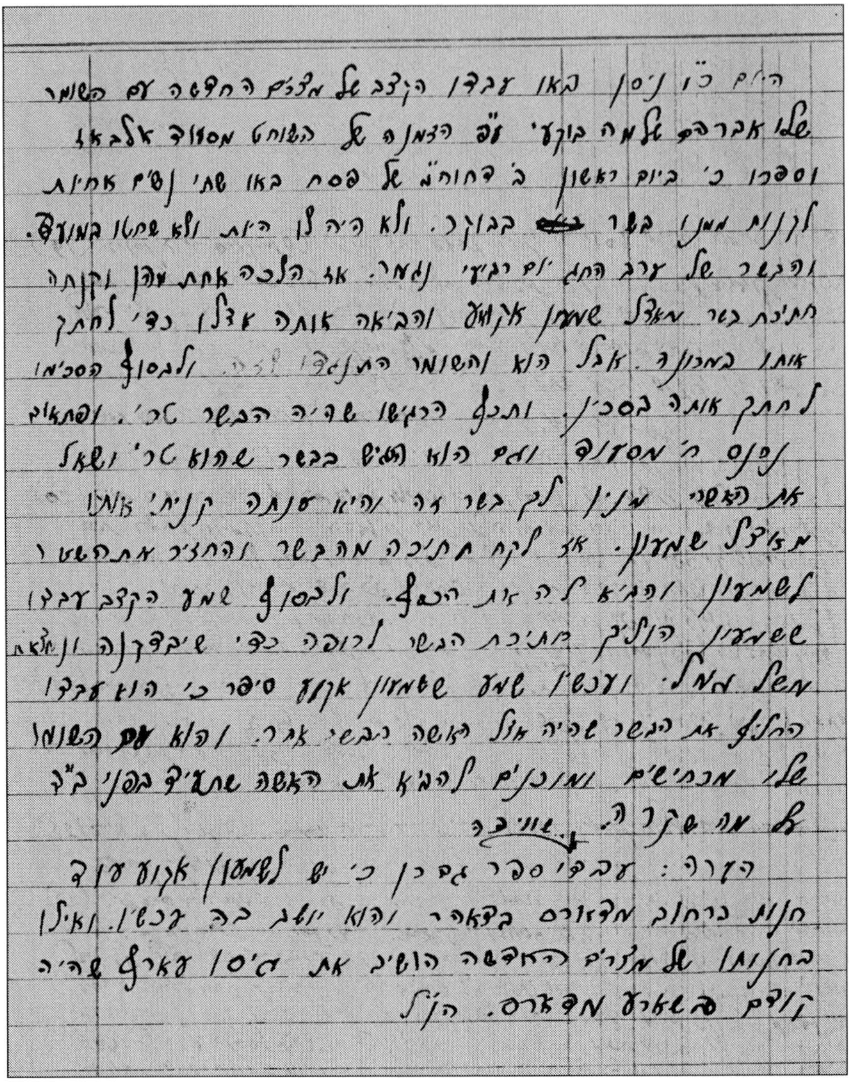

ה"ק כ"ו ניסן באו עבדו הקצב של מגדש החדשה עם השומר
שלו אברהם שלמה בוקעי נ"פ הזמנה של השוחט מסעוד אלבאז
וספרו כי ביום ראשון ב' דחוה"מ של פסח באו שתי נשים אחיות
לקנות ממנו בשר בבוקר. ולא היה לו היות ולא שחטו במועד.
והבשר של ערב החג יום רביעי נגמר. אז הלכה אחת מהן וקנתה
חתיכת בשר מאצל שמעון אקוע והביאה אותה אצלו כדי לחתך
אותו במכונה. אבל הוא והשומר התנגדו. ולבסוף הסכימו
לחתך אותה בסכין. ותכף הרגישו שהיה הבשר טר'. ופתאום
נכנס ר' מסעוד וגם הוא הרגיש בבשר שהוא טר' ושאל
את האשה מנין לך בשר זה והיא ענתה קניתי אותו
מאצל שמעון. אז לקח חתיכה מהבשר והחזיר את השאר
לשמעון והביא לה את הכסף. ולבסוף שמע הקצב עבדו
ששמעון הוליך חתיכת הבשר לרופה כדי שיבדקנה ונמצא
משל גמל. ועכשיו שמע ששמעון אקוע סיפר כי הוא עבדו
הוליך את הבשר שהיה אצל האשה ובשר אחר. והוא עם השומר
שלו מכחישים ומוכנים להביא את האשה שתעיד בפני ב"ד
על מה שקרה.
הערה: עבדו סיפר גם כן כי יש לשמעון אקוע עוד
חנות ברחוב מדזורס בקאזר והוא יושב בה עכשיו. ואילו
בחנותו של מגדש החדשה הושיב את ג'וסו עארף שהיה
קודם בשוארע מדזורס. הנ"ל

A transcription of the oral testimony against Shimon the chief *shohet*, handwritten by Rav Aharon Shwekey

that testimony could be heard from witnesses without Shimon being present,[14] and the testimony ultimately led to his dismissal from his post as *shohet*. In the first *teshuva* he wrote about Shimon's

14. Since Shimon was known to be a violent person — and he actually proved that his reputation was well-deserved by threatening, right in front of the *beit din*, to kill a butcher with whom he had had an altercation — the *beit din* could allow witnesses to testify about him in his absence.

case,[15] Harav Ovadia ends with a cryptic statement: "Behold, the end of the *shohet* and *bodek* who was dismissed proved [what had been said at] the beginning, when he exposed [his true colors] through several terrible incidents. It is the honor of God to hide this matter."

In a later update to this *teshuva*,[16] Harav Ovadia writes that Shimon was offered severance pay and persuaded to resign from his position, and that a God-fearing, competent *shohet* was installed in his stead, but he still doesn't reveal the details.

With time, however, the story came to light.

> *Rav Ovadia convinced R' Massoud Elbaz, a God-fearing shohet from Alexandria, to move to Cairo to fill Shimon's position. Shimon flew into a rage, and he and his comrades attacked and beat R' Massoud for usurping him.*
>
> *But it wasn't only R' Massoud who suffered from Shimon's violence; Shimon tried to eliminate Harav Ovadia — both directly and indirectly.*
>
> *At one point, Shimon fabricated allegations that Harav Ovadia was opposed to the Egyptian government, hoping that he would be arrested and jailed. As we have seen,[17] Harav Ovadia was already under suspicion simply because he was from Israel, but he managed to convince the authorities that the story Shimon had fed them was false.*
>
> *Shimon still refused to enter another industry. Realizing that he could no longer serve as a shohet, he opened a butcher shop to sell meat slaughtered by others. Shortly after he went into business, a woman bought a piece of meat from him. R' Massoud Elbaz happened to be standing near the butcher shop, and when he saw the meat that the woman was holding, he commented that it did not look like anything the shohtim had slaughtered that day. She told him that she had bought the meat from Shimon,*

---

15. *Yabia Omer*, Vol. 1, *Yoreh Dei'ah* 1.
16. *Yabia Omer*, Vol. 9, *Hoshen Mishpat* 2:6.
17. See p. 145.

R' Massoud Elbaz, the God-fearing *shohet* who was attacked by Arabs who mistook him for Harav Ovadia

whose store sold only kosher meat. R' Massoud's comment made her nervous that the meat wasn't kosher, however, so she told him that she was going to return the meat and get a refund. R' Massoud asked her if he could return it for her. After giving her back her money, he took the meat to a veterinarian, who examined it and declared that it was camel meat.

When he confronted Shimon with the certificate he had received from the veterinarian stating that the meat was from a camel, Shimon tried defending himself by claiming that his Arab worker had brought the nonkosher meat into the store, but when he realized that R' Massoud saw through the ruse, he began to beg him not to report the incident to Harav Ovadia. "He'll shut down my store," he cried, "and I won't be able to support my family."

R' Massoud could not allow Shimon to continue serving Jews nonkosher meat, however, so he related to Harav Ovadia what had transpired. Harav Ovadia did not shut down Shimon's store, but he did insist that a mashgiah be present at all times from then on, ensuring that only kosher meat was brought into the store.

Upon hearing this, Shimon pulled out a gun and pointed it at Harav Ovadia. "I'll take care of anyone who gets in my way," he threatened. Harav Ovadia looked him directly in the eye and responded coolly, "You want to kill me? Throughout the ages, Jews have died for our Torah. You think the gun is going to scare me?"

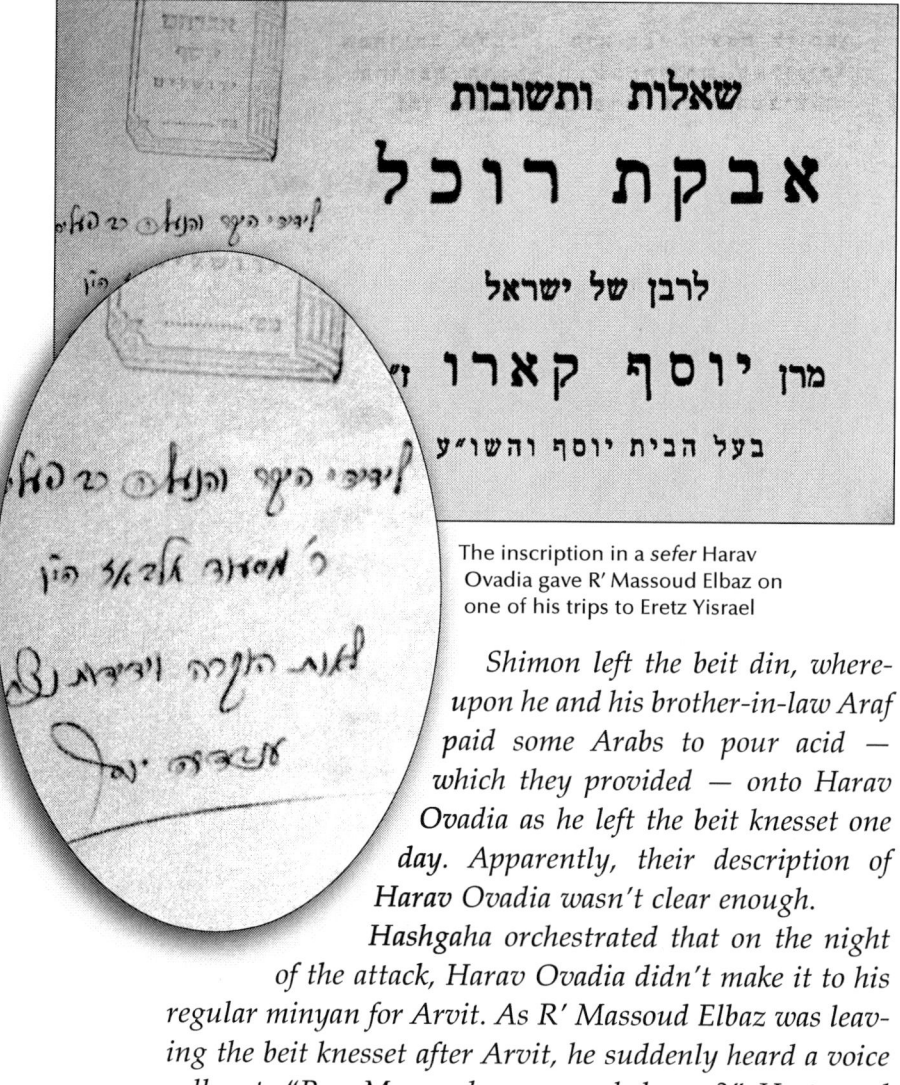

The inscription in a *sefer* Harav Ovadia gave R' Massoud Elbaz on one of his trips to Eretz Yisrael

Shimon left the beit din, whereupon he and his brother-in-law Araf paid some Arabs to pour acid — which they provided — onto Harav Ovadia as he left the beit knesset one day. Apparently, their description of Harav Ovadia wasn't clear enough.

Hashgaha orchestrated that on the night of the attack, Harav Ovadia didn't make it to his regular minyan for Arvit. As R' Massoud Elbaz was leaving the beit knesset after Arvit, he suddenly heard a voice call out, "Rav Massoud, can you help me?" He turned around, and at that moment, the Arab threw the acid at him, mistaking him for Harav Ovadia.[18]

The acid landed on R' Massoud's neck and back. Had he not turned around at that moment, he would have been blinded — or worse. He was hospitalized for a while, but he did not suffer lasting damage.

---

18. This portion of the story was related by Mr. Avraham Elbaz, R' Massoud's grandson.

> *Incredibly, R' Massoud related to his family that never before had he seen the person who called out to him, causing him to turn around just in time, and he never saw him afterward.*

Rav Ovadia felt terrible that his salvation had come at R' Massoud's expense.[19]

Some of the congregants who witnessed the incident reported it to the police, who investigated the matter and imprisoned Shimon for six months. When he was released, he agreed to hire a *mashgiah* to certify the meat in his store.

Catching Up

THE STORY DIDN'T END IN EGYPT, THOUGH. DURING THE 1950S, when Harav Ovadia served on the *beit din* of Rav Reuven Katz in Petah Tikva, Rabbanit Margalit looked out her window one day and noticed Shimon pacing outside in the courtyard. When she told Harav Ovadia about it that night, he wasn't very surprised.

Several days earlier, he had received a call from Rav Nissim Azran, who was responsible for certifying *shohtim* in Yerushalayim. A fellow had come to ask him for authorization to work as a *shohet*, and had presented rabbinic certification as well as proof that he had been working as a *shohet* in the town of Mevaseret Yerushalayim. The man's name sounded familiar, but it took Rav Nissim some time to put his finger on it. One day, it hit him: He had recently read the very first *teshuva* in *Yoreh Dei'ah* in the newly published first volume of *Yabia Omer*, and this *shohet* was the very same Shimon whom Harav Ovadia had deposed in Egypt!

In another turn of *Hashgaha*, during those same days, Harav Ovadia was attending a conference of *dayanim* in Yerushalayim,

---

19. This story has a beautiful postscript. Several years after this incident, R' Massoud visited Eretz Yisrael to collect an inheritance for his wife, whose relative had passed away, leaving her 1,000 lira. Naturally, he visited his rebbi and friend Harav Ovadia, who mentioned that he was about to print a volume of *Yabia Omer*, but he didn't have all the funds he needed for the *sefer*. R' Massoud immediately pulled out the 1,000 lira and handed it to Harav Ovadia, enabling him to publish the volume. All he asked in return was for a *beracha* for his wife, whose inheritance had funded the publication. After Harav Ovadia's passing, R' Massoud's grandson Avraham reported that his grandmother, who had received a *beracha* for long life from Harav Ovadia, was still alive and well, and had made *aliya* to Eretz Yisrael shortly before Harav Ovadia's passing.

and one of his students asked a peculiar question: May a *shohet* slaughter animals if he is not wearing a yarmulke and has not washed *netilat yadayim* upon rising in the morning?

"Why are you asking this question?" Harav Ovadia inquired.

"I moved to Mevaseret Yerushalayim recently, and we have a *shohet* who is doing so."

Rav Ovadia asked for the *shohet*'s name, and he was shocked to hear that it was none other than Shimon A. from Egypt.

He then discussed the matter with Rav Nissim Azran, who, of course, rejected Shimon's request for certification.

> *A few days after Shimon A.'s request for certification was rejected, six-year-old Yaffa Yosef was playing outside when a man approached her and asked, "Does Harav Ovadia Yosef live here?"*
>
> *"Sure," she answered. "He's my father." Thinking that the man was one of her father's students, she allowed him to follow her inside. Rabbanit Margalit froze when she saw Shimon A. in her house, but then she sprang into action and tried to block him from entering Harav Ovadia's study. He shoved her aside and barreled his way into the study, where Harav Ovadia was learning with his father-in-law, Rav Avraham Fattal.*
>
> *Shimon reached into his pocket and pulled out a gun. "It's time to get rid of you," he snarled. "You kept hounding me in Egypt, and even here, where I'm trying to turn a new leaf, you won't let me live!"*
>
> *"A new leaf?" Harav Ovadia asked. "A few days ago, someone told me that you're slaughtering animals without a head covering and without washing netilat yadayim!"*
>
> *"DON'T ROB ME OF MY LIVELIHOOD," Shimon bellowed, his eyes burning with anger. His hands shook, and he trained the gun on Harav Ovadia once more.*
>
> *The elderly Rav Avraham Fattal started to shudder violently. "Don't kill him," he begged. "If you want to kill someone, kill me. He's young, and he has little children."*
>
> *"Then why doesn't he allow me to earn a livelihood to*

"If you want to kill someone, kill me." Rav Avraham Fattal was willing to make the ultimate sacrifice for his young son-in-law.

support *my* children?" Shimon asked derisively, obviously proud of his sharp rejoinder.

"I'll find you a different source of livelihood," said Harav Ovadia, "but you must stop trying to be a shohet. I won't allow you to cause Jews to eat treif."

For some reason, Shimon placed his gun back into his pocket and left the house.

He wasn't done, though. He kept stalking Harav Ovadia, even coming to the beit din in Petah Tikva to threaten him. Eventually Harav Ovadia had no choice but to request a police escort to prevent Shimon from getting too close to him. Sometimes, the irreligious neighbors, who were amazed at Harav Ovadia's ability to go about his daily life while under constant threat, stepped in to prevent Shimon from attacking him.

One day, Shimon disappeared, and for a long time, no

one heard from him or about him. Harav Ovadia jokingly offered ten grushim to any one of his children who could explain his mysterious disappearance. A few years later, when the family had already moved back to Yerushalayim, his oldest son Yaakov was able to claim the reward when he saw a newspaper headline stating that Shimon A. had been killed. It seems that after giving up shehita, he had turned to smuggling. One day, he got into a fight with a fellow criminal, and the man killed him.[20]

And so ended a saga that had lasted more than a decade.

---

20. This story has been pieced together from several sources, including a live interview with Rav David Yosef, several *hespedim*, Harav Ovadia's own writings, and books such as *Posek HaDor*, *Abir Haro'im*, and *Ba'asher Teileich* (a biography of Rabbanit Margalit).

CHAPTER EIGHT
EXODUS FROM EGYPT

WHILE HARAV OVADIA EVENTUALLY SUCceeded, on the whole, in setting up a proper system for *shehita* in Egypt — he reported that by the time he left, 90 percent of the issues had been resolved — the other major communal problem he tried to repair culminated with his resignation and departure from Egypt.

Less than a year after his arrival in Egypt, Harav Ovadia visited the Jewish Hospital in Cairo, an institution controlled by the community council. He describes[1] his shock upon discovering that the hospital was serving nonkosher food to all of its patients — gentiles and Jews alike. The hospital did not even make a guise of providing kosher food; not only did it purchase nonkosher meat from gentile butchers, the kitchen staff cooked milk and meat together, and did not take any measures to remove blood or restricted fats from animals.

The city's religious Jews were unaware that the hospital's food was not kosher, and if they were hospitalized, they would eat the food served to them, assuming that a Jewish hospital must be serving kosher food.

When Harav Ovadia asked the manager of the hospital — a religious Jew — why the hospital served nonkosher food, he explained

---

1. *Yabia Omer*, Vol. 1, *Yoreh Dei'ah* 6.

After some time in Egypt, Harav Ovadia drew up a list for himself of religious issues that he had to tend to. Item four reads: שבית החולים יהיה כשר בלי ספק — the hospital should be unquestionably kosher.

that the hospital was maintained through the generosity of the community council, which considered the pricier kosher food to be a waste of money.[2]

At first, Harav Ovadia tried to settle the matter quietly.[3] He asked the manager to request additional funding for kosher food, and the manager agreed to do so, but each time he asked, the community council dallied in responding. Eventually Harav Ovadia approached the chief rabbi, who said he would take care of the matter, but he too was unsuccessful in convincing the council to finance kosher food. Meanwhile, Jews who were hospitalized continued eating nonkosher, unbeknownst to them.

At one point, Harav Ovadia received complaints from two women who had given birth at the hospital and had discovered only afterward that the food wasn't kosher. Had they known, they said, they would not have eaten it.

Harav Ovadia decided that he could no longer keep the issue quiet. On Shabbat Zachor 5709/1949, three-quarters of a year after

---

2. The ostensible justification for this practice was that hospital patients are in a state of *pikuah nefesh* (mortal danger), and are therefore allowed to eat nonkosher food. This claim was wrong, writes Harav Ovadia, for several reasons: (1) Even a dangerously ill patient is permitted to eat nonkosher food only if there is no other option, which wasn't true in this case. (2) Not all hospital patients are in mortal danger. (3) There were also doctors, nurses, and other staff members eating hospital food — and they certainly were not in a state of *pikuah nefesh*.

3. Unless otherwise indicated, the details in this chapter are culled primarily from three sources: Harav Ovadia's own writings, a live interview with Rav David Yosef, and the book *Abir Haro'im*, written by Harav Ovadia's grandson, R' Yaakov Sasson.

Beit Knesset Eitz Haim in Cairo, where Harav Ovadia delivered a stunning *derasha* in which he revealed that the Jewish hospital was serving nonkosher food to its patients

he first raised the issue, he spoke in the *beit knesset* about the great miracles that had transpired during that year, when the State of Israel declared independence and the Jews managed to survive the Arab onslaught and take control of the Land. At the end of the *derasha*, he started to talk about the concept of *teshuva*, and he then spoke openly about the fact that the Jewish hospital was serving nonkosher food.

His audience was stunned by the revelation, and the ensuing public outcry finally spurred the community council to action. They agreed to provide additional funding for kosher meat and to pay a *mashgiah* to supervise the hospital's kitchen. (The kitchen manager didn't keep kosher in his own home, so a *mashgiah* had to be present to ensure that meat and milk would be kept separate, fats and blood would be removed from the meat, etc.)

To avoid antagonizing the council, Harav Ovadia tried to minimize the expense of making the hospital kosher. He even wrote a long *teshuva*[4] permitting the hospital's porcelain dishes to be *kashered* even though we generally do not *kasher* earthenware, because he was concerned that if the community council would hear that they had to replace all the dishes in the hospital, they might retract their decision to serve only kosher food.

Within days of when the *mashgiah* started his job at the hospital, trouble began to brew. One day, a woman from the family of a very wealthy council member entered the kitchen, and when she saw what the *mashgiah* was doing, she shouted at him, "You're preventing them from running the kitchen properly!"

She continued hurling accusations at him, telling him that he was backward and living in the Dark Ages. When she finished her diatribe, she banished him from the kitchen in disgrace.

When Harav Ovadia heard about this incident, he asked the chief rabbi to step in and see to it that the *mashgiah* be reinstated, but the chief rabbi kept procrastinating. Finally Harav Ovadia told him that if the issue of the hospital's *kashrut* wasn't settled, he might have to pack his bags and move back to Eretz Yisrael, because he could not in good conscience remain the *av beit din* of a city where such a flagrant violation of halacha was taking place. When the chief rabbi finally tried to convince the council to take care of the issue, one of the members announced with finality, "We can't *kasher* the entire kitchen."

The chief rabbi did not want to argue with the council members, so he sent Harav Ovadia to discuss the matter with them. At the meeting, the council member who was related to the woman who

---

4. *Yabia Omer*, ibid.

had thrown the *mashgiah* out of the kitchen condescendingly told Harav Ovadia, "You did what you had to do; you spoke out against the situation. Now, you are no longer required to protest, because we're not going to do anything about it anyway."

"My obligation is not to merely suffice with a protest, but to ensure that people don't eat nonkosher," Harav Ovadia replied.

Retraction Under Threat

AS THE SUMMER OF 5709/1949 APPROACHED, MOST OF THE COMmunity council members left for vacation in Alexandria, as did the chief rabbi. Harav Ovadia continued trying to address the issue in their absence, but when he realized that his efforts were futile, he decided to publicize a proclamation, signed by all three *dayanim* in his *beit din*, stating that the food in the Jewish hospital wasn't kosher and that no one was allowed to eat it. He even had one of the other *dayanim* translate this document into Arabic for the sake of the Jews who couldn't read Hebrew well.

As they were preparing the letter, the secretary of the *beit din*, who was loyal to the community council, called the chief rabbi in Alexandria and informed him of the proclamation that the *beit din* was about to release. The chief rabbi called the other *dayanim* to the phone. "What's your rush?" he berated them. "I'm returning to Cairo in a week, and I'll take care of it when I'm back."

Upon hearing the chief rabbi's angry tone, one of the other *dayanim* grew so frightened that he told the chief rabbi that he would remove his signature from the proclamation. Once he backed down, the third *dayan* decided that it would be foolhardy for him to join Harav Ovadia, and he, too, removed his signature.

Harav Ovadia, however, was not moved by the chief rabbi's assurance. He knew that a week wouldn't be a week; he had been attempting to *kasher* the hospital for close to a year, and he was familiar with the stalling tactics used by his opponents. He therefore sent a message to all the local *batei knesset* that on that Shabbat, *Parashat Devarim* (Shabbat Hazon), he would deliver a very important address in Eitz Haim, the largest *beit knesset* in the Jewish neighborhood.

That Shabbat, before *Arvit,* some 500 people turned out to hear him speak. He rose to the podium and disclosed the recent developments in the saga of the Jewish hospital's *kashrut.* He declared that since his efforts to improve the situation had failed, he was prepared to resign from his position, because he could not be responsible for a community whose institutions were serving nonkosher food to Jews.

When the chief rabbi heard about this speech, he told the community council members that since Harav Ovadia was turning public sentiment against the community council, it would be best to accept his resignation and let him return to Eretz Yisrael.

The Resignation Letter

THAT SUNDAY MORNING, HARAV OVADIA DRAFTED A RESIGnation letter to the only council member who was not on vacation. But before he could actually deliver it, he received a phone call from the chief rabbi, who had since reconsidered his stance. "In a few days, one of the council members will visit you, and we'll take care of the *kashrut* situation in the hospital."

Harav Ovadia waited a few days, and when no visit was forthcoming, he went to the council member's office with one of the other *dayanim.* The council member began to castigate him. "You have no consideration for the chief rabbi," he shouted. "He needs to rest up from all of his work on behalf of the community. Why couldn't you wait until he returns?"

Harav Ovadia tried to convey the urgency of the issue, explaining that with every day that passed, hundreds more Jews were eating *treif,* but his explanation fell on deaf ears. He then offered to pay the salary of the hospital's *mashgiah* out of his own pocket for a few months, on condition that the community council order the hospital's officials to cooperate with the *mashgiah.*

The council member flatly refused this request.

Harav Ovadia left this man's office dejectedly. He immediately returned to his office and sent off the letter he had drafted to the community council, stating that his resignation would go into effect at the end of the month.

Over the next few days, he made the rounds of the *batei knesset* in the city, informing all of the religious residents that he was resigning from his position. He also sent a copy of his resignation letter to the chief rabbi, in the hope that the rabbi, who knew very well that there was no other rav in the city capable of administering *gittin* and *kiddushin*, would convince the community council to capitulate and *kasher* the hospital so that Harav Ovadia would remain in Egypt.

HARAV OVADIA HIMSELF WAS PLAGUED WITH DOUBT ABOUT his decision to resign over the issue of the hospital's *kashrut*. He knew that if he were to remain at his post, he could continue to see to the other religious needs of the city's sizable Jewish community. These needs could not be filled satisfactorily after his departure, because in the aftermath of Israel's War of Independence, there was no chance the Egyptian authorities would allow a rav from Israel into the country, and with the security situation as tenuous as it was, no rav from anywhere else in the world would be willing to settle in Egypt. Would it be better to remain in the city and make peace with the *kashrut* situation in the hospital, or was the fact that hundreds of Jews were eating nonkosher each day too grievous to ignore? He pined for the counsel of his rebbeim back in Eretz Yisrael and wished he could consult with them, but the Egyptian government did not allow any communication with Israel.

Plagued With Doubt

After his resignation went into effect, Harav Ovadia remained at home learning, until the leaders of the yeshiva and the *batei knesset* visited him and begged him to continue teaching Torah, even if he would not serve on the *beit din* and oversee the religious needs of the community. Harav Ovadia agreed, even though the salary they offered was a small fraction of what he had previously been paid by the community, and in the months between his resignation and his departure from Cairo, he continued to deliver *shiurim* all over the city.

He was also kept busy by the other rabbanim on the *beit din*, who suddenly realized that they were ill-equipped to issue rulings

Even after resigning from the *beit din*, Harav Ovadia remained devoted to his students at Ahava V'Ahva, delivering *shiurim* to them until he left Egypt.

without him, and visited him every few days to discuss cases that came before the *beit din*.

Many members of the community felt that the *dayanim* had betrayed their leader. Months earlier, Rav Aharon Shwekey, whose own brother was on the *beit din*, tried to convince the *dayanim* to join Harav Ovadia's battle and threaten to resign along with him, because he felt that this would sway the community council's decision. Harav Ovadia himself bore no grudge against his fellow *dayanim*, however. Despite their unwillingness to join forces with him, Harav Ovadia accepted them into his home and helped them rule on cases that were too complicated for them to resolve independently.

Last-Ditch Efforts

FOR A SHORT WHILE, IT SEEMED THAT THE CHIEF RABBI would smooth things over. When he returned from his vacation shortly before the *Yamim Nora'im* (High Holidays) of 5710/1949, he met with Harav Ovadia and told him that he was working on convincing the council members to tend to the *kashrut* situation. Before long, however, he sent a messenger to Harav Ovadia asking him to retract his resignation letter and remain at his post, but not to pursue the hospital issue any further.

After the *hagim*, the religious Jews of Cairo launched an intensive grassroots campaign to pressure the community council to accede to Harav Ovadia's conditions. There was a communal rule that if fifty paying members of the community sent a letter requesting a meeting with the community council, the council members had to convene, and the religious Jews quickly gathered over 200 signatures requesting such a meeting.

The council members flew into a rage when they heard about this petition, and in the months that followed, they pressured people who employed religious Jews to threaten to fire these employees if they didn't back off from their support of Harav Ovadia. Since the council members were very wealthy and influential with the government, a number of employers capitulated to their demands, causing their employees to back down.

In a sad irony, the power these council members wielded against their own brethren did not protect them from their Arab neighbors. Shortly after Harav Ovadia left Egypt, Islamists embarked on a campaign to usurp the wealthy Jews' influential posts. The head of the community council was one of their primary targets. His stores were burned and he was briefly jailed. After he was released, Egyptian police visited the council

One of the stores owned by the community council leader responsible for Harav Ovadia's dismissal is burned to the ground by Islamists.

A newspaper clipping from the Israeli daily *Davar* reporting on the wealthiest Jews being banished from Egypt

members and informed them that they had nineteen days to leave the country — with just one suitcase and twenty Egyptian liras each.

In Limbo

ONCE HE REALIZED THAT THE CARDS WERE STACKED AGAINST him, Harav Ovadia began preparing to return to Eretz Yisrael. Several significant obstacles stood in his way, however.

One was that the Egyptian government did not allow anyone to cross the border into Israel. This meant that he would have to travel to Israel via a neutral country. Italy, home to a large *aliya* headquarters, fit that description, but traveling via Italy posed another problem: Harav Ovadia's passport, issued by the British authorities who controlled Eretz Yisrael when he left in 1947, contained the names of his two oldest children, but not Malka and Avraham, who had been born in Egypt. Without documentation, he could not take them out of the country.

Harav Ovadia approached the British consulate in Egypt, but when the officials there found out that his final destination was Israel, they did not want to help him leave; even after they gave up control of Israel, the British were still opposed to open immigration into their former protectorate, and they kept finding excuses to delay his request.

This problem was solved when Leon Gabbai, a community member who was close to Harav Ovadia, accompanied him to the British Consulate and convinced an Arab employee to register the two younger children on the passport.

The Basis for Teshuvot

ANOTHER PROBLEM HE FACED WAS THAT THE MILITARY CENsors in Egypt would not allow any documents handwritten in a foreign language out of the country, for fear that spies could smuggle out notes containing intelligence information and share the information with Egypt's enemies.

Despite all his rabbinic duties, as well as his battles to shore up the community's religious structure, Harav Ovadia wrote hundreds of pages of Torah notes while in Egypt. Dozens of his *teshuvot*, spanning the halachic spectrum, were written in Cairo — and, in fact, begin with the address קהיר (Cairo). These *teshuvot* were later expanded or updated, and released in the various volumes of *Yabia Omer*. Even the last volume released during Harav Ovadia's lifetime contained *teshuvot* written in those years.

He was concerned that when he left Cairo with those handwritten Hebrew pages of his *teshuvot*, the authorities would search his luggage and confiscate the *teshuvot* he had toiled so hard to produce.

He was also worried about his *sefarim* library, which now contained not only the volumes he had transported with him to Egypt, but also many more that he had purchased there. In addition, the *gabbaim* in one of the *batei knesset* had presented him with 25 rare responsa *sefarim* that could not be purchased anywhere in the world, and he was particularly afraid to lose them.

Most of all, he was afraid that the council would report to the Egyptian authorities that he no longer held an official position, and the authorities would then consider him an illegal alien. They could then confiscate all his belongings and expel him immediately, without giving him time to prepare for the move and arrange to travel to a neutral country.

At the grave of Rav Yaakov Abuhatzeira (grandfather of the Baba Sali) in Damanhur, Egypt, flanked by philanthropist Lev Leviev and R' Aryeh Deri. Though he feared for his life in his final months in Egypt, in later years Harav Ovadia was welcomed back as a dignitary.

The constant fear with which he was living is evident in his introduction to the first volume of *Yabia Omer*, released just two years after he left Egypt, where he writes that he is publishing the work in fulfillment of his pledge to Hashem that if he were to make it out safely from the frightening situation he found himself in during those months in Egypt, he would publish a collection of the *teshuvot* he had written.

Finally, the family received the necessary documents to travel, and Harav Ovadia began to sell off his furniture in preparation for the move. When the religious Jews of the community heard that he was serious about moving, they renewed their efforts to reinstate him, urging the community council to convene a meeting, as per their petition.

THE COMMUNITY COUNCIL FINALLY AGREED TO MEET ON 8 Nissan 5710, but they issued an ultimatum: if the community

The Vote

would vote to keep Harav Ovadia at his post and force them to *kasher* the hospital, they would all resign. This was a frightening proposition for the community, because the council members supported almost all communal institutions.

At the meeting, Rav Aharon Shwekey delivered an impassioned speech explaining why Harav Ovadia's presence was vital to the community, but he kept being interrupted by opposing council members who didn't want him to sway any community members' votes. In truth, there were very few people present who would even

Rav Aharon Shwekey, whose impassioned plea to keep Harav Ovadia in Cairo fell on deaf ears

Chapter Eight: Exodus From Egypt ☐ 179

think of voting for Harav Ovadia, because most of the community's religious Jews didn't show up to the meeting out of fear of reprisal from their bosses.

The vote that was eventually held was phrased as follows: Do you choose Harav Ovadia, or the community council? Harav Ovadia later told his family that more than 90 percent of those present voted against him, rendering his resignation final.[5]

The Final Insult

A FEW DAYS LATER, THE COUNCIL ADDED INSULT TO INJURY by appointing a replacement for Harav Ovadia without bothering to inform him.

In each of the previous two years, Harav Ovadia had delivered the main Shabbat HaGadol speech in Cairo, and large crowds had come to hear him speak both about Aggada and about the halachot of Pesah. He had been scheduled to speak on Shabbat HaGadol of 5710, too, but as soon as the council members accepted his resignation, they found a young orator who knew nothing about halacha and offered him a monthly salary to take over Harav Ovadia's position. Although this man was actually Harav Ovadia's student, and should have realized that he was unqualified for the position, he accepted their offer. When Harav Ovadia arrived at the *beit knesset* to deliver his speech, he was shocked to see that this man had been appointed to speak in his stead.

Harav Ovadia was deeply pained at not having been notified of the change in advance. Nevertheless, when this man later approached him in Eretz Yisrael and asked him for a letter of recommendation for the *sefer* he was about to publish, Harav Ovadia gave him a warm letter.

Leaving Egypt

AFTER HARAV OVADIA MADE HIS FINAL PREPARATIONS TO leave, his students held a *seudat preida* for him on 22 Sivan 5710. Many of his students spoke at the gathering, including Rav Aharon's Shwekey's son Yitzhak, who wrote a heartwarming but sad poem about their great rebbi.

---
5. Rav David Yosef.

Five days later, on Tuesday, 27 Sivan, scores of Harav Ovadia's students escorted the family to the train station, crying bitterly as they watched him leave. Fortunately, many of them would reunite with him several years later when they immigrated to Eretz Yisrael.

The Yosef family traveled by train to the port city of Alexandria, where they boarded a boat to Italy. Harav Ovadia's fears regarding his *sefarim* and Torah notes turned out to be well-founded; when he reached the port, the authorities began to open his luggage to examine what he was taking out of the country. Suddenly, one of the officials turned to the others and said, "He is a *hacham*. Leave him alone."

Unfortunately, some of those *sefarim* were damaged in transit. After spending close to a month in the southern Italian city of Brindisi, which was home to an *aliya* camp, Harav Ovadia reached the port of Haifa on Rosh Hodesh Av 5710. To his consternation, the Jewish customs officials opened each volume to check whether he had smuggled any money between the pages, and as they finished checking each volume, they simply let it drop from their

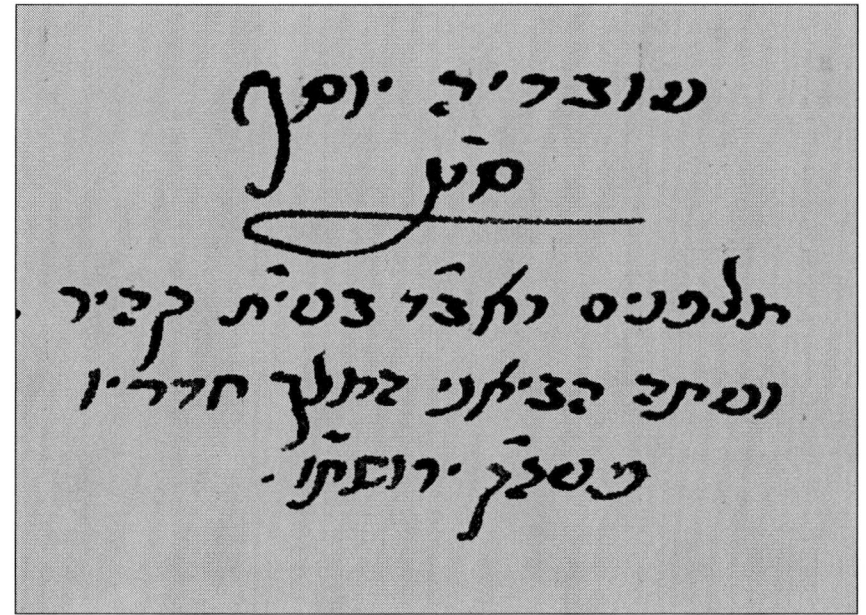

Harav Ovadia's elation at having escaped from Egypt finds expression in his signature: "Formerly Rav Av Beit Din in Cairo, and now the King has brought me to His chambers."

hands, inflicting severe damage on them. Concerned for the *kavod* of his *sefarim*, Harav Ovadia watched them the entire time, and by the time he turned around to retrieve the rest of his belongings, he realized that someone had stolen many of them while he was busy with the *sefarim*.

The horror of witnessing Jewish workers treating his *sefarim* with less respect than had the Arab workers at the port in Alexandria was mitigated only by the anticipation of being reunited with his family, his friends, and, perhaps most importantly, his rebbeim.

THE HARAV OVADIA YOSEF WHO RETURNED TO ERETZ YISRAEL was hardly the same man who had left it less than three years earlier. He had departed to Egypt with no leadership experience, and once there, he had been continually forced to defend the Torah and halacha against people many decades his senior. The courage he displayed in dealing with belligerent Egyptian officials, violent *shohtim*, and an obdurate community council would have been impressive even for an older man — all the more so for someone who still hadn't celebrated his 30th birthday.

A Changed Man

Harav Ovadia's stint in Egypt contributed to another dimension of his greatness as well. Acting as the halachic arbiter for a community in which no one else could match his level of Torah scholarship forced Harav Ovadia to become much more independent in issuing halachic rulings. Rav David Yosef relates that he noticed a significant difference between *teshuvot* that his father wrote in Egypt and those he wrote when he was back in Eretz Yisrael. While Harav Ovadia routinely cited sources that supported the halachic positions he took in his *teshuvot*, the *teshuvot* he wrote in Egypt contain many more sources than the ones he wrote in Eretz Yisrael. Rav David asked his father why, in the *teshuvot* written in Egypt, even after bolstering his argument with several solid proofs, he goes on to cite many additional authorities who agree with his opinion.

"When I was in Yerushalayim," explained Harav Ovadia, "I had people to discuss my halachic conclusions with: Rav Tzvi Pesach Frank, Rav Shlomo Zalman Auerbach, and others. In Egypt, I was

"In Egypt, I didn't have Rav Shlomo Zalman Auerbach to discuss my opinions with, so I had to make my teshuvot as airtight as possible." Harav Ovadia and Rav Shlomo Zalman conversing at a Yosef family *simha*.

young, and I was all alone. Since I had no one to discuss my opinions with, I felt that I had to make my *teshuvot* as airtight as possible."

In Egypt, he also developed his trademark fearlessness in defending Torah and halacha, establishing himself as a rav who would do everything in his power to correct halachic wrongdoing even when the matter wasn't necessarily under his direct jurisdiction. This approach played a vital role in forging the character of the nascent State of Israel, as well as its stance vis-à-vis halacha.

Finally, Harav Ovadia proved in Egypt that he could learn diligently no matter how trying his circumstances were. Even as he fought halachic battles or dealt with practical communal issues, he continued to pore over his beloved *sefarim* with utter concentration — an ability that would serve him well as the demands on his time increased and as he rose to the greatest heights of Israel's halachic leadership.

SECTION THREE

A RISING STAR

וַיְהִי ה' אֶת יוֹסֵף וַיְהִי אִישׁ מַצְלִיחַ

*Hashem was with Yosef,
and he became a successful man*

(Bereishit 39:2)

CHAPTER NINE
BACK HOME

WHEN THE YOSEF FAMILY, NOW SIX IN NUMber, moved back to Eretz Yisrael in 1950, they had no home to call their own. At first, they lived with Harav Ovadia's parents, R' Yaakov and Georgia Ovadia, who had moved into a spacious abandoned Arab home in Katamon during the Israeli War of Independence.[1]

The Ovadias had achieved financial stability by that point. Avraham, the brother who had kept the young Ovadia's nocturnal escapes to a local *beit midrash* a secret, expanded the family business by opening a successful *makolet* on Rehov David Yellin. But it was painful for Harav Ovadia to see that almost all of his siblings had been swept away by the nationalistic movements, as had so many of their peers, abandoning religious observance in the process.[2]

Approximately six weeks after returning to Eretz Yisrael, the Yosefs bought an apartment on what is now Rehov Baal Shem Tov in the Beit Yisrael neighborhood, through a system called דְּמֵי מַפְתֵּחַ

---
1. The abandoned house was discovered by his sister Shoshana, who fought off military officers to gain the rights to the house, and in which she continued to reside throughout her life.
2. He tried to influence some of his siblings to become more observant, but was unsuccessful. Later in life, however, two of his siblings, Na'im and Shoshana, did return to full observance. Na'im, with whom he had the closest relationship, predeceased him by three weeks, on the first day of Succot 5774.

Harav Ovadia learning in the tiny two-room apartment in Beit Yisrael

(lit., *key money*).³ The apartment consisted of just two small rooms. The inner room was Harav Ovadia's study, and the older two children, Adina and Yaakov, slept in that room as well. The outer room, which contained a small kitchenette, also served as the bedroom for Harav Ovadia and Rabbanit Margalit and their two younger children, Malka and Avraham. All other "amenities" were situated in the courtyard and shared with the neighbors, including the restroom and bathing facilities.

---

3. In this form of sale, a buyer who could not afford to pay the full price for a home would pay half the value of the property in exchange for the right to live in the apartment for the rest of his life, upon which it would return to the seller. Sometimes the buyer also paid a nominal monthly rent, but that amount was controlled and could not be raised. In certain cases, immediate relatives living with the buyer at the time of his or her death could continue to live in the apartment under the same arrangement.

Use of the "key money" system — which was first introduced by the British during their Mandate, after it was successfully implemented in England during World War II to help people displaced by enemy bombardments find affordable housing — is slowly petering out in Israel. As of 2013, approximately 35,000 homes were still under the system, but few are being sold for key money nowadays.

This apartment was a significant downgrade from the spacious home they were able to afford on Harav Ovadia's salary as an *av beit din* in Cairo. Although the family was now living in relative poverty, in those days, all of Israel was living under extreme austerity[4] as the fledgling country struggled to build an economy that had to include a gargantuan security budget to help protect it from its Arab neighbors. Little was left for social welfare or for generous wages in almost any industry, and those who grew up in Israel of the 1950 recalls those years as being financially dismal times.

As soon as the *gabbai* of Shaul Tzadka,[5] the *beit knesset* for Persian (Iranian) Jews in which Harav Ovadia had delivered *shiurim* before accepting his position in Egypt, heard that he was planning to resettle in their neighborhood, he informed the congregants of the opportunity. They quickly raised funds to put together a small stipend for Harav Ovadia, and they asked him to resume delivering the *shiurim* they had so sorely missed during the three years he was in Egypt. Other *batei knesset* in Beit Yisrael also took advantage of the brilliant orator living in their midst, inviting him to deliver *shiurim* on a steady basis.

Where to Enroll?

HARAV OVADIA WOULD HAVE BEEN HAPPY TO LEARN IN HIS study at home or in a shul all day while preparing his *sefarim* for print, but he had a problem: when he reentered Eretz Yisrael, he was automatically registered as a citizen of Israel, and as an able-bodied young man, he was eligible for conscription into the army. Prime Minister David Ben-Gurion had issued his now-famous exemption for yeshiva students who made Torah study their sole pursuit, but in order to qualify for this exemption, one had to be enrolled in a yeshiva.

Harav Ovadia went back to Porat Yosef, where his rebbeim and contemporaries were delighted to see him. In those days, however, Porat Yosef could hardly afford to pay stipends to *avreichim* his age, since the yeshiva had lost its impressive edifice in the Old City to the Jordanians during the War of Independence, and its administrators

---

4. In fact, the years between 1949-1959 are officially referred to as תְּקוּפַת הַצֶּנַע, *the era of austerity*.
5. See p. 93.

Scholars and laymen alike flocked to hear *shiurim* from the homegrown Rav who had returned from Egypt.

faced the considerable financial strain of purchasing a new building.

Harav Ovadia was concerned that he would be conscripted,[6] until help came from an old patron. One day, he met Rav Tzvi Pesach Frank, the rav of Yerushalayim, with whom he had developed a particularly close relationship before his stint in Egypt.[7] Rav Frank asked him where he was learning, and Harav Ovadia told him that he wasn't registered anywhere just yet, which placed him in danger of being drafted.

---

6. As Divine Providence would have it, the first law Harav Ovadia had to contend with in his introduction to the State of Israel — the right for a yeshiva student to study Torah without having to serve in the army — was also the law he would battle at the very end of his life, and the one that would cause him so much anguish, his family relates, that it would eventually cause him to pass on to the next world.

7. See p. 98.

The Porat Yosef building as it is being captured by Jordanian Legionnaires during the Israeli War of Independence

"Come learn in my kollel," Rav Frank offered.

The kollel he was referring to was called Midrash Bnei Zion, run by Rav Yitzchak Rosenthal. Its focus was primarily — but not exclusively — the mitzvot pertaining to Eretz Yisrael, which had hardly been practiced in close to two millennia of exile, and now had to be implemented properly as Israel's agricultural industries developed.

Lifelong Friendships

MOST OF THE KOLLEL MEMBERS WOULD LEARN TOGETHER all day, but Harav Ovadia joined only for the afternoon. Many of his peers in Midrash Bnei Zion would go on to become leaders of the generation, including: Rav Shlomo Zalman Auerbach, future Rosh Yeshiva of Kol Torah and the *posek hador* for Ashkenazim in Eretz Yisrael; Rav Shlomo Zalman's brother-in-law, Rav Shalom Schwadron, whose reputation as a *maggid* masked his greatness in learning; Rav Frank's son-in-law Rav Shmuel Rozovsky, who would become the Rosh Yeshiva of Ponovezh; Rav Betzalel Zolty, Harav Ovadia's old friend from the days when he learned in Hevron at night, who

The *Maggid* Rav Shalom Schwadron, one of the numerous scholars with whom Harav Ovadia (seated next to him) learned in Midrash Bnei Zion, addresses a farewell gathering for Harav Ovadia when he left Yerushalayim to become chief rabbi of Tel Aviv.

would eventually serve on the Beit Din HaGadol with Harav Ovadia and then as the Chief Rabbi of Yerushalayim; and Rav Yisrael Yaakov Fischer, who would serve as the *Raavad* (an acronym for *Rav Av Beit Din*) of the Eida Haredit for the last seven years of his life. In the kollel, Harav Ovadia learned *b'havruta* with Rav Shlomo Zalman Auerbach, with whom he developed a close, lifelong relationship, as well as with Rav Yisrael Yaakov Fischer.[8]

Rav Shlomo Zalman was the "deputy" *rosh kollel*, answering questions when Rav Tzvi Pesach was not in the kollel. But when a Talmudic debate would rage in the morning, the members of the kollel would say, "Let's wait for Ovadia to come in the afternoon." Harav Ovadia would listen to the two sides and then identify the *sevarot* (logical reasoning) of each side, using his vast memory to tell each person which earlier halachic authorities had already written his approach.

Rav Shmuel Rozovsky was particularly enamored with Harav Ovadia's encyclopedic knowledge, which was put to good use in Midrash Bnei Zion.

Rav Shmuel Rozovsky was particularly impressed with Harav Ovadia, once exclaiming to Rav Shalom Cohen, "Considering all the information he knows, I don't understand how he ever arrives at a decision."[9]

---

8. Rav David Yosef.
9. Grandson R' Yaakov Sasson. Knowing so many sides to an issue can be paralyzing, since the *posek* must eventually side with only one opinion, yet somehow Harav Ovadia was able to do so.

The feelings were mutual. Although Harav Ovadia didn't spend much time studying *"lomdus,"*[10] he related that out of all the *lomdus sefarim*, Rav Shmuel Rozovsky's is a pleasure to read, because his logic is straightforward and not convoluted.

The kollel heard *shiurim* from Rav Tzvi Pesach, and published many works on the halachot pertaining to Eretz Yisrael. One set of over a dozen volumes, *Kerem Zion*, was published over the course of many decades, setting forth guidelines for dealing with many *sh'eilot* regarding *terumot, maasrot, Shemittah*, and the like. In one such volume, published in 5712/1952, Harav Ovadia authored an essay on the halachot pertaining to one who wrote a *prozbul*[11] before the *Shemitta* (Sabbatical) year so that he could collect a loan after *Shemitta*, but subsequently lost his *prozbul*. This essay appears in a volume that contains pieces from Rav Frank, Rav Isser Zalman Meltzer, and Rav Yisrael Yaakov Fischer, among others.

The Rejected Position

NOT LONG AFTER HE RETURNED TO ERETZ YISRAEL, HARAV Ovadia was visited by a group representing the Eida Haredit. They wanted to establish a separate *beit din* for Sephardim under their aegis, and they came to offer the 30-year-old Harav Ovadia the position of *av beit din*.

Harav Ovadia mulled over the offer, but ultimately turned it down because the Eida representatives informed him that he would have to sign a proclamation against voting in Israeli elections.[12]

---

10. *Lomdus* (or *lomdut*) is the approach to learning developed in the Lithuanian yeshivot. It requires the learner to study the subject he is learning in depth, presenting as many possible *sevarot* in each direction in order to come to a valid approach to a *sugya*. Harav Ovadia wasn't particularly fond of this approach because learners generally don't follow their *sevarot* to the consequent halachic conclusion, which means that they don't learn to rule in matters of halacha.
11. The Torah states that *Shemittah* cancels loans given before the *Shemittah* year, and a lender may not collect a loan after it has been cancelled by *Shemittah*. The sage Hillel was concerned that people would be unwilling to lend money under such conditions, so he set up a mechanism called a *prozbul* in which the lender "hands over" his loan to *beit din*, and may then collect the loan after *Shemitta*. [The *Rishonim* (see, for instance, *Tosafot* to Erachin 31b, s.v. *Hillel hitkin*) explain how Hillel was allowed to enact this mechanism.]
12. The Eida Haredit, often referred to simply as "the Badatz," maintains (as did the Admor Rav Yoel of Satmar) that Jews may not set up a government in Eretz Yisrael until Mashiah arrives, and if a government is established, one may not take part in it in any way. Before each national

Harav Ovadia agreed with the stance of the Lithuanian yeshiva world — as set forth by the Hazon Ish — that religious Jews should make a point of voting, so that they could elect Knesset members who would look out for the interests of Torah Judaism.

Anything But Milah

AT THIS POINT, HARAV OVADIA HAD TO FIND SOME SORT OF livelihood, and he considered several positions. At first, since he was already an expert in *hilchot shehita*, he decided to learn the practical aspects of slaughtering. The first day he showed up for training, however, he saw a bull kick a *shohet* in the stomach, and he ran home in fright, never to return.

He had a similarly unsuccessful experience trying to become a *hazzan*.

One occupation he never tried was *milah* — because, he explained, a *mohel* spends the entire morning performing *britot*, and the entire evening running from one child to the next changing bandages. This would leave little time for learning, so it wasn't an option.[13]

An Official Dayan

IN 5711/1951, HARAV OVADIA RECEIVED OFFICIAL AUTHORIZAtion to serve as a *dayan* in Israel. Nowadays, candidates must undergo a rigorous set of exams before being appointed to such a position, but at that point, the system by which appointments were made could not be as formal, because the two chief rabbis, Rav Herzog and Rav Uziel, had to fill many positions in the Rabbanut to ensure that the State *batei din* would be fully staffed and functioning. They turned to the Roshei Yeshiva of the two main yeshivot in Yerushalayim, Porat Yosef and Hevron, and asked them to recommend candidates. Harav Ovadia topped Hacham Ezra Attia's list, and he received automatic authorization from the chief rabbis — both of whom could personally vouch for his worthiness to serve on the rabbinate — to serve as a *dayan*.[14]

---

or municipal election, the Badatz publicizes proclamations prohibiting voting.
13. Grandson R' Yaakov Sasson.
14. *Posek HaDor*.

At that time, there was an opening in the Petah Tikva *beit din*, which was led by Rav Reuven Katz *zt"l*. Upon meeting Harav Ovadia, Rav Katz was extremely impressed, and he invited the young rav to join his *beit din*. Rav Katz, who was over 70 at the time, had already served as a rav in Europe before the war. That a *dayan* approximately four decades his junior could impress him is a grand testament to Harav Ovadia's acumen as a *posek*.

At first, Harav Ovadia turned down the offer. As he explains in a *hesped* he delivered when Rav Katz passed away, "I was teaching Torah and halacha to hundreds of laymen in Yerushalayim, and I did not want to give that up. But he kept asking, until I felt uncomfortable turning him down."[15]

The other *dayanim* on the *beit din* were Rav Yisrael Sapir[16] and Rav Yitzchak Meir Ben Menachem,[17] both of whom were much older and far more experienced than Harav Ovadia.[18] Nevertheless,

---

15. Published in *Hazon Ovadia, Daled Ta'aniyot*, p. 474.
16. Rav Yisrael Aryeh Sapir was born in Russia in 5650/1890 to Rav Yaakov Moshe Sapir, the rav of Sorotov. He learned in Volozhin and spent several years in Radin, where he became close to the Hafetz Haim. He served as the Rav of Libau, Latvia, before moving to Eretz Yisrael on his own in 5676/1917. When he was offered a position on the *beit din* in Petah Tikva a year later, he was able to bring over his wife and four children. During the 1920s, with the help of Chief Rabbi Rav Avraham Yitzchak HaKohen Kook, he was able to bring his parents to Eretz Yisrael, and he then vacated his position on the *beit din* in Petah Tikva, giving it to his father. When his father passed away in 5694/1934, he once again joined the *beit din*, where he served until his passing on 30 Av 5721/1961.
17. Rav Yitzchak Meir Ben Menachem (originally Pachiner) was born in Poland in 5658/1898. In 5670/1910, he began to learn in Radin under the Hafetz Haim and Rav Naftali Tropp. He moved to Eretz Yisrael and learned first in Hevron Yeshiva (which was then located in the city of Hevron), and then in Petah Tikva's Lomza Yeshiva. In 5788/1928, he married Sara Meltzer, the daughter of Rav Isser Zalman. He served on the *beit din* in Petah Tikva from 1933-1956, after which he was appointed to the Beit Din HaGadol, a position he held until his passing in 5720/1960. He was a pioneer in republishing the works of *Rishonim*, releasing newly reworked and annotated volumes of the Rashba on *Masechet Niddah* and Rabbeinu Hananel on *Masechet Zevahim*. He also authored his own work, *Parashat Derachim*, some volumes of which were published posthumously.
18. A good indicator of just how much more experienced Harav Ovadia's three colleagues were can be found in a letter dated 17 Teves 5696/1936. In this letter, rabbanim in Eretz Yisrael express deep concern over an initiative advanced by Conservative clergy in America, who tried to enact a new custom that when a couple gets married, the husband should give his wife permission to write her own *get* if he has not lived with her for three years, and then appoint a messenger to deliver it to her, absolving her of the need to receive a *get* from her husband. Rabbanim around the world were concerned that this initiative, which is halachically unfounded, would gain traction in America, resulting in invalid *gittin* that would lead to the birth of many *mamzerim*. *Gedolei Yisrael* wrote letters to American Jewry begging them to battle this initiative. (See *Ledor Aharon*, published by Agudat HaRabbanim of America, which led the battle.)

The first three signatories on the joint letter from the rabbanim of Eretz Yisrael were Rav Katz,

they and Rav Katz accepted him as a worthy *dayan*, and he served on that *beit din* for approximately one year, commuting from Yerushalayim each day to join the sessions.

The arduous daily journey on the relatively primitive public transportation system took its toll, however, and after a short time, Harav Ovadia began to wonder whether he was using his time and energy optimally. He went to visit the Hazon Ish and asked him whether he should perhaps give up the position. The Hazon Ish replied that if he could find *parnassah* in Yerushalayim, then he should give up the position and spend his time learning and teaching Torah.

Though Harav Ovadia was serving on the Petah Tikva *beit din* alongside the likes of Rav Yisrael Sapir (above), who was some three decades his senior, his opinion was still highly valued.

Harav Ovadia was about to step down, but before he did so, he consulted with his own rebbi, Rav Ezra Attia. Rav Ezra told him that he had to keep the position. When Harav Ovadia asked him why he shouldn't follow the Hazon Ish's advice, Rav Ezra replied, "As your rebbi, I'm familiar with your abilities, and I know how much you'll be able to improve the Rabbanut. Had you told the Hazon Ish how much you could accomplish there, he would certainly agree with me that you should remain on the *beit din*."

Harav Ovadia followed his rebbi's advice, but he remained on the *beit din* for only another ten months.[19] At the beginning of

---

Rav Ben Menachem, and Rav Sapir — who were already among the leading rabbanim in Eretz Yisrael when Harav Ovadia was just 15 years old!

19. The story of Harav Ovadia's accomplishments on the *beit din* and primary reason for his resignation are the subject of Chapter 14.

the winter of 5712/1952, Harav Ovadia stepped down and began spending his days in Yerushalayim and focusing his attention on a pledge he had made in Egypt.

The Four-Month Sefer

HARAV OVADIA RETURNED TO HIS SCHEDULE OF STUDYING on his own in the morning, learning in Midrash Bnei Zion in the afternoon, and delivering his *shiurim* at night. He felt that this was the ideal time to publish a *sefer* of his *piskei halacha*, in fulfillment of a pledge he had made to Hashem when he had felt endangered in Egypt.

He realized, however, that he couldn't afford the publishing costs of a full-length *sefer* of his *teshuvot* — which would fill hundreds of pages — so he decided to write a short work, *Hazon Ovadia*,[20] on the halachot of Pesah. Since it was already winter, and he wanted to complete the *sefer* before Pesah of that year, he had to churn it out in just four months. He released it on Rosh Hodesh Nissan 5712/1952, in a limited printing of 300 copies.

The reactions of the *gedolim* of Eretz Yisrael to the *sefer* were astounding. Rav Uziel and Rav Herzog both issued approbations referring to him as *harif ubaki* (sharp and expert) as did Rav Tzvi Pesach Frank, who also responded in his letter to some of the actual material in *Hazon Ovadia*. Rav Frank was so impressed, in fact, that in his approbation to the first volume of *Yabia Omer*, which was published two years later,

In their approbations to *Hazon Ovadia*, chief rabbis Rav Uziel (C) and Rav Herzog (R) independently refer to Harav Ovadia as *harif ubaki*.

---

20. The title *Hazon Ovadia* would eventually be used for all of Harav Ovadia's halachic compendia. At the time of his passing, this series already numbered over twenty volumes, with more partially written.

he noted how warmly *Hazon Ovadia* had been received by the *talmidei hachamim* of Yerushalayim.

The most moving letter of approbation came from Rav Ezra Attia, who wrote, "The author learned in our yeshiva from his youth, beginning as a [young genius] of about 10 years old, and he served *talmidei hachamim*, rising higher and higher and learning with tremendous diligence. Night and day his candle did not go out, and he did not budge from the love [of Torah], becoming like an overpowering spring, a great expert in *Shas* and *poskim*, creating Torah novellae and dwelling in the depths of halacha."

RAV EZRA, TOO, USED HIS LETTER TO DISCUSS A SPECIFIC HALacha that Harav Ovadia had written about — one that exemplifies a basic principle of his approach to halacha.

Halacha vs. Kabbala

Harav Ovadia mentions the custom among many communities to set up the *ke'ara* (Seder plate) according to the Arizal, who designated two spaces for bitter herbs: one in the middle for *maror*, and another underneath it for *hazeret*. Harav Ovadia notes that this custom goes against the practice delineated by the Gemara and the *poskim*, because it makes the *hazeret* secondary to another form of bitter herb. In such cases, he writes, we follow the ruling of the *poskim*, not the Arizal, whose practices were based on Kabbala.

In his letter of approbation, Rav Ezra Attia argued that we don't necessarily rule *only* according to the *poskim* — especially in this specific case — since a person who eats either bitter herb fulfills his obligation, and the question is only which is the best way to fulfill the mitzva. In such a case, he writes, a person may follow the prevailing Kabbala-based *minhag*.

Unconvinced, Harav Ovadia replied, "We do not involve ourselves in the hidden [Torah]; we follow the majority of *poskim* who rule that the mitzva is to use *hazeret*, and nothing else."

He would invoke this principle many, many more times over the next six decades. Whenever halacha and Kabbala diverge, Harav Ovadia rules according to halacha, while many other Sephardic *poskim* often follow Kabbala.

Hizzuk From Rav Ezra

FOR THE MOST PART, *HAZON OVADIA* WAS RECEIVED WITH much excitement, and it sat on the tables of many *talmidei hachamim* on Pesah, just two weeks after it was released.

Some Jews of Iraqi origin, however, were disturbed by Harav Ovadia's willingness to dispute some of the *piskei halacha* of Rav Yosef Haim, the Ben Ish Hai, who was largely considered the *posek aharon* (final judge) for Iraqi Jewry.[21] A group of distinguished rabbanim of Iraqi descent drew up a declaration banning the *sefer*, and even banning Harav Ovadia himself, and they asked Rav Ezra Attia to sign the ban.

Years later, Rav Ezra related to Harav Ovadia what had transpired when they came to his house and asked him to sign the ban. "I got up and said, 'You don't come to his ankles, and you want to ban him? Leave my house!'

"Never in my life did I expel someone from my house," Rav Ezra related. "This was the only time that I did."[22]

He also warned the Iraqi rabbanim that their efforts would be futile. "The sun has already begun to shine," he said, "and you're trying to put it back into its encasement. It won't help."

"His sun has already begun to shine." Harav Ovadia recites a blessing under the *huppah* of a student, as Rav Ezra Attia presides.

---

21. This was not the first time Harav Ovadia faced opposition from Iraqi Jewry because of his stance on the Ben Ish Hai's rulings; see p. 92.
22. Rav Yitzchak Yosef, in a *hesped* delivered at Yeshivat HaKotel.

Some vigilantes in the Iraqi community, who were not particularly God-fearing, decided to fight the battle in a more extreme way. On Erev Pesah, when they burned their *hametz*, they threw in a copy of *Hazon Ovadia*. When Harav Ovadia heard about this a few days later, he came home looking ashen. "They burned my *sefer*," he whispered to Rabbanit Margalit. Feeling weak, he crawled into his bed to rest, and he became physically ill.

The Rabbanit sent a messenger to Rav Ezra Attia, who came to visit his star pupil. "Your sun is starting to shine," he said, echoing what he had told the Iraqi rabbanim, "and those who don't realize it are just blinded by its brightness."

He convinced Harav Ovadia to continue on his path, teaching Torah and publishing his *sefarim* for the benefit of Klal Yisrael.

Disputing the Ben Ish Hai

THIS WAS THE FIRST OF SEVERAL PRINCIPLED BATTLES HARAV Ovadia would fight to defend his method of arriving at halachic rulings. In his lengthy introduction to *Yabia Omer*, the first volume of which was published two years after this incident, he delves into the topic of how one goes about learning a *sugya* in depth, and outlines the rules that govern *psak* (halachic ruling).

He writes that a *posek* must first toil to understand the Gemara properly, and then learn the *Rishonim* to see how they ruled, because nowadays we are unable to rule based on the Gemara alone. He stresses that we cannot argue with a *Rishon*; when we don't understand the *Rishon*, we must realize that this stems from our own lack of wisdom. Finally, he writes, a *posek* should consult as many halachic works of the *Aharonim* as possible, even works published by contemporaries, because these often serve as a pathway to understanding the words of a Gemara or a *Rishon*.[23]

He then goes on to address the issue of people who "defend" a recent *posek* against another qualified *posek* who disputes his ruling. "[Disputing rulings] was the way of all our rabbis, from the days of the Tannaim and Amora'im until the latest *poskim*. As the

---

23. In typical fashion, he brings ample proof for each of his points, citing from both *Rishonim* and *Aharonim* extensively and showing how he developed his own approach to learning.

Gemara in *Kiddushin* states, 'Even a rebbi and his student become like enemies to one another [while arguing about a Torah topic], but they end up loving each other.'"

He cites dozens of examples of *talmidim* who disputed the words of their rebbeim: Rabbeinu HaKadosh, redactor of the Mishnah, argued with his father, Rabbi Shimon ben Gamliel; Rava argued with Rabba; the Rosh argued with the Maharam; and Rashi's own grandchildren, the Tosafists, disputed the rulings of their grandfather. "The job of a halachic authority is not to be like a donkey carrying *sefarim* [i.e., answering halachic inquiries directly from existing works he has read], but to delve into the *sh'eila* and exert his best effort to reach a halachic decision — provided that the leaders of the generation have authorized him to do so. He must be careful to take his time deliberating, because his initial impressions and logic might be wrong. And he must weigh his reasoning carefully. But after careful analysis of the matter, he may argue with the works of the *Aharonim* for the sake of Heaven — especially if he has additional *Aharonim* backing his approach."

He adds that not only is a *posek* **allowed** to dispute a matter if he sees it differently, he is actually **required** to do so. He cites both Rav Haim Palagi and Rav Chaim of Volozhin — leading Sephardic and Ashkenazic rabbanim in their respective eras — who wrote that when a rav sees an issue differently from the way his rebbi saw it, he may not rule according to his rebbi's approach. As Rav Chaim of Volozhin wrote, "It is forbidden for a student to accept his rebbi's teaching if he has questions on it, for sometimes the student will be correct, just as a little piece of wood can ignite a large one."[24]

Harav Ovadia concludes his introduction with one caveat: Every argument against an earlier *posek* must be presented respectfully, without impudence borne of arrogance.

His final paragraph contains an unusual statement: "If there appears in a work I have written until now, or in something I will write in the future with Hashem's help, harsh expressions or sharp language against an early or late authority, it is a slip of the pen, not done with forethought of its owner, and I hereby annul such

---

24. *Ruah Haim* on *Avot* 1:4.

statements with absolute annulment. I express my opinion and wish that any thought or statement that I may think, speak, or write against Hashem or those who fear Him should be null and void like a shard of pottery, because my purpose and desire in the works that I have authored and will author with Hashem's help — and, in fact, in all of my learning — is to bring pleasure to Hashem, without any ulterior motives or negative intentions."

IN TRUTH, THE IRAQI JEWS' CLAIM THAT HARAV OVADIA HAD attacked the Ben Ish Hai with impudence was baseless. It's quite likely that there was no greater expert on Ben Ish Hai than Harav Ovadia.

Respect for the Ben Ish Hai

Rav Shalom Cohen[25] recalled that when he was a youngster starting to learn in Porat Yosef, a familiar sight when you entered the beit midrash was that of Harav Ovadia standing at a bookcase poring over a volume of Ben Ish Hai.

Rav Shlomo Moshe Amar, who was the Rishon LeZion during the final decade of Harav Ovadia's life, related that he once visited Harav Ovadia to discuss a sh'eila, and the answer involved a ruling of the Ben Ish Hai. Harav Ovadia asked him to bring the Ben Ish Hai from his library. Rav Amar fetched the sefer, which was a very old edition printed in a large tome. When he opened the volume, he was shocked to find every inch of the large margins filled with tiny handwritten notes. "You couldn't find a place to stick in a pin," he recalls.

When Rav Amar expressed his amazement at the amount of work that had gone into these comments on the Ben Ish Hai, Harav Ovadia said, "People think that I considered it a simple matter to argue with the Ben Ish Hai. You should know that before I disputed any of his rulings, I learned the

---

25. The son of Harav Ovadia's mentor Rav Ephraim Cohen, Rav Shalom, learned in Porat Yosef during Harav Ovadia's time, but was about a decade younger. In 1984, Harav Ovadia pegged him to sit on Moetzet Hachmei HaTorah of Shas, and he became the leader of the Moetzet when Harav Ovadia passed away.

Rav Shlomo Moshe Amar (R) consults with Harav Ovadia in his last years.

relevant topic from the Gemara, through all of the Rishonim and the poskim until his time, a minimum of 15 times."

SOME OF THE MORE MILITANT IRAQI JEWS WERE NOT deterred by any sort of logical explanations, however. Many years after he published *Hazon Ovadia*, Harav Ovadia published a set of *sefarim* called *Halichot Olam*, which contains Harav Ovadia's *piskei halacha*, based on the rulings of the Beit Yosef, with the text of the Ben Ish Hai underneath it.

No Spot in Yerushalayim

In the introduction, he writes that after the release of *Hazon Ovadia* on *Hilchot Pesah*, he received thinly veiled threats that if he would publish more *piskei halacha* against the Ben Ish Hai, powerbrokers would see to it that he wouldn't advance to more distinguished positions in the Rabbanut.

Indeed, he wound up suffering because of his insistence on ruling according to the principles of halacha rather than following the Ben Ish Hai blindly.

A few years after the release of *Hazon Ovadia*, when Harav Ovadia was once again seeking a position on the Rabbanut, his students in Yerushalayim did not want him to have to travel out of the city each day. They approached a leading figure in the Rabbanut to request a position for Harav Ovadia in a local *beit din*, unaware that this rabbi was involved in the battle against *Hazon Ovadia*.

"How many people attend his *shiurim* in Yerushalayim?" the person asked, upon hearing their request.

"Five hundred," they answered.

"So then let them each give two shillings," he replied derisively, "and he'll have a full salary."

He refused to find Harav Ovadia a position in Yerushalayim because of the perceived slight of the Ben Ish Hai, and this refusal eventually led to Harav Ovadia's move to Petah Tikva.[26]

HIS OPPONENTS WEREN'T SATISFIED WITH STOPPING HIM from advancing in the Rabbanut.

Rav Rosenthal to the Rescue

In his *hesped* on Rav Yitzchak Rosenthal, who ran Midrash Bnei Zion, Harav Ovadia relates that at one point, Rav Rosenthal found out that a certain Iraqi rav owned a rare manuscript on *Seder Zera'im*. He went to ask the rav for permission to reprint it, and the rav agreed to give it to him on one condition: that he expel Harav Ovadia from his kollel.

Rav Rosenthal held his colleague in esteem, however. "Not only didn't he expel me," Harav Ovadia writes, "but he encouraged me to continue my work, and even helped sponsor the printing of *Hazon Ovadia* on *Hilchot Pesah* and the first volume of *Yabia Omer*."

---

26. See p. 276.

CHAPTER TEN
RESTORING THE CROWN

IF WE HAVE SEEN THAT THE HARAV OVADIA WHO returned to Eretz Yisrael after three years in Egypt wasn't the same person who left it,[1] the same could be said in the reverse even more emphatically: the Eretz Yisrael Harav Ovadia returned to was decidedly different from the one he left.

When he departed for Egypt, the British were just deciding to relinquish control of the land after being battered into submission by the Irgun and other Jewish militias, but they still maintained full authority. The Eretz Yisrael Harav Ovadia returned to was the independent State of Israel, a country run by Jews — but Jews who were, by and large, attempting to squelch or obliterate traditional Jewish commitment to Torah and mitzvot. From the laws they established to the manner in which they treated immigrants, the leaders of the new State were on a mission: to create a new Jew who would be more devoted to his homeland than to the covenant that had sustained his ancestors through 2,000 years of exile. It was up to the Torah leaders of the generation to rally the few Jews who weren't swept up in the euphoric nationalistic sentiment to

---

1. See p. 182.

A changed man returns to a changed country: Harav Ovadia upon his return from Egypt.

rebuild a Torah world decimated by the Holocaust and the hasty escape from Arab and Muslim countries, some of which had hosted Torah communities for two millennia.

But even the segment of society that was committed to Torah was facing an unprecedented challenge: Never before was there an ingathering of Jews from so many diverse backgrounds converging upon one small strip of land, toting two millennia worth of customs that reflected the various locales, climates, and government laws the Jews were subject to in their various exiles.

Could religious Jewry in Eretz Yisrael thrive if there were dozens of contradictory customs? If the Jews from France observed Judaism so differently from those who hailed from Iraq, if the American *olim* had to share a culture with Moroccans freshly arrived from Fez?

The chief rabbis, Rav Herzog and Rav Uziel, felt that it would be impossible to establish *batei din* that could rule for all the citizens of Israel unless there were guidelines that governed Jews from across the spectrum: Sephardi or Ashkenazi, new immigrants alongside natives whose families had been in Eretz Yisrael for centuries. They held a conference of a broad committee of the Rabbanut in Yerushalayim on 18-21 Shevat, 5710/1950, during which they discussed — and set concrete rules on — marriage-related issues. They then issued a statement called *Takanot Yerushalayim*[2] delineating those rules and requiring all *batei din* in Eretz Yisrael to follow them.

Rav Ovadia would quickly find himself at the fulcrum of this effort. Although he agreed with the general concept of unifying Jewry, he disagreed with a significant element in their approach — and that would soon result in his leaving his signature on how Sephardim would be governed by the *batei din* in Eretz Yisrael.

---

2. Alternatively referred to as *"Herem Yerushalayim."*

The Need for Unity

THE NEED TO SET STANDARDS FOR *PISKEI HALACHA* IN THE new State was phrased eloquently in the introduction to the statement delineating the *takanot* (decrees):[3]

> The ingathering of the exiled [is bringing Jews] from all the areas of the Diaspora, from the far ends of the earth and distant islands, who are arriving by the thousands and tens of thousands to settle in Eretz Yisrael through Hashem's great kindness, bringing along ancient customs that do not meld with the *takanot* of the sages of Eretz Yisrael and of Yerushalayim, or with the *takanot* of the community rabbanim in Eretz Yisrael who have to preside over *kiddushin* and marriages, *gittin* and divorce, and *yibbum* and *halitza*. This can cause divisiveness among Klal Yisrael and destroy the peace in the House of Israel. We therefore considered it our obligation to renew the decrees of our earlier sages *zt"l*, and to add on certain similar decrees as necessary for our times in order to maintain peace among the House of Israel, which is the underpinning of the decrees our sages passed from the days of Moshe Rabbeinu until the latest generations in their individual communities.
>
> With the permission of the Holy One, Blessed is He, and His Divine Presence, and with the permission of *beit din shel maala* and *beit din shel matta*, and with the permission of earlier sages who ruled in Eretz Yisrael and by agreement of the great *geonim* of the members of the broad council of Israel's chief rabbinate, we hereby decree and proclaim with the full force of the Torah, as was the case with all decrees passed in Klal Yisrael for their individual communities, [obligating them] for all generations....[4]

---

3. Published in its entirety in a footnote to *Heichal Yitzchak*, Rav Herzog's responsa work, *Even Ha'ezer* 1:5.
4. Aside from the example listed below, these *takanot* were:
   □ One could not betroth a woman unless he was marrying her at the same time, and that both the betrothal and marriage could only happen 10 days after they signed up for marriage in a *beit din*.
   □ No one may marry a woman who is under the age of 16, and a father may not accept a betrothal on his daughter's behalf when she is under that age.

Rav Ovadia (1) shakes hands with Ashkenazi Chief Rabbi Herzog (2) at a meeting for *dayanim*, with whom he shared a warm relationship despite differences of opinion in halacha.

There were few words in this statement that Harav Ovadia would not have agreed with. He was actually the one who proclaimed that Sephardic Jewry, which had been spread over lands throughout Africa, Asia, and even parts of Europe, had been hopelessly splintered in terms of the customs they accepted upon themselves in those lands — some of which were absolutely against halacha and had to be abolished. He felt strongly that Sephardic Jewry had to

---

☐ A man may not marry a second wife unless he has written consent for bigamous marriage from the Rabbanut.

☐ No rabbi may officiate at a wedding without written authorization from the chief rabbinate to do so.

The reasons for these *takanot*, which are beyond the scope of this book, are spelled out in the document, which was signed by Rav Uziel and Rav Herzog, representing the Sephardic and Ashkenazic communities respectively.

Sadly, toward the end of Harav Ovadia's life, several of the *takanot* that were enacted to protect the integrity of Jewish lineage came under attack by rabbis seeking to "ease" the restrictions on people of dubious heritage who wanted to marry Jews. One of Harav Ovadia's last public efforts, undertaken in the summer of 2013, shortly before his passing, was to ensure the election of chief rabbis who would uphold halacha in these areas.

unify under one common set of halachot, following the rulings of Rav Yosef Karo, author of the *Shulhan Aruch*, and he was about to embark upon a vital campaign to unite them.

He disagreed, however, with the premise that all of Klal Yisrael — i.e., Sephardim and Ashkenazim — had to operate under one set of rules. He felt that because Sephardic and Ashkenazic Jewry had constituted two distinct communities throughout the ages — even in locations where they coexisted — that pattern should continue in Eretz Yisrael.

His two goals — to ensure that the Sephardim would remain autonomous from the Ashkenazim in terms of halacha, and to unify all Sephardim under the banner of the Beit Yosef — might seem like a dichotomy of sorts. But he viewed this as both necessary and halachically mandated, and it turned into the primary campaign he led in his life.

The Yibbum That Wasn't

IN TAMMUZ OF 5711/1951, A CASE CAME BEFORE THE *BEIT DIN* in Petah Tikva that caused Harav Ovadia to analyze the *takanot* issued by the chief rabbinate a year earlier, and eventually to challenge its validity.

A family from Yemen had made *aliya*, and one of the brothers died, leaving a widow but no children. In Torah law, the wife of this person, whom we'll call Reuven, would require *yibbum*, levirate marriage. This means that one of Reuven's brothers must marry her and inherit his deceased brother's estate. The firstborn child from that union is then attributed to Reuven. If no brother wants to marry Reuven's widow, one of them must do *halitza*, which releases her from the obligation of *yibbum* and frees her to remarry outside the family.[5]

Halacha stipulates, however, that the brother who marries Reuven's widow must do so purely with the intention of keeping his brother's name alive, and not for other motives (such as monetary considerations or because he finds his brother's widow attractive). Performing *yibbum* for other motives is considered particu-

---

5. See *Devarim* 25:5-10.

larly egregious because in any circumstance other than a brother who dies childless, it is forbidden to marry one's brother's widow.

Already in the times of the Mishnah, a concern arose that men were no longer able to have the purest intentions in performing *yibbum*. There was a dispute among the sages (*Bechorot* 13a) whether the mitzva of *yibbum* should be discontinued and replaced with the alternative practice of *halitza*, and in the generations that followed, many communities abolished *yibbum*, insisting that the couple do *halitza* instead.

Many Sephardic authorities, however, ruled that even if one marries his brother's widow for a combination of two intentions — one pure and one less than pure — it is still considered proper *yibbum*. These authorities, which included the Rambam[6] and the Beit Yosef,[7] therefore considered *yibbum* a viable option even in modern times.

In establishing their *takanot*, the chief rabbinate had voted to follow the former approach, and to abolish the practice of *yibbum* in Eretz Yisrael. They phrased this injunction as follows:

> Most communities in Klal Yisrael, and the Ashkenazic communities in Eretz Yisrael, accepted upon themselves as halacha that the mitzva of *halitza* takes precedence over the mitzva of *yibbum*, and that even when both sides [the man and the woman] prefer *yibbum*, we do not allow them to do *yibbum*. And in the case in which the living brother is married to another woman, it was customary in *all* communities not to allow him to do *yibbum*.
>
> Since in our days, it is clear that most [men in the position to do *yibbum*] do not have the intention to do so for the mitzva, and in order to maintain peace and unity in the State of Israel, so that the Torah should not be like two Torahs, we decree on all those dwelling in Eretz Yisrael and on those who settle here in the future, absolutely forbidding them to do the mitzva of *yibbum*, and requiring

---

6. *Hilchot Yibbum V'Halitza* 1:2.
7. *Shulhan Aruch Even Ha'ezer* 165:1. Although the Beit Yosef cites both opinions, he first cites the ruling that *yibbum* precedes *halitza* and only then the other opinion, as "*veyesh omrim* — some say," which generally means that he ruled according to the first opinion.

them to do *halitza*. The living brother will be required to sustain his brother's widow according to the amount set by the *beit din* until he does *halitza*.

This prohibition may be annulled only in certain extenuating circumstances, with the decision of the expanded council [of the Rabbanut] and with the signatures of the chief rabbis of Israel.

Yemenite Jewry, however, had followed the ruling of the Rambam and the Beit Yosef throughout the generations. When this couple came before the Petah Tikva *beit din*, a brother, whom we'll call Shimon, expressed his desire to marry Reuven's widow. In accordance with the *takanot* issued by the chief rabbinate, the *beit din* was planning to force Shimon to do *halitza*.

Rav Ovadia at a *hachnasat Sefer Torah*.
It was important to Harav Ovadia to unite all of Sephardic Jewry through one set of halachot, but their rulings could differ from the Ashkenazi approach.

Rav Ovadia took the opportunity to examine not only the *takana* about *yibbum*, but also to challenge the entire premise of setting down one unified halachic system for Ashkenazim and Sephardim.[8]

> Regarding what the members and presidium of the chief rabbinate have written in their agreement — that peace and unity in the State of Israel and not allowing the Torah to become like two Torahs obligates them to absolutely forbid *yibbum* and require *halitza* — with all due respect, they have gone too far in this matter, and their words are not correct. Each day we encounter many rulings in matters of *shehita* or *tereifot* and other issues in *issur v'heter*, and likewise in *hilchot Shabbat* and *taharat hamishpaha*, in which each community follows the rulings of their rabbis — the Sephardim follow the ruling of Maran, the author of the *Shulhan Aruch*, and the Ashkenazim follow the ruling of the Rema.[9] The same holds true for differences in *nusah* (text of the *tefillot*), the pronunciation they use while praying and reading the Torah, the shapes of the letters in *Sifrei Torah*, *tefillin*, and *mezuzot*, etc.
>
> We have never concerned ourselves that this would seem like two Torahs, because it is well-known that each [community] can rely upon the customs of their fore-

---

8. The *teshuva* on this matter was printed in *Yabia Omer*, Vol. 6, *Even Ha'ezer* 14, which was published a quarter of a century after Harav Ovadia wrote it, when he was already serving as chief rabbi.

9. Rav Ovadia uses a catchphrase that he would often repeat: וְהָאַשְׁכְּנַזִּים יוֹצְאִים בְּיָד רמ"א, which appears fifty times in *Yabia Omer* and *Yehaveh Daat* alone. Originally coined more than 200 years ago — it already appears in the *teshuvot* of the Hatam Sofer — it is a play on the verse: וּבְנֵי יִשְׂרָאֵל יֹצְאִים בְּיָד רָמָה, *And the Children of Israel were going out with an upraised arm* (*Shemot* 14:8). It expresses the concept that Ashkenazic Jewry accepted upon themselves the rulings of the Rema (רמ"א — an acronym for Rav Moshe Isserlis), who wrote glosses on the Beit Yosef's *Shulhan Aruch* that are printed within the actual text of the *Shulhan Aruch*. In those glosses, the Rema often disputes the ruling of the Beit Yosef or writes that the custom of Ashkenazic Jewry differed from that of Sephardic Jewry in that specific halacha. (On occasion, he'll clarify something the Beit Yosef wrote without disputing it.)

Ever since the days of these two great sages — widely accepted as the greatest halachic authorities in the era of the *Aharonim* — Sephardim generally follow the rulings of the *Shulhan Aruch* in all matters, while Ashkenazim follow the Rema in instances in which he disputes the ruling of the *Shulhan Aruch*.

fathers, and that "these and these are the words of the Living God."[10]

Harav Ovadia cites proof from no less an authority than Rav Avraham Yitzchak HaKohen Kook, the Ashkenazi Chief Rabbi in the days before the State was established, who wrote that Sephardic and Ashkenazic Jews must purchase meat from separate butcher shops, because there are disputes between the Sephardic and Ashkenazic sages regarding certain halachot of *kashrut*.[11] Rav Kook explained that this was not a new phenomenon; in cities in the Diaspora in which Sephardim and Ashkenazim coexisted, there were always separate butcher shops for the two communities, and the same had held true in all of Eretz Yisrael and specifically in Yerushalayim. "Only now," Rav Kook added, "did individuals come along seeking to destroy these boundaries, and I must therefore rise up against them.

Harav Ovadia cited proof from Rav Avraham Yitzchak HaKohen Kook (below) that Israeli society would thrive with Sephardim and Ashkenazim maintaining their respective halachic traditions.

"This is not, Heaven forbid, in opposition to the value of unity and main-

---

10. *Eruvin* 13b. This phrase means that although here on earth it would seem that only one set of rules can be correct, Heaven recognizes the validity of both.
11. *Igrot Hare'iyah*, 511.

taining peace, because everyone knows that each person must follow the customs of his forefathers, due to the halachic principle of *Al titosh Torat imecha* [Do not abandon the Torah of your mother]."

Rav Ovadia felt strongly that every rav, Sephardi or Ashkenazi, must know the halachot according to both traditions, and answer each questioner according to his heritage.

He related that when he was a young rav living in the Beit Yisrael neighborhood, he came home one Hol HaMoed Pesah morning to find a woman crying outside his house. He asked her what was wrong, and she tearfully explained that her daughter had accidentally used a hametz pot to cook her husband's lunch. She had come to the neighborhood rav — who lived one flight below Harav Ovadia — to ask whether they could use the food. The rav replied that they could not, since even the smallest mixture of hametz causes food to be prohibited — even if that hametz is only absorbed into the walls of a pot.

She added that she didn't have any other food in the house to serve her husband, which was why she was crying.

"Are you Ashkenazi or Sephardi?" Harav Ovadia asked.

"Sephardi," she replied.

"I'm assuming that the pot has not been used for hametz during the past 24 hours, correct?"

"Certainly," she said. "I haven't cooked hametz since before Pesah."

"In that case," Harav Ovadia replied, "you can go home and enjoy the food."

He explained in his shiur that Maran, the Beit Yosef, maintains that hametz absorbed into the walls of a pot does not prohibit food cooked in that pot after 24 hours have elapsed since the pot was used with hametz. He used this incident to illustrate how important it is for a rav to find out who the person asking the question is, for in this case the woman was halachically permitted to serve her husband the food cooked in that pot, and had she not had food to serve her husband, that might have resulted in domestic discord.¹²

Unifying Sephardic Jewry Under Maran

TOWARD THE END OF THE *TESHUVA*, HARAV OVADIA CITED, apparently for the first time in print, a plethora of sources from some of the greatest Sephardic halachic authorities of all time. These sources served as the basis for his lifelong insistence that Sephardic Jewry must follow Rav Yosef Karo's rulings in halachic matters, even if many sages oppose him on a specific halacha:¹³

1. Rav Yaakov ibn Tzur, who lived from 5433-5513 (1673-1753), wrote¹⁴ that once the Beit Yosef's works spread throughout the Diaspora, we rule according to him even if a thousand *poskim* disagree with him.

2. Rav Haim Palagi writes,¹⁵ "It is well known throughout the world that the sages of Spain and France accepted upon them and their children to rule in all instances according to Maran Rabbeinu Yosef Karo *z"l* — *even if all the Aharonim dispute his ruling.*"¹⁶

3. The Ben Ish Hai, Rav Yosef Haim, writes that even if one hundred *Aharonim* were to disagree with the Beit Yosef, we still wouldn't be allowed to rule leniently against him — even in a case of great

---

12. Rav Ovadia stressed that the rav who lived beneath him was a great scholar who had assumed, from the woman's appearance, that she was Ashkenazi, and therefore had not bothered to ask. He warned, however, that in modern times, a rav might make that mistake out of sheer ignorance, because unworthy people were being ordained as rabbanim. In his classic humor, he phrased it as follows: "אֲבָל הַיּוֹם, גַּם תֶּבֶן גַּם מִסְפּוֹא רַב." (The last words are borrowed from a verse in which Rivka tells Eliezer that he could stay with her family overnight, and they had enough straw for them to sleep on and fodder for their cattle.) He used the turn of phrase to mean, "Today, straw and fodder are also a 'rav.'"
13. In the case of *yibbum*, many Sephardic sages agreed with the Beit Yosef, but Harav Ovadia's tendency in his *teshuvot* was to elucidate an entire halachic subject, not only the specific case that was presented to him.
14. *Mishpat U'Tzedaka L'Yaakov* 2:20.
15. *Haim BaYad* 108. Rav Haim Palagi was considered one of the greatest Sephardic sages of the last few centuries.
16. He adds an allusion from the Torah: לְכוּ אֶל יוֹסֵף אֲשֶׁר יֹאמַר לָכֶם תַּעֲשׂוּ, *Go to Yosef, and whatever he says, do.*

monetary loss: "We must follow the rulings of Maran because we accepted upon ourselves and our children [to follow them]."

[Elsewhere, Harav Ovadia cites from Hida,[17] who quotes Rav Haim Abulafia (who lived not long after the Beit Yosef passed away) as saying that when the Beit Yosef established a system for determining the halacha — which was to abide by the majority opinion among the Rif, Rambam, and Rosh (the three *Rishonim* who were the primary halachic arbiters of their era) — two hundred elders of his generation agreed with his approach.

One who argues with the Beit Yosef, concludes Hida, also disputes the opinions of two hundred Torah greats of his time.]

Since Sephardic Jewry is required to rule according to the Beit Yosef, writes Harav Ovadia, the chief rabbis did not have the right to rule against him, and their decree from the previous year is null and void. He concludes on a practical note, saying that if we are concerned that a couple eligible for *yibbum* does not have pure intentions, we should explain to them the importance of performing the mitzva without ulterior motives, and we can then allow them to perform this great mitzva.

The Mara D'Atra

IN MANY PLACES IN HIS *TESHUVOT*,[18] HARAV OVADIA ADDS one more fundamental principle for following the ruling of the Beit Yosef. There's a concept in halacha that when a city or town accepts upon themselves the ruling of a *Mara D'Atra*[19] — whether he rules stringently or leniently in a matter — that ruling becomes binding upon all the residents of that city.

Rav Ovadia explains that the Beit Yosef is considered the *Mara D'Atra* of Eretz Yisrael — especially for Sephardim — and all customs or halachic decisions followed in other countries that are in conflict with his rulings are nullified once they move to Eretz Yisrael.[20]

---

17. *Birkei Yosef, Hoshen Mishpat* 25:29.
18. See, for instance, *Yabia Omer*, Vol. 2, *Orach Haim* 25; Vol. 3, *Even Ha'Ezer* 13; and Introduction to Vol. 5.
19. Lit., *the owner of the land*, this title generally applies to the uncontested rav of a city.
20. Rav Ovadia finds a basis for this principle in *Sh'eilot V'Teshuvot Maharif* (also referred to as

According to this principle, Iraqis who followed the rulings of the Ben Ish Hai while they were in Iraq or Egyptians who followed the Ginat Vradim[21] while in Egypt must accept the Beit Yosef's sovereignty once they arrive in Eretz Yisrael.

Restoring the Halachic Crown

IN THE CASE OF *YIBBUM*, HARAV OVADIA'S OPPOSITION TO the chief rabbis' *takana* does not seem to have affected the Rabbanut's approach. But this was the opening salvo in a lifelong campaign that did meet with success in many cases. His original use of the term לְהַחֲזִיר עֲטָרָה לְיוֹשְׁנָהּ — restoring the crown to its former glory — was not intended in the spiritual sense or as a political proclamation,[22] but purely in terms of halacha: He urged Sephardic Jewry to reaccept the predominance of the Beit Yosef over all other halachic works, restoring the crown of Sephardic *psak* to its former glory.

There is wide speculation,[23] in fact, that Harav Ovadia Yosef was a reincarnation of the soul of Rav Yosef Karo.

> *While Harav Ovadia himself never made any statement to buttress that claim, when his vision suddenly deteriorated in the early 1970s and the doctors thought that he had been blinded irreparably, he traveled to Tzfat with his son-in-law Rav Ezra Bar-Shalom to visit the grave of the Beit Yosef. He sat there crying and praying. "I want to publicize your rulings in the world," he said, "but I won't be able to do that without my eyesight."*
>
> *When he returned to Yerushalayim and went for a recheck, the doctors were shocked to find that the condition affecting his vision had all but disappeared. Harav Ovadia*

Mahari Paragi), Siman 59.
21. Rav Avraham ben Mordehai HaLevi, who lived in Egypt from 1650-1712 and served as the chief rabbi of Cairo, is often referred to by the name of his responsa work, *Ginat Vradim*. His rulings were considered the basis for the customs of Egyptian Jewry during the centuries following his demise.
22. As it was used when it was adopted as Shas's party slogan three decades thereafter.
23. Cited, for instance, by Rav Benzion Mutzafi at a *hesped*.

Rav Ovadia and son-in-law Rav Ezra Bar-Shalom at a *siyum masechet*.

still took the precaution of wearing dark sunglasses almost all the time for the rest of his life to protect his eyes from harmful sunrays, but he was able to read from sefarim until his passing some four decades after the doctors had given up hope on his eyesight.

What's in a Name?

WITHIN THAT SAME YEAR that Harav Ovadia served on the *beit din* in Petah Tikva, another major issue arose that would eventually lead to his resignation from the *beit din*.

A woman from Turkey came to the *beit din* to accept a *get* her husband had sent. Her name was Rahel (רחל), but her name was pronounced as the secular name Rachelle would be enunciated. The halacha is that the names in a *get* must be spelled with absolute precision, and all nicknames must be included in the *get* and spelled in a way that people will understand from the *get* itself how to pronounce them. A problem arises, therefore, when there are different methods of spelling a name — which is especially common when either husband or wife is called by a secular name. In fact, entire *sefarim* are devoted just to the correct ways to spell names, and when there is no precedent for the correct spelling of a name, the *beit din* uses general rules regarding which Hebrew letters represent which *nekudot* (vowels) so it will be clear how the name is pronounced.

The problem in this instance was that Sephardim and Ashkenazim had different ways of spelling out this pronunciation of the name Rachelle. The Sephardim would spell it ראשיל, and the Ashkenazim would spell it רעשל. Rav Reuven Katz had instructed the *beit din* in

Turkey that wrote the *get* on the husband's behalf to spell it רעשל, and the *get* arrived at the Petah Tikva *beit din*, to be delivered to the wife, with that spelling.

When Harav Ovadia saw the *get*, his initial reaction was that he should not allow it to be delivered. He writes, however, that "For the sake of *kavod haTorah*, I kept quiet."

He allowed the *get* to be delivered, but he informed Rav Katz that in the future, he could not take part in *gittin* involving Sephardic Jews in which the names were spelled according to the Ashkenazic custom.

Not long afterward, Harav Ovadia writes, a Sephardic couple who had married in Egypt and then moved to Petah Tikva came to the *beit din* for a *get*. The husband's name was שלמה, but everyone called him Solomon. Here, too, there was a difference in the way Ashkenazim and Sephardim spelled the name. Rav Katz instructed them to spell it סלמאן, because according to Ashkenazi spelling, an *aleph* replaces a *holam*. Harav Ovadia ruled that it should be spelled סאלאמון, because Sephardim use an *aleph* in place of a *patah* and a *vav* in place of a *holam*.

This case was more critical than the one that involved the spelling of Rahel, because in this case there was room for serious error: a Sephardic Jew reading the world סלמאן, as the Ashkenazim spelled it, would read it *Silman* or *Suleman*, which are not the same name as Solomon.

In this case, writes Harav Ovadia, the other *dayanim* agreed to write the *get* according to his instructions.

But the overall issue was not laid to rest. When another Sephardic *get* came before the *beit din* and the *dayanim* wanted to spell the names according to the Ashkenazic custom, Harav Ovadia insisted that it be written according to the Sephardic spelling. The other *dayanim* — apparently concerned that if there wouldn't be a uniform system of spelling, it would be very hard to write *gittin* correctly — were equally adamant that the Ashkenazic spelling be used.

Seeing that they would not accept his opinion even though he had shown them numerous sources among Sephardi rabbanim who

Though Harav Ovadia resigned from his *beit din*,
Rav Reuven Katz loved and admired his youngest *dayan*.

ruled accordingly, Harav Ovadia reached for a napkin that was next to him on the table, and wrote on it:

> To the Religious Affairs Minister,
> I hereby resign from the *beit din*, because I cannot serve on a *beit din* that does the following ....[24]

Despite his need for the salary he was drawing as a *dayan*, Harav Ovadia chose to resign and return to delivering his *shiurim* in Yerushalayim and begin working on his *sefarim* rather than go along with what he considered a violation of halacha.

The *mahloket* between Harav Ovadia and the other *dayanim* wasn't personal; there are two obvious indications that both sides were acting for the sake of Heaven:

First, when Harav Ovadia published *Hazon Ovadia* on *Hilchot Pesah* just four months after resigning from the *beit din*, one of the warmest letters of approbation came from Rav Reuven Katz, who referred to Harav Ovadia as, "My dear friend... the insightful expert...."

---

24. Rav Yitzchak Yosef, who still has the napkin with the handwritten note.

In the body of the letter he writes, "I know his honor, who was a member of [my] *beit din*, and I have the highest esteem for his breadth of knowledge and his incisiveness, and most of all for the pure fear of Heaven that fills his heart."

Second, approximately four years after Harav Ovadia resigned, Rav Katz asked him to rejoin his *beit din*, and this time he promised that Harav Ovadia would be solely responsible for any *get* of a Sephardic couple. Had the dispute been personal, Rav Katz would never have asked him to rejoin, and Harav Ovadia would never have accepted.

RESTORING THE CROWN OF HALACHA TO ITS FORMER GLORY — by reinstating the premise that *psak halacha* among Sephardic Jewry must follow the Beit Yosef, and ensuring that Sephardim would be able to rule autonomously — was an important element in Harav Ovadia's vision for the future, but it was just one element in that quest. While he was working to achieve this, he simultaneously turned his attention to what would be yet another lifelong mission: teaching Torah to Sephardic Jewry — both old and young — through any and every available means.

Just One Element

CHAPTER ELEVEN
LEADER OF A RENAISSANCE

IN THE EARLY 1950S, THE MORALE OF SEPHARDIC JEWRY in Eretz Yisrael was at an all-time low.

Throughout the centuries of Jewish exile from Eretz Yisrael — and especially during the years of Ottoman rule — it was primarily Sephardim who maintained a connection with the land, traveling from their homelands to visit or settle there. During the early 1700s, in fact, after a failed *aliya* attempt from Europe that eventually led to Ashkenazi Jews defaulting on loans to local Arabs, the Arabs burned down the Beit Knesset of Rav Yehuda HaHassid[1] — the leader of that *aliya*, who had died shortly after the group's arrival in Eretz Yisrael — and banished all Ashkenazi Jews from Yerushalayim. For close to a century, anyone dressed in Ashkenazic garb would be beaten or imprisoned, and there are reports of Ashkenazim dressing as Sephardim in order to visit Yerushalayim.

---

1. This *beit knesset*, which came to be known as Hurvat Rav Yehuda HaHassid — or simply "the Hurvah" — was rebuilt later during the *aliyot* of the 1800s by the *Perushim* (disciples of the Vilna Gaon who settled in Eretz Yisrael).

The Hurvah was destroyed again by the Jordanian Arab Legion after they captured the Old City during the Israeli War of Independence. Although Israel regained control of the Old City during the Six-Day War in 1967, the Hurvah remained in a state of disrepair for more than 40 years, until it was finally rebuilt in recent years and opened in March 2010.

Hurva of Rav Yehuda HaHasid, after it was destroyed (above)
and after it was reconstructed (below)

In the late 18th century, the disciples of the Vilna Gaon and the Baal Shem Tov started to settle in Eretz Yisrael. At first they settled in the north, but eventually they convinced the Ottoman authorities in Constantinople to cancel the debts of the earlier Ashkenazic Jews and to abolish the decree prohibiting them from settling in Yerushalayim. Still, the Jewish population of Eretz Yisrael was primarily Sephardic, and its chief rabbi and other community officials were officially recognized by the Ottomans.

The tides began to turn during the late 1800s, when the waves of mass *aliya* from Europe began. At first, most of the *olim* were religious Jews seeking to absorb the *kedusha* of Eretz Yisrael, even if it meant living in poverty.

Survivors of Buchenwald concentration camp arrive in Eretz Yisrael illegally in 1945, as part of *Aliya Bet*, only to be arrested and incarcerated by the British.

Chapter Eleven: Leader of a Renaissance ☐ 227

As political Zionism took root at the turn of the 20th century, however, masses of irreligious Jews began to arrive and establish settlements and political movements. When the British ousted the Ottomans and imposed limits on Jewish immigration, an underground movement known as *Aliya Bet* or *hap'ala*[2] developed, aimed at bringing more and more Jews into the country illegally. As Europe became an increasingly dangerous home for Jews during the two world wars, the *aliya* movement grew exponentially, and by the time the State of Israel was established, Ashkenazim greatly outnumbered Sephardim. Moreover, they controlled the militias that had succeeded in chasing the British out of Eretz Yisrael, and they presided over the Jewish Agency and most other institutions.

Sephardic Aliya

DURING ISRAEL'S WAR OF INDEPENDENCE, JEWS IN ARAB countries — Iraq, Syria, Egypt,[3] among others — began to suffer as a backlash of the war their host countries were fighting against Israel. Jewish communities that had coexisted with Muslims for centuries in relative peace suddenly found themselves in a precarious situation. Although these Jews had historically been treated far better than their counterparts in Christian-dominated Europe, the founding of the State thrust them into immediate danger, and many sold whatever they could and hastily made *aliya*.

When these Sephardic Jews arrived in Israel, they were in for a nasty surprise: The ruling powers in Israel were extremely hostile to the immigrants' Sephardic culture — and especially toward religion. For decades, the Zionists had been carefully laying the groundwork for a secular Jewish state, toiling to eradicate the religious aspects of Judaism as much as possible — and they had largely succeeded. Most Jews who came from Europe — and even many natives of the Old Yishuv in Eretz Yisrael — were swept up by nationalistic feelings, and many of them abandoned religion.

---

2. A play on the word וַיַּעְפִּלוּ, which the Torah uses to describe Jews who attempted to reach Eretz Yisrael against Hashem's instructions after they sinned by accepting the Spies' negative report about the land (*Bamidbar* 14:44).
3. See p. 176.

Israel's declaration of independence brought on wide-scale pogroms in Arab lands, forcing many Jews to flee — some even on foot, such as this family leaving Yemen in 1949.

Beautiful synagogues, such as *Beit Knesset Eliyahu HaNavi* in Cairo, were left practically bereft.

Chapter Eleven: Leader of a Renaissance ☐ 229

The authorities weren't about to allow a few hundred thousand immigrants from Iraq and Yemen to undo all of their work. When the Sephardic Jews arrived in Israel in the late 1940s and early 1950s, they were placed in *maabarot*, transit camps, where they lived in tents for a minimum of five months. Their children were placed in educational institutions and were taught by secular educators who filled the children's impressionable minds with heresy.[4] They taught the children that Torah and mitzvot were necessary only in *galut* (exile), and here in Israel they no longer had to remain religious in order to be Jewish. They forcibly cut off the boys' *peyot* (called *simanim* by the Yemenite Jews) and the girls' braids.[5] They also introduced them to secular and immodest practices, such as mixed dancing, to induce them to drop religion.

When the parents saw what was happening to their children, they tried to protest, but they met with stonewalling or even threats that if they would insist on educating their children in the *galut* mentality, their children would be taken away from them.[6] The children,

---

4. The accounts in this section, which might seem highly exaggerated, were the subject of a Knesset investigation in the early 1950s. Although some members of the establishment — and especially then-Education Minister and future third President of Israel Zalman Shazar — denied the allegations, eyewitness reports and personal accounts by many of the children documented in the Knesset protocols are extremely damning.

The Knesset undertook to investigate the matter only after Jewish organizations from the United States and England sent telegrams expressing alarm about reports of anti-religious coercion in the *maabarot*. These telegrams caused panic among leading politicians, because Israel was reliant on donations from overseas and could not afford to have negative reports circulating in the Diaspora.

Particularly compelling is the report of Rav Yitzchak Meir Levin, Agudat Yisrael's first Knesset member. He told the investigative committee that when the initial reports of religious coercion were received, he was overseas, and he tried to soothe local Jewish leaders, telling them that it was highly unlikely that such severe abuse was being committed in Israel. To his shock, he stated, when he returned to Israel and visited the *maabarot*, he found the reports to be understated, not exaggerated.

Documentation of the saga, including much of the official Knesset protocol, is published in a pamphlet, *L'maan Daat*, by Moshe Shonfeld.

5. Braids were considered the most modest way for a girl to wear her hair. When the Knesset committee investigated reports of these abuses, the leaders of the youth divisions of the *maabarot* claimed that they only removed long hair from children infected with lice. The children stated, however, that they were never examined. They were sent to a barber for a haircut, and if they protested as they realized that the barber was about to remove their *simanim*, they were held down by a youth counselor so the barber could cut off the *simanim*.

6. One of the atrocities committed against Sephardic immigrants of that period involved the saga of the *Yaldei Teiman* (literally, children of Yemen). Young women from Yemen who gave birth in Israel were often told that their children had died, but they weren't given their children for burial. It is believed that the secular authorities kidnapped these babies and gave them to

many of whom were drawn to the free lifestyle they had been exposed to, rebelled against their parents and embraced Israeli "culture."

Rav Benzion Mutzafi[7] describes how Sephardic Jews who had so been so faithful to Torah in Arab countries were sadly forced away from religion in the Jewish state.

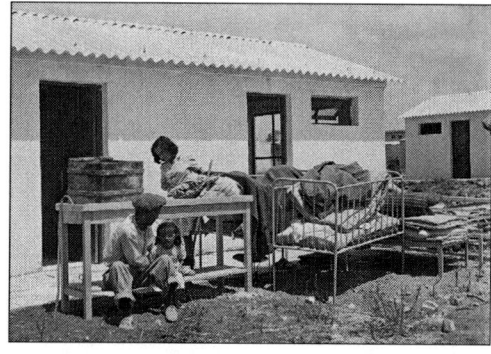

To religious parents, worse than the squalor of the *maabarot* were the concerted efforts to lure their children away from tradition.

"There were people who came here with *tefillin*," recounts Rav Mutzafi, "and they took them to kibbutzim and wrapped their *tefillin* on a horse to show them that this was 'old-fashioned,' and that this lifestyle wasn't appropriate in Eretz Yisrael.

"There were women who landed here in garments that retained the beautiful *tzeniut* standards of their original communities. As they descended from the airplane, a group of secular Israeli women tore their outer garments off them and shrieked, 'We don't dress like that here.'

"The secularists were so successful," adds Rav Mutzafi, "that even children of rabbanim didn't go to Torah schools. Hacham

---

secular couples or placed them into institutions where they would be raised as secular Jews. Several efforts to force the government to investigate the matter and release official reports were scuttled. (See *Hayeled Einenu — Parashat Yaldei Teiman*, by Shoshana Zeid.)

Harav Ovadia addressed this atrocity in *Yabia Omer*, Vol. 9, *Yoreh Dei'ah* 36. As part of the effort to uncover the true story, people wanted to open some of the graves in which the authorities had told them their children were "buried" to see whether there were really bodies in those graves. In general, one may not open a grave, because it is considered a lack of respect for the deceased. Harav Ovadia ruled, however, that in this case there was a signficant benefit to opening the graves, and he proves from the *poskim* that one may open a grave if there is a significant benefit to be gained by doing so.

7. Rav Benzion Mutzafi is a son of the great *mekubal* Hacham Salman Mutzafi. He studied in Porat Yosef under Rav Ezra Attia, and served as the yeshiva's *mashgiah* for three years in the late 1970s. About 1980, he began to expand Bnei Zion, the yeshiva his father founded first in Baghdad in 5687/1927 and then reestablished in Yerushalayim in 5702/1942.

He has authored many works, including *Sh'eilot V'Teshuvot Mevaseret Zion*, and lectures in many *batei knesset* in Eretz Yisrael. He is also widely respected for his ability to answer impromptu questions on any Torah topic on radio shows and similar forums.

Greeting lifelong friend Rav Yehuda Tzadka

Yehuda Tzadka [*Menahel Ruhani* of Porat Yosef] related that in those early years of the State, he once gave a Sephardic Jew a blessing that his child should grow up to be a *ben Torah*.

"'Don't curse me!' the man replied indignantly. 'Curse your own son!'

"'Why is it a curse?' Rav Tzadka asked.

"'Because a person who learns Torah is poverty-stricken,' the man retorted."

By the time Harav Ovadia returned from Egypt in 1950, tremendous damage had already been inflicted on Sephardic communities.

Few families were interested in having their children enrolled in a serious Torah environment; they didn't see any future in Torah study, and they wanted their children to have an easier, more comfortable life.

In addition, there were few Torah role models for Sephardic children to look up to, and even the official religious bureaus discriminated against Sephardim. In his eulogy on Rav Yaakov Moshe Toledano,[8] who preceded him as chief rabbi of Tel Aviv, Harav Ovadia described how the early Ministers of Religious Affairs would appoint Ashkenazi rabbanim to positions of "chief rabbi," while Sephardic rabbanim of equal or greater scholarship were deemed "community rabbis," and received a salary that was miniscule compared to those of chief rabbis. This changed only when Rav Toledano accepted the role of Minister of Religious Affairs in 1958.

Rav Yaakov Moshe Toledano, who finally gave equal recognition to Sephardic rabbis

Filling the Void

A TELLING PICTURE OF the state of Sephardic Jewry in those years was painted in 1955 by Rabbi Shlomo Yosef Zevin,[9] a member of the board that awarded Harav Ovadia's first volume of *Yabia Omer* the Rav Kook Prize for Torah Literature:

---

8. Published in *Hazon Ovadia, Arba Taaniyot*, p. 471.
9. Rabbi Zevin was an extraordinary Torah scholar with a rare background, having studied in both Lithuanian and Hasidic yeshivot. He was highly respected by all streams of religious Jewry. A prolific author and deep thinker, he was a founding editor of *Encyclopedia Talmudit* and the author of many Torah works.

Rav Shlomo Yosef Zevin (L) foresaw a beautiful future for Sephardic Jewry in the young Harav Ovadia.

We have grown accustomed to thinking that Torah has dwindled in the Sephardic communities.... It is not so. The light of God has yet to become extinguished among our Sephardic brethren; from time to time we see this in their creation of Torah literature. One of the best and most prominent of these creations is *Yabia Omer*. The author is but a young man, but he is already a *gadol baTorah*....

Into this Torah void stepped Harav Ovadia, with the second prong in his campaign of *Lehahzir Atara Leyoshna*. Much as he deemed it vital to unite the Sephardim under one halachic umbrella, he also recognized that there was a more immediate need: to impress upon Sephardim the importance of keeping halacha and teach them the halachot a Jew must keep.

By the time Harav Ovadia passed away, says Rav Mutzafi, the entire Torah world recognized that Harav Ovadia had singlehandedly taken a community that seemed to have no future in terms of Torah study and observance, and had developed it into a proud community of tens of thousands of Torah-true families.

WHEN HARAV OVADIA BEGAN TO DELIVER *SHIURIM* AGAIN in Beit Knesset Ohel Rahel in 1951, he realized that he wouldn't

"We Want a Story!"

necessarily have an audience unless he could draw people through some gimmick. The people who came to the *shiur* were simple laborers, and while they did want to learn Torah and halacha, they weren't likely to last day after day at a *shiur*. Harav Ovadia came up with an ingenious strategy: In addition to the humor and stories he always injected

Although Harav Ovadia's audience included serious scholars, he was willing to tell a serialized story in order to draw laymen to study Torah.

into his *shiurim*, he would tell a serial story. Each day, he would tell his students part of a story, so that they could hear the entire story only if they came to the *shiur* every night.

While the serialized story succeeded in drawing the crowd back each night, the promise of a story at the end still couldn't keep simple laymen interested in a 2½-hour *shiur* with no break. They would often interrupt Harav Ovadia, saying, "*Lo hamidrash ha'ikar, ela hamaase.*" What *Hazal* intended with these words is that studying Torah is not enough; one must also follow through in *maase*, action. *Maase* also means a story, however, and Harav Ovadia's audience was trying to tell him that the Torah portion of the lecture was less important to them than the story.

ONE WOULD IMAGINE THAT HARAV OVADIA — WHO DEVOTED his mornings to writing the most complex *teshuvot* on halachic issues of the day, spent his afternoons studying with some of Yerushalayim's greatest scholars, and had already served as rosh yeshiva for advanced students for three years — would soon tire of having to

Beginning of a Revolution

descend to the level of these laymen. But he didn't. He would show up each night and deliver his *shiur* with zest, placing his own personal advancement in learning aside for hours each day because he realized that in order to draw Sephardim back to Torah, he had to create a social revolution that would start with the adults. Even Sephardim who had resisted the forceful secularization and remained religious wanted to give their children vocational training or educate them as professionals. "If they don't get trained, how will they have *parnassa*?" they wondered. Instead of sending their children to Porat Yosef, they enrolled them in *dati-leumi* (national-religious) high schools, which would eventually lead to their entering the army and then earning a degree or learning a vocation.

Harav Ovadia realized that he first had to impress upon the adults the importance and beauty of Torah, and only then could he influence them to send their children to institutions where they could become true *bnei Torah*. Even some of his most devout students were still concerned about their children's future, but Harav Ovadia soothed them. "Soon, the country will need lots of rabbanim and *dayanim*. If you send your children to Torah institutions, they'll become leaders of Klal Yisrael."

> *One participant in Harav Ovadia's shiur was willing to send his children to yeshivot, but he wasn't ready to make the commitment quite yet. "My oldest is in eighth grade now, and I'm sending him to a national-religious high school," he told Harav Ovadia. "I need to know that at least one of my children will have parnassa."*
>
> *"Today," relates Rav Yitzchak Yosef, "this man's three younger sons are highly respected rabbanim in three different cities. The oldest son, who trained as an electrician in deference to his father's wishes to have one son with parnassa, is a fine Jew who learns Torah and fulfills mitzvot, but he is envious of his younger brothers, who are great Torah scholars — and have at least as much parnassa as he does."*

RAV AVRAHAM YOSEF, THE OLDEST OF HARAV OVADIA'S SONS to survive him,[10] recalls those days with nostalgia:

The Nightly Shiur My father would take me and my brother Yaakov to his *shiur* even when we were five or six. I can't say that we really understood much, but he took us along every night.[11]

Who came to the *shiur* back then? A couple of Iraqis, one Moroccan, mostly Isfahanim[12] (Persians) — a conglomerate of Jews from different nationalities, with a grand total of about twenty-five participants. That was all! It was the only *shiur* of its kind in Yerushalayim back then. It lasted for two-and-a-half hours: one hour was Gemara, and the rest was halacha.

Eventually, the *shiur* started to gain fame through word-of-mouth, and yeshiva students also started to attend: a few from Porat Yosef, some from Novardhok [the most famous of whom is Rav Reuven Elbaz], and a few

Rav Reuven Elbaz (R), Rosh Yeshivat Ohr HaHaim, one of the scholars who attended Harav Ovadia's *shiur* in the 1950s, at the wedding of Rav Yaakov Yosef, Harav Ovadia's oldest son

10. Rav Yaakov passed away a few months before Harav Ovadia.
11. Rav David Yosef, who was born in the 1960s, recalls his father taking him to the nightly *shiur* as a young child. The *shiur* would end at 11 p.m., and little David would invariably fall asleep during the *shiur*. Rabbanit Margalit asked Harav Ovadia why he continued to take his young son. "Wouldn't it be better to let him fall asleep in his bed?" she wondered.
 "I want him to hear the words of Torah, to get used to the sound of learning."
 Rav David relates, however, that he still remembers some of the actual halachot that he heard back then.
12. Isfahan is a large city in Iran.

Chapter Eleven: Leader of a Renaissance

from Hevron. The subject matter was *hilchot issur v'heter*, and these students would prepare beforehand, studying the Tur and Beit Yosef intensively, because they knew that if they wanted to pass an exam from Abba, they had better know Beit Yosef inside and out.

They weren't young *bahurim* — they were in their 20s, already accomplished scholars — and yet they would walk out of a *shiur* that was aimed primarily at simple laymen amazed by the depth and clarity of the *shiur*. They would take deep pleasure in listening to his analysis of the halachot.

One of the participants had previously served as a rav in France, and when he decided to move to Eretz Yisrael, the community presented him with a Citroen car as a parting gift. This rav would pick up my father and drive him to the *shiur*, a Grundig tape recorder with giant reels in tow, and he would record the *shiur*.

Once, Abba asked him, "Why do you record the *shiur*?"

"The Rav speaks quickly," he replied, "and I understand slowly. If I listen two or three times, I understand."

This rav never told Abba that as he listened to those *shiurim*, he took copious notes, filling dozens of notebooks. Rav Shlomo Moshe Amar[13] told me that decades later, he reviewed these *shiurim* with that rav, and he was amazed by the *hiddushim* (novel interpretations) Abba was delivering all the way back then.

"But what was Abba's primary intention in delivering those *shiurim*?" concludes Rav Avraham. "To turn an eclectic group of laymen into *poskim* in *Hilchot Issur V'Heter*? Certainly not. He wanted to have an effect on their children."

Harav Ovadia lived to see the fruit of these efforts.

Eight or nine years before his passing, relates Rav Avraham, Harav Ovadia was working on a volume of *Hazon Ovadia* on *Hilchot Succa*. As was his wont when writing his *sefarim*, he asked his assistants to get him all the printed works available on

---

13. The Rishon LeZion for the last decade of Harav Ovadia's life.

the topic — even those of modern-day scholars far younger than he. He would take a *sefer* with him when he retired for the night, which meant that he would spend a few hours reading the volume, and by morning he would have memorized everything the author wrote.

"One morning," says Rav Avraham, "as soon as he got up, he asked my brother Rav Moshe[14] to find out who this author was. 'His name is Raz,' he said.

"'Can you find out if he is related to Benzion Raz?' my father asked.

"My brother said, 'Abba, how am I supposed to find out now, at this early hour?'

"'I'm relying on you to find him,' my father answered simply.

"Heaven ordained that on that very morning, Benzion Raz — the person Abba was looking for — came to the *tefillah* in Abba's *beit knesset*. My brother brought him over to Abba, who asked, 'Is this author your grandson?'

"'Yes,' Benzion answered.

"Abba beamed with joy. 'Why is the rav so happy?' R' Benzion asked.

"'It was worth investing all of those nights giving that *shiur*,' replied Abba, 'just to get one gem such as your grandson, who knows how to present material in such a well-organized, clear manner. I so enjoyed reading his *sefer*!'

"And R' Benzion's grandson wasn't the only one. Abba wasn't focusing only on those actually participating in the *shiur*; his eyes were on the future generations that would come from those participants.

"There was a fellow named Yehuda Naki, who used to give out tea at those *shiurim*. A few years before Abba passed away, a *ben Torah* came to visit him and said, "I'm the grandson of Yehuda Naki, who used to bring you tea." Abba hugged and kissed him, and said, 'Had I invested in that community only to see the grandchildren and great-grandchildren that came forth from them, *dayenu*.'"[15]

---

14. Harav Ovadia lived with his son Rav Moshe for the last twenty years of his life. See Chapter 31.
15. Lit., *it is enough*; paraphrased from the Pesah Haggada.

Yeshivat Ohr Torah

IN ADDITION TO HIS EFFORTS TO TEACH TORAH TO THE MASSes of uneducated Sephardic Jews, Harav Ovadia identified two other systemic failures in his community, and he endeavored to solve both in one go.

One problem, he felt, was that although Yeshivat Porat Yosef excelled at training students to learn, they learned at a slow pace. The Sephardic community urgently needed rabbanim to teach Torah and rule in halacha, and at the pace of study in Porat Yosef, they wouldn't develop quickly enough to fill the gaping need for Torah teachers and *poskim*. The second issue was that the learning at Porat Yosef ended at 6 in the afternoon, and there was no organized place for Sephardic boys and married men to learn in the evening.

It appears that these two considerations led him to establish Yeshiva Ohr Torah, the first night kollel for Sephardim.[16] He released a *Kol Koreh* (proclamation) before the inauguration of Ohr Torah on 1 Adar 5714, explaining that "the purpose of the yeshiva is to fill the spiritual void that has been created, specifically among Sephardim and those of the Eastern communities."[17]

The inauguration was graced with the presence of Rav Ezra Attia and Rav Ephraim Cohen, Harav Ovadia's rebbeim from Porat Yosef, along with Rav David Jungreis and Rav Pinchas Epstein of the Eida Haredit. Rav Herzog and Rav Tzvi Pesach Frank were considered the patrons of the yeshiva, although it was run exclusively by the 33-year-old Harav Ovadia.

Harav Ovadia speaks at the inauguration of Ohr Torah, with many of the greatest Torah leaders of Yerushalayim in attendance.

---

16. *Posek HaDor*, pp. 31; 36-37.
17. The term ספרדים, in a technical sense, refers to Jews of Spanish descent (in Hebrew, Spain is ספרד). In an effort to include Sephardim hailing from the Middle East and Africa, a broader term has developed over the years: ספרדים ועדות המזרח, Sephardim and Communities of the East.

In the 1950s, they learned in his Kollel Ohr Torah.
Thirty years later, Harav Ovadia tapped
Rav Shalom Cohen (R) and Rav Shimon Ba'adani (M)
to join him on the *Moetzet Hachmei HaTorah*.

A contractor by the name of Shlomo Cohen took upon himself the administrative end of the yeshiva, providing twenty *avreichim* (married men) with a stipend of five Israeli lira each month to enable them to devote their evenings to learning. This group of scholars was joined by an ever-increasing cadre of laymen who were already attending Harav Ovadia's nightly *shiurim*.

The studies at Ohr Torah began at 7 p.m. and lasted well into the night. Harav Ovadia's official title was *nasi* (leader) of the yeshiva, though he didn't draw a salary from the position. His old friend Rav Benzion Abba Shaul served as the *meishiv* in the yeshiva, answering questions from the other *avreichim*.

Harav Ovadia insisted that the *avreichim* learn at a swift pace, instructing them to learn Gemara with just two commentaries, *Rashi* and the *Rosh*, and then move on to studying the halachic ramifications of the *sugyot* they were learning. This was the beginning of another lifelong goal: to get *avreichim* to learn practical halacha. He grew increasingly outspoken about men who spent many years in the *beit midrash* learning *sugyot* with all the *lomdut*, but did not even know halacha for themselves, let alone to rule for others.[18]

Two of the *avreichim* in Ohr Torah were Rav Shalom Cohen (son of Rav Ephraim Cohen) and Rav Shimon Ba'adani — both of whom would become the founding members of Shas's *Moetzet Hachmei HaTorah*, along with Harav Ovadia and Rav Shabtai Aton, in the early 1980s.

THE *SHIURIM* DELIVERED IN OHR TORAH, BOTH TO THE Torah scholars and the laymen, were building blocks for adult Torah education, one of Harav Ovadia's passions throughout his life. Incredibly, not once did he request payment for delivering *shiurim*. Although some *batei knesset* in which he delivered steady *shiurim* did gather funds to pay him a small salary, Harav Ovadia was equally ready to deliver a *shiur* without pay.

Unpaid Positions

In fact, his most famous *shiur* — the weekly Motza'ei Shabbat lecture in Beit Knesset HaYazdim in Yerushalayim — was an unpaid endeavor.

> A fellow had recorded Harav Ovadia's Motza'ei Shabbat shiur for many years, and began to produce tapes and sell them in batei knesset. A few months after he began this enterprise, another fellow began to record the shiurim and sell the recordings. The first fellow claimed that the second was infringing on his business, which is prohibited under the halacha of hasagat gvul.
>
> "There is no hasagat gvul here," Harav Ovadia ruled immediately upon hearing the claim. "The Torah that I teach here belongs to me, and I make it hefker (free) for all takers. Anyone who wants to disseminate this Torah — whether in recorded or written form — is welcome to do so!"[19]

---

18. In his lengthy introduction to the first volume of *Yabia Omer*, published during the same year as Ohr Torah was established, he details his vision for the correct approach to learning — and especially the vital need not to suffice with understanding the *sugyot* on an intellectual level, but to know the halacha that emerges from those *sugyot*.
19. Rav David Yosef.

ANOTHER PRINCIPLE HARAV OVADIA SET FOR HIMSELF WAS that he was willing to deliver a *shiur* to even a small group of people. His children tell incredible stories of how he was willing to travel to far ends of the city — and even the country — to teach Torah.

No Shiur Too Small

> *Rav David Yosef relates that when he was a young married man, he would learn with his father each night. One day, Harav Ovadia summoned him and said, "It's time for you to begin teaching Torah as well, not just learn for yourself. I want you to start delivering a shiur somewhere."*
>
> *Following his father's instructions, Rav David began to deliver a shiur in Katamon, under the aegis of Agudat Yisrael's "Torah La'am" movement that organized Torah lectures throughout Israel.*
>
> *Shortly thereafter, Rav David was learning with his father one night, when he suddenly excused himself. "Abba," he said, "I need to go prepare for the shiur I'm supposed to deliver."*
>
> *"But I want to continue learning with you," Harav Ovadia replied. "I'll tell you what — continue learning with me now, and I'll deliver the shiur in your place tonight."*
>
> *When it came time to deliver the shiur, Harav Ovadia instructed Rav David to continue learning, telling him that they would resume their study session when he got back.*
>
> *This wasn't the only time this happened; in those years, Harav Ovadia, who was already Rishon LeZion, often offered to "substitute" for Rav David.*
>
> *"Mine quickly became the most popular shiur in Yerushalayim," recalls Rav David, "because everyone came in the hopes that the substitute would be there that week!"*

Harav Ovadia's readiness to run to the other end of Yerushalayim to deliver a *shiur* had nothing to do with family bonds.

> *Rav Avraham Yosef relates that there was a young man studying in Yeshiva Mercaz HaRav, a hesder yeshiva, who*

"Everyone came to hear the substitute maggid shiur!" Rav David Yosef with his father.

was just beginning to grow into a Torah scholar. Bursting with energy and spiritual zeal, he decided to start a Daf Yomi shiur in his neighborhood. "Daf" and "Yomi" turned out to be impossible with the group that attended his shiur, so it morphed into a nightly Gemara shiur in which he taught a few lines of Masechet Berachot — but he taught them well. It took over a year to learn the entire masechet, and when it was time for the siyum, he wanted to make a memorable celebration to encourage more people to join his shiur. He told the rav of the neighborhood that he wanted to invite a widely respected figure to speak at the event. "Whom do you have in mind?" the rav asked.

"Harav Ovadia Yosef," the young man answered.

"Are you kidding?" the rav replied incredulously. "You think the Rishon LeZion has time to come to a siyum for a handful of men?"

This young man was not easily deterred, however, and he decided to visit Harav Ovadia's office to invite him. No sooner did he explain the circumstances than Harav Ovadia summoned his secretary. "When do I have an opening for a siyum?" *he asked. She told him when there was an opening, and the budding scholar scheduled the siyum for that date.*

"This young man is now one of the leading teachers of Torah in Eretz Yisrael," relates Rav Avraham Yosef, "and he attributes it all to that moment when Abba showed him that his efforts to teach Torah — even to a small group — were important enough for the Rishon LeZion to make time to attend the siyum."

No Kids, No Goats

HARAV OVADIA'S TORAH TEACHING WAS FOCUSED ALMOST exclusively on adults, for he felt that teaching them the beauty of Torah would lead them to send their children to Torah institutions. He didn't rely entirely on this indirect method of encouraging enrollment in Torah institutions, however. During those same busy years, while writing his *sefarim*, learning in Midrash Bnei Zion, and teaching Torah at night, he somehow found time for another important endeavor that would turn into an endless mission: enrolling more and more children into Torah institutions. Toward this end, he was willing to travel the length and breadth of the land, risking both his livelihood and his own future prospects in order to benefit the Jewish people.

CHAPTER TWELVE
FOR THE FUTURE OF KLAL YISRAEL

WHILE ADULT EDUCATION WAS IMPORTANT to Harav Ovadia, he realized that the only way to reconnect Sephardic Jewry to the Torah was to ensure that the next generation would receive a Torah education. From the early 1950s until his passing, he devoted an inestimable amount of time and effort to encourage Sephardi parents to send their children to Torah schools, rather than the seemingly glittering alternatives that beckoned — especially in the early days of the State of Israel.

IN ORDER TO UNDERSTAND THE DIFFICULTY HARAV OVADIA faced in signing children up for Torah-true education, one must first understand the background of the educational system in place in Eretz Yisrael in those days.

Four Streams

During the early 1920s, when Mandatory rule took effect, the British authorities did not set up a school system in Israel. Rather, they recognized three streams of Jewish education, controlled by Jewish organizations that were active in the country:

Harav Ovadia being greeted by schoolchildren in a town in the South, as part of his effort to grant every child in Israel a Torah education

1. *Zerem Haklali* — the general stream. The stated educational objective of this school system, which comprised the overwhelming majority of school-age children, was to teach "secular studies according to the culture of Israel."[1]

2. *Zerem Ha'ovdim* — the workers' stream. This second-largest stream belonged to the socialist movement, which was extremely active in building *kibbutzim* and *moshavim* throughout the land. Their doctrine was to train children to follow in the footsteps of the *halutzim* (pioneers) who were laboring to cultivate the land under a purely socialist economic model.

3. *Zerem HaMizrahi* — Named for its affiliation with the Mizrahi movement, this stream of schools taught Torah studies alongside secular studies. Their official goal was to encourage children graduating from their elementary schools to attend Bnei Akiva yeshiva high schools, where Torah studies were primary and secular studies were secondary, but they also created high schools for young men who wanted to focus more on their secular studies than on their Torah studies.

At that point, the hareidi *hinuch* institutions, often called Talmudei Torah, were in a no-man's land. They were not recognized by the British authorities, and therefore received no funding from them. On the other hand, since they received no fund-

---

1. "Israel" here refers not to the state, which only came into existence close to three decades later, but to a vague concept of *Am Yisrael* as a nation, without specification of what defines a person as part of "Israel."

ing, they were not required to submit to any sort of curriculum regulation.²

The "Status Quo"

WITH UNREST MOUNTING IN ERETZ YISRAEL, THE BRITISH government asked the UN to send an investigative committee to make recommendations regarding the future governance of the land. The committee, called UNSCOP (United Nations Special Committee on Palestine), spent a few months gathering testimony from various leaders. The Arabs boycotted the committee, while Jewish officials cooperated with it.

In an effort to secure the broadest-possible support base for Israeli independence, David Ben-Gurion, then-chairman of the Jewish Agency and soon to be the country's first prime minister, exchanged letters with R' Yitzchak Meir Levin, son-in-law of the Gerrer Rebbe and the lay leader of Agudat Yisrael in Eretz Yisrael. In one letter, R' Levin asked Ben-Gurion to delineate the future state's stance toward religion. Ben-Gurion wrote back a famous letter, called the "Status Quo Letter," in which he issued four assurances:

Rav Yitzchak Meir Levin, who secured a "Status Quo" agreement from future Prime Minister David Ben-Gurion

1. Shabbat would be the official day of rest in Israel.³

---

2. One myth that has led to great misunderstanding on the part of Diaspora Jews in recent years is that children in Torah schools in Israel do not receive any secular education, even in math and language. This is generally untrue; even in schools that will not allow their curriculum to be dictated by the government, students are taught the basic subjects needed to communicate and interact with society in business and other settings.
3. This eventually became anchored into law in 1951, when the Knesset passed a bill, *Hok Sha'ot Ha'avoda Vehamenuha*, the Hours of Work and Rest Law, which governs when an employer is

2. Official government bodies would guard the laws of *kashrut*.⁴
3. Marriage and divorce would be under the control of the religious authorities.⁵
4. Religious Jews would retain autonomy over the education of their children, with a minimal requirement to teach language, some history, and some science.

With that letter in hand,⁶ R' Levin —under the guidance of the Agudah's Rabbinic leadership — joined those who recommended to UNSCOP that a Jewish state should be created in the region.⁷

Exemption for Talmud Torahs

FROM 1948, WHEN ISRAEL DECLARED INDEPENDENCE, UNTIL 1953, the educational system continued to operate under the "streams" arrangement, with the addition of a fourth stream: the Agudat Yisrael school system. In keeping with Ben-Gurion's fourth assurance, this system was autonomous, but it had to include a minimum of secular studies. At the same time, however, there were many Talmud Torahs and yeshivot that did not become part of this *Zerem Harevi'i* (fourth stream), and remained completely autonomous in terms of the subject matter they taught and even in the

---

allowed to employ workers. Part of the law prohibits employers from employing workers on Shabbat.

4. This manifested itself in all government kitchens, including the kitchens on IDF bases, being at least nominally kosher. In addition, it has been the generally accepted practice that government officials do not eat obviously nonkosher food while on official state missions.

5. This was anchored into law in 1953, when the Knesset passed a bill requiring all marriages and divorces to be administered by the rabbinical *batei din*. As explained elsewhere (see p. 141, fn. 15), this bill was vital in ensuring the integrity of Jewish lineage.

6. Many religious Jews were pleased with the Status Quo Letter, but R' Levin himself was more concerned than excited. In response to a congratulatory letter from Moreinu R' Yaakov Rosenheim, he wrote, presciently, "How my heart is pained that we have descended to the point that a pledge of a status quo on religious matters is considered an accomplishment. I am trembling and full of prayer to Hashem: trembling in fear of Jewish blood that will be shed in a war with the Arabs, and trembling in fear of the war with the secularists following that war. I am concerned that there will be no escaping this war despite the guarantees of a status quo. How difficult this battle will be for us in our current state, when dissent, confusion, and a blurring of the minds reign among us…" (*Ha'ish Ufa'alo*, a biography of R' Yitzchak Meir Levin, p. 48).

7. Ultimately, UNSCOP recommended that the British end their Mandate and proposed the Partition Plan, which would establish two new states in the region, one Jewish and one Arab. The Jews accepted the proposal, but the Arabs rejected the plan, insisting that there be only one state under full Arab control. When the British ended their Mandate, the Jews declared independence, prompting an immediate attack by seven Arab nations.

language of instruction.⁸ Although Ben-Gurion had never officially exempted these schools from the requirement to teach some secular studies, the government did not enforce the secular studies stipulation in schools that were not part of the government educational system.

Aside from the transit camp schools, in which the government attempted to institute *hinuch ahid* (unified education) with no religious studies,⁹ the state generally kept its pledge granting autonomy to the Agudat Yisrael stream.

The Chinuch Atzmai System

IN 1953, AS THE KNESSET SLOWLY ANCHORED THE NASCENT country's official policies into law, the government decided to replace the four-stream system with a simplified system that included only two options: *mamlachti* and *mamlachti-dati* schools.

The *mamlachti* (national) system subsumed the first two of the four streams, which included some 80 percent of Israel's schoolchildren when the state was founded, and the *mamlachti-dati* (national-religious) system was meant to include all religious schools. Both systems would be officially recognized by the government, which meant that they would receive full funding from the state, freeing parents from the need to pay tuition.

Gedolei Yisrael strongly opposed government control over religious schools. The Hazon Ish was one of the most outspoken leaders of this opposition, stating that Torah teachers could not be employees of the state, because they would then be subject to government interference. He also foresaw that the state would insist on dictating the curriculum of the schools it was funding.

Eventually, an alternative to the *mamlachti* and *mamlachti-dati* systems was developed, called Chinuch Atzmai (lit., *independent education*). Schools in the Chinuch Atzmai system were governed

---

8. Some Ashkenazi schools preferred to continue teaching in Yiddish, because they viewed the adoption of Modern Hebrew as an everyday language as part of the Zionist effort to secularize the Jewish people. This intention was actually expressed openly by some secular Zionist leaders, who saw the adoption of a common language as a way to replace Torah, *has veshalom*, as the unifying bond connecting the Jewish people.
9. See p. 230.

The Hazon Ish (center) was extremely outspoken about government involvement in the curriculum for Torah schools.

by the same set of rules that had applied to the Agudat Yisrael system until then: they were autonomous, but they had to guarantee some minimal secular studies. Since it was not in control of the curriculum, the state agreed to fund only 60 percent of the Chinuch Atzmai budget; the rest had to be raised through tuition or private donations.

Most Beit Yaakov girls' schools in Israel became part of the Chinuch Atzmai system, as did a large network of boys' schools. There were still Talmud Torahs, however, that were categorically opposed to *any* government interference in their curriculum, and those institutions remained outside the official educational system. Some Talmud Torahs did receive minimal funding,[10] but most of them covered their budgets through tuition and fundraising — mostly abroad.[11]

---

10. These schools are called מוּכָּר שֶׁאֵינוּ רִשְׁמִי — recognized, but unofficial — as opposed to schools governed by anti-Zionist streams, which fall under the classification of לֹא מוּכָּר — not recognized — and receive no government funding whatsoever.

11. In recent years, the government has attempted to force these schools to include a mandatory core curriculum by threatening to cut the minimal funding they receive. This effort has met with

The Battle for the Country's Future

ALL OF THE PROTAGONISTS IN THE EARLY DAYS OF THE STATE rightly viewed the school system as the progenitor of the future Israeli society. The Mapai[12] leadership felt that if they could indoctrinate as much of society as possible with their concept of the "new Jew" who was no longer tied to Torah, they would eventually succeed in squelching all attachment to religion and creating a fully secular state. Torah leaders, *lehavdil*, realized that if they could maintain a school system in which children were taught Torah in its purest form, that would eventually lead to a religious renaissance in Eretz Yisrael.

Since national-religious schools accepted the secular government as a force in shaping future generations, their curriculum reflected a departure from traditional Torah values and an effort to design a new Jew — albeit one who was not as distant from Torah Judaism as the one the secularists were seeking to create. The Torah leaders in Eretz Yisrael — the young Harav Ovadia among them — determined that it was vital to sign up as many children as possible to Chinuch Atzmai schools, but they faced several major obstacles.

First, they had to ensure that the other 40 percent of the funding for the schools would be covered without burdening families with a heavy tuition bill. They realized that many families would not be willing — or able to afford — to pay tuition for their children,

Every soul was precious to Harav Ovadia, seen here surrounded by children at a *hachnasat Sefer Torah* in Beit Yisrael, Yerushalayim.

---

sharp opposition by the hareidi sector.

12. Mapai (מפא״י) is an acronym for Mifleget Poalei Eretz Yisrael. Led by Ben-Gurion, the party controlled the government for nearly 30 years. It eventually became the modern-day Labor party.

which meant that they would have to raise funds overseas to cover the deficit. Many of the greatest Torah leaders of the time, from both Eretz Yisrael and abroad, devoted prodigious energies to this effort. Rav Aharon Kotler was especially dedicated to the cause of Chinuch Atzmai; it is widely reported that he gave Chinuch Atzmai fundraising priority over that of his own fledgling yeshiva, Beth Midrash Govoha of Lakewood. Harav Ovadia eventually joined the fundraising circuit, raising many millions of dollars for the Chinuch Atzmai system — especially during his years as a Rishon LeZion.[13]

Second, they had to convince parents to sign their children up for the Chinuch Atzmai schools, and this was no easy task. Many parents were convinced that children who attended national-religious schools would eventually find jobs and a livelihood, while those who attended Chinuch Atzmai schools would be left without any prospects for earning a living.

On top of these difficulties, the government made it extremely difficult to transfer a child to a Chinuch Atzmai school. They allowed parents to switch their children only during one specific week of the year; anyone who missed that short window had to wait until the following year.

Furthermore, stories abound of how the government deliberately sabotaged efforts to enroll or transfer children to Chinuch Atzmai. For instance, bareheaded fathers who came to a municipal office to sign up their children for school were given the requisite form to fill out, because the officials assumed they were enrolling their children in the government-run school systems, but when a father walked in wearing a *kippa* on his head, the official would say, "We ran out of forms." This sly tactic was discovered when some fathers removed their *kippot* before walking into these offices, and the missing forms were suddenly available.[14]

---

13. It took great courage for a rav who, as a member of the Rabbanut, was an employee of the State, to raise funds for a school system that was competing with the official government-funded educational system.
14. *Hashorashim Le'ohr HaYahadut*, p. 17, as related by Shlomo Malka, who tried to help parents overcome the obstacles in switching their children to Torah schools.

HARAV OVADIA REALIZED THAT SEPHARDIC PARENTS WERE particularly vulnerable to government interference in their educational choices. Many of them had fled their home countries on little notice and had arrived in Eretz Yisrael practically penniless. The poverty they suffered caused many of them to place their children's financial future ahead of their spiritual success.

The Threat

Harav Ovadia embarked on a one-man campaign to sign up children for Chinuch Atzmai schools.[15]

The one-week period of the year in which parents could switch their children to Chinuch Atzmai was extremely intense for Harav Ovadia; each day he spent hours traveling on the primitive transportation system. One day he went to Rehovot, another day to Ashdod, then Ashkelon, then Yavneh — all in one week — to convince as many parents as possible to make the switch.

> R' Shlomo Lorincz, a Knesset member for the Agudat Yisrael party, met Harav Ovadia on a bus from Beer Sheva to Yerushalayim during the early 1950s. He asked Harav Ovadia what he was doing in Beer Sheva, and the latter explained that he had gone to convince parents to sign their children up for Chinuch Atzmai.
>
> "Which organization do you work for?" R' Lorincz asked.
>
> "No organization," Harav Ovadia replied.
>
> "And how do you get people to transfer their children to Torah schools?" R' Lorincz continued.
>
> "In each city," explained Harav Ovadia, "I gather as large a group as I can, and I speak to them between Minha and Arvit. I tell them stories of tzaddikim and some divrei Torah, and then I explain how much better their children will turn out if they send them to Torah schools."
>
> "Who pays your bus fare?" asked R' Lorincz.
>
> "I pay it myself," Harav Ovadia replied.
>
> That Harav Ovadia, who was himself poverty-stricken at

---

15. Much later on, in the early 1980s, he founded a school system run on the Chinuch Atzmai model, Maayan HaHinuch HaTorani, geared specifically toward Sephardic families, offering them an education based on Sephardic customs; see Chapter 22.

Rav Ovadia at a cornerstone-laying ceremony for Mayanei HaYeshua Medical Center in Bnei Brak. MK R' Shlomo Lorincz is second from right.

the time, would spend his own money to travel all over Israel for this endeavor, is one level of mesirut nefesh, but R' Lorincz could hardly believe just how selfless the young rav actually was. "Recently," Harav Ovadia shared, "I received a message from the Mizrahi party: They are upset that I'm encouraging parents to switch out of their national-religious school system into Chinuch Atzmai. They warned me that if I continue to travel from city to city doing this, they're going to scuttle any opportunities for me to advance in the Rabbanut."

"If this will affect your livelihood," suggested Rabbi Lorincz, "then maybe you're not required to continue?"

"This is pikuah nefesh for Sephardic Jewry," Harav Ovadia replied. "I'm prepared to forgo any future positions and overlook any considerations of my own livelihood to ensure that Sephardim learn in Talmud Torahs and yeshivot."

Leaders of the Mizrahi party followed through on their threat. For years, they prevented Harav Ovadia from receiving a position as a *dayan* in Yerushalayim, which would have enabled him to continue to deliver *shiurim* to his devoted students while earning the salary his family so desperately needed. And more than a decade after this encounter with Rabbi Lorincz, when Harav Ovadia was the only candidate for Sephardic chief rabbi of Tel Aviv,[16] the Mizrahi party delayed elections for months as they tried to convince others to run against him.[17]

HARAV OVADIA'S EFFORTS TO ENSURE THAT CHILDREN WOULD

For One Jewish Soul

receive a Torah education weren't limited to mass lectures in which he could convince dozens of parents at a time, nor were they limited to his younger years when he was relatively unknown. Even as chief rabbi, he would drop everything and run to convince one parent to transfer a child to a Torah school.

> *Once, a principal of a Torah school in Ramot visited Harav Ovadia to discuss an issue he was grappling with. There were two brothers enrolled in his school, and the parents had just informed him that they were switching their sons to a national-religious school for the following school year. The principal was extremely disappointed, because these children were showing great potential in their Torah studies. He came to ask Harav Ovadia for advice on how to convince the parents not to transfer their boys to the other school.*
>
> *"Did you come by car?" Harav Ovadia asked.*
>
> *"Yes," the principal replied.*
>
> *"I'm sorry," said Harav Ovadia, "but my driver is not here. Would you mind driving me to this family's home?"*
>
> *The principal shifted uncomfortably. "Kevod haRav," he stammered, "My car is a jalopy. It's not appropriate for the honored rav to travel in such a beat-up car."*
>
> *Harav Ovadia waved his hand dismissively; the state of the principal's car made not a whit of a difference when*

---

16. See p. 329.
17. Rav Yitzchak Yosef.

Harav Ovadia was willing to travel far and wide for Torah education.
Visiting schoolchildren of Persian descent in Los Angeles.

Jewish souls were at stake. He donned his glima and, accompanied by the shocked principal, headed out to the car.

"As I was driving," the principal later recalled, "I kept seeing the same reaction. Passersby glanced into the passenger seat, then turned their heads for a better look, their eyes opening wide. What was Harav Ovadia Yosef, the Rishon LeZion, doing in such a clunker?

"We arrived at the home and knocked on the door. The boys' father opened the door in his undershirt. He took one look at Harav Ovadia standing there in his glima and dashed back into his apartment to put on a shirt. Harav Ovadia waited patiently, and after the fellow invited him in, he sat at the table and discussed the importance of a Torah education. By the time he finished, the man was convinced, and the boys were reenrolled in our school."[18]

---

18. Rav Zamir Cohen of Hidabroot.

The Visit Does the Trick

EVEN AS HIS PHYSICAL CONDITION DETERIORATED AS HE grew older, Harav Ovadia still made "house calls" if that would grant another Jewish child a Torah education.

Once, in his later years, on his way out of his weekly Motza'ei Shabbat shiur, Harav Ovadia heard a man shouting, "Let me talk to the rav! Let me talk to the rav!"

Harav Ovadia turned to see who was shouting, and he saw some other people pushing the man away from him. "Why are you pushing him?" Harav Ovadia reproved them. "Let him speak."

"I have a problem," the man cried. "I want to enroll my child into a Torah school, and they won't accept him."

"Why won't they accept him?" Harav Ovadia inquired.

"Because we have a television in our home."

"So why don't you get rid of it?"

"I want to," the man sighed, "but my wife won't hear of it."

"What's your address?"

The man turned white. "The rav doesn't have to come to my home," he whispered.

"Just tell me your address," Harav Ovadia repeated.

The man gave him the address, and then tore out of the beit knesset in a mad rush. He jumped into a cab and raced home. "Quick," he told his wife, "we have to clean up. Harav Ovadia Yosef is coming to our house."

His wife thought he had lost his mind. "Harav Ovadia Yosef has nothing better to do with his time than to come to our home?" she asked incredulously.

"Don't ask questions," her husband replied, as he ran around straightening up the house. "Just trust me and get the house ready."

No sooner had they finished tidying the house than there was a knock at the door. It was Harav Ovadia.

They invited him in, and before he could even begin to speak about how much nahat the woman would have if her children would attend a Torah school, she said, "If this is so important to the rav that he's willing to come to my house, I'm getting rid of the television right this minute so we can enroll my son in a Talmud Torah."[19]

The Adopted Street Youth

OVER THE YEARS, HARAV OVADIA WOULD REAP HIS OWN *nahat* when he would see the *talmidei hachamim* who developed as a result of his efforts to enroll them in Torah schools as children.

Sometimes, his role was far more active than just convincing parents to send their children to Torah schools.

A few years before Harav Ovadia's passing, a young man named Elisha was traveling on a bus to Teveria, and an older man with an obviously rabbinic appearance sat down next to him. They struck up a conversation, and Elisha

Testing students who attended his *shiur* in *Beit Knesset Ha'orpalim* during the 1950s, with his father-in-law Hacham Avraham Fattal seated next to him. Harav Ovadia would derive personal pride when his students grew into *talmidei hachamim*.

---

19. Rav Avraham Yosef.

mentioned that he worked with street youth, attempting to bring them closer to Judaism. The rav took an avid interest in these activities, and when Elisha expressed surprise that he would be so curious about his work with street youth, the rav explained, "You don't realize — I didn't always look like this.

"I grew up in the aftermath of World War II. My parents were Holocaust survivors who were just trying to make ends meet, and were too broken from the war to raise me. I ended up spending more time on the street than in my home, and even before my bar mitzva, I had earned the title, 'Ha'avaryan' (the criminal). Each Shabbat, my friends and I would spend hours hanging out or playing soccer. Our 'soccer field' was the street right next to a beit knesset, and one Shabbat morning, as I kicked the ball into the air, a rabbi walked out of the beit knesset. The ball scored a direct hit on his hat, knocking it off and making it sail a few feet away, sending me and my friends into uproarious laughter. The rav calmly retrieved his hat and placed it back on his head. Then he walked over to me.

"Full of street swagger, and wanting to prove my mettle to my friends, I asked him, 'Do you want to join our game?'

"My friends laughed again, but to my surprise, the rav wasn't angered by our gall. 'Would you like to come to my house to eat?' he asked me.

"'Actually,' I admitted, 'I'm starving. I wouldn't mind eating something.'

"The rav took me to his home, made Kiddush, and gave me some food. When I finished my portion, he asked whether I would like some more. I rarely got such good food, so I said yes. Only later on did I find out that I had eaten his portion.

"When I finished eating, he asked whether I wanted to rest. I said yes, and he set up a bed for me.

"I woke up many hours later, when Shabbat was over. 'What would you like to do now?' the rav asked.

"'I want to go to the cinema,' I said, 'but it costs 1½ lira.'

"The rav took out some money and gave it to me, but only on condition that I would return to his home.

"When I returned, I realized that I was one of twelve boys that he had 'adopted' in this manner, giving of his time and his money to make them feel at home.

"I slowly began to learn how to live as a Jew, and when I grew close enough to Judaism, he bought me tefillin. He paid someone to study Torah with me, and he also learned with me on occasion. Eventually he enrolled me in a yeshiva, and when it came time for me to marry, he was the mesader kiddushin. A few years later, when I wanted to take the tests to become a dayan on the Rabbanut, he encouraged me and helped me, and eventually I became a dayan."

Turning to Elisha, the rav said, "I'm interested in helping you in your work with street youth. I'm about to retire from the Rabbanut, and I would like to do for others what the rav did for me half a century ago."

They exchanged phone numbers, and as they descended from the bus and were about to part ways, Elisha said, "You never told me — who was that rav who saved you from the street?"

"Not was," the rav corrected him. "He's still alive. His name is Harav Ovadia Yosef."[20]

---

20. Rabbi Boaz Shalom, Hidabroot.

Chapter Thirteen
The Home Front

While the years of 5710-5714 (1950-1954) were extremely productive for Harav Ovadia on many spiritual fronts — serving as a *dayan*, studying Torah at Midrash Bnei Zion, teaching Torah to the masses in the evening, signing children up for Torah schools, and writing *sefarim* — financially, these were the most trying years for the growing Yosef family. Within a few years of returning from Egypt, two more children were born: a daughter, Yaffa, and a son, Yitzchak, who would eventually be elected as Rishon LeZion, shortly before Harav Ovadia's passing.

During those years of austerity, the government rationed food by handing out coupons that entitled families to certain items. Most of the coupons were for staples, such as flour, but coupons for certain nonessentials, such as chocolate, were distributed as well. Rabbanit Margalit would trade these nonessential coupons for items that were more vital, or sell them for money that she would then put aside for more important needs.

"Needs" is a relative term. One woman might need a new kitchen, another might need a gold necklace, a third some new clothing. The Rabbanit made do without any of these "needs," but she did have one particularly pressing need: Her tiny two-and-a-half

Hacham Avraham Fattal at the bar mitzva of Yitzchak Yosef, with Yaakov Yosef in the background. Hacham Avraham would redeem his ration coupons for treats for the Yosef children.

room apartment on Rehov Be'er Sheva didn't contain a closet to store the family's clothing. Not that there was all that much to store — her daughters recall owning one weekday dress and one Shabbat dress each — but clothing piled up on open shelves in every corner was impossible to ignore.

For months, the Rabbanit sold her coupons for chocolate and other nonessentials, and saved up the money, waiting for the day when she would be able to afford a closet.

In 1954, she finally reached her goal. She had saved up 200 lira, and she would finally have a closet in which to store the family's clothing.

Seventeen Years in the Making

THAT VERY SAME YEAR, HARAV OVADIA WAS CLOSING IN ON a long-term goal of his own. From the age of 17, Harav Ovadia had been writing halachic responsa — but he realized that it wasn't proper for someone his age to publish them.[1] In Egypt, he had spent countless hours writing *teshuvot*, putting aside his struggles with both the Egyptian authorities and members of the Jewish community. When he returned to Eretz Yisrael, he continued working on his *teshuvot*, despite his poverty and the busy life he led.

And now his *sefer* was finally ready for publication. There was one problem: He was missing 200 lira of the total publication costs.

The new closet was beckoning. But the Rabbanit understood that this was her chance to show her husband how much his scholarship meant to her. She took out her savings, the 200 lira she had scraped together with such difficulty, and handed it over to Harav Ovadia.

The closet could wait.

---

1. See p. 90.

Rabbanit Margalit was willing to forgo her own needs so the world could benefit from her husband's writings.

The world needed the first volume of *Yabia Omer* more than her home needed a closet.

THE PUBLIC'S RESPONSE TO HARAV OVADIA'S SECOND PUBlished *sefer* was even more overwhelmingly positive than the

Yabia Omer

response to *Hazon Ovadia*.[2] In *Yabia Omer*, his brilliance shone forth from every page, as he dealt with "old" halachic dilemmas — for example, whether one may wear two sets of *tefillin* at the same time[3] — alongside "modern" *sh'eilot*

---

2. See p. 198.
3. Many people have a custom to wear two types of *tefillin*, in which the primary difference is the order in which the *parshiyot* are written. The two types are referred to as "Rashi" and "Rabbeinu Tam," after the Rishonim who wrote clearly about the subject (although the two opinions existed long before their times). Ashkenazim who wore both generally wore them separately, one after another, while many Sephardim made their *tefillin* very small and wore both types together. Although this Sephardi practice wasn't a new phenomenon, Harav Ovadia considered it wrong and set out to correct it. After examining all of the related *sugyot*, he determined that this custom had developed because of a Kabbalistic opinion that refers to both types

that related to electricity and technology. In the first volume, which comprises two sections[4] containing some 70 full-length *teshuvot*, he deals with ten *sh'eilot* regarding new technologies that are commonplace or perhaps even archaic today, but were then the latest innovations. For example:

- ☐ If one is praying or reciting *Kriat Shema* and he hears a woman singing over a radio or gramophone, must he stop because *kol b'isha erva*, or is that a problem only with live singing?
- ☐ May one pray or recite *Kriat Shema* in the presence of a photograph of an immodestly dressed woman?
- ☐ Does one determine whether to recite *tefillat haderech* (the wayfarer's prayer) based on the distance traveled, or on the amount of time on the road?[5]
- ☐ May one use a thermos on Shabbat, or is it prohibited as *hatmana* (insulating)?
- ☐ May one read by the light of an electric lamp on Shabbat?[6]

In the *Yoreh Dei'a* section of *Yabia Omer*, most of the *sh'eilot* Harav Ovadia discussed were issues that had existed for centuries, but even in that section there were some *sh'eilot* that involved innovations. For example, as air travel gained popularity, it became commonplace to bring deceased people to Eretz Yisrael for burial. A *sh'eila* arose as to whether the casket used to transport the deceased

---

of *tefillin* as equally valid, even though the halacha maintains that "Rashi *tefillin*" are primary and "Rabbeinu Tam *tefillin*" could be worn as a stringency. Harav Ovadia applies his general rule that in disputes between halacha and Kabbala, we follow halacha, and he therefore recommends that everyone who wears Rabbeinu Tam *tefillin* should don them separately.

4. In this first volume, Harav Ovadia published *teshuvot* on two sections of *Shulhan Aruch*: *Orah Haim*, the laws of daily living, and *Yoreh Dei'a*, the laws of *kashrut*, family purity, conversion, and the like. All later volumes would contain *teshuvot* not only on these two sections, but also on the other two sections of *Shulhan Aruch*: *Hoshen Mishpat*, monetary law, and *Even Ha'ezer*, the laws of marriage, divorce, and the like.

5. This *sh'eila* became extremely relevant as cars and buses became the primary forms of transportation, cutting travel to a fraction of the amount of time it had taken on foot or by horse and buggy.

6. The Tannaic Sages enacted a *gezeira* (decree) that one may not read by the light of a flame because he may forget that it's Shabbat and tilt the lamp to cause more oil to enter the wick, which is akin to lighting a flame. In his *teshuva*, Harav Ovadia examines the method in which *gezeirot* are enacted, and whether we would enact a *gezeira* today that is not exactly the same as a *gezeira* enacted by the earlier Sages, even if our reason for enacting it stems from a similar concern.

to Eretz Yisrael is considered designated for the use of the *niftar* (in which case it couldn't be used for any other purpose), or whether it does not become designated for that purpose because the family of the deceased knew that the body would not be buried in the casket, since the custom in Eretz Yisrael is to bury without a casket.

In each case, before ruling on the actual *sh'eila*, Harav Ovadia examines the overall halachic approach to these vital issues — for instance, whether the use of electricity on Shabbat would be a Torah-level or a Rabbinic prohibition. The principles he establishes can often be used to resolve many more *sh'eilot* than what the questioner actually asked.

Wall-to-Wall Approbations

BY THE TIME HE WAS READY TO RELEASE *YABIA OMER*, Harav Ovadia had made an impressive name for himself among Eretz Yisrael's elite scholars. The *sefer* carries *haskamot* from a veritable who's who among the Torah luminaries of those times — including Harav Ovadia's two primary mentors, Rav Ezra Attia and Rav Tzvi Pesach Frank, as well as several leading Sephardic rabbis and rabbanim of the Eida Haredit, all of whom expressed their admiration for the work in their glowing approbations.

The work was awarded Tel Aviv's "Rav Kook Prize for Torah Literature," in Elul of 5715/1955. In expressing why *Yabia Omer* was selected, Rav Shlomo Yosef Zevin wrote:

> The author is unique in his incredible breadth of knowledge. He cites myriad sources from the *Rishonim* and *Aharonim* for each detail and logical step in the subject he examines, and all the responsa works — from both Sephardic and Ashkenazic sages — are open and well-known to him. He offers the Torah public a wealth of knowledge and sources through this work, and many hidden works are revealed by him.
>
> Our author also exhibits a keen mind for developing a halachic approach, using straightforward and correct logic, until he reaches a practical halachic conclusion.

A newspaper clipping of the winners of the Rav Kook Prize for Torah Literature in 5715. Harav Ovadia (middle, left) appears alongside his lifelong friend Rav Betzalel Zolty.

Rav Zevin alludes to an extremely useful feature of Harav Ovadia's works: He provides the Torah world with access to sources that would otherwise be unavailable. Blessed as he was with an incredible memory,[7] Harav Ovadia cites dozens of sources for each point he makes in a *teshuva*, quoting from *sefarim* that were long out of print or had fallen to disuse over the generations.

Upon Harav Ovadia's passing, Rav Benzion Mutzafi remarked that authors whose works would no longer have been quoted if not for Harav Ovadia were surely greeting him in heaven:

He brought to life the words of *Gedolei Yisrael* from throughout the ages. Some of the *geonim* he quotes in his *sefarim* were never even heard of by many *talmidei hachamim*; but even the well-known *geonim* were not widely studied. Rav Ovadia opened windows into the words of Rav Hai Gaon, Rav Paltai Gaon, Rav Natrunai Gaon, and others.

In Turkey alone, in the last 500 years, there were more than 5,000 phenomenal *talmidei hachamim* who wrote *sefarim*. This may sound like an exaggeration, but I have seen a detailed list of these *hachamim*. Many of them would never be remembered if not for the fact that Maran Ovadia quotes them in his *sefarim*.

---

7. See Chapter 25.

SHORTLY AFTER *YABIA OMER* WAS PUBLISHED, HARAV Ovadia approached the Brisker Rav, Rav Yitzchak Zev Soloveitchik, who was one of the greatest geniuses of recent times in the Lithuanian Torah world, and handed him a copy. "Who are you?" the Brisker Rav asked. But Harav Ovadia was too shy to respond, and he just walked away.

"I Couldn't Sleep All Night"

The next morning, the Brisker Rav remarked to one of his confidants that he hadn't slept all night, because he had become totally absorbed in the phenomenal gift he had received the day before. "Who knew that there were such great *geonim* among the Sephardim today?" he remarked.⁸

A similar incident was recounted by Rav Henoch Padwa,⁹ a future leader of London Jewry who was then serving as a *dayan* on the Eida Haredit. Rav Padwa was a *talmid muvhak* of the great Tchebiner Rav,

Rav Yitzchak Zev Soloveitchik, the Brisker Rav, was so absorbed in the first volume of *Yabia Omer* that he couldn't sleep all night.

---
8. *Posek HaDor*.
9. Told by Reb Benzion Reich, who heard it from a *talmid* of Rav Padwa.

Rav Dov Berish Weidenfeld, the Tchebiner Rav, on *Yabia Omer*: "There has not been such *bekiut* since Rabbi Akiva Eiger."

Rav Dov Berish Weidenfeld. One morning, when Rav Padwa walked into Rav Weidenfeld's house, he saw him pacing the floors in a state of obvious emotional upheaval. When he noticed Rav Padwa, the Tchebiner Rav said, "I must show you something amazing." He handed him a copy of *Yabia Omer*, which he had just received. "I can't believe that an author from our times can write a *sefer* on this level," the Tchebiner Rav exclaimed.

The Tchebiner Rav also remarked that there had not been such *bekiut* (breadth of Torah knowledge) since Rabbi Akiva Eiger.[10]

Spiritual Highs, Financial Lows

WHILE HARAV OVADIA WAS THRIVING IN TERMS OF HIS learning and teaching, the family was going through its most difficult times in terms of finances. Harav Ovadia himself needed almost nothing; those who learned with him recall him subsisting on the same menu of bread with a drop of margarine for his main meal every day for years. But the well-being of his family was of great concern to him.

His father-in-law, Hacham Avraham Fattal, who realized the great value of the work his beloved son-in-law was doing, tried to ameliorate the family's poverty. His weekly visits were a highlight in the upbringing of the Yosef children, who would dance around

---

10. Rabbi Hersh Goldwurm.

him excitedly when he arrived. Whereas their mother would trade any nonessential ration cards for more important staples, their grandfather Hacham Avraham would redeem his cards to bring some treats for his grandchildren. One child would get a small piece of chocolate, another a candy, a third an apple, and a fourth a sugar cube. Small comforts, but so important to the Yosef children, who had little else.

There was also an unwritten understanding between father and daughter. Each week, before he left the house, Hacham Avraham would hide a five-lira note somewhere, and indicate to Adina that she should show it to her mother after he left. He didn't want Margalit to thank him, and he certainly didn't want to give her the opportunity to refuse the money she so desperately needed.[11]

The Fire

ONE EXPENDITURE THAT HARAV OVADIA INSISTED ON MAINtaining was cleaning help. He deeply respected and appreciated all that Rabbanit Margalit did for the family, and he felt that under no circumstances should she do the heavy housework, such as washing the floors. No matter how they struggled financially, Harav Ovadia insisted that she hire a cleaning woman to help with such chores.

One day, that decision would help save the family's meager possessions.

> *During the winter, the Yosef apartment was heated by kerosene space heaters — the only form of heat the family could afford. While working on his writings one afternoon, Harav Ovadia rose quickly to retrieve a sefer from his library. He was so absorbed in the sugya he was working on that he didn't notice that as he passed the heater, he accidentally knocked it over. The kerosene spilled all over the floor, and quickly caught fire. All that was in that room was an old wooden table — and Harav Ovadia's hundreds of sefarim, which would have made excellent fodder for the fire.*

---

11. *Ba'asher Teileich*, a biography of Rabbanit Margalit, written by granddaughter Margalit Katzir, daughter of Yaffa (Yosef) Cohen.

Harav Ovadia looked on in horror as the flames spread, getting closer to the sefarim shelves. The rational thing to do might have been to run for his life, but Harav Ovadia simply couldn't bring himself to abandon the only possessions he valued. He tried to put out the flames with his feet and bare hands, but that did little to contain the fire.

Eight-year-old Adina, who had witnessed the entire chain of events, ran into the other room, where the cleaning woman had just hauled a pail of water to start washing the floor. Dumbstruck, she silently tried to drag the pail into her father's study, but it was too heavy for her. The cleaning woman realized what was transpiring, and she lifted the pail, ran into Harav Ovadia's study, and quickly poured it onto the flames. Although water would generally cause a kerosene-fueled fire to spread, the water from the pail somehow smothered the flames and extinguished the fire.

Everyone stared at the strange scene, shocked.

"An open miracle," the awed cleaning woman finally whispered.

"Abba," added Adina, finally finding her tongue, "we saved the sefarim."

"My daughter," Harav Ovadia corrected softly, "we didn't save the sefarim. They saved us."

Tragedy Strikes

IN 1955, RABBANIT MARGALIT GAVE BIRTH TO ANOTHER daughter, Rahel. The Rabbanit immediately noticed that her baby's lips were a sickly blue.

To her surprise, the hospital midwife suddenly asked, "How many children do you have at home?"

"Six," Margalit answered.

"Six is a nice number," the midwife said in a strange voice.

Shortly thereafter, a doctor arrived to examine the baby. It didn't take long for him to diagnose the problem. "This baby has a serious heart defect," he said resolutely. "She won't live for long, and each day she lives will be painful for her — and for your family. I would advise you to stop feeding her."

The Rabbanit fixed him with an equally resolute gaze. "There's only One Who determines how long we live," she replied, "and He commands us to do all we can to continue our lives and those of the people around us until the day He decides to terminate them."

All the other doctors on staff were equally pessimistic, and discouraged her from trying to keep her baby alive. After two days of hearing their dismal "advice," she took Rahel home. Thus began a three-month marathon. Rabbanit Margalit had to make a difficult decision: She could call on her husband when she needed help with the younger children, or she could keep her daughters Adina and Malka home from school to help her. She decided that her daughters could manage, on occasion, without the lessons they would absorb in Beit Yaakov — lessons that inculcated the message of sacrificing one's own needs for Torah, a message that resounded from the very walls of her home. For the next three months, whenever Rahel's condition worsened and Rabbanit Margalit had to run with her to the hospital, she left Adina and Malka in charge of their younger siblings, without uttering a word to Harav Ovadia.

The doctors couldn't understand why she kept coming to the hospital on her own. "Next time," one of them told her angrily, "I want to see your husband here with you."

The Rabbanit remained silent. What could she tell the doctor — that her husband would certainly have escorted her to the hospital had she not shielded him from the developments and left the house without his knowledge?

On Lag Ba'Omer 5715/1955, Rahel's condition deteriorated rapidly. The Rabbanit rushed back to the hospital with her, but nothing could be done to save her life.

The other Yosef children knew nothing about their sister's passing until after the burial. The Rabbanit couldn't bring herself to share the news with them, and 10-year-old Adina, the eldest, who had been on a school trip in honor of Lag Ba'Omer when her mother left to the hospital, didn't comprehend the meaning of the candles or the significance of her parents sitting on the floor. When she asked her mother where Rahel was, the Rabbanit choked on her words. "She had to go to the hospital again," she finally croaked out.

"Why aren't you there with her?" Adina asked.

"Maybe I'll go tomorrow," the Rabbanit answered, averting her eyes.

The next morning, Adina demanded to go visit Rahel. She still didn't understand why her parents were sitting on the floor. Finally, Malka summoned her to another room. "I think I know a secret," she said. "Rahel was *niftar*. You know what *niftar* means? It means that she died."

"*How can you talk like that?*" Adina shouted at her. "Don't even say such a thing out of your mouth!"

The Rabbanit, who had overheard the entire conversation, turned to her husband and asked him to break the news.

Harav Ovadia sat the family down and began to explain the concept of *neshamot* and their missions on earth, and the concept of a *gilgul* that must come down to complete its mission for a matter of months so that it can then ascend to a special place in Gan Eden.

The young children barely understood their father's explanation, but Harav Ovadia's words hit their mark elsewhere. The Rabbanit, who had devoted endless physical and emotional energy to the tiny, sickly child, found solace in his words.

The children understood only one part of Harav Ovadia's explanation: Rahel's carriage was empty — and it would remain empty forevermore.

Double Consolation

LESS THAN A YEAR WAS ALL IT WOULD TAKE FOR THE FAMILY to receive some consolation from Above, in the form of not one daughter, but two. The Rabbanit gave birth to twins, Sara and Rivka, on 9 Iyar 5716/1956, just nine days before the first anniversary of Rahel's passing.

While the birth brought a *simha* to the family, the Rabbanit herself was completely drained, both physically and emotionally. She spent hours each day in bed, but could not get back to herself. Harav Ovadia provided sympathy and encouragement, and reiterated the promise he had made to her when they were engaged: In exchange for all the time and effort she was putting into raising the family, she would merit half of the portion in Gan Eden he

Harav Ovadia and Rabbanit Margalit in happier times, on a trip abroad. After her infant daughter passed away, only her husband's explanation about a soul's mission in this world brought solace to the Rabbanit.

was working so hard to amass. His words did wonders for her, as did those of the *mekubal* Rav Ephraim Cohen, who, during one of his visits to Harav Ovadia, wished the Rabbanit a full recovery and gave her a *beracha* and pledge that she would yet give birth to additional children who would light up the world with their Torah.

A Lifeline

THE APARTMENT ON REHOV BE'ER SHEVA, WHICH HAD BEEN small even for the six people who had first inhabited it in 1951, was now home to another four children. The walls didn't expand to accommodate the additions, and neither did family's meager earnings.

It was clear to all that this period in the life of the Yosef family had to come to an end; they would have to find additional income in the form of an official position for Harav Ovadia. The option had been there for years, but Harav Ovadia and Margalit had delayed this inevitable decision because they both felt that he was accomplishing too much in Yerushalayim to warrant a move. Now, Harav Ovadia would have to accede to Rav Reuven Katz's repeated requests that he return to the *beit din* in Petah Tikva — but that he also move to the growing city with his family, so that he could serve as a spiritual leader in more ways than one.

CHAPTER FOURTEEN
IN THE EIM HAMOSHAVOT

PUBLISHING *SEFARIM* AND TOILING TO CLARIFY halacha were personally satisfying to Harav Ovadia, but they certainly weren't bringing in much income. In the spring of 1956, a few months after the release of the second volume of *Yabia Omer*, Harav Ovadia accepted Rav Reuven Katz's invitation to rejoin the *beit din* in Petah Tikva. This time Rav Katz pledged to place Harav Ovadia in charge of all marriage-related cases that involved Sephardim, thus avoiding the issues over which he had resigned from the *beit din* close to five years earlier. Rather than commuting back to Yerushalayim each day, however, he moved the entire Yosef family out to Petah Tikva.

The *moshava* Petah Tikva was the first settlement of its kind in Eretz Yisrael. As opposed to a *moshav*, in which the land is owned communally, in a *moshava*, each parcel of land is owned by an individual. The founders of Petah Tivka were religious Jews from the Old Yishuv[1] in Yerushalayim, who wanted to try their hands at farming the land of Eretz Yisrael rather than subsist off the *haluka*

---

1. The term "Old Yishuv" refers to Jews who lived in Israel before the days of the Zionist-affiliated *aliyot* that began in the late 1800s.

Petah Tikva, Eim Hamoshavot, "Mother of the Moshavot"

system.[2] They bought land in the central region of Eretz Yisrael, near the source of the Yarkon River, in 1878. Their first attempt to settle there failed, however, because they couldn't tame the malaria-ridden swamps. They were forced to move to an area farther south, where they established a village called Yehud. In 1883, with the financial backing of Baron Edmund de Rothschild, they were able to drain the swamps and move back.

In the decades that followed, groups of Hovevei Zion who immigrated to Eretz Yisrael bought parcels of land in Petah Tivka. By 1937, the settlement had expanded to the point that the British Mandatory government upgraded its status to that of a full city. When Israel declared independence in 1948, several nearby villages were officially subsumed into the borders of Petah Tikva, raising its population to 22,000.

---

2. In the *haluka* system, Jews who were willing to sacrifice and live in the difficult conditions in Eretz Yisrael were supported by their brethren back in Europe, who received a portion of their reward for the mitzva of living in Eretz Yisrael in exchange for monthly donations. The system was set up through a network of "kollelim" (*kollel* in the sense of community, not in the more modern sense of a group of scholars studying Torah) and each country in Europe had its own *kollel* in Eretz Yisrael (e.g., *Kollel Polin* supported Polish Jews and *Kollel Ungarin* supported Hungarian Jews).

A New Experience

WHEN THE YOSEFS MOVED TO PETAH TIVKA, ITS ORIGINAL status as a religious *moshava* was long forgotten. The city was inhabited by both religious and irreligious Jews, with the latter being the overwhelming majority.

The Yosefs moved into a relatively spacious apartment — it had three bedrooms, proper facilities they didn't have to share with neighbors, and a living room with space for the children to play. The older children still shared their bedroom with Harav Ovadia's library, but they were used to falling asleep to the sound of their father working through a difficult halachic topic.

The comfort came at a price, however. In Yerushalayim, the Yosefs had been immersed in a thoroughly religious environment; in Petah Tikva, they experienced their first real exposure to the secular Israeli lifestyle. The neighborhood they moved into was irreligious, and they were the only Torah-observant family in their building.

At first, the neighbors were suspicious of the rabbinic presence in their midst. Aware of the religious tensions that often ran high in other areas of the country, they were concerned that the rabbi and his family would demand that they change their lifestyle to accommodate the Yosef family's religiosity. Harav Ovadia went out of his way to ease their suspicion. Painful as it was for him to hear the neighbors deliberately turn up the volume of their radios as he walked up the steps on Shabbat, or take the opportunity to light a cigarette just as he and the children returned home from shul, he never reproached any of them. In fact, when a child of one of the neighbors asked to join the Yosefs for Kiddush on Shabbat, Harav Ovadia first asked that child's parents for permission, lest they think he was trying to "convert" their child against their will. And when the Rabbanit wanted to ask one of the neighbors to refrain from sunbathing outdoors in an extremely immodest garment, Harav Ovadia insisted that she not say a word. "She lived here before us," he said. "We can't dictate our rules to her. She'll have to feel uncomfortable herself and decide to change on her own."

"How will you pass by?" the Rabbanit asked, knowing how careful Harav Ovadia was not to view anything even remotely immodest.

"I'll close my eyes," Harav Ovadia replied.

Eventually, the suspicions abated, and the neighbors developed warm feelings for the family. When they noticed the Yosefs walking into the building on Shabbat, they turned down their radios, and they tried not to be seen with lit cigarettes on Shabbat.

THE SEPHARDIC CHIEF RABBI OF PETAH TIKVA, RAV AMRAM Aburavia, was already over 70, and was not well. He was only too happy to have the assistance of a young, energetic rav in administering the needs of the Sephardic Jewry in the city, and he took a deep liking to Harav Ovadia. In a letter addressed to Harav Ovadia several years after the latter arrived in Petah Tikva, Rav Amram confers the highest accolades on a rav more than three decades his junior: "Our great rabbi, the fortress

"He Can't Help But Spread Torah"

Rav Amram Aburavia, the Sephardic chief rabbi of Petah Tikva, welcomed the assistance of the energetic Harav Ovadia.

and tower, genius of the generation and its splendor, the entire nation travels by his light...."

When the family moved to Petah Tikva, Harav Ovadia's students in Yerushalayim begged him to continue delivering *shiurim* to them on a steady basis, and he agreed to make the arduous bus journey to Yerushalayim once a week for this purpose. That weekly *shiur* didn't slake his thirst to spread Torah, however. He also established a *shiur* in Petah Tikva's Beit Knesset Aram Naharayim, and eventually he and Rav Aburavia "split up" the city, ensuring that every *beit knesset* that wanted some sort of *shiur* would have one of the two address its members.

Some saw this as an absolute *need* on Harav Ovadia's part: No matter where he went, he *had* to deliver Torah *shiurim*. His children took note. At Harav Ovadia's funeral, his son Rav Avraham shared with the audience that his father taught them not to suffice with learning to develop their own scholarship or even to write *sefarim*; they had to go out to the simple folk and teach them Torah as well. "You taught us to go down to the nation," he wailed, "to use anything — stories, parables — whatever it took to teach them Torah."

After being elected chief rabbi of Holon in 5760/2000, Rav Avraham followed in his father's footsteps, running from one *beit knesset* to another to teach Torah, adroitly peppering his Torah content with stories and light humor to keep his audience attuned. In a eulogy in honor of Harav Ovadia's *sheloshim*, he related that a few years before his father's passing, a member of the family urged Rav Avraham to broaden his sphere of influence. "You can't continue to give these small *shiurim*," the relative insisted. "It's time to graduate to something bigger and better."

Rav Avraham didn't accept this criticism. "Let's go to Abba and ask," he said.

When Harav Ovadia heard the question, he turned toward the relative who had criticized Rav Avraham. "Where did you get this idea from?" he said sharply. "Did I ever demand a certain size audience in order to teach Torah?"

Convinced by a Snake

IN RECENT DECADES, PETAH TIVKA HAS BECOME HOME TO many commercial enterprises, but in the 1950s, agriculture was still the primary source of revenue for many residents. Once, Harav Ovadia gave a *shiur* in which he discussed the prohibition of milking a cow on Shabbat. Unbeknownst to him, one of the regular attendees of this *shiur* owned a number of cows, which he milked on Shabbat. When Harav Ovadia heard from a participant that even after this *shiur*, this man continued to milk his cows, he sat down with him and discussed the matter at length, explaining the severity of Shabbat desecration. The man kept protesting that he didn't want to sell his cows, and creating a halachically acceptable partnership with a gentile would be too difficult.

The Shabbat after this conversation, when the man entered his barn to milk his cows, a venomous snake bit him. He was rushed to the hospital, and it took three weeks for the venom to leave his system. Harav Ovadia went to visit him in the hospital, and he spoke to him gently. "You see how much HaKadosh Baruch Hu loves you?" he remarked. "He prevented you from desecrating Shabbat!"

His words struck a chord with the farmer, and when he left the hospital, he sold his cows to a non-Jew[3] for Shabbat.

Rav Avraham Yosef follows in his father's footsteps, teaching Torah to audiences throughout the country no matter the size.

---

3. *MiShiurei Maran HaRishon LeZion*, 1:30 (*Parashat Bo*).

Long-Term Investments

HARAV OVADIA'S INVESTMENT INTO HIS *SHIURIM* IN PETAH Tikva didn't produce results only for the short term; the *shiurim* had an impact on many participants for years to come, as was the case with his followers in Yerushalayim.[4]

Rav David Yosef, who was born in Petah Tikva in 5717/1957, returned to the city to learn in Yeshivat Ohr Yisrael in 5730/1970, when the family was living in Tel Aviv. One day, he boarded a bus with a few friends, and was surprised to see a driver with a long beard and a large black *kippa*. The boys struck up a conversation with the driver, and when he heard that one of them was Harav Ovadia's son, he exclaimed, "I became hareidi because of him!"

The driver told the boys that he worked in Egged to keep busy, not for the money, because he had a large farm through which he supported his family.

When David recounted this conversation to his father, Harav Ovadia called this man, whom he remembered from the *shiurim* thirteen years earlier, and invited him for a visit. During the visit, Harav Ovadia asked this man to support Torah in his home city by giving a generous donation to Yeshivat Ohr Yisrael. [One of Harav Ovadia's "pet projects" was to raise money for Torah institutions, even if he was not directly affiliated with the institution and had not been asked to raise funds for it.] "Rather than give a donation," the man replied, "I will provide all the fruits and vegetables the yeshiva needs, free of charge."

Harav Ovadia instructed David to relay this offer to the administration of the yeshiva. When the Rosh Yeshiva, Rav Yaakov Neiman, heard about the pledge — which would save the yeshiva a great deal of money — he kissed David on the forehead and asked him to tell his father that he did not have to pay tuition for his son. David dutifully called Harav Ovadia to deliver the message. Within an hour, Harav Ovadia arrived at Ohr Yisrael and marched straight over to the Rosh Yeshiva. "I *want* to pay tuition for my son," he declared, withdrawing the entire year's tuition from his pocket and handing it to Rav Neiman.

---

4. See p. 290.

Harav Ovadia at the grave of the Rambam, with sons Yitzchak, David, and Moshe

Secularization Becomes a Factor

IN HIS WORK AS A *DAYAN* IN PETAH TIKVA, HARAV OVADIA spent much of his time dealing with *sh'eilot* pertaining to marriage and divorce — many of which required him to take into account the mounting trend toward secularization in the country, and especially in the kibbutzim from which *sh'eilot* were arriving.

Shortly after his move to Petah Tikva in Sivan of 5716/1956, a *get* presided over by the great Rav Eliezer (Leizer) Silver of Cincinnati arrived at the *beit din* to be delivered to the wife, who lived in Petah Tikva. Harav Ovadia noticed an issue: Because in Eretz Yisrael the woman was known only by her nickname, the way in which her name was written in the *get* posed some question.

In his ruling, after delving into the question of whether the *get* could be used as is, Harav Ovadia adds that since the *beit din* had heard rumors that this woman was seeing other men, they did not want to delay the delivery of the *get*. They therefore decided to rely on the authorities who ruled leniently in this matter and hurried to present her with the *get* her husband had sent, even though it wasn't written in the most ideal way.

In another *teshuva*, written in Heshvan 5717/1956, Harav Ovadia describes a case that came before the *beit din*, in which the *dayanim* had to take into account the fact that the lifestyle on secular kibbutzim in Israel was often immoral, and determine whether that affected the halachic status of children born on such kibbutzim. Harav Ovadia's denunciation of the secular lifestyle didn't earn him accolades from the media, who jumped on this responsum as proof that Harav Ovadia didn't respect the irreligious. But Harav Ovadia wasn't looking for a fan club; he had to consider all relevant factors in order to issue a halachic ruling, and he would not mince words in his quest to arrive at the correct halacha.

THERE WERE ALSO SOME GENERAL QUESTIONS THAT AROSE, one of which was a sort of throwback to his first stint on the *beit din*.

Torah Law or Rabbinic Law? When he arrived in Petah Tikva, he noticed that the rabbanim were writing in the *ketubot* of both Ashkenazi and Sephardi couples that should the marriage terminate, the husband would give the wife, "*kesef zuzi ma'atan dehazu leichi* **mide'oraita** — 200 *zuz* that are owed to you [based on] **the Torah law**." Harav Ovadia pointed out that because Sephardim follow the opinion of the Rif and Rambam that a *ketuba* is not mandated by Torah law, but only by Rabbinic law, the word *mide'oraita* should be replaced in Sephardic *ketubot* with the word *mide'rabbanan*, or should at least be left out. Since Rav Katz had agreed to give Harav Ovadia authority over marriage issues involving Sephardim, he was able to make this change to the *ketubot*.

IN SOME OF THE *TESHUVOT* WRITTEN DURING THE PETAH Tikva era, Harav Ovadia displays not only his acumen in halacha, **Soft Skills** but also an uncanny ability to work with people and sidestep possible problems.

One case involved a couple who emigrated from Russia, where they had been married in civil court twenty years earlier, without *huppa* and *kiddushin*. The husband wanted a divorce, but the wife demanded that he give her *mezonot* (support). A disagreement arose on the *beit din* over whether the husband was required to give her *mezonot*, considering that the couple had been married in a civil ceremony, without a *ketuba*.

Harav Ovadia relates that he discussed the matter with Rav Shlomo Shimshon Karelitz, a nephew of the Hazon Ish, who had joined the *beit din* shortly before Harav Ovadia returned, and he agreed wholeheartedly with Harav Ovadia. As *Hashgaha* would have it, on the day when the couple returned for the verdict, Rav Katz wasn't in the *beit din*, and Rav Sapir and Harav Ovadia needed a third *dayan* to rule in this matter. Rav Karelitz, who generally wasn't in the same triumvirate as Harav Ovadia in those days, joined for this case, and they ruled in favor of the husband.[5]

Nevertheless, writes Harav Ovadia, they convinced the man that even if this woman would have served as no more than a housekeeper for twenty years, it would be appropriate to give some sort of parting gift, and he should therefore give her something. Thanks

After rejoining the *beit din* in Petah Tikva, Harav Ovadia occasionally sat on a triumvirate with Rav Reuven Katz (C) and Rav Shlomo Shimshon Karelitz (L).

---

5. Harav Ovadia writes that Rav Sapir ended up agreeing with him and Rav Karelitz, making it a unanimous decision.

to Harav Ovadia's intervention, the couple eventually agreed on an amount, and they were able to avoid any further acrimony in their separation.

Another case involved a bizarre circumstance. The daughter of a wealthy man had become engaged, and during her engagement, a swindler decided to defraud her father. He hid two witnesses in a certain location, and arranged for the girl to come to that location. He then tricked her into accepting an item from him, while making "*kiddushin*," which turned her into a married woman and prevented her from marrying the man to whom she was engaged. This swindler then demanded a huge sum from the girl's father in order to give her a *get* to release her.

Harav Ovadia goes into great detail as to why this *kiddushin* is invalid and not a halachic concern, but he writes at the end that even though this woman didn't need a *get*, the *dayanim* were able to convince the swindler to settle for a small payoff and give the *get* just in case there was some meaning to his *kiddushin*.

In both these cases, Harav Ovadia found a clever way to work around a problem rather than confronting it head-on or issuing a ruling that would be difficult to enforce.

A Sudden Loss

DURING THE WINTER OF 5717/1957, MRS. GEORGIA OVADIA, Harav Ovadia's mother, started to get terrible headaches. She summoned her oldest son from Petah Tikva, and he accompanied her to the hospital for a battery of tests. After the initial tests were done, she began to feel bad for taking Harav Ovadia away from his learning, and she sent him back to Petah Tikva. A few weeks later, the headaches became worse, and she called Harav Ovadia back to Yerushalayim. This time, the doctors discovered a growth in her head, and they told Harav Ovadia that in order for her to survive, she would need immediate surgery.

Harav Ovadia didn't have much time to think, and he felt that he should go along with the doctors' recommendation. Unfortunately, Mrs. Georgia never woke up from the surgery. Her *petira* on 21 Adar I was a crushing blow to Harav Ovadia, who considered her the primary figure in encouraging his growth in learning as a child. In the introduction to Volume Three of *Yabia Omer*, which he published several years after her passing, Harav Ovadia included an epitaph to his mother, writing poignantly about the pain of the loss, and describing her devotion to raising her children in the path of Torah and the reward for her efforts that would certainly be hers in the World to Come.

Forgoing the Promotion

HARAV OVADIA'S TWO YEARS IN PETAH TIKVA WERE EXTREMEly productive. In fact, he made such a mark on the *beit din* that when Rav Reuven Katz decided to retire, he summoned Harav Ovadia and asked whether he would succeed him as *av beit din*.

In his eulogy on Rav Katz,[6] Harav Ovadia related that he immediately refused the request, out of concern for the feelings of Rav Sapir,[7] who had already been on the *beit din* for twenty years before Harav Ovadia joined.

He adds that Rav Katz pretended to be upset at him for not accepting the position, but he told others that he was impressed that Harav Ovadia was humble enough to turn down such a prestigious position.

"Ultimately," writes Harav Ovadia, "this was for my own good. In 5718, Rav Waldenburg invited me to serve on his *beit din* in Yerushalayim, and I was able to accept a position under him without having to step down from a more prominent position as *av beit din*."

---

6. Printed in *Hazon Ovadia, Dalet Taaniyot*, p. 474.
7. Rav Sapir had passed away two years before Rav Katz, so Harav Ovadia was now able to mention his reason.

CHAPTER FIFTEEN
RETURN TO MY FATHER'S HOME

THE YOSEF FAMILY'S RETURN TO YERUSHALAYIM IN 5718/1958 heralded a new era, one that the family would eventually refer to as the "years of plenty." Although they were hardly wealthy, the two years they spent in Petah Tikva had enabled Harav Ovadia to stabilize the family's finances, to the extent that they were now able to afford an apartment of their own — the first they were able to purchase outright.

The city of Yerushalayim was undergoing a construction boom in those days, with new neighborhoods springing up on land that had become part of Israel in 1948. One such neighborhood was Tel Arza, which is alternately known nowadays as Ezrat Torah or Shikun Habad. The Yosefs bought two small, first-floor apartments at 8 Rehov Elkana, which they combined into one unit, and they became neighbors with one of Harav Ovadia's closest friends, Rav Benzion Abba Shaul, who bought an apartment on the third floor of the same building. The apartment had three bedrooms — one for the Rav and Rabbanit, one for the boys, and one for the girls — as well as an extra room that could serve as a study, without Harav Ovadia having to sidestep sleeping children as he went to retrieve a *sefer*.

The Yosefs, who had always seen their stint in Petah Tikva as a necessary way station, but not a final port of call, were excited to return to Yerushalayim. In many *teshuvot* written upon returning to the Holy City, Rav Ovadia writes the year as: וְשַׁבְתִּי בְשָׁלוֹם אֶל בֵּית אָבִי, *I will return in peace to my father's home* (*Bereishit* 28:21), because the word וְשַׁבְתִּי has the same numerical value as תשי"ח, the year they were able to return to Yerushalayim.

Harav Ovadia immediately resumed delivering nightly *shiurim* to his old group of followers, some of whom had been with him since he began teaching Torah in Beit Knesset Ohel Rahel as a 17-year-old, about twenty years earlier. Harav Ovadia had slowly raised the level of scholarship of this core group, cultivating them into accomplished *talmidei hachamim*; this was no small feat, considering that some attendees had originally joined to hear the serialized stories he told each night.[1] One member of that group admits that in the early years of the *shiur*, he and his friends occasionally came to the *shiur* with a cinema ticket in their pockets, but were so enthralled by the *shiur* that they stayed in the *beit knesset* as

Harav Ovadia participates in a *siyum* at the home of one of his longtime students. The child next to him is his son, future Rishon LeZion Rav Yitzchak.

---

1. See p. 235.

Harav Ovadia went overtime, missing the movie. Over the years, Harav Ovadia insisted on testing the participants on what they had learned, and some erstwhile simple laymen had by this point mastered large sections of *Shulhan Aruch*.

By now, the group numbered in the hundreds, and the *shiur* moved into Beit Knesset Borochov in the Bucharim neighborhood, where there was room for the entire group.

THE OFFICIAL POSITION HARAV OVADIA RETURNED TO Yerushalayim to fill was a vacancy on the Rabbanut *beit din* led by Rav Eliezer Yehuda Waldenburg, author of *Tzitz Eliezer*.

My Friend, My Brother

Rav Waldenburg was only six years older than Harav Ovadia, but he had been serving on the Rabbanut in Yerushalayim since 5711/1951. By the time the 37-year-old Harav Ovadia returned from Petah Tikva, Rav Waldenburg was already making a name for himself as an eminent authority on all halachic matters, and especially for his groundbreaking rulings regarding modern medicine. His *Sh'eilot V'Teshuvot Tzitz Eliezer*, which would eventually fill 22 volumes written over the course of five decades, include several long sections (called *kuntreisim*) that focus on specific topics, such as the use of electricity on Shabbat and *hagim*, civil marriages, taxes, autopsies, and many others.

From the way the two wrote to and about each other in letters printed in their respective works, it's clear that there was a natural kinship and mutual respect between them. Already in the introduction to the third volume of *Yabia Omer*, published within two years of Harav Ovadia's return to Yerushalayim, he writes, "When I sat in the council of sages with my dear friend, my beloved guide and intimate, a friend like a brother to me… Rav Eliezer Waldenburg *shlita, av beit din* in Yerushalayim, I arrived at several new conclusions regarding how *beit din* should work."

For his part, Rav Waldenburg addresses Harav Ovadia as, "My friend and colleague with whom I shoulder the burden, the Western light, a vessel of Torah… Harav Ovadia Yosef."[2]

---

2. *Tzitz Eliezer* 8:36.

In Rav Eliezer Waldenburg, Harav Ovadia found a kindred spirit in halachic approach.

Harav Ovadia enjoyed his work in the Yerushalayim *beit din*, where he tackled some highly complex *sh'eilot* with his colleagues, and issued rulings in hundreds of cases. Some of these rulings he wrote up and published in later volumes of *Yabia Omer*.

Another relationship that began in those days was between Harav Ovadia and Rav Yosef Shalom Elyashiv, whom he would

Harav Ovadia and Rav Yosef Shalom Elyashiv (C) at the *hachtara* of Chief Rabbi Yisrael Meir Lau (R)

join on the Beit Din HaGadol not long thereafter. Rav Elyashiv began to write him letters regarding *teshuvot* that appeared in *Yabia Omer*, and he would respond. The mutual respect between the two is plainly evident in the admiring words with which they address each other.

Always Awake

HARAV OVADIA QUICKLY BECAME A MAINSTAY OF HIS NEW neighborhood as well; Tel Arza residents and visitors spoke in those days of the rav who was awake whenever you passed his house. Rav David Yosef relates that Rav Moshe Shmuel Shapira, Rosh Yeshiva of Be'er Yaakov, had a daughter who lived in Tel Arza. He told Rav David that when he was visiting his daughter, he would occasionally pass Harav Ovadia's home at 10 p.m. and see him bent over his *sefarim*, learning with deep concentration. It amazed him that when he would pass by a few hours later, he would see him in exactly the same position.

The students of the Tchebin Yeshiva, located one block away on Rehov Hanna, also got used to the idea of Harav Ovadia being available into the wee hours of the morning. Rav Yitzchak Yosef relates that once, on a Friday night, someone in the yeshiva noticed that the *hamin* (cholent) was burning, and he added water to the pot. Someone else saw him doing it, and realized that this was a clear violation of the prohibition of *bishul* (cooking) on Shabbat. This threw the yeshiva students into a quandary: Were they allowed to eat the *hamin* the next day, or were they required to wait until Motza'ei Shabbat (which is often the halacha regarding food that was cooked in violation of *hilchot Shabbat*)? If they could not eat the *hamin* on Shabbat, all the students of the yeshiva would have to find an alternate day *seuda*, which would pose no small challenge.

Rav Yitzchak, who was a child at the time, recalls being awakened by a knock at the door at 2 a.m. From the windows of the yeshiva, the boys were able to see Harav Ovadia learning in his study, and they figured that they could ask him the *sh'eila*. After hearing all the details of the case, Harav Ovadia was able to find them a *heter* to eat the *hamin* in this specific instance.

Hundreds Come Streaming

THE ADMINISTRATION OF THE PORAT YOSEF YESHIVA ALSO decided to capitalize on their famous alumnus's return to Yerushalayim. The yeshiva, which had been forced out of the Old City when the Jordanians captured the area in 1948, had spent several years moving from one *beit knesset* in Yerushalayim to another, while raising money to build their own building. The ceremonial laying of the cornerstone for the building took place in 1955; during that ceremony, Rav Ezra Attia had seated the 34-year-old Harav Ovadia, whom he had begun to refer to as "the Prime Minister of Torah,"[3] right beside him on the dais. By the time of the building's completion in 1956, Harav Ovadia had moved to Petah Tikva, but shortly after his return to Yerushalayim, the yeshiva's administration asked him to deliver a *shiur* each Friday night that would be open to the public. Harav Ovadia, who was always seeking additional opportunities to teach Torah, gladly acquiesced.

The *shiur* quickly became one of the most popular weekly events in Yerushalayim. Over a thousand people — men, women, and even children — would pack into the new building to hear Harav Ovadia deliver a combination of halacha, *mussar*, Midrashic teachings, and *divrei Torah* on the *parasha* of the week — peppered, characteristically, with stories and humor. The *shiur* served as a prototype for what would later become the most listened-to Torah lecture in the world, Harav Ovadia's Motza'ei Shabbat *shiur*.[4]

The *shiur* in Porat Yosef grew so popular that a curious journalist, Reuven Kashani, decided to join one week, and he wrote an article colorfully depicting the scene[5]:

> I was surprised to see the large *beit midrash* filled from end to end. Sitting side by side were elderly men, some bearded and some clean-shaven; youths beside scholars and working men. All seats were taken, and there was a rush to add spots to sit. People were dragging benches

---
3. The *mekubal* Rav Benayahu Shmueli, at a *hesped*.
4. See Chapter 30.
5. The article was printed in *Herut*, the official newspaper of Menachem Begin's right-wing party by the same name.

and chairs from side rooms, while others stood lining the walls of the *beit midrash*. A quick glance at the women's gallery showed that it, too, was full. Among the audience were Ashkenazim who know the Rav and come to hear his Torah.

The audience doesn't sit quietly, arms folded, as they wait for the *shiur* to begin. They sing in unison, fervently humming tunes of Shabbat Kodesh as they look forward to the beginning of the *derasha*.

At the designated hour, the Rav walks in, and the crowd rises in his honor. The Rav walks in measured steps toward the platform and sits down. He is of medium height, wearing a long black coat and a black hat. His face seems serene and sports a trimmed beard. His eyes shine behind his glasses, and his entire bearing commands respect. After

"*The shiur lasts a full hour, and the Rav's words flow forth calmly and confidently, softly and with dignity.*"
A journalist describes Harav Ovadia's Friday night *shiur* in Porat Yosef's new building in Geula, which drew hundreds of men, women, and children out of their homes to hear *divrei Torah*.

short introductory remarks by another scholar about issues of the day, the Rav rises to deliver his *derasha*.

Quiet reigns as the Rav begins his *derasha* with a discussion of *parashat hashavua*. From there he moves on to his main topic: halacha. The *shiur* lasts a full hour, and the Rav's words flow forth calmly and confidently, softly and with dignity. He intersperses words of Aggada and *mussar*, brings parables and Midrashim, and quotes the words of the *geonim* and poskim from memory, drawing parallels from one subject to another.

All these elements flow from his mouth with clear logic, in a definite sequence, each piece in its correct place, and you sit there enthralled, enjoying the experience but wondering at the same time how he can be so well-versed in every branch of Jewish knowledge. Most of all, you are astonished by his infallible memory, as he cites sources chapter and verse. Although the *derasha* is long, the audience shows no signs of fatigue. No one moves or stirs — so powerful is the thirst to hear his beautiful words.

Indeed, Harav Ovadia Yosef's *derasha* is a profound experience for his audience and draws their hearts close [to Torah]. Although I have heard the Rav speak on other occasions, that evening remains engraved upon my mind.

Harav Ovadia continued to deliver this Friday night *shiur* until 1968, when he moved to Tel Aviv.

The Rav on the Radio

IN THOSE YEARS, ANOTHER INTERESTING OPPORTUNITY TO disseminate Torah arose. Each Friday, Kol Yisrael, the official government radio station, broadcasted a program called *Kabbalat Shabbat*. At the time, it was the country's longest-running program. *Kabbalat Shabbat* drew a broad audience, who listened avidly to the mix of *divrei Torah* on the *parasha*, discussions of practical halacha, and other Torah programming. The host, Moshe Levi, was Harav Ovadia's friend from when they were youths in Porat Yosef, and

Harav Ovadia leaving a *beit din* session during the 1960s

when a spot for halachic questions-and-answers was introduced to the program, Harav Ovadia was the natural choice to answer questions. At first, he alternated with an Ashkenazi rav, Rav Tzefania Drori, but Rav Drori had to give up the spot after a while and Harav Ovadia became the weekly host.

The lively question-and-answer sessions kept Harav Ovadia on his toes. He could never know before he entered the studio what questions he would face, yet he was never fazed by a question. Queries would also come in by mail, and he enjoyed answering these relatively straightforward questions, many of which would eventually appear in his second series of responsa, *Yehaveh Daat*.

For example, in the same radio program he could be asked, in quick succession, questions such as:

- ☐ If one attended a Daf Yomi *shiur* for a while, and he would now like to switch to a *shiur* in halacha, does his regular attendance at the Daf Yomi *shiur* take on the halachic status of a vow that he must annul before switching *shiurim*?
- ☐ Our *beit knesset* shipped an old, beautiful *aron kodesh* from our former country to Eretz Yisrael, and it was installed in our *beit knesset*. For a long time, the doors of the *aron kodesh* were covered with a cloth *parochet*, as is customary. Now, a member of our congregation has refurbished the doors of the *aron kodesh* and decorated them, and he would like to remove the *parochet* so the doors will be visible. May we allow him to do so?
- ☐ If someone wrote cantillation or punctuation marks in a *Sefer Torah*, did he render it invalid?

Harav Ovadia would answer these questions fluidly, citing chapter and verse to source his ruling. At one point, when he held a special pre-Pesah question-and-answer session and callers were bombarding the program, the host suddenly interrupted and said, "I just want to clarify to the public, because you can't see what I see: The rav is sitting here without a single *sefer* in front of him."

The Beit Din HaGadol Calls

IN 1965, FIVE YEARS AFTER HARAV OVADIA JOINED RAV Waldenburg's *beit din*, and following the publication of the third and fourth volumes of *Yabia Omer*, a position opened on the Beit Din HaGadol Le'irurim (the highest halachic court in the country), which was also situated in Yerushalayim. Rav Betzalel Zolty and Rav Yosef Shalom Elyashiv, both of whom were already *dayanim* on the *beit din* and held Harav Ovadia in high esteem, wanted him to fill the position.

Some powerful people in the Rabbanut wanted to prevent Harav Ovadia from joining the Beit Din HaGadol, and they tried to influence other members of the council responsible for electing new *dayanim* to vote against Harav Ovadia. During a particularly rancorous debate between the council members, Rav Zolty suggested that the vote be held by secret ballot, and Harav Ovadia's primary detractor threatened to walk out of the session. Although this council member was extremely influential, Religious Affairs Minister Zorach Warhaftig refused to cave in to his threats. "We won't allow anyone to be terrorized into voting a certain way," he declared, "and anybody who doesn't like that can leave."

The secret ballot was held, and Harav Ovadia was voted onto the Beit Din HaGadol by a large margin.

THE BEIT DIN LE'IRURIM (*BEIT DIN* FOR APPEALS) WAS ESTABlished in 5679/1919 as a branch of the Rabbanut HaRashit (Chief

Appeals in Beit Din?

Rabbinate). It was established because the British Mandatory government was willing to grant official recognition to the Rabbanut's *beit din* system only if it was modeled after the British judicial system. *Batei din* already existed in cities in Eretz Yisrael with large Jewish populations, but in order to meet the British criteria, there had to be a "higher" *beit din* in which a party in a *din Torah* could appeal a verdict of a lower *beit din*.

At the opening session of the Beit Din HaGadol with the new *dayanim*. (R-L): Harav Ovadia, Rav Salman Hugi Aboudi, Rav Betzalel Zolty, Rishon LeZion Rav Yitzhak Nissim, Rav Yosef Shalom Elyashiv, and Rav Eliezer Goldschmidt

Chapter Fifteen: Return to My Father's Home ☐ 299

Originally, the three-member appeals court consisted of one or both chief rabbis, along with either one or two members of the Moetzet HaRabbanut HaRashit, the Chief Rabbinate Council (who were not *dayanim*). It operated this way until Heshvan 5711/1950, two years after the State was founded, when Rav Herzog, the first Ashkenazi chief rabbi of Israel, established an appeals court composed entirely of *dayanim* unaffiliated with the Chief Rabbinate Council, and with the chief rabbis serving as its head.[6]

The establishment of a *beit din* for appeals was no simple matter in halacha, because there is a rule that one *beit din* is not allowed to nullify another *beit din*'s rulings. A dispute erupted when the Chief Rabbinate was established in 1919, with the Eida Haredit, led by Rav Yosef Chaim Sonnenfeld, declaring a fast on the day it was established, because they felt that its appeals court was in clear violation of halacha. Those in favor of creating an appeals court argued that if a regular *beit din* is aware that there is a higher court that can review its verdicts, that is considered a de facto agreement that their ruling is not binding if one of the two parties in a *din Torah* wants to lodge an appeal.

Harav Ovadia himself had already addressed the issue of the halachic validity of an appeals court, in a *teshuva* he wrote in Cairo in 1948, published in Volume Two of *Yabia Omer*.[7] He offers an additional reason why the existence of an appeals court is halachically permissible — one that Rav Elyashiv held as well.

There are two ways that a *beit din* can reach a decision in a case. Sometimes the circumstances are clear-cut and there is a halacha in Shulhan Aruch clearly addressing the matter. In other instances, however, the circumstances are murky, and there is also no clear halacha in *Shulhan Aruch* addressing the specific case. In such instances, the *dayanim* on the *beit din* must use *shikul hadaat*, their own judgment, drawing parallels from similar cases that have been addressed over the years, in order to reach a conclusion.

The rule stating that one *beit din* may not nullify another's ruling

---

6. The name of the appeals court was also changed at the time, from Beit Din Le'irurim to Beit Din **HaGadol** Le'irurim, reflecting the Mishnaic term, "Beit Din HaGadol of Yerushalayim."
7. *Hoshen Mishpat* 3:8.

refers to rulings that are dependent on the judgment of the *dayanim*. In such cases, the second court has no right to say that their judgment is better than that of the previous *beit din*. If, however, the second *beit din* does not seek to override the first *beit din*'s judgment, but rather to review the ruling of the first *beit din* to ensure that it was not in contravention of a clear halacha in *Shulhan Aruch*, that is not a violation of the rule that one *beit din* may not nullify another's decision, because a decision rendered against a ruling in *Shulhan Aruch* is not considered valid to begin with.

Harav Ovadia cites a slew of sources indicating that a *beit din* may be established to review judgments to ensure that they do not contradict a clear halacha. He cites from *Noda B'Yehuda* that only a rav who believes that he may have ruled against halacha would be opposed to having his decisions reviewed.

His appointment to the Beit Din HaGadol at the age of 44 — when most *dayanim* were appointed to this post in their 60s, at the very end of their *dayanut* career — was a clear nod to Harav Ovadia's accomplishments over the years, and a recognition that he was destined to become a leading figure in the Rabbanut. He would end up retaining his position on the Beit Din HaGadol for over twenty years, until he was required to step down in 1987 because his involvement in the Shas party precluded him from holding any government position.

To Harav Ovadia, this appointment was particularly attractive because he had to appear in the *beit din* only several mornings a week, for a few hours on each of those days, and the salary he earned was generous enough to enable him to devote the rest of his days to learning and teaching Torah.

It was also an extremely enjoyable type of work for Harav Ovadia, because instead of spending hours listening to the two parties in a case present their arguments, the *dayanim* on the Beit Din HaGadol spent their time examining all the angles of the relevant halacha, so his time in the Beit Din was also spent learning. In addition, he was in the company of some of the most brilliant Torah minds in the world, and they would often discuss Torah and halacha matters that were not directly related to the cases they were reviewing.

WHILE HARAV OVADIA WAS BECOMING RECOGNIZED AS ONE of the Torah pillars of Eretz Yisrael, Rabbanit Margalit was running her own empire: an empire of *hessed*, run with nearly militaristic precision.

The Neighborhood Hessed Hub

Like any good army commander, Rabbanit Margalit had an intelligence unit: she would find out which families needed help, and what sort of help they needed. Then she would dispatch her troops:

> "Malka, Mrs. Cohen doesn't feel well today. Go help her feed the children and put them to sleep."
>
> "Adina, Mrs. Hecht's husband is traveling today. Go see if she needs any help."
>
> "Yaffa, please bring these meatballs to the Mualems. But wait, first go ask Rabbanit Abba Shaul if she needs to throw another load into the washing machine."

The Yosef family's washing machine and telephone — two rarities in those days — turned the apartment on 8 Elkana into public property. Not by the public's overstepping of boundaries, but by the Rabbanit's insistence. "The machine does all the work anyway," she would tell her neighbors. "Why should you do all that work by hand? Give me your laundry and I'll just throw it in."

Little did the neighbors realize, as they gratefully handed over their laundry, that the Rabbanit didn't just "throw it in." She often checked the clothing for stains, scrubbing out spots that she knew wouldn't come out in the machine.

And her *hessed* didn't come only in the form of physical assistance with household tasks; the Rabbanit's door was also open to any woman seeking a sympathetic ear.

> One morning, the Rabbanit heard a frantic knock on the door. Miriam, a neighbor, was standing there, an anxious look on her face. "May I use the telephone?" she asked.
>
> "Sure," the Rabbanit said, welcoming her into the apartment. Something told her that this conversation was private, so she left the room.

She returned a few minutes later, after noting that Miriam's voice had gone still, to find her standing at the phone looking dejected.

Suddenly, Miriam placed her head in her hands and began to weep uncontrollably. The Rabbanit quickly handed her a cup of water and sat down next to her. She waited for Miriam to calm down, then waited some more, unsure what to say.

Finally, Miriam broke the silence. "I have two mute daughters. Two...."

The Rabbanit was confused. Miriam's had two mute daughters, yes, but they were almost entering adolescence. Sad as the situation was, why had Miriam chosen this morning to bemoan her fate?

The answer wasn't long in coming.

"If the first two were mute, then the third..." Miriam's voice trailed off. She couldn't get the frightful words out of her mouth.

Now the Rabbanit understood — Miriam was expecting.

"Do you think that it has been decreed from Heaven that all of your children will be mute?" she asked, setting off another round of tears from Miriam.

"I'm certain that my next child will also have some sort of handicap," she sobbed. "If not muteness, then deafness. But something."

"Miriam," the Rabbanit soothed, "first of all, your daughters don't only give you pain. They also give you nahat. They're sweet girls, they help you a lot, they do well in school...."

"You don't understand," Miriam answered sharply. "You don't know how my heart sinks each time I see an adult cast a pitying glance at my girls, or when I watch them suffer from the taunts of thoughtless children."

"I didn't finish what I was saying," the Rabbanit said softly. "What I mean is that even if your child is born with some sort of handicap, it doesn't mean that you won't have

nahat. But more importantly — why expect the worst? Genetics are complex. You have no reason to assume that this child will be born with a handicap."

"And if it has been decreed that the child will have a handicap?" Miriam persisted.

The Rabbanit caught Miriam's eyes and uttered words that only a mother who had suffered the loss of her own child had the right to say. "If that's what will happen, then that will be the best thing for the child — and for you. Hashem does only good for people. We might not understand why it's good for us. But we know that it is."

Coming from the Rabbanit, this message struck a chord with Miriam. She thanked the Rabbanit and took her leave.

For the next eight months, Miriam prayed as she had never prayed before, and, following the Rabbanit's advice, she visited the graves of great tzaddikim to beseech Hashem in their merit. When Miriam stopped by the Yosef home on her way to the hospital to request a beracha from Harav Ovadia, the Rabbanit's heart skipped a few beats. *What if the baby is born with a defect?* she thought, reaching for her Tehillim. *Will Miriam ever forgive me?*

A few hours later, the news arrived: Miriam's baby was perfectly healthy! The Rabbanit breathed a sigh of thanks to Hashem, and celebrated the baby's brit — and eventually his bar mitzva — feeling almost like a grandmother.[8]

Expansion on Two Levels

IN 1959, ON ADINA'S FOURTEENTH BIRTHDAY, A NEW DAUGHter, Leah, was born, bringing the number of the children in the family to ten. The older boys were away at yeshiva much of the time, but the Rabbanit still had her hands full with the younger children and the older girls.

Before the Yosefs could turn around, their daughter Adina was 18, and the *shadchanim* started to call. It was not long before the wedding band was playing its melodies as Adina walked down to

---

8. *Ba'asher Teilech.*

At the wedding of Rav Ezra Bar-Shalom to Harav Ovadia's oldest child, Adina. The *hattan* (R) would eventually follow in his father-in-law's footsteps and serve on the Beit Din HaGadol.

the *huppa* to be married to R' Ezra Bar-Shalom, a budding *talmid hacham* who would eventually follow in his father-in-law's footsteps and sit on the Beit Din HaGadol.

A year later, Adina gave birth to a son, and a year after that, she gave birth to a daughter. The Rabbanit herself felt too young to be a grandmother; she still wanted to be a mother. In 1966, Hashem answered her prayers and granted her a *ben zekunim*, Moshe.

CHAPTER SIXTEEN
A UNIQUE RELATIONSHIP

THE SPECIAL RELATIONSHIP BETWEEN HACHAM Ovadia[1] and Hacham Benzion Abba Shaul — which began when the two were youngsters in Talmud Torah Bnei Zion and lasted until Hacham Benzion's passing more than six decades later on 19 Tammuz 5758/1998 — was one that was unique among *gedolei Yisrael*.

One of the most remarkable aspects of the relationship was that the two were absolute opposites in terms of how they ruled in halacha, disputing hundreds of each other's *piskei halacha* over the course of their lives, yet never losing an iota of respect for each other.

Their divergent approaches in halacha most likely stemmed from a difference of opinion on how to learn a *sugya*. Rav Yehoshua Abba Shaul, a grandson of Hacham Benzion and the author of five *sefarim* of his own, tells a story to illustrate this difference:

> *Hacham Ovadia was once sitting at a wedding, and a sh'eila arose regarding the validity of the ketuba. He took two*

---

[1]. Although in general we have been referring to Harav Ovadia by the title "Harav," reflecting the title most commonly conferred upon him in his life, in this chapter we refer to him as Hacham Ovadia to reflect the title by which Hacham Benzion addressed him.

Though they differed in halachic approach, the love and respect shared by Hacham Ovadia and Hacham Benzion Abba Shaul was legendary.

>   papers. *On one he wrote out all the sources that would consider the ketuba valid, on the other he wrote out the sources that would invalidate it, and he ruled based on this listing.*
>
>   *My grandfather, on the other hand, learned a sugya thoroughly — from the Gemara, through the Rishonim and the Poskim — and he ruled according to the way he understood the halacha when he finished the sugya, without seeking the opinions of numerous Aharonim.*

Although each one knew that the other would likely disagree with his ruling, they still sought each other's opinions on halachic issues. Already in a *teshuva* published in the *Orah Haim* section of the first volume of *Yabia Omer*, Hacham Ovadia quotes a point Hacham Benzion raised regarding the topic he was dicussing, and one of the *teshuvot* in *Yoreh Dei'a* is a response to a *sh'eila* posed by Hacham Benzion.[2] In the third volume of *Yabia Omer*, Hacham Ovadia prints a full *teshuva* written by Hacham Benzion permitting

---

2. *Teshuvot* 40 and 2, respectively.

Hacham Ovadia and Hacham Benzion celebrated their differences in learning. Seen here in a Torah conversation at a *simha*.

corneal transplants only if the donor is a non-Jew, and Hacham Ovadia responds with a *teshuva* ruling that the cornea may be taken from a Jew as well.[3]

Respecting the Differences

NOT ONLY DID THE TWO RESPECT EACH OTHER'S RIGHT TO argue, they actually celebrated the differences in their styles of learning.

Hacham Benzion once took part in a siyum Hacham Ovadia made upon completing Masechet Mo'ed Katan. After the siyum, Hacham Benzion spoke, and he said, "I have merited to learn many masechtot many times each with Hacham Ovadia, but I merited to learn Mo'ed Katan with him only once. I can tell you, however, that he knows every single daf in the masechet by heart."

Hacham Ovadia rose immediately and said, "I may know what's written on the daf, but Hacham Benzion

---

3. *Teshuvot* 20 and 21, respectively.

knows what's under the daf (i.e., the deeper levels of understanding)."

This exchange actually represented a deeper disagreement the two had regarding how one should learn. Hacham Ovadia felt strongly — from the youngest age — that yeshivot were learning too slowly, and their students would never develop into true *talmidei hachamim* at that rate. He wrote about this topic in several places in *Yabia Omer*, and he tried to convince Hacham Benzion and Rav Yehuda Tzadka to speed up the pace of learning in Porat Yosef.

Interestingly, though, when the two *hachamim* learned together, they followed Hacham Ovadia's approach.

> At the shiva for Hacham Benzion, Hacham Ovadia mentioned that they used to walk to school together and review a daf each way. One of Hacham Benzion's brothers said, "You learned much more than two daf each day together. I remember him saying that the two of you learned 40 (!) daf each day!"
>
> Hacham Ovadia waved his hand and said, "I remember learning a daf each way."
>
> When he left and returned to the car, his attendant R' Tzvi Hakak asked how it could be that Hacham Benzion remembered learning 40 daf if it was actually only one daf each way.
>
> "I should admit that we learned 40 daf each day?" asked Hacham Ovadia. "There's nothing to be gained by people knowing that."

Two Matmidim

BOTH *HACHAMIM* WERE KNOWN FOR THEIR INCREDIBLE *hatmada* (diligence). If as youths they would use their walks to review their learning by heart,[4] by the time they were teenagers they were using every waking moment for learning. They even had a weekly learning session while they prepared *lichvod Shabbat* — Hacham

---

4. See p. 106.

Benzion would ask a question while Hacham Ovadia prepared, and Hacham Ovadia would answer as Hacham Benzion got ready.

From the time Hacham Ovadia moved to Egypt a few years after marriage, until he moved back to Yerushalayim in 5718/1958, his contact with Hacham Benzion was intermittent, as the two built their respective homes and charted their own paths. Hacham Ovadia was focusing primarily on becoming a *posek* and teaching halacha to simple Jews, while Hacham Benzion was developing as rosh yeshiva of Porat Yosef and teaching generations of students how to study Gemara in-depth. Becoming neighbors in 8 Rehov Elkana afforded them new opportunities to cultivate their friendship and reignite the learning partnerships they had enjoyed in their youth.

After reuniting on Rehov Elkana, Hacham Ovadia and Hacham Benzion began an all-night learning session each Thursday night that continued as they walked home together Friday morning.

The Timely Theft

SHORTLY AFTER HACHAM OVADIA MOVED BACK TO Yerushalayim, he and Hacham Benzion began a weekly all-night study session in Beit Haknesset Shoshanim L'David on Thursday nights. They would pray *k'vatikin* (at sunrise) Friday morning and then walk the 15 minutes back to Rehov Elkana together, continuing to discuss the topic they had been studying until they arrived home.

> One week, two minutes after they parted, Hacham Benzion heard a knock at his door. Hacham Ovadia was standing there, sans hat and rabbinic frock, smiling from ear to ear.
>
> "What brings you here so soon?" Hacham Benzion asked.
>
> "Last night," Hacham Ovadia replied, "while we were away, thieves broke into my apartment while everyone else was asleep and stole everything."

Chapter Sixteen: A Unique Relationship □ 311

"Everything" in those days wasn't much. Although Hacham Ovadia's financial standing had stabilized by that point, the family still didn't have extras. The thieves stole pots, pans, cups, and cutlery, leaving the family without a dish to their name.

"So why are you smiling?" asked Hacham Benzion.

"I don't understand how these burglars knew to come this week of all weeks," exclaimed Hacham Ovadia. "How did they know that this week is Parashat Vayishlah, when we'll read in the Haftara: אִם גַּנָּבִים בָּאוּ לְךָ אִם שׁוֹדְדֵי לַיְלָה, *If thieves have came upon you, if plunderers of the night*" (Ovadia 1:5)!

Respecting Hacham Ovadia's Five Minutes

LATER ON IN LIFE, WHEN HACHAM OVADIA WAS RISHON LeZion and had a chauffeur-driven car, he and Hacham Benzion both attended an event outside Yerushalayim. When it ended, Hacham Ovadia offered Hacham Benzion a ride home. "I need to stay here for a while," Hacham Benzion demurred.

Having attended Hacham Ovadia's *shiur* in Beit Knesset Shaul Tzadka during their younger years, Hacham Benzion (seated beside the standing Hacham Ovadia) valued each moment of his friend's life.

No sooner had Hacham Ovadia's car pulled away than Hacham Benzion sought a different ride leaving to Yerushalayim immediately. "Why did you tell Hacham Ovadia that you're not ready to leave?" someone asked Hacham Benzion.

"I knew that if I would accept the ride," Hacham Benzion explained, "he wouldn't suffice with taking me back to Yerushalayim; he would drive me all the way home. I didn't want to take him out of the way."

"It's not much of a bother in a car," the questioner persisted. "How long does it take? Five minutes?"

"You don't realize how much five minutes of Hacham Ovadia's life is worth," Hacham Benzion answered pointedly. "You can't fathom how much he accomplishes in five minutes!"

PERHAPS THIS RESPECT FOR HACHAM OVADIA'S TIME explains a story told by both Hacham Ovadia and his son Rav Avraham in their respective eulogies of Hacham Benzion.

Who Took the Child for Stitches?

One Friday afternoon during the winter, an hour before sunset, the young Avraham was playing outside with his friends when he was hit by a rock thrown by one of the boys. Some of his siblings saw the incident, and they ran inside to summon the Rabbanit. When she saw Avraham's face covered in blood, she thought that he had been hit in the eye, and she started to scream for help.

Hacham Benzion heard her cries and came running down the steps. He grabbed Avraham, took him to a sink, and rinsed off his face, wrapping the wound in a cloth. He assuaged the Rabbanit's fear, assuring her that the cut was above the eye, and that while Avraham needed to go to the hospital for stitches, there wouldn't be any long-term damage. Without uttering another word, he left the apartment with Avraham, taking him to Bikur Holim hospital on Rehov HaNevi'im and sitting with him while the doctor stitched him up. By the time they were ready to head back

At the bar mitzva of Avraham Yosef, some years after Hacham Benzion escorted him to the hospital. (R-L) Grandfather Rav Yaakov Ovadia, Hacham Ovadia, the bar mitzva boy, and grandfather Hacham Avraham Fattal

home, it was already Shabbat, and they had to walk the 25 minutes to Tel Arza.

The temperature had dropped while they were in the hospital, and Hacham Benzion asked Avraham whether he was cold. "I was embarrassed to answer that I was," recalls Avraham, "so I just kept quiet.

"Hacham Benzion understood my silence, and he took off his coat and put it on me."

As they neared their beit knesset, Hacham Benzion turned to Avraham and said, "I don't want your father to be concerned about you, nor do I want him to blame you for the difficulty I incurred. Don't come into the beit knesset until I have spoken to him."

Avraham followed Hacham Benzion's instructions. For his part, Hacham Ovadia was astonished to hear that his son had gotten hurt and that no one had told him about it.

"This was my son," he said in wonderment in his eulogy for Hacham Benzion. "I'm the one who should have been taking care of him."[5]

---

5. *Tiferet Zion*, pp. 143, 310.

Perhaps Hacham Benzion decided to take Avraham to the hospital because he knew something that others didn't.

Years earlier, when the teenaged Hacham Ovadia and Hacham Benzion learned together in Beit Haknesset Shoshanim L'David on Friday afternoons, Benzion would get up to go prepare for Shabbat half an hour before candle-lighting, and Ovadia would say, "Just a few more minutes." Often, when Benzion returned to the *beit knesset* for Minha, he would find that Ovadia had become so engrossed in his learning that he had simply forgotten to go home and get ready for Shabbat.

On that wintry Friday afternoon a few decades later, Hacham Benzion may have determined that unless someone would actively disrupt Hacham Ovadia from his learning, he would never realize that his wife was screaming in fear that their son would lose his eyesight, and Hacham Benzion therefore resolved to take Avraham to the hospital himself.

"I Was Afraid to Live Above Him!"

WHEN RAV DAVID YOSEF FIRST ESTABLISHED HIS BEIT Midrash Yehaveh Daat, it was situated in two conjoined apartments in a residential building in Har Nof, with other apartments on top of one part of the *beit midrash*. One of the residents who lived in an apartment above the *beit midrash* — a sweet, sincere person — protested against the establishment of the *beit midrash* there. He quoted the Taz (*Orah Haim* 151:4), who writes that when he lived in Krakow, several of his children died, and he attributed it to the fact that he lived above a *beit knesset*.

Rav David replied that the Rema (ibid. 151:12) states that the prohibition of living above a *beit knesset* applies only if the building was built specifically as a *beit knesset*, and predated those who lived in the building. If, however, the residents lived there before part of the building was turned into a *beit knesset*, they need not be concerned.

Furthermore, Hacham Ovadia had already written a *teshuva*[6] on the matter, and he quoted a *teshuva* from the Rambam, who states

---
6. *Yabia Omer*, Vol. 6, *Orah Haim* 26.

that it is permissible to live above a *beit knesset* as long as the area directly above the *heichal* in which the *Sifrei Torah* are kept is not used for sleeping. Hacham Ovadia quotes the Hida,[7] who points out that Maran, the Beit Yosef, did not have access to the Rambam's responsa, and had he been familiar with this *teshuva*, he would certainly have ruled similarly.

The man's fears were not allayed, however, and he insisted that Rav David come with him to Hacham Benzion, to whom he addressed all of his halachic queries.

"I knew what Hacham Benzion would rule," says Rav David, "because at some point when Abba and Hacham Benzion lived in 8 Rehov Elkana together, the bomb shelter was converted into a *beit knesset*. Hacham Benzion himself lived on top of the *beit knesset* that was established after he had moved into the building."

Sure enough, when the two posed the question, Hacham Benzion turned to Rav David. "You're referring to me, right?" he said laughingly, before assuring the resident of the upper floor that he could live there without worry.

But then, he became very serious. "To tell you the truth," he added, "living on top of the public *beit midrash* three floors below me is not what made me fearful in those days. You know what I was worried about? Two floors beneath me there was a *beit midrash* of a single person who studied Torah day and night, and I was petrified to sleep above him as he learned.

"It was much more frightening to live above Hacham Ovadia than to live above a *beit knesset*."

Learning Amid the Bombs

RAV DAVID YOSEF RECALLS THE UTTER TERROR THAT GRIPPED Yerushalayim during May and June of 1967. Three Arab countries — Egypt, Jordan, and Syria — were preparing to do battle with Israel, although Egypt was by far the most belligerent of the three. These forces also had support from an additional nine Arab armies, and all twelve armies were equipped with advanced Soviet weap-

---

7. *Sh'eilot V'Teshuvot Haim Sha'al* 1:56.

onry. The total Arab forces threatening Israel were two-and-a-half times the size of the Israeli Army.

The country was in a state of near panic. Ten thousand graves were dug in advance of the war, and 14,000 hospital beds were prepared. Jews throughout the Diaspora prayed for the safety of the people and donated money for the war effort.

The first attack during the war was actually a preemptive strike by the Israeli Air Force, at approximately 8 a.m. on June 5, that miraculously knocked out almost all of Egypt's fighter planes on the ground. A few hours later, Jordan began to shell residential neighborhoods in Yerushalayim. The city's residents had spent weeks preparing their bomb shelters, but when the strike actually began, Sara and Rivka Yosef were in school, and David was in Talmud Torah — all in the Beit Yisrael neighborhood, a 15-minute walk from Rehov Elkana.

Harav Ovadia's daughter Yaffa took matters into her own hands, and began to run toward the schools. A soldier stopped her on Rehov Ezra, however. "Where are you going?" he shouted, and motioned with his finger toward the Spitzer school, where Harav Ovadia and Rabbanit Margalit had married 23 years earlier. "Get into this bomb shelter!"

"I need to find my sisters and brother," she panted.

"You're not going anywhere," the soldier retorted. "It's too dangerous."

Suddenly, a woman appeared on the street. "Aren't you Harav Ovadia Yosef's daughter?" she asked.

Yaffa nodded.

"If you're looking for your sisters, they're in there," she said, pointing to the school. "They were walking toward your home, and a soldier directed them inside."

Yaffa entered the bomb shelter and found her 11-year-old twin sisters huddled together in fright. She told them to stay put, and then, casting a furtive glance into the street to ensure that the soldier was nowhere in sight, she ran out toward David's Talmud Torah, ignoring the shouted commands of other soldiers along the way. She found David at his school, and, clutching his hand, she ran back to the Spitzer school to pick up her sisters.

By the time they arrived home, the Rabbanit was pale from anxiety. Relieved to see them safe and sound, she pulled them down the steps to the bomb shelter, where the building's other residents were already vying for space.[8]

Terror. Desperation. Anxiety. Despair.

Words can't do justice to the feelings of defenseless men, women, and children crouching in a bomb shelter, wondering if the next shell will bring the entire building down on their heads. Some twenty civilians would lose their lives and hundreds more would be injured in the three days before the Israeli Army would manage not only to turn back the Jordanian Legion, but, with Divine assistance, to regain control of the Old City and capture the West Bank as well.

> *One woman in the bomb shelter of 8 Rehov Elkana was crying hysterically. Her only son had been called up to serve on the front lines, and she was terrified that he wouldn't return. The Rabbanit sat down next to her, holding seven-month-old Moshe on her lap and clamping her hands over his sensitive ears to protect them from the deafening shell blasts. She tried to soothe the forlorn mother, but each blast set off a fresh wave of sobbing.*
>
> *Only two people in the shelter were seemingly unfazed by the noise: Hacham Ovadia and Hacham Benzion, who had decided that they would devote the days in the bomb shelter to studying Masechet Hullin.*

"When scholars want to learn *Masechet Hullin* today," notes R' Yehoshua Abba Shaul, "they'll find themselves an air-conditioned *beit midrash*, a *sefer* with pictures to help them understand the *sugyot* that discuss blemishes on an animal's internal organs, and perhaps a cold drink to keep them focused."

The Six-Day War was fought in June, in summer weather. The heat was stifling even on the upper floors; all the more so in the windowless bomb shelters. Yet the two *hachamim* sat there and learned the difficult *halachot* of *treifot* — regarding which Hacham

---

8. *Ba'asher Teileich.*

While all Israelis huddled in fear in bomb shelters during the Six-Day War, Hacham Ovadia and Hacham Benzion were able to focus on *Masechet Hullin*.

Ovadia often consulted with Hacham Benzion because of his expertise in the area — as though there was nothing going on around them.[9]

Yet despite their seeming nonchalance, both of them would remember their learning sessions in the bomb shelter for years to come.

Hacham Benzion's students relate that shortly after the war, he began to deliver a *shiur* to the *bahurim*, and then he suddenly veered in a different direction. "Tell me," he challenged them, "is Hacham Ovadia a human or an angel?" He told the boys about how Hacham Ovadia had sat and learned, seemingly unperturbed by the shelling. "Is he a human or an angel?" he repeated in wonderment.

Hacham Ovadia, for his part, was equally amazed by Hacham Benzion's ability to focus during those days, even mentioning it in his eulogy of Hacham Benzion some three decades later.[10]

---

9. R' Yehoshua Abba Shaul, who heard it from his grandfather.
 In his eulogy at the end of Hacham Benzion's *shiva*, Hacham Ovadia recalled that during the shelling, Hacham Benzion would tell him his *hiddushim* (novellae) in *Masechet Yevamot* — one of the most complex and difficult *masechtot* in all of *Shas*.
10. *Tiferet Zion*, p. 118.

Chapter Sixteen: A Unique Relationship ☐ 319

SO POWERFUL WERE THE FEELINGS OF MUTUAL LOVE AND respect between these two leaders of Sephardic Jewry that neither could bear to see the other one disrespected in the least.

Mutual Love and Respect

After a particular halachic dispute between the two — one that later became famous — a certain rav approached Hacham Benzion and tried to rile him up against Hacham Ovadia's ruling. Hacham Benzion pinned him with his gaze, and said, "You and I together don't come to Hacham Ovadia's ankles."

Anyone who learned in Porat Yosef during those decades was witness to the respect the two accorded each other in public. Rav Benzion Mutzafi relates that he was once at a gathering in which both were in attendance, and at one point, Hacham Benzion had to leave the room. When he returned, Hacham Ovadia was speaking, and rather than disrupt by going back to his seat at the eastern wall, Hacham Benzion sat down among the crowd. Hacham Ovadia motioned for him to come forward, but Hacham Benzion remained seated, so as not to interrupt the *shiur*.

"I cannot continue," Hacham Ovadia declared, "until Hacham Benzion is seated in a place that befits his stature."

> *Rav Gideon Ben-Menashe[11] recalled a gathering in Porat Yosef that Hacham Ovadia was scheduled to attend. He noticed that Hacham Benzion made sure to find a seat before Hacham Ovadia walked in, so that he could rise fully in his honor when he walked in. As Hacham Ovadia walked through the door and spotted Hacham Benzion, he ran toward him, and both of them opened their arms in greeting even before they reached each other. Hacham Benzion then seated Hacham Ovadia in his own place at the eastern wall of the yeshiva, facing the crowd, and took a seat facing forward, with the rest of the crowd. "His honor should sit here," Hacham Ovadia protested.*
>
> *"No," Hacham Benzion replied. "His honor should sit there. I'll sit here."*

---

11. One of the leaders of Rav David Yosef's Beit Midrash Yehaveh Daat.

Rav Ovadia eulogizing Hacham Benzion at his funeral, with Rav Eliyahu Abba Shaul standing next to him.

Hacham Ovadia had to pull him by the hand to sit next to him at the eastern wall.

"That day," recalls Rav Ben-Menashe, "We learned what it truly means to love talmidei hachamim, to abnegate oneself to other talmidei hachamim — even if you disagree with them on many matters."

PERHAPS THE GREATEST SIGN OF HACHAM OVADIA'S RESPECT for Hacham Benzion is the longest *teshuva* in all of *Yabia Omer*, in which Hacham Ovadia devotes dozens of pages — comprising more than 50,000 words — to refuting 195 *piskei halacha* published in Hacham Benzion's second volume of *Sh'eilot V'Teshuvot Ohr LeZion*.

The Longest Teshuva

It is clearly evident from this *teshuva*, published after Hacham Benzion's passing, that Hacham Ovadia respected his old friend so much that it was important to him to devote so many pages to setting down his own rulings on these matters.

The dispute didn't end even after Hacham Ovadia passed away. Shortly after his passing, Hacham Benzion's grandson published a pamphlet defending his grandfather's halachic positions against Hacham Ovadia's refutations.

And in the spirit of the loving relationship between the two, he dedicated his pamphlet to… Hacham Ovadia!

SECTION FOUR

LEADER OF THE LAND

וְיוֹסֵף הוּא הַשַּׁלִּיט עַל הָאָרֶץ

Yosef was the ruler over the land

(Bereishit 42:6)

CHAPTER SEVENTEEN
ON THE BIG STAGE

THROUGHOUT THE 1960S, HARAV OVADIA'S FAME CONtinued to spread throughout Eretz Yisrael, via his *shiurim*, his weekly radio program, and eventually through a widely circulated publication called *Kol Sinai*. In its second issue, Shevat 5722/1962, Harav Ovadia was profiled as the "cover story," and its editors later asked him to write a monthly halacha column for the everyman, in simple and clear language.

Through this popular column, a much broader audience was introduced to his phenomenal knowledge and clarity in all areas of halacha. This wider recognition would serve him well as he was propelled into the national limelight during the election campaign for chief rabbi of Tel Aviv.

Private Coronation

IN 5715/1955, RABBI YITZHAK NISSIM WAS ELECTED TO THE position of Rishon LeZion,[1] In that capacity, he would serve alongside Rav Yitzchak Isaac Herzog, who was reelected as the Ashkenazi chief rabbi.

Five years later, when elections for chief rabbi were supposed to be held again, many leading Sephardi rabbanim

---

1. The position of Rishon LeZion predated the State by a few hundred years, and Sephardim therefore view the position as one of great distinction and authority. In fact, the Rishon LeZion is considered the de facto head of Porat Yosef, the first and foremost Sephardi yeshivah.
   In his role, he is expected to lead the Rabbanut and improve the spiritual standing of society at large.

The second issue of *Kol Sinai*, featuring Harav Ovadia on the cover. His column in the publication would bring his clear *piskei halacha* to a much broader audience.

wished to replace Chief Rabbi Nissim. Their choice: Harav Ovadia Yosef, who hadn't even celebrated his 40th birthday. Before the official election was held, the Vaad Ha'Eida HaSepharadit held a *maamad hachtara* (coronation ceremony) in Yerushalayim and appointed him as "Rosh HaRabbanim HaSephardim" (Sephardi Chief Rabbi) and "Rishon LeZion."[2]

---

2. The Rabbanim who attended this event included: Harav Ovadia's primary mentor, Rav Ezra Attia; the *dayan* Rav Yosef Babliki; Chief Rabbi of Yerushalayim Rav Eliyahu Pardes; Chief Rabbi of Teveria Rav Meir Vaknin; Chief Rabbi of Haifa Rav Nissim Ohanah; Chief Rabbi of Acco Rav Shalom Lofes; Chief Rabbi of Ramle-Lod Rav Yitzhak Abuhatzeira; and Chief Rabbi of Beit Shemesh Rav Yosef Buskila.

After the ceremony, the rabbanim signed a letter proclaiming their support of Harav Ovadia for the position, and the letter was posted publicly throughout Yerushalayim.

Harav Ovadia at the private coronation ceremony, surrounded by the Sephardic chief rabbis of several cities in Eretz Yisrael

Harav Ovadia took part in the ceremony, but did not want to run for the government-recognized position of chief rabbi because he felt extremely uncomfortable about opposing a sitting chief rabbi — a feeling that would remain with him even ten years later when he finally did run against Rav Nissim, upon the insistence of many rabbanim.[3]

The Religious Affairs Minister in those years was the chief rabbi of Tel Aviv, Rav Yaakov Moshe Toledano, the only non-Knesset Member ever to serve as Religious Affairs Minister. In 1960, shortly after the *maamad hachtara*, Rav Toledano began to prepare the groundwork for elections, setting up a *guf habocher* — the committee that would elect the chief rabbi. Judging by the makeup of that committee, Harav Ovadia should easily have won the election.

But Rav Toledano passed away of a sudden heart attack on Shabbat Bereishit, 24 Tishrei 5721/1960, and the elections were delayed — first for ten months, then an additional year, and so on, until they finally took place in 5724/1964.[4] During those delays, Harav Ovadia's name was consistently floated as a candidate for the

---
3. See pp. 356-357.
4. During that period, Rav Nissim continued as the sitting chief rabbi. He was actually the only chief rabbi at the time, because Rav Herzog had passed away in 1959, and no one could be appointed to replace him without elections.

post. The secular press, which had hardly heard of Harav Ovadia before the coronation ceremony, suddenly took a deep interest in this young rav whom much older Sephardi rabbanim had anointed as their leader. In 1962 and 1963, several secular newspapers ran profiles about Harav Ovadia.

By the time the elections were actually held in 1964, however, Harav Ovadia decided that it would be wrong to oppose a sitting chief rabbi, and he withdrew his candidacy. Rav Ovadia Hadaya[5] ran in his place, and Chief Rabbi Nissim won the election.

The Void in Tel Aviv

RAV TOLEDANO'S PASSING HAD LEFT A VOID NOT ONLY IN THE Religious Affairs Ministry, but also at the helm of the Rabbanut in Tel Aviv, and rabbanim and lay leaders from Tel Aviv tried to convince Harav Ovadia to run for chief rabbi of the city.

Harav Ovadia was torn regarding this position, too, but for a different reason. On one hand, Tel Aviv had the largest population of any Israeli city — the city boasted over 400,000 residents, compared to 250,000 in Yerushalayim — and he knew that he could accomplish a great deal as its chief rabbi. On the other hand, his students in Yerushalayim begged him not to run for the post. Their bond with him had deepened significantly in the seven years since he had moved back from Petah Tikva, and they couldn't fathom losing him again. Furthermore, he felt an urge to keep putting out his *sefarim*, through which his approach to halacha would be preserved for generations to come, and he was concerned that his obligations as chief rabbi of the largest city in Israel would keep him too busy to write.

Harav Ovadia discussed the matter with Rav Ezra Attia, who asked for some time to think about it. Several days later, he summoned Harav Ovadia and issued an unequivocal reply: Harav Ovadia must run for chief rabbi of Tel Aviv. Hacham Ezra felt that the Rabbanut needed to be revolutionized, and that only Harav Ovadia could turn it around. This was so vital, he felt, to the spiri-

---

5. See p. 62 fn 5.

tual future of the State, that when another candidate announced that he was running against Harav Ovadia, Hacham Ezra visited him and strongly encouraged him to withdraw his candidacy.

When Harav Ovadia's students heard about Rav Ezra's instructions to their beloved rav, they tried to persuade him to relent. "He's going to leave us like sheep without a shepherd," they complained.

"I'll send someone else to deliver the *shiur*," Hacham Ezra promised. He foresaw that if Harav Ovadia would take this position in Tel Aviv, he could then run for chief rabbi of Israel, a position through which he could revitalize the spirit of the Sephardi community and strengthen halachic observance in the State. Harav Ovadia's students would therefore have to forgo hearing his *shiurim* for the benefit of the broader public.

IN THE TEL AVIV ELECTIONS, TOO, HARAV OVADIA'S DETRACtors tried desperately to prevent him from becoming Sephardi chief rabbi. They filed one Knesset motion after another to delay the elections, in the hopes that they would find a candidate who could run against him and win, but they did not succeed. Elections were held on 11 Sivan 5728/1968, with Harav Ovadia as the lone candidate for Sephardi chief rabbi. He was voted in unanimously, and IDF Chief Rabbi Goren was elected as the Ashkenazi chief rabbi.

More Delays

Harav Ovadia was ready to begin his work in Tel Aviv immediately after the elections, but Chief Rabbi Goren was reluctant to give up his position as the founding chief rabbi of the IDF. The years after the overwhelming Israeli victory in the Six-Day War were exciting ones in the army, and he preferred — for the meantime — to devote his time to the military rabbinate.

The two chief rabbis were initially supposed to have a joint *hachtara* (coronation), but when a year passed and Chief Rabbi Goren still wasn't ready to give up his position in the military, city officials decided to hold a ceremony for the Sephardi chief rabbi alone.

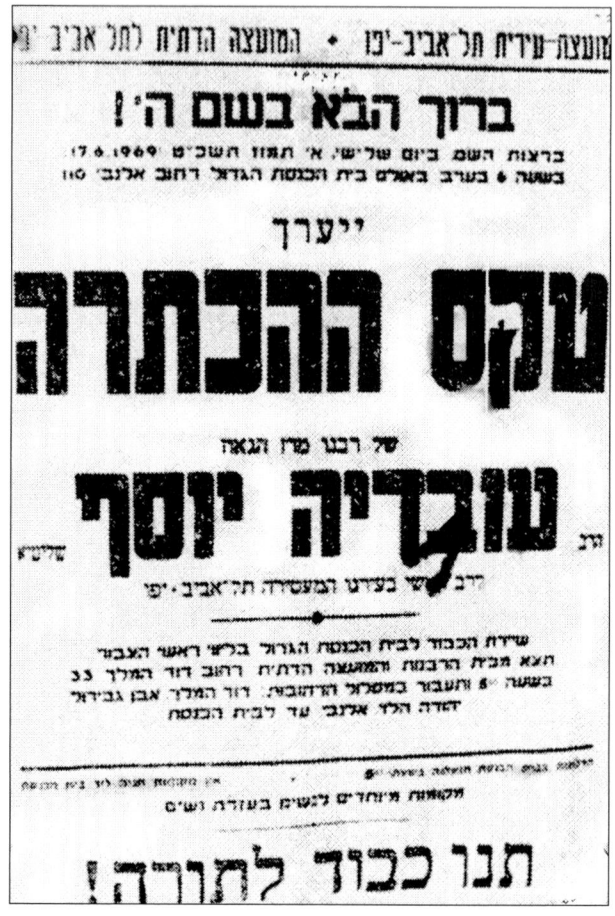

A street placard posted by the Tel Aviv-Yaffo municipality announcing the coronation ceremony for Harav Ovadia as the city's chief rabbi

HARAV OVADIA'S CORONATION CEREMONY, ON ROSH HODESH Tammuz 5729/1969, was held with great fanfare. Tel Aviv had been without a Sephardi chief rabbi for close to nine years, and the pomp surrounding the ceremony reflected the enthusiasm of the residents. The coronation began in the building of the Mo'atza Hadatit (religious council), where Harav Ovadia was welcomed by city officials.

"His Honor, the Chief Rabbi"

On hand for the ceremony was a holdover from Ottoman days, a *"kavas"* — an honor guard who accompanies key government figures. Yosef Shalit, the *kavas*, banged three times on the floor with his silver staff and announced "His honor, the Chief Rabbi!"

Harav Ovadia being driven in a convertible to the coronation ceremony

After the welcoming ceremony, Harav Ovadia entered a chauffeur-driven convertible and was driven to Tel Aviv's Great Synagogue. Children lined the streets, waving flags in honor of the occasion. The exterior of the Great Synagogue was under renovation, and the thousands of men and women who came to take part in the coronation ceremony had to step over building materials and walk through mud to enter the building, but that didn't deter them. The *beit knesset* was festively decorated with flowers, and there was a special platform for the rabbanim, covered by a blue *huppa*.

Rav Yehudah Meir Abramovitz, the deputy mayor of Tel Aviv, read the proclamation stating that the people of the city accepted Harav Ovadia as their rav:

At the coronation ceremony in Tel Aviv's Great Synagogue. The *kavas* is at right behind Harav Ovadia. Seated next to him are Rav Eliyahu Pardes, Sephardic chief rabbi of Yerushalayim, and Tel Aviv's Mayor Yehoshua Rabinowitz.

In the name of the residents of Tel Aviv-Yaffo, the great city with its hundreds of thousands of residents, I have been appointed an emissary to express their will and trust, the desire of the entire public, with all its strata and communities, to accept the authority of our master and rabbi, the *gaon* Harav Ovadia Yosef *shlita*, to listen and follow all of his rulings and decisions, and to accept from him advice and counsel. ... We wish upon our master that Hashem Yitbarach should enable him to do a great service and uplift the glory of Torah and Israel, to bring glory to the honor of the Rabbanut and those who carry the flag of Torah and halacha, to strengthen the walls of Judaism and the eternal values of the nation; to encourage keeping our holy Shabbat and family purity, and to bring *kashrut* to every Jewish table. In particular, he will deliver Torah discourses to the youth, to teach and raise them to the light of Judaism, of Torah, and of *yirat Shamayim*....

Harav Ovadia's *ktav rabbanut* from the city of Tel Aviv

Chapter Seventeen: On the Big Stage ☐ 333

Rav Yihye Mahbub blows the *shofar* in indication that the city of Tel Aviv was officially accepting Harav Ovadia as their rav.

R' Pinchas Sheinman, the head of Tel Aviv's religious council, greeted the participants, and R' Avraham Bauer read the official *ktav rabbabut* (rabbinic installation letter), which was then handed over to Harav Ovadia by a group of prominent leaders of the Tel Aviv community. Absolute silence reigned as Rav Yihye Mahbub of the Yemenite community, wrapped in a *tallit*, blew thirty sounds from a long, winding shofar.

Harav Ovadia was then accorded an impressive welcome by a group of leaders, including Ashkenazi Chief Rabbi Isser Yehuda Unterman; Interior Minister Chaim Moshe Shapira, who spoke on behalf of the government; Tel Aviv Mayor Yehoshua Rabinowitz, who read a blessing from Israel's President Zalman Shazar; and the Chief Rabbi of Yerushalayim, Rav Eliyahu Pardes.

Harav Ovadia then donned the traditional *glima* (robe) and *mitznefet* (turban) worn by Sephardic chief rabbis,[6] and rose to address the audience. He began with an in-depth Torah discourse and then spelled out his plans for his term as chief rabbi of the city, stating that he would work with the city's existing rabbanim to:

- ☐ Rectify any *kashrut* violations in the city.
- ☐ Ensure that *mikvaot* were being tended to properly.
- ☐ Supervise the process of officiating at marriages.

---

6. Though the *mitznefet* was the same as the one he wore later, when he became Rishon LeZion, the *glima* was not as elaborate.

Harav Ovadia wearing the *glima* and *mitznefet* for the first time, flanked by Tel Aviv's deputy mayor Rabbi Yehuda Meir Abramowitz and the *kavas*.

He delineated his goal of finding solutions to halachic issues — but only solutions that would be in full accordance with the *Shulhan Aruch*, ruling for Sephardim according to the Beit Yosef and for Ashkenazim according to the Rema.[7]

He also pledged to work with the *dayanim* in the city's *batei din* to speed up the process so that litigants would have their cases dealt with efficiently.

Harav Ovadia announced that he would travel throughout the city delivering *derashot* and lovingly drawing his constituents closer to Torah and halacha. He expressed his hope that these efforts would bring the youth of Tel Aviv closer to their glorious heritage. He also stated his intention to visit the transit camps and encourage new *olim* during the rough times that an *oleh* typically endures, by sharing Torah thoughts and spiritual ideals that would empower them to overcome the physical hardships of settling into a new country.

Harav Ovadia devoted the final segment of his introductory address to the importance of encouraging the growth of yeshivot and kollelim.

---

7. See p. 214.

AFTER THE CEREMONY IN THE GREAT SYNAGOGUE, A SMALL *seudat mitzva* was held in Harav Ovadia's honor in the Deborah Hotel, where he was further toasted by public officials and rabbanim, including his longtime friend Rav Betzalel Zolty.

A Servant, Not a Master

Toward the beginning of the year 5729/1968, Harav Ovadia began to tackle the agenda he had set for himself. By this time, his children Yaakov and Yaffa had also married, but the family still needed an apartment large enough to house their remaining seven children, as well as Harav Ovadia's ever-expanding library. Adina Bar-Shalom, who was living in Tel Aviv at the time, undertook the task of finding her parents a suitable apartment. Meanwhile, Harav Ovadia commuted from Yerushalayim, and slept three nights a week in the hareidi-owned Deborah Hotel to minimize the travel time. His son Avraham, who was still single, would travel with him, serving as an informal secretary.

The attendees of his *shiurim* in Yerushalayim were devastated that he was no longer going to teach them. His friend, the *mekubal* Hacham Mordechai Sharabi, Rosh Yeshivat Nahar Shalom, in

At Harav Ovadia's farewell gathering at Yeshivat Nahar Shalom, seated next to the *mekubal* and Rosh Yeshiva Hacham Mordechai Sharabi.

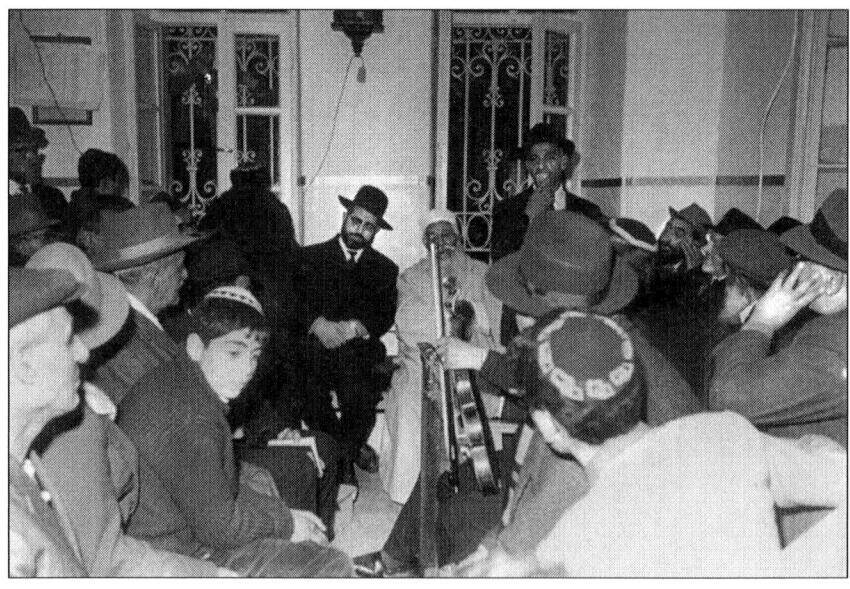

Yerushalayim, made a *seudat preida* (farewell gathering) for him in the yeshiva. Such a large crowd thronged to see him off that people were forced to stand outside and watch through the windows. When Rav Sharabi heard many other speakers mention how much Harav Ovadia would be missed, he rose to the podium and said, "*Rabbotai*, Harav Ovadia Yosef is *ours*. When he finishes his mission in Tel Aviv he will return to Yerushalayim with great glory and honor."[8]

Kashrut First

ONE OF HARAV OVADIA'S FIRST ITEMS OF BUSINESS WAS TO establish an active presence in the *kashrut* department of the Tel Aviv Rabbanut, which had stagnated in the years during which there was no chief rabbi. He knew that this was not the sort of task that could be executed while sitting at an office desk; he would have to establish a physical presence in the city's markets. One day, he told the staff of the Rabbanut's *kashrut* department that they were going to make an unannounced appearance in the Shuk HaCarmel (the Carmel Market), the largest market in the city, to check the *kashrut* of the butcher shops. The heads of the *kashrut* department blanched. "We can't go there," they said. "These people are extremely violent, and if we try to check their merchandise, they might attack us."

Anyone who thought that the threat of violence from a butcher would deter Harav Ovadia obviously hadn't heard about his decade-long battle with Shimon A., the *shohet* from Egypt whom he had deposed several times.[9] Harav Ovadia went to the market and walked from one vendor to another, determining whether their meat and poultry were actually under the *hashgaha* of the Rabbanut, and investigating how the food was handled in the shop.

When he found a few vendors guilty of selling nonkosher products, he immediately removed the *hashgahot* from those shops. Each time he declared that a vendor had lost his *hashgaha*, he set off additional waves of panic among the workers in the Rabbanut,

---

8. His words would ring prophetic in less than five years, when Harav Ovadia returned to Yerushalayim upon becoming the Rishon LeZion.
9. See pp. 156-161.

who were afraid for their safety. But Harav Ovadia was undaunted.

The fears of the Rabbanut employees turned out to be unfounded. The vendors in Shuk HaCarmel realized that they were dealing with a fearless man of integrity, and they came to his office to beg him to restore their certification. Harav Ovadia gave them a set of strict guidelines and insisted that they submit to more rigorous supervision to ensure that they wouldn't repeat their indiscretions.[10]

Harav Ovadia traveled to Kibbutz Saad, which was then home to one of the largest poultry processing plants in the country, to review the procedures in place there. He determined that the *meliha* (salting) process was lacking, and he developed a new system that became the norm for Rabbanut processing plants.

He also turned his attention to the separating of *terumot* and *maasrot*, appointing R' Moshe Karp, whom he trusted implicitly, to oversee the operations at the Tnuva fruit and vegetable distribution facility. When Tnuva managers protested that they couldn't afford to discard more than 1 percent of their produce, Harav Ovadia devised a viable solution to allay their concerns.[11]

Harav Ovadia at a meeting with Tel Aviv rabbanim in advance of Pesah

---

10. Rav David Yosef.
11. Ibid.

At the Helm of the Batei Din

UPON SETTLING IN TEL AVIV, HARAV OVADIA GATHERED THE chief rabbinic judges of the various Sephardi and Ashkenazi *batei din* to discuss how to streamline the *beit din* process. Among those in attendance were Rav Mordechai Yaffeh-Shlesinger, Rav Shlomo Teneh, Rav Shmuel Baruch Werner, and Rav Yitzchak Kulitz — some of the greatest halachic minds in the country[12] — who unanimously agreed to consult with Harav Ovadia regarding difficult cases that were taking a long time to adjudicate, thus freeing them to expedite the simpler cases. Harav Ovadia also set up a special *beit din* for *gittin*, under the leadership of Rav Rafael Abo, instructing Rav Abo to summon him any time a difficulty arose, so as to avoid any delays.

Shiurim, Shiurim, Shiurim

TO ENSURE THAT ALL OF TEL AVIV'S RESIDENTS WOULD FEEL A connection to learning, Harav Ovadia advertised a *shiur* schedule that is almost dizzying to read, and would have been hard to maintain even if he had not had so many other duties as chief rabbi.

Yet he managed to keep to a schedule that included delivering over three hours' worth of *shiurim* each day from Sunday through Thursday, except on Tuesdays, when he delivered a weekly *shiur* to his devoted students in Beit Haknesset Shaul Tzadka in Yerushalayim, who had begged him to give them a *shiur* at least once a week.[13]

Each Friday night, he prayed in a different neighborhood in Tel Aviv, so that he could regularly speak in all the city's *batei knesset*. Often, his driver would drop him off at a distant *beit knesset* before Shabbat, and he would walk home with his sons for over an hour.

On Shabbat day, he would pray at Beit Knesset Ohel Moshe, where he would deliver two *shiurim* — one in the morning after *Kriat HaTorah*, and another after Minha. Most of his *shiurim* lasted 1½ hours; some lasted two hours.

---

12. Rav Kulitz would later serve as Chief Rabbi of Yerushalayim.
13. He would also spend a few hours during those trips in the Beit Din HaGadol, because he had not relinquished his position there when he became chief rabbi of Tel Aviv.

A partial listing of Harav Ovadia's shiur schedule

היום	השעה	המקום	סוג השיעור
בכל יום ראשון	8—6.30 בערב	ביכ"נ "אור תורה" רח' אליאסף, מול סונדק שאול	הלכות שבת ודברי אגדה על פרשת השבוע
בכל יום שני	10.30—9 לפנה"צ 8—6.30 בערב	ישיבת "תורה והוראה" רח' זבולון 18 תל-אביב מדרש רשב"י דרך לוד שכונת התקוה	אבן העזר (מיוחד לאברכי הישיבה) הלכות שבת ודברי אגדה על פרשת השבוע
בכל יום רביעי	6.30—5.30 בערב 8—6.30 בערב	ביהכ"נ "מגן דוד" רח' אונג 15 שכ' התקוה מדרש רשב"י דרך לוד שכונת התקוה	שיחה מוסרית ודברי אגדה הלכות שבת ודברי אגדה
בכל יום חמישי	10.30—9 לפנה"צ 10—8 בלילה	ישיבת "תורה והוראה" רח' זבולון 18 תל-אביב ישיבת "תורה והוראה"	אבן העזר (מיוחד לאברכי הישיבה) הלכות טהרת המשפחה
יום שבת	שחרית אחרי קריאת התורה אחרי מנחה	ביהכ"נ הגדול "אהל מועד" רח' שד"ל 5 תל-אביב ביהכ"נ "אוהל מועד"	דרשה על פרשת השבוע, עונג שבת ודברי התעוררות

The range of topics he discussed is astounding. In one week, he would deliver *shiurim* in *hilchot Shabbat, Yoreh Dei'a, Even HaEzer, mussar,* as well as *derashot* on the weekly *parasha,* and more.

A group of doctors asked him to teach the halachot pertaining to the medical profession. Rav Yitzchak Zilberstein, himself a great authority in medical halacha and a longtime lecturer on the subject, related that even decades later, doctors would speak of their astonishment at this young rav, who "walked into the room without a *sefer,* without notes, and quoted entire passages from memory. He could speak for over an hour in an organized fashion, keeping us enraptured throughout."

How long could a rav keep up such a busy lecture schedule while handling all the *batei din* and Rabbanut matters in the city? Half a year? A year?

An advertisement sponsored by Beit Haknesset Ohel Moed begins with the words, "We would like to inform the public of the schedule of *shiurim* that the chief rabbi has been delivering for *the last three years*" [emphasis added].

When a family member, concerned for the rav's well-being, suggested that he reduce the amount of time he devoted to *shiurim*, Harav Ovadia replied, "*Ki lekach notzarta* [loosely: This is what I was created for]."[14]

Restoring Sephardic Psak

HARAV OVADIA ALSO REINSTATED SEPHARDI HALACHIC practices that had been ignored or overridden by the city's Ashkenazi rabbanim during the preceding decades. For instance, the Ashkenazi rabbanim had instructed the government authorities who registered marriages that they could not register a marriage that was to take place between the 17th of Tammuz and Rosh Hodesh Av, in accordance with the Rema's ruling that one may not marry during that period. Harav Ovadia pointed out that in Eretz Yisrael,[15] this ruling applies only to Ashkenazic Jewry; Sephardim are allowed to marry until Rosh Hodesh, and he adjusted that policy accordingly.

During Harav Ovadia's first year in Tel Aviv, the head of the city's *kashrut* department showed him the *Hilchot Pesah* that the Tel Aviv Rabbanut published each year. Since this list had traditionally been authorized by the chief rabbi, he asked Harav Ovadia to sign. Harav Ovadia read the list, and then said, "I can't sign until you change one line."

The line in question read: "Rice and beans are prohibited, and the Sephardim have a custom to eat them."

"This is untrue," explained Harav Ovadia. "Rice and beans are halachically permissible, but the Ashkenazim have accepted upon themselves a stringency not to eat them."

"But this has been the text for years," protested the head of the *kashrut* department. "Why should we change it?"

To Harav Ovadia, this was irrelevant. He would not sign a document that misrepresented halacha.

---

14. *Posek HaDor*.
15. Some Sephardic communities have local customs established by their rabbanim not to marry during this period. Harav Ovadia was ruling for those in Eretz Yisrael who did not have this custom and were prevented from marrying during that period only because of the Ashkenazic custom. Obviously, Sephardic communities whose rabbanim rule that they may not marry during this period must follow their custom.

The head of the *kashrut* department then approached the document's author, Rav Isser Yehuda Unterman, who was then the Ashkenazi Chief Rabbi of Israel, to discuss it with him, and Rav Unterman told him, "Harav Ovadia is correct."

In his eulogy on Rav Unterman,[16] Harav Ovadia recalls this incident and praises Rav Unterman for being courageous enough to admit to a mistake.

In the case of other foods regarding which the halachic traditions of the two commuties diverged, Harav Ovadia instructed that the labels on the product read, "Kosher for Pesah for Sephardim only." This is still the Rabbanut's policy on such products.

Sharing the Duties

SEVERAL FACTORS[17] INFLUENCED CHIEF RABBI GOREN TO become active in the Tel Aviv Rabbinate in late 1971, although he continued to retain his position as chief rabbi of the military. Harav Ovadia tried to share his duties with his Ashkenazi counterpart, so when managers of the various departments of the Rabbanut posed *sh'eilot* to him, he would send them to consult Chief Rabbi Goren.

Harav Ovadia with Ashkenazi Chief Rabbi Isser Yehuda Unterman.

---
16. *Hazon Ovadia, Dalet Taaniyot*, p. 470.
17. We will discuss most of these in the coming chapters.

Once, before Rosh Hashana, a serious *sh'eila* arose in a slaughterhouse serving the Tel Aviv area. The *shohtim* had slaughtered approximately 100 sheep in order to provide enough *roshei keves*[18] for the city's residents. The innards of one of the animals was then determined to be *treifa*, unfit, but it was impossible to determine from which animal they had come. Would all the animals be rendered unusable?

Chief Rabbi Goren deliberated at length, but could not come to a decision. Someone told Harav Ovadia what was being discussed in the room down the hall, and, drawing from his encyclopedic memory and keen understanding of the concepts, he explained why the sheep were permitted.[19]

Despite his overarching knowledge in almost all matters of halacha, Harav Ovadia tried as much as possible to include his Ashkenazi colleague in all decisions — an effort that would soon become impossible due to two unfortunate cases that were about to shake the entire country.

---

18. Heads of sheep, which many use as a *siman* on Rosh Hashana Eve as a remembrance of *Akeidat Yitzhak*.
19. *Ein Yitzchak*, by Rav Yitzchak Yosef, Vol. 3, p. 78.

CHAPTER EIGHTEEN
JEWISH LAW VS. JEWISH STATE

DURING THE EARLY 1970S, TWO NOTORIOUS CASES pitted the political agenda of the State of Israel against Torah law, bringing to the fore an inherent problem with the Status Quo concession Ben-Gurion had made to the religious Jews in the country.[1] These two cases marked the first time that politicians openly expressed a demand that rabbanim "create solutions" to the "problems" posed by halacha.

In truth, the conflagration was inevitable. Ben Gurion had agreed to allow the *batei din* to handle all matters related to marriage and divorce in Israel, but there was bound to come a day when secular Jews would insist that they not be restricted by halacha regarding marriage and divorce.[2]

In 1964, a 34-year-old gentile woman named Helen Zeidman moved to Israel.[3] She settled on Kibbutz Nachal Oz, a secular

---
1. See p. 249.
2. This issue applied equally to secular Jews who were living abroad if and when they decided to make *aliya* and suddenly found that Israeli law mandated that they follow Torah law in issues of marriage and divorce.
3. The facts of this case are based on the book *Sha'aruriyat Hagiyurim Hamezuyafim* (*The Outrage of the Spurious Conversions*), published by the *Vaad HaRabbanim Ha'olami L'inyanei Giyur*, an international body created by *gedolei Yisrael* and spearheaded by Rav Chaim

Harav Ovadia and Rav Shalom Mashash, Sephardic chief rabbi of Yerushalayim, writing a *ketuba*. Would the government renege on David Ben-Gurion's Status Quo letter granting *batei din* control of marriages?

kibbutz, where she met a Jewish man, and they decided to marry. Since they couldn't marry in Israel, where intermarriage was forbidden by the Rabbanut, they married abroad in a civil ceremony.

Several years after her marriage, Mrs. Zeidman applied to be converted by the Rabbanut. The rabbanim who reviewed her case rejected her application because she would not accept the Torah and commit to keep halacha.

In 1967, undeterred by the Rabbanut's rejection, Mrs. Zeidman turned to a Reform clergyman in Israel, who was only too happy to convert her. With her conversion certificate in hand, she approached the Interior Ministry and requested that she and her children be registered as Jewish. Interior Minister Chaim Moshe Shapira of Mafdal[4] refused to register her as a Jew, in compliance with the British mandate-era law that the body overseeing Judaism was the Rabbanut, which had rejected her Reform conversion. She

---

Kreiswirth *zt"l*, the Rav of Antwerp, in response to the crisis caused by halachically invalid conversions. The citations from the secular newspapers below appear in that work, pp. 54-62.

4. As is the case with almost all parties in Israel, the Mafdal has undergone several name changes over the years. It has been known as the Mizrachi party, the National Religious Party (NRP), and, in the iteration in which it appears as of the date of publication of this book, Bayit Yehudi (Jewish Home). In this chapter, we use the name Mafdal (short for Miflaga Datit Leumit), which was the official name of the party during the period in which these events took place.

took her case to the Israeli Supreme Court, petitioning the court to force the Interior Ministry to recognize her as Jewish.

This set off a political crisis in Israel, because Mafdal threatened that if the Supreme Court would rule in favor of Mrs. Zeidman, they would leave the government coalition. Prime Minister Golda Meir could not afford to lose the Mafdal, because that could have toppled her coalition.[5] As the ruling in the Supreme Court loomed, the leaders of the government swung into action, seeking any possible solution to the crisis.

This case caused a huge uproar, and eventually became part of a larger battle often referred to as *"Mihu Yehudi* — Who is a Jew?," in which secularists demanded an end to the Rabbanut's control over defining who is Jewish.

In a telling op-ed published during the heated national debate, Gershom Schocken, editor of the left-wing newspaper *Haaretz*, wrote:

> It is in Israel's interest to ease the conversion process here in Israel, not in the Diaspora.[6] Anyone who settles here and

---

5. In Israel, the prime minister rules with a coalition composed of political parties representing a majority of the 120 members of the Knesset (Israeli Parliament). If at any point a coalition partner resigns from the government and the coalition comprises less than half of the Knesset members, the government is in danger of a "no confidence" vote, in which case the government is disbanded and early elections are held.

Although Golda Meir originally had 102 out of 120 Knesset members in her governing coalition, during the spring of 1970 her coalition was under threat of dissolving. Her party, Hama'arach (the reformed Mapai party, Hama'arach would eventually become the Labor party), had 56 Knesset members. She brought Menachem Begin's Gachal (forerunner of the Likud party) into her government, along with Mafdal and several small parties. During the months when the Helen Zeidman case was brewing, there was a political crisis on another front as well: The government was considering accepting a peace initiative called the "Rogers Plan," named for U.S. Secretary of State William Rogers. The plan called for Israel to accept UN Security Council Resolution 242, which required Israel to withdraw from territories it had captured during the Six-Day War, and in return, the Arab countries would sign peace agreements with Israel.

Begin refused to even consider the Rogers Plan, and threatened to quit the government if the plan was brought up for debate — which he did in August 1970. Since he controlled 26 seats, the government was already poised to drop to 76 seats. The Mafdal comprised 12 seats, which meant that if no resolution could be found for the Helen Zeidman case and Mafdal would resign, the coalition would be reduced to 64 seats — an extremely fragile government, especially considering that eight out of the 64 seats were split among three small parties, each of which could then demand all sorts of concessions from the government.

Prime Minister Meir took it as a given that Begin would resign, so at this specific juncture, it was vital to her to keep Mafdal in her government.

6. Schocken refers here to the law that required the government to recognize all conversions performed outside the country, even though the only government-recognized conversions in Israel were those performed under the auspices of the Rabbanut.

connects his destiny with this nation should be allowed to join the Jewish people immediately.

What does the Mafdal want from Mrs. Zeidman? As a member of a kibbutz, she can't possibly undergo a conversion through the Rabbanut, because she'll have to declare that she'll keep *kashrut*, something that is impossible for her as a member of an irreligious kibbutz.

What does the Mafdal want from people like Mrs. Zeidman? That they leave Israel? That they leave their kibbutz? That they live a lie?

The Rabbanut was under tremendous pressure from politicians and the general population to "find a solution" for this case, but with the Supreme Court ruling scheduled for June 16, 1970, no solution seemed forthcoming. As far as the Rabbanut was concerned, the only way for Mrs. Zeidman to be considered Jewish was for her to undergo a full conversion, one that included a commitment to keep Torah and mitzvot.

And yet a "solution" did materialize on June 15, one day before the Supreme Court was to rule. Mrs. Zeidman underwent a sudden "Orthodox" conversion, presided over by IDF Chief Rabbi Goren and a hastily assembled *beit din*. In exchange for the conversion, she promised to withdraw her petition to the Supreme Court.

Her retraction enabled the Mafdal Knesset members to remain in the government.

The solution seemed to work — but almost no one was happy with it.

The secular newspaper *Maariv* tells the story from one side of the political spectrum:

> How was the "happy ending" of the Helen Zeidman saga contrived? Members of Hama'arach related in the Knesset yesterday that during a meeting of the party's ministers on Shabbat eve, Defense Minister Moshe Dayan casually remarked, "Go to [IDF Chief Rabbi] Goren; he'll solve the problem for you."
>
> And it seems that's exactly what they did….

> Most of the Knesset members refused to believe that such a "magic trick" could occur.

One might have expected secularist Knesset members to rejoice, but their reaction was actually quite the opposite:

> Hama'arach Knesset Members did not try to hide their anger at what had transpired. "They always tell us that a conversion process takes at least a year, until the candidate proves her consistent interest in being part of the Jewish nation and her love for us, and demonstrates her Jewish knowledge. Primarily, [we were told] that the waiting period had to be long enough for the candidate to regret the decision. Reform conversion was rejected because it was a 'quick conversion' — and suddenly it turns out that it's possible to perform an Orthodox conversion even faster, within a few hours — a true express conversion. This is serious? This brings honor to the Rabbanut?"

But *Maariv* also cited Mafdal's defense of the conversion:

> The Deputy Interior Minister [Yosef Goldschmidt, of Mafdal], said, "We can assume that [Chief Rabbi] Goren also took into account the issue of *pikuah nefesh* from a political standpoint."[7]
>
> If not for the government crisis and the Mafdal's threat to quit the government, Helen Zeidman would not have been able to undergo a conversion through Orthodox rabbis. She was converted only through a new low in the politicalization of religion in Israel.
>
> Even the Reform movement in Israel screamed foul, releasing this statement the next day:
>
> "The council of progressive rabbis sees the so-called solution for the conversion crisis as a political trick that shows how low the establishment is willing to stoop in order to retain its monopoly over religious matters."

---

7. I.e., the possibility of the governing coalition disintegrating might somehow pose a security risk to Israel.

The crisis largely began because of the Orthodox claim that Reform conversion is too quick and undiscerning, a "paper conversion." Suddenly it became clear that Helen Zeidman's knowledge of Judaism, which she had studied under a Reform rabbi, was so great that she was able to receive an Orthodox conversion within three hours.

In the Torah world, both in Israel and abroad, the "conversion" was met with shock and consternation. *Poskim* from all over the world immediately issued a statement against IDF Chief Rabbi Goren for "making a laughingstock out of conversion."

Harav Ovadia was largely unaffected by this debate while it was raging. Although Chief Rabbi Goren was officially sharing the helm of the Tel Aviv Rabbanut, he had yet to officially commence his duties in that capacity, and had performed the Zeidman conversion under the auspices of the military rabbinate.

Soon, however, Harav Ovadia would find himself in the midst of another difficult case involving Chief Rabbi Goren — one that would culminate with him running for, and winning, the title of Rishon LeZion.

The "Brother and Sister" Saga

CHANOCH AND MIRIAM LANGER WERE A BROTHER AND SISter enlisted in the Israeli Army in the late 1960s and early 1970s. Their mother, Chava Langer, had originally married a convert named Avraham Borokovsky in Europe, and she separated from him without a *get* (Jewish divorce). She subsequently married a Jew-from-birth named Otto Langer and bore two children from him. But since she was still halachically wed to Borokovsky, her children were *mamzerim*, born of a forbidden union, and were therefore not permitted to marry regular Jews.

Chief Rabbi Isser Yehuda Unterman first became aware of this problem in 1955, when he was chief rabbi of Tel Aviv. On 28 Heshvan 5716/1955, Chava Langer and Avraham Borokovsky took part in a *beit din* session in Tel Aviv, where the *dayanim* ruled that the children, then 11 and 9 years old, were *mamzerim*. Rav Unterman circulated this information among marriage registrars, and when the children reached adulthood and wanted to marry, they were prevented from doing so.

In Iyar 5726/1966, 20-year-old Chanoch Langer requested that the Tel Aviv *beit din* convene to find a *heter* for him to marry. Over a period of four years, four rabbinic courts reviewed that case, holding numerous sessions, interrogating many people, and deliberating long and hard, but they were unable to find grounds for permitting him to marry.

Considering the devastating consequences to the lives of Chanoch and Miriam Langer, however, the Petah Tikva *beit din* recommended that the Beit Din HaGadol probe the matter. The triumvirate of *dayanim* on the Beit Din HaGadol who reviewed the case were Harav Ovadia, Rav Yosef Shalom Elyashiv, and Rav Shaul Yisraeli. After deliberating at length, they unanimously upheld the original ruling: the Langers were unfit to marry regular Jews.

Political Machinations

OVERLAPPING, AS IT DID, WITH THE ZEIDMAN CASE, THE SAGA of the Langer children presented yet another public challenge to the Status Quo granting the Rabbanut control over marriage and divorce. The secular political leadership openly began to seek ways to circumvent the Rabbanut and allow Chanoch and Miriam Langer to marry. To do so, they needed to find someone with rabbinic authority who was amenable to coming up with a "solution" that would bypass the ruling of the *batei din*.

Defense Minister Moshe Dayan came to the rescue yet again, suggesting that IDF Chief Rabbi Goren could pave the way for the two to marry.

Chief Rabbi Goren, working under the auspices of the military rabbinate, then convened a "field" *beit din*, which, he claimed, found a *heter* releasing the Langer children from their status as *mamzerim*. The composition of his *beit din* remains a secret until this day. This *heter* didn't actually free the two to marry, however, because IDF Chief Rabbi Goren did not have the legal authority to reverse the Rabbinate's ruling.

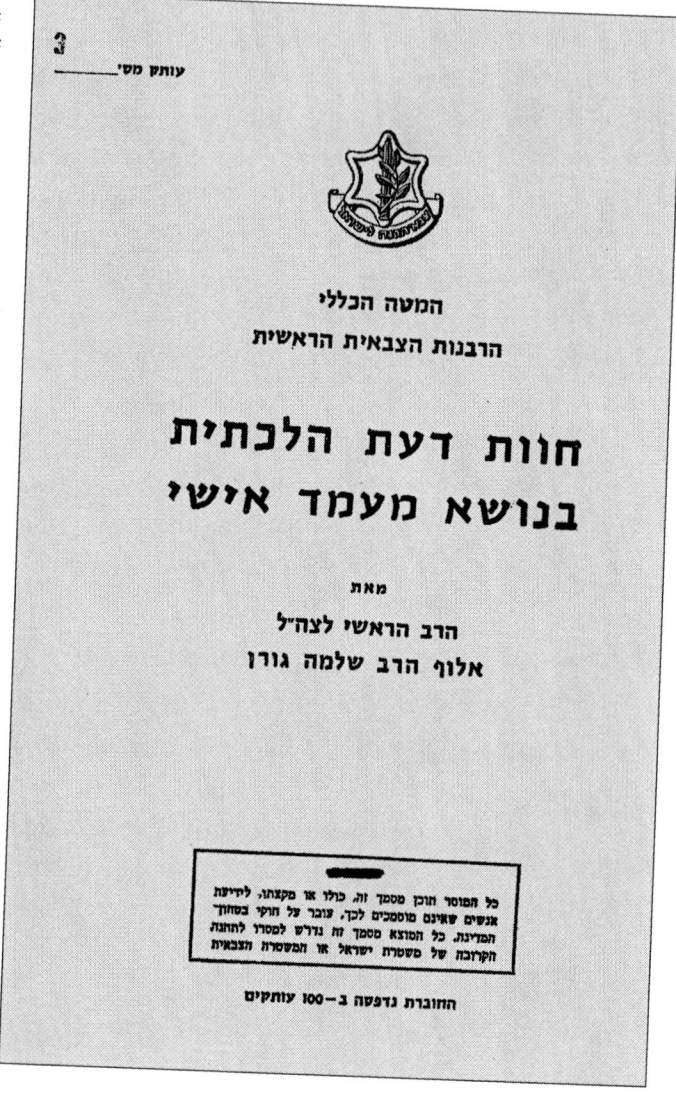

A copy of IDF Chief Rabbi Goren's *"Mahberet,"* explaining why the Langers could marry, was kept classified under military censorship.

Prior to issuing his *heter*, Rav Goren rushed out a booklet containing the background of the case, including the relevant documents and halachic underpinnings according to his view. One hundred copies of the booklet were printed by the government printer, and all 100 were kept classified as "military information that could not be publicized." A warning on the cover, which prominently featured the insignia of the IDF, read, "Anyone who relays the content of this document, in whole or in part, to unauthorized individuals, violates state security laws. Anyone who finds this document is required to transfer it to the nearest Israeli police or military police station."

This secret booklet was nicknamed "the *Mahberet*" (notebook), and its writer, IDF Chief Rabbi Goren, was subsequently referred to (in religious publications) as the "Baal HaMahberet."

Moshe Dayan embarked on a protracted effort to keep delaying the elections, so that he and his supporters could organize support for Rabbi Goren to be elected as Chief Rabbi of Israel. It was widely presumed that IDF Chief Rabbi Goren, who had no experience in the civilian rabbinate and had few followers among the rabbanim on the *guf habocher*, had no chance of winning against incumbent Chief Rabbi Isser Yehuda Unterman, who had already defeated him in 1964. However, the governing coalition would not allow the elections to go forward as planned, because the shoo-in candidate Rav Unterman had been the first person to circulate the Langers' *mamzeirut* status, while IDF Chief Rabbi Goren was guaranteeing to free them from it.

The problem of no civilian experience was easily rectified: During the spring of 1971, IDF Chief Rabbi Goren finally handed in his army beret and assumed the role of chief rabbi of Tel Aviv, to which he had been elected nearly three years earlier. Meanwhile, the government worked to change the makeup of the *guf habocher*, the body that elected the chief rabbi, to assure that Rabbi Goren would have a majority.

The "Heter" Is Revealed

SOMEHOW, ALTHOUGH THE *MAHBERET* WAS STILL A CLASSIfied document subject to military censorship, its contents were leaked to the secular press.

IDF Chief Rabbi Goren's "*heter*" was based primarily[8] on the claim that Avraham Borokovsky, Chava Langer's first husband, was not really Jewish, because his

---

8. Although there were other parts to the *heter* as well, this was the only one that was even somewhat worthy of consideration, and the scholars who dismantled the claims made in the *Mahberet* focused primarily on this one.

conversion was invalid. If he was a gentile, his marriage to Chava Langer was null and void, and her marriage to Otto Langer was permissible.

In April 1971, while addressing a rabbinic conference in Tel Aviv, Harav Ovadia lashed out against this *heter*, relating that he had been on the Beit Din HaGadol triumvirate that had reviewed the case, and they had found Borokovsky's conversion to be valid. He also noted the irony inherent in the military censorship that had prevented the *Mahberet* from reaching the *batei din*, which actually had the power to act based on the booklet's contents.

Pledges and Expectations

IN THE LATER PART OF 1971, GOVERNMENT OFFICIALS OPENLY expressed their faith in Tel Aviv's new chief rabbi to solve all issues that arose between the State and the Torah. When Ram Caspi, the Langers' lawyer, wrote to Prime Minister Golda Meir to ask her to intervene in his clients' case, she replied that their problem would "receive a positive solution once new elections for chief rabbis have been held." She even agreed to meet with Caspi and the Langers to reassure them that Chief Rabbi Goren would provide the solution.[9]

Now officially ensconced in the Tel Aviv Rabbanut, Chief Rabbi Goren embarked on a campaign to defeat Chief Rabbi Unterman in the elections, which kept being delayed further and further as the government sought ways to ensure his election. He made no guise of hiding his plans upon being elected, in speeches that were touted for their bravery in the secular press, while shaking religious Jews worldwide to the core:

> Addressing members of the Guild for Religion and Spirit of B'nai B'rith, Rabbi Goren, who holds the rank of general, said that halacha in this generation had not advanced hand-in-hand with the times and technology nor did it incorporate any innovations.... The Chief Rabbi was referring apparently to the recent case in which marriage

---

9. "Brother, Sister Labeled *Mamzerim* to Meet with Mrs. Meir" (*Jewish Telegraphic Agency*, 13 Aug. 1971).

licenses were denied to two young Israelis because the religious authorities deemed them to be of illegitimate birth. The case aroused widespread anger against the Orthodox establishment. Rabbi Goren referred to the problem of conversion when he called for "deep and flexible tolerance" to solve the problems of every Jew who wants to return to his ancestral land.[10]

Harav Ovadia Called to Arms

ANOTHER FULL YEAR WENT BY BEFORE THE ELECTIONS FOR chief rabbi of Israel were actually held, and by that time, the government had managed to change the composition of the *guf habocher*, thus ensuring that Rabbi Goren's election was a foregone conclusion.[11]

Hareidi rabbanim and *dayanim* were particularly anxious over this development. Rav Elyashiv, specifically, felt obligated to prevent the Rabbanut from becoming a laboratory for concocting *heterim*, as Chief Rabbi Goren had essentially promised to do. By this point, Sephardic Chief Rabbi Yitzhak Nissim had agreed to join forces with Chief Rabbi Goren, creating a bond in which each would help the other with their respective campaigns. Torah leaders were deeply concerned about this alliance and its implications with regard to Chief Rabbi Goren's "flexible" approach to halacha.

There was an additional concern that worried the Torah community in Israel.

Aside from electing the chief rabbis, the *guf habocher* also chooses a 10-member Chief Rabbinate Council, which convenes together with the two chief rabbis to vote on measures that affect the public. The council comprises five Sephardim and five Ashkenazim. Rav Unterman saw an unsolvable problem with the council[12] that would render his victory pointless unless the Sephardi chief rabbi was replaced, and Rav Unterman wanted to withdraw from the race.

---

10. "Rabbi Goren Says Halacha Behind Times" (*Jewish Telegraphic Agency*, 2 Nov. 1971).
11. "Bitter Contest Expected in Rabbinate Elections" (*Jewish Telegraphic Agency*, 5 Oct. 1972).
12. Described below.

When the hareidi leadership begged him to run, he agreed on only one condition: that Harav Ovadia run against Rav Nissim for the post of Rishon LeZion.

The Quandary

RAV UNTERMAN'S INSISTENCE THAT HE JOIN THE RACE PREsented a dilemma for Harav Ovadia, who described his quandary in a *teshuva*:[13]

The chief rabbi of Israel, Rav Unterman, was asked by the rabbanim to run in the elections that will be held on 7 Heshvan 5733, against the second candidate [Tel Aviv Chief Rabbi] Shlomo Goren, so that he can maintain his post and preserve the holiness.

He acceded to their request, but only on the condition that I, the young one, run for the post of chief rabbi against [Sephardi Chief Rabbi] Yitzhak Nissim. He explained that Rav Yitzhak Nissim has taken control of the Chief Rabbinate Council, and the members of the council have taken to boycotting sessions when Rav Nissim commands them to do so, because of internal disagreements between him and Rav Unterman.

The Chief Rabbinate Council is therefore frozen, because they don't have a majority participating in the sessions. Therefore, even if Rav Unterman were elected, what benefit would there be, for as long as Rav Nissim, who is currently the sole candidate [for Sephardi chief rabbi], retains control, what have the wise accomplished with their decree? The Rabbanut will remain paralyzed!

A meeting was held among all the members of the Beit Din HaGadol, including the renowned *geonim*, Rav Yosef Shalom Elyashiv, Rav Betzalel Zolty, Rav Eliezer Goldschmidt,[14] and other rabbanim, and they decided that

---

13. *Yabia Omer*, Vol. 9, *Hoshen Mishpat* 9. As was his wont, although he had received an unequivocal ruling from Rav Elyashiv exhorting him to run for chief rabbi, Harav Ovadia spent days deliberating the *sh'eila* from every halachic perspective, until he was absolutely convinced that he was permitted to run.

14. This meeting took place in Rav Elyashiv's home on Hol HaMoed Succot. When the rabbanim reached their unanimous decision to urge Harav Ovadia to run, Rav Elyashiv called his home

The members of the Beit Din HaGadol who convinced Harav Ovadia to run for chief rabbi, at a Yosef family *simha*. (R-L): Rav Eliezer Goldschmidt, Rav Yosef Shalom Elyashiv, Rav Yitzchak Yosef, Harav Ovadia, and Rav Betzalel Zolty.

I should accede to Rav Unterman's request and present my candidacy for chief rabbi, running against Rav Nissim, and "the one Hashem chooses will be the holy one."[15]

Although they urged me strongly to present my candidacy, I was extremely torn, because, thanks to Hashem Yitbarach, I have been serving the holy community in Tel Aviv for several years, and they have not budged from their love, fondness, and respect for me, for I have found favor in their eyes as I guide them and disseminate Torah throughout the city. Blessed is His Name forever, for His kindness has overwhelmed me, and I sit among my people in peace and serenity.

I could not ignore the constant urging of the aforementioned *geonim*, however. I expressed my concerns in a letter to the great Rav Yosef Shalom Elyashiv *shlita*: Was it

and asked if Harav Ovadia could come visit him in his *succa*. When Harav Ovadia arrived, he found his three colleagues from the Beit Din HaGadol waiting to convince him to announce his candidacy.

15. Paraphrased from *Bamidbar* 16:7.

permissible to cause the demotion of a rav, which would seem to contravene the principle of *maalin bakodesh ve'ein moridim* — we are only allowed to promote in matters of holiness, not to demote.[16]

He answered that since Rav Nissim sought every possible way to have Rav Unterman deposed, and is using all his power to support [Tel Aviv Chief Rabbi] Shlomo Goren — with whose actions the Beit Din HaGadol takes issue — there is no question that it is permissible for me to run against him, and it is even a mitzva.

The holy *gaon* Rav Yisrael Abuhatzeira[17] wrote similar words to me, and he expressed his unhesitating support for me.

Convinced that he was required to run for the post of Sephardi Chief Rabbi, Harav Ovadia submitted his candidacy, although he felt that he had no chance of winning. By the time he joined the race, there were just two weeks to campaign, and the entire leftist establishment was behind the ticket of Rabbis Nissim and Goren.

The campaign quickly turned bitter, with the secular politicians and journalists attacking Rav Unterman and Harav Ovadia, claiming that they were too closed-minded to serve the needs of a modern state — a claim that was particularly ludicrous when leveled against Harav Ovadia.

---

16. See, for instance, *Yoma* 12b.
17. Commonly known as the Baba Sali.

CHAPTER NINETEEN
A STUNNING VICTORY

THROUGHOUT HARAV OVADIA'S SEVEN DECADES AS A *posek*, he consistently championed one ideal: the Talmudic precept of *koha d'heteira adif* (lit., the power of permitting is preferable). This concept — and Harav Ovadia's application of it — has been widely misunderstood to mean that a rav should find a *heter* no matter what the circumstances.[1]

The concept actually means, as *Rashi*[2] explains, that anyone can rule *l'humra* (stringently), but only a rav who is certain about the teachings transmitted to him from his rabbis has the right to rule leniently. *Tosafot*[3] add that the *posek* who rules leniently must find proof for his leniency, while the one who rules stringently can just rely on the fact that he is not causing the questioner to transgress any prohibition. It therefore takes greater acumen for a *posek* to find a valid halachic *heter*, rather than simply ruling stringently so as not to lead the questioner to transgress because of his ruling.

---

1. See Chapter 27, which is devoted entirely to explaining the concept and Harav Ovadia's application of it.
2. *Beitza* 2b, s.v. *D'heteira adif lei.*
3. Ibid., s.v. *Vechi teima.*

The claims of the Israeli leftists — and the suggestions by his Ashkenazic counterpart — that Harav Ovadia was unwilling to toil to find *heterim* was demonstrably ludicrous. In the five volumes of *Yabia Omer* that had been published prior to the election campaign, Harav Ovadia had consistently exhibited his *koha d'heteira*, even writing toward the end of dozens of *teshuvot* that he was ruling with *koha d'heteira*,[4] having established that there was ample halachic basis to rule leniently.[5]

Specifically when it came to issues of *agunot* or *mamzeirut*, Harav Ovadia labored endlessly to find a *heter*, citing earlier *poskim* who wrote of the importance of finding a proper halachic basis for these people to marry.[6]

Particularly rankling was Chief Rabbi Goren's suggestion that Harav Ovadia and his fellow *dayanim* on the Beit Din HaGadol were remiss in their duties to find *heterim* for *mamzeirim* because they didn't care about those unable to marry. Years before the Langer case reached the Beit Din, Harav Ovadia presided — along with Rav Betzalel Zolty and Rav Shaul Yisraeli — over a case that involved an intricate *sh'eila* of a woman who been suspected of bearing a child with her brother-in-law after her husband died. Harav Ovadia wrote a 14,000 word *teshuva*,[7] which was signed by the other two *dayanim*, permitting the child to marry a regular Jew.

It should have been amply clear that if Harav Ovadia and his colleagues could not find a *heter* for the Langer children, it was because no such *heter* existed. But those campaigning for Chief Rabbis Nissim and Goren's ticket spent the short weeks before the elections besmirching Harav Ovadia's reputation, suggesting that he and the other rabbanim on the Beit Din HaGadol were coldly ignoring the plight of the Langers.

---

4. In some instances, as additional proof to his position he cites other *poskim* from earlier generations who ruled with their *koha d'heteira*.
5. See, for instance: Vol. 1, *Orah Haim* 32, *Yoreh Dei'a* 14; Vol. 2, *Orah Haim* 15, *Even Ha'ezer* 1; Vol. 3, *Orah Haim* 24, *Even Ha'ezer* 4; Vol. 4, *Orah Haim* 34, *Yoreh Dei'a* 24; Vol. 5, *Orah Haim* 25, *Yoreh Dei'a* 10.
6. See, for instance, Vol. 4, *Even Ha'ezer* 15, and Vol. 7, *Even Ha'ezer* 7.
7. Printed in both *Yabia Omer* (Vol. 5, *Even Ha'ezer* 2) and *Piskei Din Rabbaniyim*, a compendium of rulings issued by the Rabbanut, Vol. 6, p. 131.

SHORTLY AFTER SUCCOT, HARAV OVADIA WENT TO VISIT THE Baba Sali, Rav Yisrael Abuhatzeira, in Netivot. As he walked in, the Baba Sali leaned over and whispered something to a family member, and then tried to kiss Harav Ovadia's hand. Harav Ovadia refused to allow the octogenarian *mekubal* — close to thirty years his senior — to kiss his hand as a show of respect. Years later, this family member revealed that the Baba Sali had told him that Harav Ovadia possessed a *neshama* from the times of the Geonim.[8]

The Baba Sali's Blessing

The Baba Sali bestowed his blessing upon Harav Ovadia and asked him to stay for a *seuda*. Harav Ovadia demurred, however, because he was scheduled to deliver a *shiur*. The Baba Sali insisted that he drink something, and as he handed Harav Ovadia the glass, he grabbed his hand and kissed it. He also wrote a letter calling on all the members of the *guf habocher* to vote for Harav Ovadia.

A TEAM QUICKLY ASSEMBLED TO CONVINCE THE MEMBERS OF the *guf habocher* to vote for Harav Ovadia. The group included: Rav Yaakov Ades, Rosh Yeshivat Kol Yaaakov; Rav Eliyahu Shrim, Rosh Yeshivat Torah VeHora'a; and Rav Yitzchak David Grossman, then a 33-year-old rabbi just starting his campaign to rehabilitate the Galilean town of Migdal HaEmek.

The Candidate Sits Out the Campaign

Harav Ovadia himself did not take part in the campaign, opting instead to learn at home during those frenetic weeks. Two days before the elections, he finally made an appearance at the makeshift headquarters that had been set up for his campaign. When he inquired how things were going, the team told him that they did not see much chance for him to win, because most of the *guf habocher* had committed to vote for Rav Nissim. "I only need one vote," Harav Ovadia replied. "HaKadosh Baruch Hu's!"[9]

---

8. Rav David Yosef.
  The Geonim lived in a period between the closure of the Talmud and the *Rishonim*, more than a millennium before Harav Ovadia was born.
9. *Minhagei Harasha"l*, p. 85.

Harav Ovadia's only involvement in the campaign was to release an official document outlining an 11-point plan to revitalize the country's rabbinate, as he had done for the rabbinate of Tel Aviv. In the document, released on Rosh Hodesh Heshvan 5733, he committed to:

- ☐ Improve the image of the chief rabbinate, and work to solve halachic issues according to Torah spirit.[10]
- ☐ Fill vacant rabbinic slots in cities that had long been without a rabbi.
- ☐ Appoint more *dayanim* and establish more *batei din*, and work to close the gap between the number of Ashkenazi and Sephardi *dayanim*.[11]
- ☐ Establish an institute of higher learning designed to train rabbanim, and devote time to improving the yeshivot in Eretz Yisrael.
- ☐ Raise the spiritual levels of existing rabbanim — and especially those serving in peripheral cities designed for *olim* — by offering them *shiurim* from *gedolei Yisrael*.
- ☐ Improve *kashrut*.
- ☐ Spend time with the everyman; be *mekarev* those distant from Torah and strengthen the already religious by establishing Torah *shiurim* throughout the land.
- ☐ Draw Israeli youth closer to Torah by organizing lectures in all schools — both religious and irreligious.
- ☐ Quell the contention between the various sectors in Israel.
- ☐ Strengthen the bond between Israel and Jews throughout the Diaspora.
- ☐ Encourage *aliya* to Israel and provide for the spiritual needs of *olim*, for "not on bread alone will man live."[12]

---

10. In reference to the *geirut* and *mamzeirut* issues that were front and center in these elections, Harav Ovadia committed to rule with *koha d'heteira*, citing his work in the five volumes of *Yabia Omer* published until that time as proof that he could do so, but also cautioning that this could be achieved only by following the rules governing *psak halacha*, not circumventing them.
11. At the time, there were 70 *dayanim* serving in Eretz Yisrael, and only 20 were Sephardim.
12. *Devarim* 8:3.

The Outcome

HARAV OVADIA ARRIVED AT THE VOTING STATION IN HEICHAL Shlomo on 7 Heshvan — not to do some last-minute campaigning, but to fulfill his duty to vote, as one of the 150 members of the *guf habocher*. After submitting his votes for each of the two chief rabbi positions as well as for the ten-member chief rabbinate council, he went to the house of his

Harav Ovadia arrives at the Kotel to thank Hashem for his election as chief rabbi and is greeted with spontaneous dancing by well-wishers.

daughter Yaffa in Katamon and sat down to learn as though no important vote was taking place. His son Yitzchak remained in Heichal Shlomo to wait for the vote tally. When it was announced that Harav Ovadia had received 81 votes to Rav Nissim's 68, Yitzchak ran to his sister's home to inform Harav Ovadia that he had been elected alongside Chief Rabbi Goren, who had been victorious by an 89-57 margin.

Harav Ovadia immediately traveled to the Kotel to thank Hashem, and was greeted there by a large group of his students and well-wishers.

THE DAYS THAT FOLLOWED SAW HARAV OVADIA BEING FETED in venues throughout Eretz Yisrael. In Heichal Shlomo he was welcomed by several *dayanim*, as well as by religious government officials, including Religious Services Minister Zorach Warhaftig, and secular officials, such as Jerusalem Mayor Teddy Kollek. His alma mater, Yeshivat Porat Yosef, held a special ceremony to recognize his achievement, and Rosh Yeshiva Rav Yehuda Tzadka blessed Harav Ovadia with success. The ceremony was graced with the presence of the three

"Halacha Is Not Determined at Dizengoff"

Rabbanim participate in Porat Yosef's ceremony to honor Harav Ovadia upon his election as Rishon LeZion. (R-L): Rav Yosef Shalom Elyashiv, Rav Betzalel Zolty, Harav Ovadia, Rav Yehuda Tzadka, Rav Eliezer Goldschmidt, and Rav Yaakov Fink (Chief Rabbi of Haifa).

colleagues who had convinced the new Rishon LeZion to run for election — Rav Elyashiv, Rav Zolty, and Rav Goldschmidt — along with philanthropist Suleiman David Sasson, who flew in from London to take part in the celebration.[13]

Not all of the welcoming ceremonies retained a good-natured, congratulatory spirit. At a reception for Harav Ovadia at the home of Israel's president attended by the Cabinet and the leaders of the military, President Zalman Shazar and Prime Minister Golda Meir both urged the new Rishon LeZion to find some way for the Langer children to marry. Defense Minister Moshe Dayan was particularly open about the government's expectations, declaring, "I don't care how you find a *heter*, the bottom line is that we have to rule leniently for those who were prevented from marrying."[14]

By the time Harav Ovadia rose to address the crowd, the atmosphere in the room had grown tense, and it seemed at first that he would capitulate and guarantee to provide the solution they

"Halacha is determined in the beit midrash and by the Shulhan Aruch."
Rav Ovadia clarified his position at the reception at the home of President Zalman Shazar, with all of Israel's political leaders in attendance.

---

13. Similar ceremonies were hosted, most notably: in the Kings Hotel by the Vaad Ha'eida HaSepharadit, which had already anointed him Rishon LeZion 14 years earlier; in the Central Hotel in Yerushalayim by Agudat Yisrael; in Haifa by Chief Rabbi Yosef Mashash; and in Teveria by Chief Rabbi Avraham Dov Auerbach.
14. *Posek HaDor*.

sought. His opening words were: "I am from a line of Rishon LeZions dating back more than 300 years," he began, "all of whom worked with *koha d'heteira* to try to solve halachic issues that arose." But before anyone could misinterpret his words, Harav Ovadia declared, "However, halacha is not determined at Dizengoff Square; it is determined in the *beit midrash* and by the *Shulhan Aruch*. If there is any way to be lenient and permit something, the Sephardic *hachamim* will be the first ones to rule leniently. But if there is no way to permit something, and after all the probing, investigating, and halachic examination that we do, we still cannot find a basis to allow it, we cannot permit something that is prohibited, Heaven forbid."

The Fallout

IT DID NOT TAKE LONG FOR CHIEF RABBI GOREN TO FOLLOW through on his pledge to tend to the Langer saga. At first he tried to convince Harav Ovadia to join him and one more *dayan* and set up a new *beit din* to adjudicate the matter, but Harav Ovadia refused, because he felt that this would contravene the halachic process. The existing *batei din*, he maintained, had held their sessions in good faith and had attempted to find a *heter*. No fewer than nine *dayanim* — including some of the most experienced *dayanim* in the country — had taken part in the effort to find a *heter*, and not one had managed to find one. If there was anything to be done about the case, it would not be accomplished by overriding the existing *beit din* system, but rather by returning the case to the *batei din* that had first reviewed it and having those *dayanim* examine the new evidence Chief Rabbi Goren claimed to have uncovered in his *Mahberet* — which he was still guarding as a state secret. Harav Ovadia agreed that if the lower *beit din* couldn't find a *heter*, the matter could then be brought to the Beit Din HaGadol, whose ranks included both chief rabbis.

On November 15, exactly one month after their election, Harav Ovadia felt that he had no choice but to report to the press that his Ashkenazi counterpart had issued an ultimatum four days earlier: If Harav Ovadia would not join him on a new three-man *beit din*,

Chief Rabbi Goren would cut off all contact with him and refuse to participate in a joint inaugural ceremony.

Chief Rabbi Goren denied issuing the ultimatum, but Harav Ovadia Yosef repeated the charge in an interview published in the *Jerusalem Post*.[15]

Four days later, on November 19, in a shocking maneuver, Chief Rabbi Goren assembled a *beit din* of an additional nine rabbanim and "removed the taint of *mamzeirut*" from Chanoch and Miriam Langer — who were immediately wed to their respective fiancés in a joint ceremony attended by Defense Minister Moshe Dayan and celebrated by many government officials, including Prime Minister Meir, who sent a congratulatory telegram to the two siblings.

Chief Rabbi Goren held a press conference, stating that he would not publicize the names of the nine *dayanim* "for fear of reprisals against them by religious extremists." Since he was still officially the chief rabbi of Tel Aviv, he was able to order the local authorities to register Chanoch and Miriam Langer as marriageable under halacha. Chanoch, who was then 27, married Yehudit Kinspon, and Miriam, 25, married Danny Levin.[16]

Several members of the Beit Din HaGadol who were interviewed that day openly expressed their doubts that Chief Rabbi Goren's *beit din* had been given any time to examine the evidence and hear testimony from witnesses who knew firsthand information pertinent to the case. They described the maneuver as "devastating to the rabbinic judicial system."[17]

> *As these dramatic events were unfolding, Harav Ovadia was delivering a shiur in Netivot's Yeshivat HaNegev. Journalists quickly determined the whereabouts of the Sephardic Chief Rabbi and traveled to Netivot to record his reaction to the news that his Ashkenazi counterpart had circumvented him and the entire beit din system by issuing his heter.*

---

15. "*Mamzerim* Case Sparks Bitter Row Between Chief Rabbis" (*Jewish Telegraphic Agency*, 15 Nov. 1972).
16. "Goren Clears *Mamzerim*: Hanoch and Miriam Langer Wed Their Fiances" (*Jewish Telegraphic Agency*, 20 Nov. 1972).
17. As reported by *Hamodia* on November 20, 1972.

Rav Yissachar Meir, Rosh Yeshivat HeNegev, was astonished that Harav Ovadia remained levelheaded and completed his *shiur* while the media waited outside for his comment.

> Someone informed the rosh yeshiva, Rav Yissachar Meir, about the members of the press waiting outside, and he wrote a note to Harav Ovadia. Harav Ovadia read it, folded it, and placed it in his pocket. He continued to deliver his shiur, an in-depth examination of a halachic matter that, in his classic style, included citations from dozens of poskim. When the shiur ended, Rav Meir expressed his wonderment that Harav Ovadia was able to remain levelheaded and concentrate on

the shiur while the entire world was in an uproar, waiting anxiously for his reaction.[18]

Taking It to the Courts

TORAH LEADERS IN ISRAEL AND THROUGHOUT THE WORLD protested against Chief Rabbi Goren's *heter*. But while the damage caused by Chief Rabbi Goren's actions was largely irreversible, the Torah leaders – Harav Ovadia among them – felt that it was vital to do everything possible to prevent his actions from setting a precedent for future tampering with the halacha.

Avraham Borokovsky was encouraged to take his case both to *beit din* to affirm his status as a Jew, and to the Israeli Supreme Court to prevent the chief rabbi from continuing to slander his name by claiming that he was not Jewish.

The *beit din* in Petah Tikva, which Borokovsky petitioned to review his case, requested that the Beit Din HaGadol transfer the Langer file to its possession so they could view all the documents pertinent to the case. Chief Rabbi Goren, in his capacity as one of the new heads of the Beit Din HaGadol, rejected the request, claiming that the *dayanim* were tainted and couldn't be trusted to judge the case. Harav Ovadia responded, characteristically, with a well-documented halachic *teshuva* delineating why the *beit din* **was** qualified to review the case again, and instructing that the files should therefore be transferred to them. For the time being, however, the secretary of the Beit Din HaGadol could not release the documents, because he could not act against one of the heads of the Beit Din.

Four months later, the Supreme Court ruled that Chief Rabbi Goren's ruling in the Langer case had no effect on Avraham Borokovsky, and ordered Rabbi Goren to hand over to the Petah Tikva *beit din* all documents pertinent to the case. The court also ordered Chief Rabbi Goren to pay 1,000 shekels toward Borokovsky's litigation costs.[19]

---

18. *Posek HaDor*, p. 218.
19. A complete review of the Langer case and its aftermath can be found in *Rav Elyashiv*, (Artscroll/Mesorah Publ., 2013).

HARAV OVADIA REITERATED THAT THE ISSUES CROPPING UP between the two chief rabbis were not due to his intractability or to his refusal to help those in difficult situations. "I am opposed to extremism," he related in a media interview, "but I believe halacha should be dispensed without publicity and without sensationalism. I cannot make halacha so plastic that it can fit into any mold. I cannot tell the public that everything is permissible, everything is forgivable." [20]

Halacha Is Not Plastic

As spring of 1973 gave way to summer, the Torah community continued trying to mitigate the damage of Chief Rabbi Goren's *heter*. But with the outbreak of the Yom Kippur War, the public's attention would soon be diverted away from the Langer case and the tension between the two chief rabbis. And in the aftermath of the catastrophic war, the entire Israeli public would begin to appreciate Harav Ovadia's brilliance and his ability to resolve thorny halachic issues without bending halacha in the slightest.

---

20. "Yosef Denies He Will Resign" (*Jewish Telegraphic Agency*, 8 Jan. 1973).

CHAPTER TWENTY
THE FATHER OF AGUNOT

AFTER THE INTOXICATING ISRAELI VICTORY OVER three massive Arab armies in the 1967 Six-Day War, the prevailing sentiment among the Israeli public was that the decisive beating inflicted on Egypt, Jordan, and Syria would prevent those nations from ever attacking Israel again. Even as Egypt and Syria once again mobilized large battalions on Israel's borders in the summer and fall of 1973, the upper echelons of the IDF (Israel Defense Forces) repeatedly ignored the warnings, preferring to rely on intelligence estimates that the enemy troops were performing military exercises and were not preparing for war. Advance warnings by Arab collaborators were dismissed, and although the weeks before Yom Kippur 5734/1973 saw tens of thousands of Arab troops being mobilized at the Suez Canal and similar numbers setting up camp near the Golan Heights in Syria, Israel's leaders continued to believe that the threat of an Israeli offensive would ultimately deter Egypt and Syria from attacking. The hubris of army leaders lulled both the military and the civilian public into a false sense of security.

The war, which began at 2 p.m. on Yom Kippur, saw more than

2,500 Israelis killed in action and thousands more injured. The war shook the confidence of the Israeli people, and destroyed their trust in their government to protect them from their neighbors. As a result, almost every official in a position of power during the war was forced to resign, including Prime Minister Golda Meir, Defense Minister Moshe Dayan, several generals of the army, and the leaders of Aman, Israel's intelligence unit. As recently as 2013, government agencies were still arguing about which minister was most responsible for *"hamehdal* — the neglect" that led to the losses in war. The national wound inflicted during the Yom Kippur War was still raw, even four decades later.

At no small personal risk, Harav Ovadia traveled to the front lines several times during the war to provide much-needed encouragement to the soldiers. Both religious and irreligious personnel streamed to hear his words of *hizuk*, and then lined up to receive his blessing. He also visited many hospitals to sit at the bedsides

Rav Ovadia visiting the front lines during the Yom Kippur War to encourage the soldiers.

and shore up the spirits of soldiers wounded in battle.

One of the most painful consequences of the war was the many *agunot* — "chained women" — it left in its wake. According to halacha, if a woman's husband goes missing and there is no evidence of his death, she may not remarry. If she does remarry and her first husband returns, she would not be permitted to remain married to either man, and children born from the second marriage would be *mamzerim* (illegitimate children) and would not be permitted to marry regular Jews.

Heter agunot — finding a halachic basis to free women whose husbands' whereabouts were unknown — is one of the most complex areas of halacha. Historically, the greatest rabbis of each generation were called upon to rule on such cases.[1] Each such case calls not only for sensitivity to the plight of the chained woman, but also for a great deal of fealty to halacha and *yirat Shamayim*. A rav seeking to free an *aguna* cannot lose sight of the devastating long-term consequences of issuing a *heter* to remarry if the woman's husband is actually still alive.

Yom Kippur War Agunot

IN THE CASE OF THE YOM KIPPUR WAR *AGUNOT*, THE STAKES were especially high because of the youth of the *agunot*; close to 1,000 soldiers presumed to have fallen in battle were young married men. In many cases, however, the soldiers' remains were unidentifiable or impossible to locate. Many of the recovered bodies were charred beyond recognition, and scores of others were not found. Statisticians might have predicted that anyone who disappeared in the gruesome

---

1. In fact, *heter agunot* is, quite likely, the most common topic in major responsa works written throughout the ages; each case is weighed considering as many precedents as possible.

Although in most halachic issues, one is supposed to weigh the halacha without attempting to rule in one direction or another, when it comes to cases of missing husbands, there is a deliberate stress on finding a *heter*, which is why the topic is referred to in Rabbinic literature as **heter** *agunot*. In *Sh'eilos V'Teshuvos Heichal Yitzchak* (*Even Ha'ezer* 1:30), Rav Yitzchak Isaac HaLevi Herzog quotes from Rabbeinu Gershom Me'or HaGola, one of the earliest *Rishonim*, who writes, "According to what our Rabbis taught us, in this matter our sages were lenient, in order to aid the *agunot* and ascertain that they don't stray into bad ways."

Rav Herzog points out that matters have only gotten worse in our times; since non-Orthodox strains of Judaism are willing to issue "*heterim*" without any sort of halachic consideration, he posits that rabbanim have to try even harder to find proper *heterim*.

battlefield conditions of the Yom Kippur War could not possibly return, especially since both Egypt and Syria were known to have executed the prisoners they captured. But halacha does not rely on statistical projections.

To free the wives of these presumed-dead soldiers, each case had to be studied individually. Evidence had to be gathered, medical and dental records that might help identify the soldier had to be reviewed, and witnesses to the exact circumstances of the soldiers' disappearance had to be located and questioned.

It was imperative that the rav who would take on the daunting task of freeing the hundreds of Yom Kippur War *agunot* would have broad enough shoulders for everyone to rely on his *heterim* — and he had to be acknowledged by the greatest rabbis to be qualified, so that his rulings would be accepted. This rav would need to possess sufficient *yirat Shamayim* and halachic proficiency, as well as deep sympathy for the *agunot* — some of whom were married for only weeks or months before their husbands disappeared. While every *aguna* case requires sensitivity, the prospect of an 18-year-old woman condemned to a life of solitude is all the more devastating.

Since Ashkenazi Chief Rabbi Goren had been the longtime chief rabbi of the IDF, it was assumed that he would be called

Harav Ovadia and Moshe Dayan (second and third from right) at a memorial ceremony for soldiers who had fallen in battle during the Yom Kippur War. Dayan charged Harav Ovadia with the task of determining the halachic status of the *agunot* of the married soldiers.

upon to rule on these cases. Surprisingly, however, army officials approached Harav Ovadia, the Sephardic Chief Rabbi, and asked him to take on the responsibility. There was much speculation as to why Harav Ovadia was chosen for the task, but what is known is that leading rabbis in the IDF were instrumental in this decision. They explained to Defense Minister Moshe Dayan — an ally of Chief Rabbi Goren since the days of the Langer case[2] — that it was pointless to issue *heterim* if the rabbanim who would have to officiate at subsequent marriages of these *agunot* wouldn't be willing to rely on those *heterim*. The rulings had to be issued by a rabbinic figure who was respected by *all* communities in Israel, and only Harav Ovadia fit that bill.

IN A NEARLY 13,000-WORD *TESHUVA*,[3] HARAV OVADIA acknowledges that it was extremely difficult for him to assume this responsibility:

Nightly Sessions

On the heels of the Yom Kippur War, I was asked by my friends, IDF Chief Rabbi Mordechai Piron and Deputy Chief Rabbi Gad Navon, to lead a *beit din* to deal with the issue of *agunot*, to deliberate and rule on close to 1,000 files of *kedoshim*,[4] IDF soldiers *Hy"d* who were married and left behind young wives.

...I am certain that I am too small to rule on matters of *erva* (illicit relationships), and especially on cases of *eishet ish*.[5] I realize the great responsibility in this matter, and it is extremely difficult to grasp all the concepts.

In the next 700 words of the *teshuva*, Harav Ovadia cites dozens of sources about the importance of finding *heterim* for *agunot*, and how terrible it is if a person who is able to find *heterim* refrains from doing so. He closes the section with a prayer that Hashem should save him from erring in any of the cases.

---

2. See p. 362.
3. *Yabia Omer,* Vol. 6, *Even Ha'ezer* 3.
4. The term *kedoshim,* holy ones, is an appellation used to describe someone who was killed *Al Kiddush Hashem,* sanctifying Hashem's Name.
5. I.e., the possibility of a married woman remarrying while her first husband is still alive.

Rabbi Gad Navon (R), who was deputy chief rabbi of the IDF during the Yom Kippur War, worked with Harav Ovadia to establish the facts of each *aguna* case. Also pictured is Moshe Yosef, Harav Ovadia's youngest, welcoming his father back to Eretz Yisrael after a long trip abroad.

Harav Ovadia accepted the mission, and began working to free the *agunot*. Each evening, after a long day dealing with his regular workload in the Rabbanut, he would sit with Rabbis Piron and Navon, who served as the other two *dayanim* on this *beit din*, and sift through all the evidence that had been prepared for them. Most of the cases were straightforward: there were two or more witnesses who testified that they knew the deceased soldier while he was alive and that they saw and and recognized his lifeless body within three days of his death, as required by halacha.[6] Such cases took as little as ten minutes to resolve.

In many instances, however, there were no witnesses who could testify with certainty that the husband was dead. Then, the three rabbanim would examine pictures, dental records, bone structure analyses, and other medical records. In some cases, they did not have "hard evidence." In the case of an airplane that had been shot down on the way back from a sortie, for instance, they had to rely

---

6. After three days, there is concern that the body has decomposed to the point that it can no longer be identified properly.

on the testimony of another pilot who witnessed the plane go down and didn't see anyone parachute out of it.[7]

The ID-Tag Heter

HARAV OVADIA HAD TO ESTABLISH CERTAIN PRINCIPLES AS the basis for *heterim*, and each of these principles was based on precedents found in universally accepted responsa literature from previous generation.

One of his guiding principles was that if a body couldn't be identified, the *"diskit,"* a metal ID tag worn around the soldier's neck — popularly referred to as a dog tag — could be relied on to establish the soldier's identity. Before issuing this groundbreaking ruling, Harav Ovadia had to resolve a number of thorny halachic questions, among them:

1. May an object be used for purposes of halachic identification altogether?
2. May the name engraved on the ID tag, which stated the soldier's given name and surname, be used in place of the person's given name and father's given name, as is usually required for halachic identification?
3. Is there a concern that a soldier lent his ID tag to someone else, and the person whose name is on the ID tag is actually still alive?
4. In some cases, the ID tag was found not around the soldier's neck, but in his pocket. Would this constitute additional grounds for concern that this was not actually his ID tag?
5. If other identification that corroborated the information on the ID tag was found in the soldier's pockets, did that prove with certainty that the ID tag belonged to him?

> At one point, Harav Ovadia almost despaired of resolving these serious sh'eilot. He knew that he could not "invent" a new heter on his own; he had to find some earlier recognized posek who had freed agunot whose husbands had died in

---

7. The full *teshuva* for this *heter* is in *Yabia Omer*, Vol. 6, *Even Ha'ezer* 4.

Harav Ovadia had to determine whether soldiers who were caught in tanks that blew up could be presumed dead.

similar situations. One night, one of the greatest halachic authorities of previous generations appeared to him in a dream and told him, "Look in my sefer in such-and-such teshuva, where I rule that we don't have to suspect that someone loaned another person an item used for identification purposes, and I freed an aguna based on that heter."

Harav Ovadia woke up and ran to find the sefer, relieved that he would be able to free more agunot based on that heter.[8]

IN THE COURSE OF FINDING *HETERIM*, HARAV OVADIA QUOTed from dozens of halacha works, building a case to allow each *aguna* to remarry.

Other Forms of Evidence

The ID-tag issue was only one of the halachic challenges Harav Ovadia grappled with. In some cases, there were photographs taken of the deceased soldier within three days of his passing, and Harav Ovadia had to deal

---

8. *Posek HaDor*, which states that Harav Ovadia told this story at a gathering of Agudat HaRabbanim, where he explained the halachic underpinnings of the *heterim* he had granted to *agunot*.

with the question of whether photographs are considered equivalent to a live witness testifying that he recognized the soldier.

In other cases, the only evidence available by which to identify a soldier were fingerprints or dental records.

Harav Ovadia labored to ascertain whether these forms of evidence were halachically valid, and he was then able to apply appropriate *heterim* to dozens of cases.

But for a person who cared so deeply about people, the process never got easier. Each case was gut-wrenching, and Harav Ovadia was barely able to sleep during the months in which he was involved in finding *heterim*. His family would sometimes find him going through photographs on his own, sobbing uncontrollably as he tried to find the elusive piece of evidence on which a *heter* could be based.

Sometimes, after issuing a *heter*, Harav Ovadia faced an additional difficulty: meeting family members who were unaware of the exact condition in which their son, brother, or husband's body had been returned. The bodies were delivered in closed caskets, and the families generally didn't know that the bodies were virtually unidentifiable. Rav David Yosef relates that there was one man who prayed with the Rav regularly, and Harav Ovadia could barely look him in the face because he knew that the casket he had buried contained almost no remains.

HARAV OVADIA DIDN'T DEAL WITH THESE CASES ONLY ON a technical level; he would truly feel the pain of each widow.

Feeling the Pain of the Agunot *One night, after he finally found a heter for one aguna, he summoned his son, Rav David, and asked him to find the woman's telephone number. The woman's verdict would be handed down in the beit din the following morning, but Harav Ovadia did not want her to have to wait until the morning to learn that she was free to remarry.*

"Abba," Rav David asked, "it's so late at night. Are we not taking the chance of waking her up?"

Chapter Twenty: The Father of Agunot ☐ 379

"I'm certain that she is not able to get any sleep tonight," Harav Ovadia answered. "She's too busy worrying about what the ruling will be tomorrow."

By law, however, Harav Ovadia was not allowed to tell the woman what the ruling would be until she was back in beit din the next morning, just as a judge would not be allowed to telephone a defendant and notify him of the verdict ahead of time. Yet Harav Ovadia could not bear to leave the woman in the agony of uncertainty all night. He called her and said, "I just want you to know that you can rest easily tonight." He didn't tell her the exact ruling, but he did convey to her that she would no longer be condemned to solitude.

"The woman began to cry," recalls Rav David, "and my father cried along with her."

The World Trade Center Case

LONG AFTER HIS TENURE AS RISHON LEZION ENDED, HARAV Ovadia continued to be called upon to resolve *aguna* cases. In the last decades of his life, appeals on behalf of *agunot* poured in from around the world. Some were from *agunot* or their families, asking him to find a *heter*; others came in the form of *teshuvot* from other rabbanim who felt they had a viable *heter* but sought Harav Ovadia's approval because they did not feel comfortable taking responsibility themselves for the woman remarrying.

The last few volumes of *Yabia Omer* contain *teshuvot* regarding *agunot* in France, Belgium, Russia, and other places around the world. But perhaps the most famous of these cases came from the United States.

After the destruction of the World Trade Center on September 11, 2001, a Sephardi *aguna*, Mrs. S., whose husband Eliyahu worked at Cantor-Fitzgerald,[9] asked that Harav Ovadia review her case to determine whether she was permitted to remarry.

---

9. Cantor-Fitzgerald was a large financial services corporation whose New York headquarters were housed on floors 101-105 of World Trade Center One, or the North Tower, which was the first building hit in the terror attack that day; 658 employees of Cantor-Fitzgerald were killed in the attack.

Harav Ovadia describes the circumstances in detail:[10]

Eliyahu S. worked on the 104th floor of the North Tower, well above the point of impact (which was somewhere between floors 93-99). He called his wife, apparently from his office phone, at 8:20, to wake her up. At 8:46, approximately one minute after American Airlines Flight 11 hit the building, she tried calling him on his cellphone and did not get through. She left a message, and he called back at 8:52 and told her that they were evacuating the building. She never heard from him again.

A list of Eliyahu's phone calls, generated by his cellphone provider, corroborated the account.

There was additional proof that Eliyahu was in his office that morning,[11] because he received an email at 8:17 and replied at 8:21,

Could the wife of a man trapped above the point of impact of the airplane that hit the North Tower of the World Trade Center on 9/11 remarry? The *sh'eila* found its way to Harav Ovadia.

---

10. *Yabia Omer*, Vol. 10, *Even Ha'ezer* 10:18.
11. The cellphone records didn't prove conclusively that he was in his office that morning; he could have made those phone calls from the street.

Chapter Twenty: The Father of Agunot ☐ 381

and records proved that the email was sent to his office and the reply was generated from his office.

Harav Ovadia quotes the professional opinion of an engineer, Mr. Tzemach, who stated that there was no doubt that everyone who was trapped above the point of impact died, either as a result of the immense conflagration, or due to smoke inhalation even before the fire reached their floor. Furthermore, the smoke was so thick that even if people were still conscious after the impact, they would not have been able to find their way to an exit route. There was also a report of a Cantor-Fitzgerald employee who called his family and said that they were trapped inside and couldn't escape.

Harav Ovadia had to weigh two primary factors in this case:

1. Would halacha recognize the professional opinion that a person couldn't possibly survive an explosion beneath him caused by the impact of an airplane carrying 50 tons of jet fuel?
2. Would Mrs. S.'s testimony that her husband had called her from his office phone serve as a solid-enough basis to establish that he was indeed inside the building at the time?

In a brilliant *teshuva*, Harav Ovadia explains the halachic factors involved in relying on estimates and *rov* (majorities). But what also emerges from this *teshuva* is that even as an octogenarian, he understood all the nuances of modern technology and was able to apply this knowledge to issue a *heter* for Mrs. S. to remarry.

HARAV OVADIA WAS WILLING TO DEAL WITH *AGUNA* CASES even when they came at a personal risk.

When HaKablan Closed Down

Rehov HaKablan, where he lived for the last two decades of his life, is a quiet, winding, residential street in the tranquil neighborhood of Har Nof. It came as a surprise to Har Nof residents and visitors to find the entire street closed down one day by the police, with squadrons of officers patrolling the block.

As an octogenarian, Harav Ovadia was still being called upon to deal with the most difficult *aguna* cases.

No one divulged the reason for the street closure at the time, but the story later came to light.

It seems that a man had disappeared many years before, and his wife had been an aguna ever since. Now, evidence had emerged that he had been killed by organized crime operatives, and his body had been embedded into the pillars of a large edifice in Yerushalayim built during the 1970s. His wife wanted to know whether the proof the police had could be relied upon halachically in order to free her to remarry.

The police were reluctant to release the criminal file containing the evidence, even for the shortest time. They were concerned that if the criminals would find out that the evidence was out of police hands, they might try to steal it and destroy it, to prevent prosecution. In deference to the woman's anguished plea, however, they set up a "military zone" on Rehov HaKablan, shutting it entirely to traffic, and brought the file directly to Harav Ovadia. He pored over the evidence as police officers remained in his apartment, returned the material to them, and ultimately found a heter for the aguna to remarry. The threat of a mafia attack during his examination of the evidence didn't deter him from trying to free this aguna.[12]

The "Other" Agunot

ALTHOUGH MOST OF THE *AGUNA* CASES FOR WHICH HARAV Ovadia became famous involved husbands who went missing under tragic circumstances, he also championed the cause of women whose husbands refused to give them a *get* (halachic bill of divorce). Such a woman is equally chained to her husband, and cannot remarry unless the husband agrees to issue a *get*.

A *dayan* in the Rabbanut recalled a case in which a husband threatened that he would not give his wife a *get* for 50 years, but subsequently agreed to release her if she paid him $50,000. The wife's family could not afford to pay this outrageous sum, and the rabbanim tried to persuade the man to abandon these extortionist tactics, but he absolutely refused. This *dayan* expressed to Harav Ovadia his frustration at not being able to obtain a *get* for the woman.

"Have you never heard of the *mitzva* of *pidyon shevuyim* (redeeming prisoners)?" Harav Ovadia asked.

"*Pidyon shevuyim*?" the *dayan* asked, puzzled.

"Yes," Harav Ovadia replied. "This woman is a prisoner in her marriage. Go raise the funds to free her."

---

12. Heard from R' Shlomo Zevihi, Harav Ovadia's driver.

"Here we were, throwing up our hands in despair," recalls the *dayan*, "and the solution was right there before our eyes."

But raising the sum was still a daunting task. Shortly after Harav Ovadia recommended that they raise the funds to free her, this *dayan* heard that a philanthropist who was close to Harav Ovadia was visiting Eretz Yisrael. The *dayan* reminded Harav Ovadia about the case, and asked whether he'd be willing to ask the philanthropist for a donation for this cause.

"Good idea," Harav Ovadia replied. "Tomorrow night I'll be at a gathering with him. Come to the gathering and remind me, and I'll ask him."

At the gathering, the *dayan* reminded him and he immediately approached the philanthropist and explained the situation. "Can you help us free this righteous woman?" he asked the philanthropist.

"How much do you need?" he asked.

"$50,000," the *dayan* replied.

"Give me the wiring instructions, and the money will be deposited tomorrow."

Upon receiving the money, the husband gave his wife the *get*. She subsequently remarried and raised six children who are now building Torah homes themselves.

"I was shocked that Harav Ovadia was so willing to approach this philanthropist and ask for the money," the *dayan* related. "This man was a donor to Harav Ovadia's network of schools, and asking him to give to this cause could easily have made him less willing to donate to the rav's institutions. But the rav's pity for this woman overrode any other considerations."

The Erev Yom Kippur Get

RAV DAVID YOSEF RECALLED THAT ONE EREV YOM KIPPUR afternoon, a recalcitrant husband visited Harav Ovadia, who spent a long time convincing him to give a *get*. The man finally agreed, but Harav Ovadia was concerned that by the time Yom Kippur was over, the husband might regret his decision and continue to withhold the *get*.

While most people were busy eating the *seuda hamafseket* and getting ready for Yom Kippur, Harav Ovadia got to work writing the *get* himself and sending his family members to gather kosher witnesses so that the *get* could be issued before the husband would renege.

PERHAPS THE STORY THAT BEST CAPTURES HARAV OVADIA'S dedication to freeing *agunot* is one that occurred approximately 14 years before his passing.[13]

Heter Aguna Before Surgery

The elderly rav wasn't feeling well one day, and Rav David and R' Aryeh Deri took him to the hospital to be examined. The doctors determined that he had suffered a heart attack, and they told him that he needed an emergency stent procedure to open his arteries.

"I need to go home for three hours," Harav Ovadia replied. "Then I'll return for the procedure."

Rav David and R' Aryeh were concerned that the delay would be dangerous, and they tried to dissuade him from leaving the hospital. "Why does the rav need three hours?" R' Aryeh asked.

"I'm not sure that I'll come out of this procedure alive," Harav Ovadia explained, "and I'm in middle of writing a *teshuva* to free an *aguna*. If I don't finish writing the *teshuva*, who will take pity on this woman and release her from her loneliness?"

They brought him home, and he finished writing the *teshuva* permitting the *aguna* to remarry. Only then did he return to the hospital for the lifesaving procedure.

HISTORICALLY, THERE HAVE BEEN SOME DEVASTATING SITUAtions in which a rav issued a *heter* to an *aguna* to remarry, and then

No Returns

"*ba harug beraglav* — the dead man walked in on his own two feet." While such situations were few and far between, they are certainly the nightmare of not only the *aguna* herself, but also of the rabbanim who issued *heterim* to women to remarry.

---

13. This story was told by Rav David Yosef at Harav Ovadia's funeral.

With grandson and biographer R' Yaakov Sasson, to whom Harav Ovadia remarked with relief that no husband whose *aguna* he had freed later returned.

Shortly before his passing, Harav Ovadia was conversing with his grandson and biographer R' Yaakov Sasson, and the discussion turned to Harav Ovadia's work freeing *agunot*. He mentioned two historical cases in which presumed-dead husbands returned after their wives had remarried. "*Baruch Hashem*," he said, "I have merited to free hundreds of *agunot*, and I have never had a husband return."

This comment reflected the great *yirat Shamayim* with which he approached every subject — especially one as enormously significant as *heter aguna*. While he certainly empathized with the women he sought to free, that empathy never caused him to veer ever so slightly off the path of halachic truth.

CHAPTER TWENTY-ONE
AT THE SUMMIT

BY THE TIME HARAV OVADIA RESOLVED ALL OF THE Yom Kippur War *aguna* cases, nearly a year and a half had passed since his election as chief rabbi. Because most of his duties were now centered in Yerushalayim, his family felt compelled to find a residence that befit the Rishon LeZion, who sometimes hosted heads of state in his home. As far as Harav Ovadia was concerned, whatever apartment they would settle in had to have one feature: space for his still-growing *sefarim* library. The Rabbanit eventually chose an apartment on Rehov Rothschild in Rehavia. When Harav Ovadia saw the apartment for the first time, he noticed that an inordinate amount of space had been designated for a grand piano that had been left behind by the previous owner, and he asked that the piano be removed so he could use the space for more *sefarim*.

In Nissan 5734, Harav Ovadia was officially installed as the Rishon LeZion. The ceremony, while moving, was relatively simple compared to the fanfare surrounding his installation as chief rabbi of Tel Aviv. It took place in Beit Knesset Rav Yochanan ben Zakkai in the Old City, a venue used to inaugurate many a Rishon LeZion over the years, and was attended by many *gedolei Torah*. In a display of respect, Rav Rafael Abo, Rav Isser Yehuda Unterman, and Rav

Harav Ovadia is helped into his *glima* by Ashknezic Chief Rabbi Unterman (R) and Rav Eliezer Goldschmidt (above).

Harav Ovadia wearing the gold *luhot habrit* medallion

Eliezer Goldschmidt helped Harav Ovadia into a black *glima* (robe) with branches and leaves of gold thread embroidered on it. This robe would become emblematic of Harav Ovadia, as he would wear it, or others like it, when appearing in public for the rest of his life. In honor of the occasion, he also donned a pure-gold medallion in the shape of the *luhot habrit* traditionally gifted to the Rishon LeZion.

Harav Ovadia's intensive efforts to free the Yom Kippur war *agunot* had changed the country's view of him — and, by extension, their opinion of rabbanim in general. The public now perceived him to be a rav who, while being concerned with the needs of the people, considered himself primarily accountable to the Torah. While the next eight years would still be rocky in terms of his relationship with Ashkenazi Chief Rabbi Goren and the ten members of the Chief Rabbinate Council,[1] by this point Harav Ovadia had much of the public — and many politicians — squarely planted in his corner. He was now able to embark on the goals he had committed to in the campaign material he had released a week before his election.[2]

Strengthening the Rabbanut

ONE OF THE PRIMARY BATTLES HARAV OVADIA FOUGHT DURing his years as Rishon LeZion was over who could be appointed to serve on a Rabbanut *beit din*. He and Chief Rabbi Goren disagreed fundamentally in this regard, as the latter wanted to pass a resolution in the Chief Rabbinate Council that only *dayanim* who had served in the IDF could qualify for the Rabbanut. Harav Ovadia insisted that serving in the IDF was a nonsensical prerequisite for serving on a *beit din*, and that a *dayan's* Torah knowledge and *yirat Shamayim* should be the only deciding factors in his appointment. He ultimately won this battle, only because each newly appointed *dayan* needed the approval of both chief rabbis, and Chief Rabbi Goren eventually capitulated because he realized that Harav Ovadia wasn't willing to back down on this issue.

In the course of his tenure as Rishon LeZion, Harav Ovadia succeeded in appointing dozens of new, competent *dayanim* who would reinvigorate the Rabbanut and help bolster the prestige of the *batei din*.[3]

Harav Ovadia also convinced the Chief Rabbinate Council to grant any *dayan* who had served on a *beit din* the automatic right

---

1. The Chief Rabbinate Council had been elected at the same time as the two chief rabbis, but the team that worked to gain Harav Ovadia's election did not have time to work on a slate for the Chief Rabbinate Council, and nearly every rabbi elected to the council was from the ranks of his opposition.
2. See p. 329.
3. *Posek HaDor*, p. 217.

to run for election as chief rabbi of a city. By doing so, he succeeded in bringing about the election of two rabbanim who would become legendary leaders of Yerushalayim: Rav Betzalel Zolty and Rav Shalom Mashash.

Rav Zolty and Rav Mashash

ON 21 KISLEV 5721/1960, RAV TZVI PESACH FRANK, THE LEGENDary rav and *av beit din* of Yerushalayim and one of Harav Ovadia's mentors and avid supporters, passed away.[4] For the next 11 years, Yerushalayim had no chief rabbi to take responsibility for the city's religious infrastructure. Without a chief rabbi, stores could sell non-kosher food with impunity and hotels could feed their guests meat and other food prepared without supervision. Although the Rabbinate's *kashrut* department was led by prominent qualified rabbanim who strove to maintain acceptable standards, they needed the backing of a chief rabbi invested with the power to enforce halacha.

In 1972, government officials started to talk about appointing an interim chief rabbi of Yerushalayim until elections could be held. The Torah leaders of the time were concerned that if left to their own devices, these politicians might not choose someone God-fearing and well-versed in halacha, and they decided to preempt that eventuality.

The leading roshei yeshiva and rabbanim of Yerushalayim, with Rav Yechezkel Abramsky[5] at their helm, chose Rav Betzalel Zolty to serve in that capacity. Rav Zolty was then the youngest *dayan* on the Beit Din HaGadol, but he was second in seniority to Rav Elyashiv.

In an assembly of rabbanim and Agudah *askanim* at Yerushalayim's Merkaz Hotel during Chanuka 5732/1972, Rav Zolty was crowned the chief rabbi of Yerushalayim. Although the official elections

---

4. See *Hazon Ovadia*, pp. 464-466, for Harav Ovadia's *hesped* on Rav Frank. It appears from that *hesped*, as well as from stories Harav Ovadia told, that much of his approach as a rav and leader was taken from Rav Frank.
 More specifically, Rav Frank was famous for speaking out against municipal or national violations of halacha even though he was employed by the State — something Harav Ovadia would do many times during his tenure as Rishon LeZion. For instance, they both spoke out against public *hillul Shabbat* in Eretz Yisrael and against drafting yeshiva students into the army.
5. Rav Abramsky, who had served as the chief rabbi of London before moving to Eretz Yisrael, was the Rosh Yeshiva of Slabodka and the author of *Hazon Yehezkel* on the *Tosefta*.

would take place only six years later, Rav Zolty's appointment by *gedolei Yisrael* was seen as binding, to the extent that no other hareidi rav would dare to run against him.

When the time came for elections, the Mizrahi party wanted to see their own rabbanim elected to both the Ashkenazi and Sephardi chief rabbi positions. Some leaders of the Mizrahi movement tried to prevent Rav Zolty from running, on the grounds that he had never served as a community rav, only as a *dayan*, but Harav Ovadia had forestalled their efforts by ensuring that any rav who had served on a *beit din* could run for election.

Harav Ovadia came out in vociferous support of Rav Zolty, his longtime colleague on the Beit Din HaGadol whom he knew to be both God-fearing and fearless enough to enforce *kashrut* and all other Rabbanut concerns in Yerushalayim.

As the elections neared, Harav Ovadia personally invited the chief rabbi of Morocco, Rav Shalom Mashash, to visit Eretz Yisrael and present his candidacy for the Sephardic chief rabbi position. He had come to know Rav Mashash primarily through the latter's

Rav Shalom Mashash and Harav Ovadia loved and revered each other.

writings, and was very impressed with him — even though he disagreed with him on many halachic matters.

When the Mizrahi leaders saw that their preferred candidates would lose handily to Rav Zolty and Rav Mashash, they attempted to delay the elections. The head of the Religious Council in Yerushalayim, R' Gedalyah Schreiber, sent a query to Harav Ovadia, asking him what to do about the repeated requests for delayed elections, and Harav Ovadia responded with a *teshuva* examining whether their request was halachically valid:[6]

> The heads of the National Religious Party are exerting heavy pressure on [R' Gedalyah Schreiber] and the other members of the Religious Council, demanding that they refrain from preparing the groundwork for elections for chief rabbi of Yerushalayim and halt the election process, because the candidates with the greatest chances of being elected are not acceptable to the National Religious Party, for despite their greatness in Torah and pure *yirat Shamayim*, they don't subscribe to the Mafdal philosophy. [R' Schreiber] has asked me whether he should yield to the pressure exerted by the heads of the party and halt the election process, or continue with the plans to the best of his ability….

This *teshuva* constitutes a fascinating illustration of Harav Ovadia's general approach: that everything must be examined through the lens of halacha. Rather than answer from a *hashkafa* perspective, he cites halachic sources extensively to underscore the gravity of a city not having a rav and to prove that appointing a rav is a halachic obligation that takes precedence over other communal expenses. He then establishes that even if only a minority of a community would like to appoint a rav, they may force the majority to comply — both in terms of choosing a rav and in terms of paying his salary. He also states that anyone who prevents a city from appointing a rav is worthy of excommunication.

---

6. *Yabia Omer*, Vol. 7, *Yoreh Dei'a* 18.

He then continues:

> I am personally aware of the problems that exist in the Holy City, Yerushalayim of Gold, in areas of *kashrut* and *mikvaot*, regarding which we can apply the principle: "That which is holier than its counterpart is in a greater state of destruction than its counterpart."[7] The *kashrut* of many hotels [in the city] has been particularly neglected.... Since the passing of the previous chief rabbis,[8] hundreds of thousands of our Jewish brethren who stay at hotels in Yerushalayim have transgressed by eating forbidden foods. There is no doubt that if the two candidates who are currently running... the great *gaon* Rav Betzalel Zolty and the renowned *gaon* Rav Shalom Mashash (previously chief

Harav Ovadia knew that his lifelong friend Rav Betzalel Zolty would mend the decaying *kashrut* supervision as chief rabbi of Yerushalayim.
Here, they visit a food production factory together and issue guidelines to *mashgihim*.

---

7. This principle means that wherever there is great potential for holiness, there is proportionately great potential for spiritual devastation. Rav Ovadia was intimating that since Yerushalayim has the most potential for holiness of any city in the world, its potential for spiritual devastation is proportionately great, which explains the appalling state of *kashrut*, *mikvaot*, and Shabbat observance in the city.

8. Actually, there hadn't been a Sephardic chief rabbi of Yerushalayim serving alongside Rav Tzvi Pesach Frank since 1939, when Rav Yaakov Meir, who had served as the Sephardic chief rabbi for 18 years, passed away.

rabbi of Morocco) are elected, they can certainly contribute greatly, applying their wisdom and piety to the areas of *kashrut* and *mikvaot* and establishing bulwarks and repairing breaches [of halacha]. They can also prevent egregious public desecration of Shabbat in hotels, for now there is no one to speak up against [the management of these hotels], who will do anything to sate their desire for money.

Harav Ovadia added that although there were many great rabbanim, *dayanim*, and roshei yeshiva in Yerushalayim at the time, only a chief rabbi, with power invested in him by the government, could stand up to powerful commercial entities and threaten to strip them of their *kashrut* certification if they didn't comply with the Rabbanut's regulations.

Harav Ovadia signed off on the *teshuva* by encouraging R' Schreiber to forge ahead with the preparations for the elections, and to expedite the process as much as possible. "Strengthen and fortify yourself," he concludes. "Do not fear or tremble before them, for Hashem will be with you in all that you do."

When the *teshuva* was later published, Harav Ovadia added a few lines stating that his words had made their mark: R' Gedalyah Schreiber withstood the pressure and held the elections on 3 Kislev 5738, as scheduled. Rav Zolty and Rav Mashash were indeed elected, and served with great distinction as the rabbanim of Yerushalayim.

UNFORTUNATELY, RAV ZOLTY'S TENURE AS CHIEF RABBI OF Yerushalayim was short-lived. On 30 Heshvan 5743/1982, he suddenly passed away, at the age of just 62. His passing came as a shock to everyone, for he was vibrant until his last day. In his *hesped*,[9] Harav Ovadia related that on the day of his passing, Rav Zolty spent a long, hard day tending to Rabbanut matters, yet he still had energy to deliver an in-depth *shiur* to a group of advanced scholars.

Group Decisions

---

9. Printed in the *Sefer HaZikaron* published in honor of Rav Zolty's fourth *yahrzeit* (*Machon Yerushalayim*).

Harav Ovadia and Rav Zolty inspect the Matzot Yehuda factory.

If Rav Zolty was sorely missed by Yerushalayim's scholars and laymen alike, how much more was his loss felt by his friend and colleague, Harav Ovadia. The lives of the two had intersected many times during their nearly five-decade friendship — and especially during the last five years of Rav Zolty's life. During that last period, the two had collaborated to revamp the *kashrut* system in Yerushalayim that had been neglected for so many years. They would visit factories together and discuss important practical *sh'eilot* with each other — often involving Rav Elyashiv, Rav Goldschmidt, and Rav Shaul Yisraeli, their other colleagues from the glory days of the Beit Din HaGadol — to ensure that reliably kosher food was readily available in Yerushalayim.

The Carmel-Mizrahi Question

About two months before Pesah 5735/1975,[10] a major sh'eila arose that was liable to cause a shortage of a Pesah staple: wine. At that point, approximately 95 percent of wine used in Israel on Pesah was produced by Carmel-Mizrahi,[11] which also exported large quantities of kosher-for-Pesah wines.

---
10. The bulk of the facts of this case are taken from Rav Ovadia's *teshuva* in *Yabia Omer*, Vol. 8, *Orah Haim* 43.
11. Rav David Yosef, who reports that the other 5 percent were wines produced by small vintners under the *hashgaha* of the Badatz Eida Haredit. The *sh'eila* also affected the Eliaz Winery, a much smaller wine producer that now markets under the name Binyamina.

The sh'eila therefore affected not only the vast majority of Jews in Israel, but world Jewry as well.

Naturally, Harav Ovadia was called upon to clarify the status of the wine. Seeking the largest consensus possible to ensure that the eventual decision on this sh'eila would be accepted by Jews from across the religious spectrum, he called together a group of the greatest poskim in Eretz Yisrael: Rav Yosef Shalom Elyashiv,[12] Rav Betzalel Zolty, Rav Shlomo Zalman Auerbach, Rav Eliezer Goldschmidt, and Rav Shaul Yisraeli. They heard testimony from Rav Yedidyah Yanovsky,[13] the mashgiah of the Vintners Association at Carmel-Mizrahi's original and primary production plant in Rishon LeZion, and Rav Eliyahu Bakshi-Doron, who would serve as the Sephardic chief rabbi 20 years after Harav Ovadia, but at the time was chief rabbi of Bat Yam and responsible for one of the two plants that had encountered the sh'eila. They also heard from vintners and other industry experts.

The issue started at the Asis plant in Ramat Gan and the Paka plant in Bat Yam, both of which produced the spirits that would later be added to the fermenting wine in Carmel-Mizrahi's Rishon LeZion plant to boost the alcohol content of the wine.

There are many raw ingredients that can be used to create spirits, one of which is grain starch. Grain-based spirits are hametz, and any wine produced with such spirits cannot be used for Pesah. In order to produce Pesah wines, Carmel-Mizrahi would send actual wine to the Asis and Paka plants to ferment into spirits, and the spirits would then be shipped back to Carmel-Mizrahi to be added to the wines.

For wines used during the year, the Asis and Paka factories would alternate between the raw ingredients used for the spirits. That year, after a production run of grain-based spirits, they switched to sugar beet as their raw ingredient,

---

12. Listed in the order in which they appear in Rav Ovadia's *teshuva*.
13. Rav Yanovsky was widely respected by the *gedolei hador*, to whom he turned frequently with *sh'eilot* regarding all the mitzvot governing produce grown, processed, and exported from Eretz Yisrael.

and only afterward did they produce the wine-based spirits. Before producing the wine spirits, they cleaned all of the production equipment with caustic soda,[14] an extremely powerful cleaning agent, which would certainly render the equipment kosher for Pesah use.

In the next stage of the process, the various forms of spirits would be stored in two huge tanks. The problem was that that year, after storing first the grain-based spirits and then the sugar beet spirits, they used the very same tanks for the wine-based spirits without cleaning the tanks.

The sh'eila actually affected more than just wine, since the sugar beet spirits had been used to produce liquor and arak[15] for Pesah, while the wine spirits had been used to produce wine. Did the fact that they were stored in the same tanks used to store grain-based spirits render all of the wine, liquor, and arak produced in Israel unusable for Pesah, because they contained traces of hametz derivatives?

The first fact the rabbanim were able to establish was that the *sh'eila* did not pertain to the grape juice produced by Carmel-Mizrahi, because grape juice was produced on equipment that had been cleaned for Pesah and had not come into contact with any of the problematic spirits.

After spending a few days deliberating the matter, the group of rabbanim accepted Harav Ovadia's approach, which resulted in all the wines and brandies produced in the factories being ruled kosher for Pesah use, even *l'chatchila*. With regard to the liquors, arak, and vodka in question, the ruling was that these were permitted *b'dieved*, but Harav Ovadia strongly urged people to be stringent and not drink them on Pesah. He wrote, however, that these beverages could be stored and used after Pesah, even for those who generally do not keep *hametz*-based liquors over Pesah.

Because Harav Ovadia was both savvy and humble enough not to simply release this *psak* himself, but to gather this group of

---

14. Scientifically termed sodium hydroxide (NaOH).
15. Arak is an extremely sharp alcoholic beverage (up to 80 percent alcohol content), originally produced in the Arabic Middle-Eastern lands.

Torah giants to discuss the case with him, his *psak* was relied upon throughout Eretz Yisrael and the world.

ANOTHER MAJOR *SH'EILA* AROSE WHEN THE HEALTH Ministry issued a directive requiring all day-old chicks to be inoculated against certain illnesses that were spreading through poultry farms all over Israel.

Chicken Inoculations

The inoculation could only be given in the neck area, and many religious Jews were concerned that the needle could puncture the trachea (windpipe) of a chick as it was inserted, thus rendering it a *treifa*. Since this inoculation had become mandatory for all chickens, those who scrupulously keep halacha were refraining from eating chicken altogether.

> Harav Ovadia invited Rav Elyashiv,[16] Rav Yisraeli, Rav Abba Shaul (whom he regarded as the preeminent authority on treifot),[17] Rav Zolty, and Rav Goldschmidt to a meeting to discuss the sh'eila. He then asked a top veterinarian in the Health Ministry to perform a live demonstration of the inoculation, so the rabbanim could see exactly which area of the neck the needle entered.
>
> They noticed that the veterinarian first lifted the skin around the neck and then inserted the needle. Since precautions were taken not to insert the needle anywhere near the trachea or esophagus, it seemed that there was no sh'eila after all.
>
> In reality, however, this demonstration only served to minimize the sh'eila, not to eradicate it, because most of the inoculations were not performed by veterinarians, but by the chicken farmers themselves, who were given a quick course in how to inoculate their own fowl. The sh'eila confronting the group of rabbanim was whether the farmers could be relied upon to insert the needles with the same care as a professional, or whether the bulk of chickens were being inoculated in a way that might render them treifot.

---

16. Listed in the order in which they appear in Rav Ovadia's *teshuva*.
17. See p. 319.

The group unanimously agreed with Harav Ovadia's opinion, which was to permit the use of all the chickens. This opinion was based on *teshuvot* from generations past, and also drew on a *teshuva* in *Tzitz Eliezer*, written by Harav Ovadia's close friend, Rav Eliezer Yehuda Waldenburg.

IN SOME INSTANCES, HARAV OVADIA OVERRODE CONCERNS raised by his friends and colleagues. One such case was when Rav Waldenburg issued a ruling that the Rabbanut could not provide *kashrut* certification at a hotel that would serve dairy desserts to guests who had just eaten a meat meal (in violation of the halacha that requires a waiting period between eating meat and dairy), even if the hotel was willing to follow all Rabbanut policies and maintain a *mashgiah* on premises.

Unwitting Consumers Take Precedence Over Flagrant Sinners

Harav Ovadia disputed this ruling, because he considered it vital that the Rabbanut continue issuing certification to these hotels. Those who specifically chose to eat dairy after meat could not be stopped, he felt, but it was important nonetheless that the food be certified kosher, to prevent people from eating forbidden foods unwittingly.

Some irreligious media outlets misinterpreted this ruling as a sign of Harav Ovadia's "moderate" stance to halacha. Had they read his *teshuva* explaining the ruling, they would have understood that it had nothing to do with being "moderate"; it was the result of an awareness of the limits as to what could be achieved when dealing with a mostly secular public in the modern era:

> If it would be possible for us to raise the flag of religion, we would certainly be obligated to protest with all our power, and to force those who sully their own souls in sin — and especially those who cause others to sin — to comply with halacha. In our orphaned generation, however, due to our numerous sins, there is nobody who knows how to admonish properly — and certainly not how to protest

— especially in times when freedom, liberty, and permissiveness reign supreme.

Furthermore, Harav Ovadia felt that the Rabbanut had to look out for the man on the street who *would* choose to eat kosher if it was available to him, but might not have the wherewithal to determine what is kosher and what isn't. He felt that the Rabbanut couldn't prevent a person who *wanted* to violate halacha from doing so, but they did have the capability to ensure that those who wanted to keep halacha could do so easily:

> Hotels in the country are at full occupancy during many months of the year, and numerous God-fearing but unwitting tourists who come to Israel cannot fathom that a hotel in the Holy Land would serve nonkosher food. They walk into these establishments and eat and drink without thinking twice. If there will not be a God-fearing *mashgiah* and *kashrut* certification at each hotel, the hotel owners will bring in *neveilot* and *treifot*,[18] actual mixtures of milk and meat,[19] and all sorts of other [forbidden foods]. It would turn out, then, that we are causing many God-fearing people to unsuspectingly eat *neveilot* or *treifot*.[20]

Entebbe in Halacha

HARAV OVADIA'S INFLUENCE ON THE ENTIRE POPULATION OF Israel went far beyond *kashrut* issues. Shortly into his term as chief rabbi, after inquiries into the leadership breakdown during the Yom Kippur War forced Prime Minister Golda Meir to resign, Yitzhak Rabin began his first term as prime minister, and he and Harav Ovadia forged a relationship that lasted — with occasional ups and downs

---

18. I.e., animal meat that is not kosher for one reason or another.
19. I.e., foods that are not kosher because they contain both milk and meat — as opposed to offering kosher meat and milk products and relying on consumers to wait the required amount of time between eating them.
20. Rav Ovadia cites a similar ruling from Rav Moshe Feinstein (*Igrot Moshe, Yoreh Dei'a* 1:52) as support for his opinion. Rav Moshe points out that there is a benefit in ensuring that those who don't know anything about *kashrut* or are unaware of the gravity of eating nonkosher will still eat kosher as frequently as possible, and he also states that we should be more concerned with such people than with flagrant sinners who choose to violate halacha.

— until the latter's assassination.[21] In those years, long before political leaders would visit Harav Ovadia because they needed the backing of his Shas party to win elections or form a government, Rabin already began to consult with him when he wanted to know how Jewish law would approach certain security issues.

One such instance was during the drama that would ultimately become known as Operation Yonatan.

> *On June 27, 1976, an Air France flight from Israel to Paris, with a stopover in Athens, was hijacked by two Palestinian and two German terrorists who had boarded during the stopover. After forcing the pilot to make a refueling stop in Libya, the hijackers had him fly to Entebbe, Uganda, where they were welcomed by dictator Idi Amin, who offered the terrorists tactical support and backup by his army. Once there, the hijackers separated the non-Jewish and Jewish hostages, freeing the non-Jews over the course of the first two days in Entebbe. They demanded the release of 40 imprisoned PLO terrorists[22] in exchange for the more then 100 Jewish and Israeli hostages, and threatened to start killing the hostages on July 1 if the terrorists were not released. The Israeli government negotiated an extension of this deadline until July 4. In the interim, Prime Minister Rabin turned to Harav Ovadia to find out what Jewish law said about releasing terrorists in exchange for hostages.*

Harav Ovadia convened a group of *gedolei Yisrael*[23] to examine this particularly sensitive *sh'eila*. At stake were two serious questions: Would capitulating to the terrorists cause more hijackings in the future? And would the released PLO prisoners — all of whom had been involved in terror attacks against Israel — try to infiltrate

---

21. Their relationship was such that when someone passed a note to Rav Ovadia in the middle of his *shiur* on Motzaei Shabbat, 12 Heshvan 5756 (November 4, 1995), informing him that Rabin had been shot and critically wounded, he interrupted the *shiur* — which was broadcast to thousands across the country — to immediately recite a *Mi Shebeirach* for Rabin, and then roundly condemned the hatred among Jews that would lead to such an act.
22. Most of these terrorists were held in Israeli prisons, but others were scattered in prisons throughout the world.
23. He does not name the group in the *teshuva*.

A C-130 Hercules, the type of aircraft used by the Israelis to free the hostages in Uganda, parked in front of the old Entebbe terminal. Bullet holes from the Israeli raid still pockmark the terminal building.

Israel yet again to attack Jews? These questions involved serious issues of *sakanot nefashot* (risk to life), but so did the prospect of leaving the hostages at the mercy of the hijackers.

The resolution of the hostage crisis turned out to be very different from what the rabbanim envisioned as they deliberated the *sh'eila*. The outcome of this story from Harav Ovadia's inside view is fascinating:[24]

> While we were still deliberating the various angles of the issue, Prime Minister Yitzhak Rabin visited to bring us the glad tidings that the IDF had succeeded in killing all of the evil hijackers and their helpers in Uganda. They had freed the hostages and were in the midst of transporting them to Eretz Yisrael.

He adds words of praise to Hashem for enabling the success of the mission, and for showing the nations of the world that, with His

---

24. *Yabia Omer*, Vol. 10, *Hoshen Mishpat* 6.

Hand guiding them, the Jewish people could rescue hostages who were on their way to certain death.

Positivity Wins

DESPITE HIS INVOLVEMENT IN MAJOR GLOBAL AND NATIONal events, Harav Ovadia still considered it his personal responsibility to encourage every Jew to keep Torah and mitzvot — and he realized that this could be achieved only by presenting the Torah to the masses in a positive light.

Although he did speak out openly against the Reform and Conservative movements that were trying to gain traction in Israel,[25] his primary efforts were directed at making the Torah beloved to all of Klal Yisrael. For instance, he set up a system ensuring that every *kalla* in the country received some lessons in the laws of family purity before she was married. In a *shiur* delivered many years after his tenure as chief rabbi, he related that when he was the chief rabbi of Tel Aviv, his daughter Adina Bar-Shalom, who also lived in Tel Aviv, would give private classes to irreligious *kallot* before their weddings. Once, a *kalla* turned to her at the end of a class and said, "Before you started teaching me, I resented the fact that you were mixing into my personal life. But after hearing what you taught, I'm seriously considering keeping these *halachot*."

Harav Ovadia considered this story a paradigm for what could be accomplished if the correct systems and people were in place to represent Torah ideals and present them to the secular public in a positive way. He begged all *talmidei hachamim* who were capable of teaching Torah to go out and establish *shiurei Torah*, and his own family members knew that if they wished to follow in his footsteps, they had to be out teaching Torah, not just learning for the sake of their own advancement.

> Rav Mordechai Toledano recalls that when his family moved to Haifa after his appointment to the Rabbanut beit din, his father-in-law Harav Ovadia exhorted him to establish as many shiurei Torah as possible, not to suffice with serving on the beit din and learning for his own sake. When

---
25. *Minhagei Rasha"l*, p. 105.

"The sun shines for everyone."
Harav Ovadia appears in the window of his office to bless a crowd gathered below to receive his blessing on Hol HaMoed.

it became known in Haifa that Rav Toledano was willing to deliver shiurim upon public request, invitations started streaming in from the entire city. Once, he was invited to speak at a particular school, and only after accepting the invitation did he learn that the school was co-ed. He felt uncomfortable delivering a shiur in that type of environment, but he was also loath to renege on his commitment, so he called his father-in-law for advice.

"When he heard my query," Rav Toledano relates, "he answered in one line: 'The sun shines for everyone.'

"He felt that to bring Torah to the masses, you had to be like the sun, which does not differentiate between the various peoples of the world; it shines for everyone. So, too, I would have to get used to the idea of delivering shiurim to all sorts of audiences if I was to have an effect on the masses."

Taking It to the Top

EVEN WHEN PAINED BY BREACHES OF HALACHA, HARAV Ovadia tried as hard as possible not to come into direct conflict with the individuals in question, but rather to lobby at higher levels to repair the breaches. When a law permitting abortions was under consideration in the Knesset in 1976, Harav Ovadia called a gathering at Porat Yosef for rabbanim from all over Israel. Harav Ovadia and Rav Yehuda Tzadka addressed the hundreds of rabbanim in attendance and discussed the halachic ramifications of the law, until the group adopted an official policy on the matter.

When the law passed in the Knesset, Harav Ovadia took his protest all the way to the top. He arranged a meeting with Prime Minister Rabin to discuss the issue, and took along his "rabbinic board": Rav Yisraeli, Rav Zolty, and Rav Goldschmidt. Rabin listened attentively and asked many questions.[26] Their efforts to overturn the law did not succeed, however, so Harav Ovadia refocused his efforts on making the public aware of the severity of the sin. Later in life, he would make himself available to the heads of Efrat, an organization that tries to convince expectant women not to terminate their pregnancies. Though he rarely interrupted his set learning schedule, he told the heads of Efrat that they could call him anytime — day or night — if he could somehow help them prevent an abortion.[27]

No Changes

EVEN MATTERS THAT MIGHT HAVE SEEMED OF MINOR SIGnificance to others didn't escape Harav Ovadia's attention, for he understood well that a small change to tradition could eventually morph into something much more serious.

Immediately after Israel recaptured the Old City from Jordan in 1967, then-IDF Chief Rabbi Goren instituted a new text for the *Nahem* prayer,[28] removing mentions of the desolation of Yerushalayim, which he felt were no longer true.

In the first volume of *Yehaveh Da'at*,[29] Harav Ovadia responded to a questioner who asked the following:

> Isn't it time to change the text of the *tefilla* of *Nahem* that is recited on Tisha B'Av? Specifically, how can we say the

---

26. *HaPardes*, Year 50, Issue 8 (Iyar 5736).
27. Rav Zamir Cohen of Hidabroot, at a *hesped* delivered on his network the day Rav Ovadia passed away, before the funeral.
28. *Nahem* is a supplication added to the *Shemoneh Esrei* on Tisha B'Av, beseeching Hashem to rebuild Yerushalayim and the *Beit HaMikdash*.
29. Based on questions asked on his radio show; see pp. 297-298.

words: הָעִיר הַחֲרֵבָה וְהַבְּזוּיָה וְהָאֲבֵלָה וְהַשּׁוֹמֵמָה, *the city that is mournful, ruined, scorned, and desolate*, which is an inaccurate description of the circumstances today? To our great joy, we see Yerushalayim expanding rapidly, with constant construction of buildings that are immediately occupied upon their completion with thousands upon thousands of Jews. Furthermore, we see tens of thousands streaming to the Kotel HaMaaravi with joyous, festive song on their lips.

Harav Ovadia examines this question from two fronts:

One, is it proper for us to change the text of any *tefilla* nowadays? And two, is the claim that Yerushalayim is no longer desolate an accurate one?

In answer to the first question, he quotes extensively from sources throughout the ages that vehemently opposed changing any *nussah hatefilla*, even if we no longer see how the phraseology applies on a practical level.

However, he continues, in this case we *can* understand the text on its most simple level. The area where the *Beit HaMikdash* stood remains a stomping grounds for anti-Semitic gentiles, and the Old City of Yerushalayim is still filled with symbols of idolatry in its many churches. Furthermore, it would be impossible to consider Yerushalayim rebuilt as long as it is forbidden for Jews to ascend to Har HaBayit.[30]

He bemoans the fact that people view the ability to visit the Kotel as the ultimate privilege, when in reality the Kotel should serve as a sobering reminder of the destruction of the *Beit HaMikdash* and cause a Jew to yearn for it to be rebuilt.

He concludes by pointing out that even if we consider the physical restoration of the city a great achievement, the text of *Nahem* could easily be understood to refer to the spiritual state of the city, which he points out, is at a terrible nadir:

---

30. This, too, was a battle against Chief Rabbi Goren, who, in opposition to the opinion of nearly every Torah authority in Eretz Yisrael, insisted that it was permissible to ascend Har HaBayit and even went up there himself.

"The Kotel should serve as a sobering reminder of the destruction of the Beit HaMikdash, not be seen as the ultimate privilege."
Harav Ovadia deep in prayer at the Kotel HaMaaravi.

How depressing it is to the heart of any God-fearing Jew to see the distance of the Jewish people from the path of Torah and mitzvot; to see hundreds of thousands of Jewish children educated without Torah and mitzvot; to see the devastation of the strictures of modesty and ethical living, the mass desecration of Shabbat, the rampant violation of *kashrut* laws, and many more examples like these.

Unlike those who considered the State of Israel to be the answer to all the historic ills of the Jewish people, Harav Ovadia — even as its chief rabbi — courageously spoke out against the blows the State was inflicting on religion. Twice during his tenure as chief rabbi, he issued an official statement before Tisha B'Av reminding Israel's citizens that the country was still in need of salvation and that the original text of *Nahem* should still be recited.[31]

Spiritual State of the State

HAVING EARNED THE ADMIRATION OF THE PUBLIC, HARAV Ovadia raised a host of issues that others may have felt uncomfortable addressing while officially seated as chief rabbi of Israel. When it came to *hillul Shabbat*, for instance, Harav Ovadia did not suffice with general statements regarding the importance of Shabbat, but

---

31. *Minhagei Rasha"l*, pp. 93, 103. Rav Ovadia also ruled, following the ruling of the Beit Yosef, that *Nahem* should be recited during all three *Shemone Esrei* prayers on Tisha B'Av, not only during the *Minha* prayer, as had become customary even among Sephardic communities.

rather joined other hareidi leaders in fighting to prevent mass *hillul Shabbat*. He allied himself with those who denounced the opening of the Ramot Road, which ran adjacent to Yerushalayim's religious neighborhoods and would be open on Shabbat. He also wrote a letter condemning the plans to build a stadium in what is currently the Ramat Shlomo neighborhood of Yerushalayim. While Jerusalem Mayor Teddy Kollek[32] was dead-set against constructing the stadium elsewhere, the public pressure eventually forced him to back down and agree to have it built in the Malha neighborhood, far from any residential neighborhoods that would have to witness large-scale *hillul Shabbat* when fans drove to the stadium.

Say No to TV

HARAV OVADIA ALSO FOUGHT TO BOLSTER THE MORAL underpinnings of society. When a TV show in Israel made light of the sanctity of marriage, Harav Ovadia wrote a letter to the Minister of Education and Culture, Zevulun Hammer of Mafdal, sharply protesting the program and asking him to intervene and ensure that no such shows be aired in the future.

In a *teshuva* written in those years, in the context of a *sh'eila* that was sent to him regarding the permissibility of reciting *Kriat Shema* in front of a television broadcasting immodest images, Harav Ovadia not only categorically forbids the recitation of *Kriat Shema* under such circumstances, he also addresses the permissibility of watching television in general:

> Know that all that we have been discussing [regarding reciting *Kriat Shema*] refers only to those who are placed into a circumstance in which they are [compelled to] view a television. Bringing a television into one's home, however, is absolutely forbidden. Anyone who is willing to admit the truth [realizes] that besides placing him into the category of scoffers and causing him to waste time that could be used for Torah study, the television will also lead him astray.

---

32. For whom the stadium was eventually named.

Harav Ovadia reciting *Kriat Shema*

This stance might not seem surprising today, but it should be noted that this *teshuva* was written in the 1970s, when most people, even observant ones, considered television relatively innocuous.

HARAV OVADIA DID NOT LIMIT HIS VOICE AS THE CHIEF RABBI to matters of religious concern. He spoke out frequently about safety issues, such as the dangerous driving habits of Israelis. Several times during his ten years as chief rabbi, he issued official proclamations urging drivers to exercise greater caution on the road, and urged all the rabbanim in the country to devote Shabbat lectures to the topic.

Slow Down!

He would remain concerned about this topic long after his term as chief rabbi was over, bringing it up every so often at his Motzaei Shabbat *shiur*, where he also discussed the halachic ramifications of causing a car accident because of unsafe driving.

THROUGHOUT HIS LIFE, HARAV OVADIA REMAINED FOCUSED on the individual, even as his scope of influence continued to broaden. After his successful efforts to free the Yom Kippur War *agunot*, he managed to open a smooth line of communication with Defense Minister Moshe Dayan — and he used that connection to help many religious girls avoid army service.

Under Fire

In order to be exempted from mandatory army or national service, young women had to declare that their religious beliefs prevented them from serving. While girls who attended Beit Yaakov high schools were granted exemptions without having to prove their religious convictions, girls who had become more religious while attending public or national-religious schools were not granted exemptions so easily. Many girls approached Harav Ovadia with the concern that army or national service would have a detrimental spiritual effect on them. Because Dayan trusted Harav Ovadia implicitly, all it took was one phone call from Harav Ovadia's office to the Defense Ministry, and the girl would automatically receive her exemption.[33]

When the secular media uncovered this story, all the players came under fire for what the media considered a scandal, but Harav Ovadia courageously stood his ground against the onslaught.

Term Extension and Term Limits

NEW ELECTIONS FOR CHIEF RABBIS WERE ORIGINALLY SCHEDuled for 1978, five years after Harav Ovadia was first elected to office. At that point, a large majority of the *guf habocher* was against the reelection of Chief Rabbi Goren, but Harav Ovadia was considered a national asset and his reelection was guaranteed. Harav Ovadia urged Rav Shaul Yisraeli, who was highly respected by rabbanim from across the political spectrum, to run against Chief Rabbi Goren. Rav Yisraeli announced his candidacy, but the Mafdal, the only party still squarely in Chief Rabbi Goren's camp, came out against Rav Yisraeli. Realizing that they didn't have enough votes on the *guf habocher* to elect their candidate, the Mafdal took the legislative route, introducing a bill in the Knesset that extended the term of the chief rabbis to ten years — thereby delaying the elections until 1983 — but also imposed a limit of one 10-year term.

While Agudat Yisrael tried to fight the bill, Mafdal — which was then considered the key partner in building any coalition because it was the third-largest party in the Knesset — was able to convince both the left- and right-wing parties to vote for the bill.

---

33. *Posek HaDor*, p. 217.

Before the extended terms of Chief Rabbis Yosef and Goren actually ended, there was a grassroots effort to overturn the law and allow the chief rabbis to run again. Agudat Yisrael introduced a bill in the Knesset overturning the one-term limit, but Justice Minister Moshe Nissim, a son of former Rishon LeZion Rav Yitzhak Nissim, convinced his Likud party to join the Mafdal and vote against the bill. The bill was defeated by a small majority (47-40), and Harav Ovadia was unable to run for an additional term.

While most of the country had come to admire and love him by this point, Harav Ovadia still had a few detractors, mostly in the upper echelons of the government, who were thrilled to see him relinquish his role as chief rabbi.

Little did they realize that by forcing him out of his position as chief rabbi, they were actually freeing him to lead the most ambitious project of his life — one that would restore the pride of Sephardi Jews throughout Israel and bring thousands upon thousands to enhanced Torah study and observance.

Chapter Twenty-Two
Shas: Actualizing a Dream

NOT LONG AFTER BECOMING THE OFFI-cial leader of the Shas party, R' Eli Yishai was discussing the latest developments with Harav Ovadia. "I appointed So-and-so to lead this initiative, and So-and-so to run our bureau in such-and-such city..."

Harav Ovadia folded his arms on the table in front of him and with a warm but firm look, said, "This is not why I'm involved in Shas; it makes no difference to me who is appointed to which positions. I want to hear about how many shiurei Torah you started, how many more classrooms in Torah schools we have funded, and how many mikvaot we've built."[1]

There's a common misconception that was a natural consequence of Harav Ovadia's name becoming inextricably bound to the Shas party he led for the last three decades of his life: almost everyone — from media pundits to politicians, from foreign leaders to local

---

1. Rabbanit Yehudit Yosef.

journalists — began to think of him as a political leader. When discussing his involvement in the party that would bring him to the front pages of Israel's daily papers hundreds of times over the last 30 years of his life, it is vital to bear in mind what his son Rav Avraham told a secular interviewer who referred to Harav Ovadia as a political leader. "My father, a politician?" Rav Avraham Yosef asked, clearly shocked by the question. "My father spends a maximum of 10 minutes of the day directing the party."

Indeed, for all that Shas would reshape Israeli politics and bring both local and foreign government leaders to Harav Ovadia's study, he himself had only one purpose in building Shas: to increase the number of Torah-observant Jews in Israel and create frameworks in which Jews could easily keep Torah and mitzvot throughout the country.

Channeling the Vigor

HARAV OVADIA CONCLUDED HIS TERM AS CHIEF RABBI AT the age of 63, full of vigor and energy. While he was content spending most of his time writing *sefarim*, serving on the Beit Din HaGadol, and learning and teaching Torah, he also felt a burning need to find new ways to bring Jews closer to Torah, as he had done when he was chief rabbi. The means to that end would not be long in coming.

In 1982, a small new political party was formed in Yerushalayim, to run in municipal elections. The founders of the party, Nissim Ze'ev and Shlomo Dayan, felt that hareidi Sephardic Jews in the city who were voting for hareidi parties were not receiving their fair share of representation in the municipality. They planned to target not only hareidi voters, but also Sephardim from across the religious spectrum — a population that had been discriminated against in many ways since the State's founding 34 years earlier.

Harav Ovadia was originally hesitant to become involved with this new party, because he did not want to highlight divisions between Sephardim and Ashkenazim.

That changed in 1983, however. A young man by the name of R' Aryeh Deri[2] developed a connection with Rav Eliezer Menachem

---

2. Aryeh Deri first became known to Harav Ovadia when the former learned in Hevron with

Rav Eliezer Menachem Mann Shach convinced Harav Ovadia to lead Shas.

Mann Shach, the rosh yeshiva of Ponevezh and the leader of the Lithuanian Torah community. R' Aryeh and Rav David Yosef, with whom he had learned in Hevron Yeshiva, approached both Harav Ovadia and Rav Shach and laid out a plan to breathe new spiritual life into Israeli society and the Sephardic community in particular. They felt that if they could garner enough support for a political party, they would be able to use the party to advance Torah study and observance throughout Israel. Rav Shach immediately agreed that this was a great idea, and he appealed personally to Harav Ovadia to lead the movement.

"When we approached Abba and asked him to lead the party, he was very hesitant," recalls Rav David. "But then we laid out our plans for a complete overhaul of Israel's Torah infrastructure. We planned to open a network of Torah schools, establish *shiurim* for *baalebatim* throughout the country, and ensure that the basic religious needs of every Jewish citizen would be met.

"In order to succeed in building this Torah empire, we needed funding, and funding in Israel is dependent on political clout.

Rav David Yosef during the late 1970s. When Harav Ovadia was looking for a private rebbi to advance Moshe, his youngest son, in learning, Rav David urged him to hire Aryeh, who was extremely dynamic and a brilliant learner. Harav Ovadia was immediately impressed with Aryeh, who had a wide array of inborn talents and leadership skills, and the young man quickly became one of Harav Ovadia's closest disciples and advisers. The two were so close, in fact, that when Aryeh Deri married in 5741/1981, Harav Ovadia risked becoming stranded in a snowstorm in order to attend his wedding in Bat Yam.

"When we explained to Abba that our only interest in getting involved in a political party was to build Torah, he acceded to Rav Shach's request to lead Shas."

Even when Harav Ovadia agreed to lead the party, he did not want to take sole responsibility for it. He set up a body of leading rabbanim known as *Mo'etzet Hachmei HaTorah*, the original members of which were Rav Shalom Cohen, Rav Shimon Ba'adani, and Rav Shabtai Atoun, with whom he would sit to determine policy for the movement.

IN ADVANCE OF THE 1984 KNESSET ELECTIONS, SHAS TOOK ITS platform to the national level, putting forth a list of candidates to serve in the Knesset. It was entirely unclear whether the party would succeed in garnering the minimum number of votes necessary for Knesset representation. Harav Ovadia agreed to travel around the country on behalf of the party, under the banner: "לְהַחֲזִיר עֲטָרָה לְיוֹשְׁנָהּ, restoring the crown to its original glory." He had originally used this slogan to describe the need to restore Sephardi *psak halacha* to

A Shocking Victory

"Restoring the Crown" takes on its third meaning: Harav Ovadia at a Shas rally.

the rulings of the Beit Yosef[3]; later, it had been used to describe the return of Sephardic Jewry to Torah study and mitzva observance.[4] As a campaign slogan, the phrase encompassed the two original uses as well as a third: to free Sephardic Jewry in Eretz Yisrael from the discrimination that had been rampant in the newly formed State of Israel and to restore their pride in their heritage.

In order to gain any seats in the Knesset, the party had to pass the *ahuz hasima* — a threshold number of votes without which the party does not earn recognition as an official party and remains a nonentity. Running on a very low budget and without any real experience, a ragtag team of volunteers managed to canvass the country and ignite a fire among Sephardic Jews. Voters were concerned, however, that their votes would go to waste because the party would not pass the *ahuz hasima*, and the campaign directors assumed that these people would continue to vote for the parties they had supported until then.

On the morning of the elections, a surprising announcement was made in Bnei Brak. The Steipler Gaon, Rav Yisrael Yaakov Kanievsky, declared that every *ben Torah* should vote for Shas.

By that evening, this last development delivered a stunning result: Shas had garnered four seats, while Agudat Israel, which had sent four MKs to the Knesset for several terms running, won only two seats.

Thus began what would become one of Harav Ovadia's main projects over the last three decades of his life: to leverage his party's political clout to build Torah, Torah, and more Torah.

The True Purpose

ONE ASTOUNDING ASPECT OF HARAV OVADIA'S LIFE WAS that nearly every major effort he undertook could fill a biographical volume of its own. In fact, during his lifetime, separate books were written about his early years; his years as a key figure in the Rabbanut; his extensive writings; and his leadership of Shas.

---

3. See p. 219.
4. See p. 234.

Without a shadow of a doubt, the latter volume is the one in which Harav Ovadia himself would have taken the least pride. His moves as the head of Shas may have given political pundits fodder for their newspaper columns and eventually material for full tomes, but many of these commentators missed the entire point: Harav Ovadia was involved in Shas only because it would help Torah Jewry in Eretz Yisrael, and specifically Sephardic Torah Jewry. Where they saw political genius, he saw only one consideration: Would this cause more Torah to be studied and more mitzvot to be observed?

Since this was Harav Ovadia's vision for the party he led, our discussion of Shas will focus on its role in making Torah more accessible to all of Israeli society.[5]

The Numbers

THE WAY THE PARLIAMENTARY SYSTEM IN ISRAEL IS STRUCtured, even a small party can be the linchpin that determines whether a government remains in power.[6] The government will typically be willing, therefore, to provide funding for the needs of any party willing to sign onto a coalition agreement.

This system may seem ethically questionable if a party's special interest funding is spent on frivolous projects that benefit only a narrow slice of the country's population. In Shas's case, however, the party's "special interests" were to benefit the entire citizenry by championing Jewish causes. All Jews in Israel stand to gain from increased Torah study and mitzva observance — whether they recognize that or not — and Harav Ovadia therefore considered it his responsibility to ensure that the monies that were so freely distributed to coalition partners be used to build Torah infrastructure in Israel.[7]

---

5. Most of the facts and figures regarding Shas's achievements were culled from an interview with Rav David Yosef, who was closely involved in building the party and its various branches.
6. A government must have a coalition comprising a majority of the 120 Knesset members. Even a party with only four seats can wield tremendous power if the government coalition would number 57 without it. See p. 347.
7. In later years, Shas also championed the cause of social welfare, advocating on behalf of the ever-increasing number of Israeli families that were suffering from poverty.

ONE OF SHAS'S FIRST ACHIEVEMENTS WAS THE ESTABLISHment of Maayan HaHinuch HaTorani,⁸ a network of elementary schools throughout the country.

Maayan HaHinuch HaTorani

Harav Ovadia's two lifelong friends from Porat Yosef — its rosh yeshiva Hacham Benzion Abba Shaul and its *menahel ruhani* Rav Yehuda Tzadka — joined him in leading the school system, whose objective harked back to Harav Ovadia's efforts during his younger years: to ensure that every Sephardi child had access to a Torah education.⁹ That meant making the Maayan HaHinuch HaTorani schools at least as attractive — and financially viable — to parents as the *mamlachtidati* (religious-public) schools. The religious component of these schools, which Harav Ovadia had already considered faulty in the 1950s, had only deteriorated over the course of the passing decades, and the three leaders of Maayan HaHinuch HaTorani considered it vital that they offer easily affordable tuition so that no parents

The inaugural meeting to launch Maayan HaHinuch HaTorani. Harav Ovadia is addressing Rav Yitzchak Peretz, the first Knesset leader of Shas (R), with Rav Yehuda Tzadka (between them) and Hacham Benzion Abba Shaul (L) participating.

---
8. Literally, "the Wellspring of Torah Education."
9. See pp. 255-260.

would be tempted to send their children to the *mamlachti-dati* schools that were funded completely by the government.

Since Maayan HaHinuch HaTorani operated under the *mukar she'eino rishmi* (recognized but unofficial) rubric,[10] there was a significant gap between the amount of funding the government would provide for each child and the amount that parents could be expected to pay. Each of the three founders of the network agreed to fundraise to help cover this gap.

Unfortunately, both Hacham Benzion and Rav Yehuda Tzadka were unable to make trips abroad due to illnesses and other reasons, and the lion's share of the fundraising responsibility fell upon Harav Ovadia. Despite the taxing burden this added to his already overwhelming schedule, he never regretted his decision to establish the system. He was glad to go abroad as many times as necessary to ensure that every Jewish child in Israel could be offered a Torah education.

Harav Ovadia wasn't satisfied with overseeing the network from afar. He was actively involved in the educational decisions, and, as he had done throughout his life, he would travel across the country to encourage parents to enroll their children in Torah schools.[11]

Harav Ovadia would often relate a story — which may have been allegorical or may actually have happened — to illustrate why it was vital that parents enroll their children in Torah schools:

> *A farmer once approached me and said, "Rabbi, it's not fair. My neighbor's field grows the most beautiful flowers, which he exports for a huge profit, and my field only turns out onions. Why can't I grow something more profitable?"*
> *"What did you plant?" I asked him.*
> *"Onions," he answered.*
> *"Well," I replied, "if you plant onions, you're going to*

---

10. See p. 252, fn. 10,
11. Although he oversaw Maayan HaHinuch HaTorani, Harav Ovadia didn't advocate that parents send their children only to "his" school system; he wanted to see as many Jewish children as possible receiving a Torah education, regardless of whether they were enrolled in Maayan HaHinuch HaTorani or in other Torah school systems, such as Chinuch Atzmai.

"If you plant flowers, you'll grow flowers." A child kisses Harav Ovadia's hand as he arrives at an event.

get onions. If you want to grow flowers, you have to plant flowers."

Harav Ovadia would then describe the sad results of a non-Torah education. "If you want your children to grow up to be flowers," he would conclude, "then you have to plant flowers."

Harav Ovadia's ability to speak to the hearts of even the simplest Jews bore fruit. During the three decades that elapsed between the establishment of Maayan HaHinuch HaTorani and Harav Ovadia's passing, the network would grow to include 650 schools. In 2010, some 40,000 boys and girls were enrolled in the system. The network also included 300 *ganim* (preschools), in which an additional 13,000 children were enrolled.

Fittingly, both Harav Ovadia and Rabbanit Margalit were immortalized in these school systems. After Rabbanit Margalit's passing in 5754/1994, the girls' division was named Beit Margalit, and after Harav Ovadia's passing, the boys' division became known as Bnei Yosef.

El HaMaayan

ONCE THE MAAYAN HAHINUCH HATORANI NETWORK OF elementary schools and preschools was up and running, Shas leaders turned their attention to an additional frontier: adult and adolescent Torah education.

For many years, Harav Ovadia had been horrified by the increasing trend among Israeli teenagers toward dangerous — and even criminal — activities, such as drug and alcohol abuse. He realized that many of these adolescents were from underprivileged homes and did not succeed in the regular school environment. Sometimes the reason for their embrace of criminal activity was a relatively easy problem to solve: sheer boredom. In other cases, the cause was a deep-seated antipathy for society, which they felt had dealt them an unfair hand. In any event, these children needed somewhere to go in the afternoon after school, for entertainment, for attention, and for their own safety.

Shas established a separate unit called El HaMaayan, which opened *mo'adonim* (clubs) throughout the country. Their objective was twofold: to provide opportunities for both Torah study and positive social activities for Israeli youths who were not enrolled in Torah schools.

Many Israeli schools offer a variety of extracurricular enrichment classes, but parents must pay privately for those extra hours of instruction. Children from poverty-stricken families that could barely pay their monthly bills were unable to attend those classes, until El HaMaayan stepped in and established free enrichment classes, thereby keeping children and adolescents off the streets. They also organized *kaytanot*, day camps, to keep children occupied during the summer.

But from Harav Ovadia's perspective, the ultimate goal of the *mo'adonim* was to offer public-school children Torah classes in which they could taste the sweetness of their heritage — often with life-altering results.

> *Many stories are told of children who first joined the mo'adonim for the fun-filled extracurricular activities, but also took part in the Torah classes. Once they learned a little bit about Judaism, however, they thirsted for more, and begged their parents to enroll them in a Maayan HaHinuch HaTorani school. Before long, these children came home and asked their parents to allow them to keep Shabbat. In due time, entire families joined in, eventually becoming religious.*

Adult Education

EL HAMAAYAN ALSO INCLUDED AN ADULT EDUCATION DIVIsion, aimed at *baalebatim* who were either religious or seeking to learn more about religion. In a matter of years, El HaMaayan built a database of over *two thousand* Torah classes throughout Israel, with a minimum of ten attendees in each group. These classes were taught by a corps of Sephardic *talmidei hachamim* who were paid a modest stipend. Many of these young men developed their teaching skills by giving these small *shiurim* and later went on to use those skills in more public settings.

Rav David Yosef wrote a standard curriculum for these *shiurim* in the form of booklets on halacha and *parashat hashavua*, which were distributed free of charge to the groups.

The cost of all of these initiatives was steep, but thanks to Shas's political success — they gained seats steadily in elections through 1999, when their list included 17 Knesset members — they were able to secure government funding for their educational programs.

In 1993, for example, the government agreed to pay for the construction of 440 classrooms in Maayan HaHinuch HaTorani schools. Each classroom cost $110,000, for a total cost of $50 million just for classrooms.

Kiruv Infrastructure

DURING THE EARLY 1980S, THE *KIRUV* MOVEMENT IN ISRAEL was at its height. Seminars organized by the various *kiruv* organizations would typically bring dozens back to religion, and an overwhelming majority — some place the number at 90 percent — of these returnees were Sephardi.[12] What happened to these fresh *baalei teshuva* when a seminar ended? Shas stepped into the picture, providing long-term adult education to teach them halacha and other areas of Torah they needed to master in order to live as religious Jews.

Many of those returning to the fold lived in small towns or cities that did not have a significant religious infrastructure. Shas lobbied the government to build hundreds of *batei knesset* and no less than one thousand *mikvaot*, to ensure that these newly religious families would be able to maintain their Torah observance.

Atzarot Teshuva

IN ELUL 5748/1988, HARAV OVADIA UNDERTOOK A NEW CAMpaign: to visit as many cities and towns as possible during Elul and host an *atzeret teshuva* (repentance gathering) in each one. To allow him to reach multiple cities each night, organizers would rent a helicopter to shuttle him from one venue to another. In each city, the *atzeret teshuva* would generally be held in the local soccer stadium, with the cost of renting the facility covered either by El HaMaayan or by the local municipality. The mayor of the city would often sit next to Harav Ovadia at the *atzeret*, which would typically draw thousands of people. This enabled Harav Ovadia to address hundreds of thousands of Jews — live and in person — each year.

On days when these events were scheduled, Harav Ovadia would leave Yerushalayim at 6 p.m. by helicopter and head to the first city on his itinerary. Rav David Yosef would leave Yerushalayim earlier

---

12. Historically, Sephardic Jews who strayed from Torah observance often did so due to financial pressure or government coercion in the early days of the State of Israel (see p. 228). Even those who succumbed to this pressure generally did not harbor anti-Torah feelings. Ashkenazic Jews, on the other hand, typically dropped religion for "ideological" reasons, having bought into one ism or another during the period of the Enlightenment or in the eras that followed. Nonobservant Sephardic Jews were therefore much more traditional, closer to religion and more easily drawn back to Torah, than their Ashkenazi counterparts.

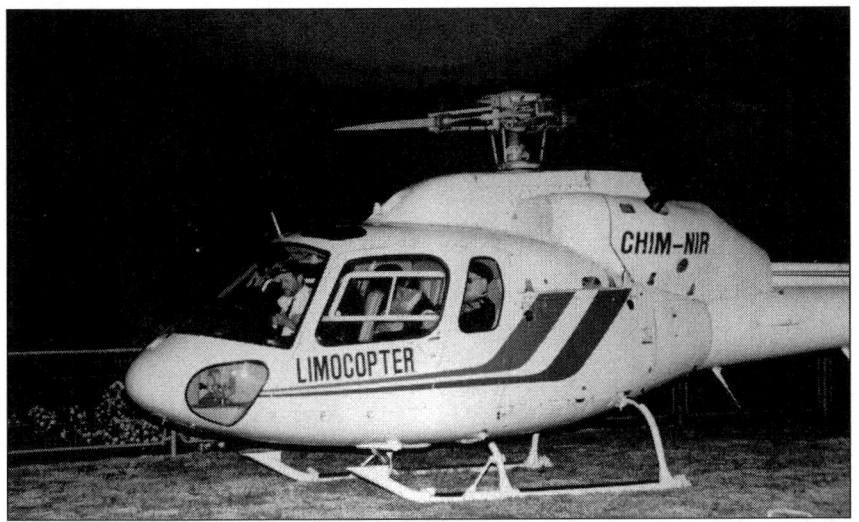

Harav Ovadia is in the helicopter, about to lift off to an *atzeret teshuva*.

in the day, by car, and would begin addressing the audience at the first event prior to his father's arrival. When Harav Ovadia arrived, Rav David would be driven to the next venue while his father kept the audience enthralled for about an hour.

Harav Ovadia's speeches at these events were full of warmth; he would speak of the love HaKadosh Baruch Hu has for each Jew, and how He waits for His children to repent. In his classic style that was so beloved by the masses, he would pepper the speeches with stories and wit.

> At the beginning of a gathering in Tzfat, he apologized to the audience for arriving late. "The Gemara states that one who eats ketzach[13] [קצח] will not suffer from heartache," he said. "Tonight, we have accomplished this, for I have already visited Kiryat Shemoneh and Hatzor. Ketzach can be an acronym for קרית שמונה, צפת, חצור!"

After concluding his speech, he would lead the audience in *Kabbalat Ol Malchut Shamayim*, and then recite a *Mi Shebeirach*, blessing all the attendees to merit a healthy and prosperous new year. In later years, he would bring the elderly *mekubal* Rav Yitzhak

---

13. A type of seed, possible nigella.

Harav Ovadia greets Rav Yitzhak Kadouri, who would join him on *atzarot teshuva* even when he was well over 100.

Kadouri, who was already over 100 at the time, along on these trips, and Rav Kadouri would bless the audience as well.

THE SELFLESSNESS AND DEDICATION HARAV OVADIA exhibited on these trips was astounding.

Devotion to the Masses *R' Tzvi Hakak, Harav Ovadia's personal assistant in the last decades of his life, related that one night in Elul, Harav Ovadia was scheduled to speak in Naharia and Acco on the same night. When the helicopter landed in Naharia, there were people waiting at the landing pad to receive berachot from the Rav. Harav Ovadia greeted each one warmly and blessed him, but then, as the assistants were about to usher the Rav into the car to take him to the soccer stadium for the actual event, he suddenly asked them to call an ambulance, because he was not feeling well.*

"This was shocking to us," related R' Hakak, "because the Rav never even agreed to see his doctor unless it was absolutely necessary."

After a quick exam, the medics on the ambulance

Addressing the crowd at an *El HaMaayan Atzeret Teshuva*

determined that Harav Ovadia had suffered a heart attack. They rushed him to the hospital in Naharia, where he underwent an angioplasty to clear his arteries, as well as the insertion of a coronary stent.

When Harav Ovadia began to recover, R' Hakak asked him when he had first begun to feel ill.

"It was five or ten minutes after the helicopter left Yerushalayim," he replied.

"Why didn't Maran tell me right away?" R' Hakak asked. "We could have diverted the flight and touched down at the nearest hospital!"

"I knew that there were hundreds of people waiting for me in the stadium in Naharia," he said. "How could I disappoint them?"

"But when Maran realized when we landed that he could not make it to the event, why didn't he tell us then to call an ambulance, instead of blessing all of those petitioners?"

"Those people, too, waited for me for a long time. I couldn't just send them away without blessing them."

Back to Learning

ALL THIS TRAVEL WAS EXTREMELY TAXING ON HARAV OVADIA. As Rav David Yosef puts it, "A helicopter ride is perhaps the most dubious pleasure known to man."

Yet despite the noise of the rotors overhead and the unsteady movement of the helicopter, Harav Ovadia's head would be firmly planted in his *sefer* from the beginning of the ride to the end. And when they finally returned home each night at 2 a.m., Harav Ovadia would throw off his *glimah* and run to his study, "as an alcoholic would run to wine," in Rav David's words.

> "Once," Rav David Yosef recalled, "when Abba returned home from one of these exhausting trips, Ima urged him to take a break and eat and drink something before returning to his study.
>
> "Abba excused himself, saying, 'During the flight, I thought of a hiddush, and I'm afraid that I'll forget it. I have to write it down immediately.'"

After Israeli security forces uncovered, in 2005, an Arab plot to assassinate the Rav, the government hired bodyguards to stay with him at all times. An irreligious bodyguard in his 20s once commented that by the time he returned from these trips, he could barely keep his eyes open. Yet the octogenarian Harav Ovadia would run straight back to learn as though he had just enjoyed a night's sleep.

Over the years, Shas was able to launch many more government-funded initiatives, thanks to its status as a key coalition partner. And while many government ministers — and often the prime ministers themselves — would seek Harav Ovadia's opinion on a wide array of matters, as far as Harav Ovadia was concerned, only one thing could justify Shas's existence and the time he devoted to it: the steady growth of the Torah community in Eretz Yisrael.

SECTION FIVE

BELOVED BY HIS PEOPLE

וְיִשְׂרָאֵל אָהַב אֶת יוֹסֵף

Yisrael loved Yosef

(Bereishit 37:3)

Chapter Twenty-Three
Channeling the Gifts

AT A *HESPED* SHORTLY AFTER HARAV OVADIA'S passing, his son, Rishon LeZion Rav Yitzchak Yosef, offered a window into what set his father apart:

> Abba addressed a famous question: The Midrash states that when Rivka Imeinu passed by a house of *avoda zara*, Eisav wanted to run out, and when she passed a *beit midrash*, Yaakov Avinu wanted to run out to start learning. But the Gemara (*Nidda* 30b) states that in the womb, the unborn child studies the entire Torah with an angel. If Yaakov wanted to learn Torah, why wouldn't he remain in the womb and continue to study Torah with the angel?
>
> Abba offered two answers to this question:
>
> One: The *Beraita* (*Avot* 6:4) uses a phrase, וּבַתּוֹרָה אַתָּה עָמֵל — *you should **toil** in Torah*. The point of Torah study is not to acquire knowledge effortlessly, but to toil in it. It's true that Yaakov was able to study vast amounts by learning with an angel, but that wasn't his own *ameilut*, his own toil. He wanted to leave the womb in order to toil in Torah on his own.
>
> Two: An essential part of studying Torah is to follow through in action and keep the mitzvot of the

Harav Ovadia with his son, subsequent Rishon LeZion Harav Yitzchak Yosef, at a *simha*

Torah. A person can study the laws of *lulav* and *etrog* extensively, but if Succot comes and he doesn't actually shake a *lulav* and *etrog*, even the studying he did is considered deficient. Yaakov wanted to leave his mother's womb so he could follow through in action after studying with the angel.

I feel that both of these points were Abba's "mottos" in life.

Upon hearing about Harav Ovadia's incredible memory and the lightning-quick mind he was born with, people tend to attribute all of his success in learning to those gifts. But many people are born extremely gifted and don't grow in Torah and become *gedolim*. Harav Ovadia, however, was determined from the youngest age to use his gifts for Torah. Moreover, he didn't rely only on his gifts; he toiled in Torah far more than many others who were less gifted.

> *In a personal diary he kept as a teenager, he wrote the words, "I know that I am destined for greatness."*
>
> *Far from being an expression of haughtiness, these words were intended to remind him of the responsibility that came along with his Divine gifts. He realized that he could use those gifts for Torah, or use them to amass fame or fortune in a different venue.*
>
> *He chose Torah. Only Torah.*

Later in life, in an address to thousands who assembled at special events organized by Shas on Hol HaMoed, he recalled that when he was a teenager and he started to write sefarim, other teens in Porat Yosef would laugh at him. "Yet by now I have released forty sefarim," he said.

Again, this was not a self-congratulatory statement. He wanted to imbue a young generation of budding talmidei hachamim with the idealism to succeed in Torah and the confidence to set goals and achieve them.

He would often recount that Napoleon would gather young troops and say, "Is there anyone in this group who does not dream of being a general one day? If there's even one of you who doesn't harbor such aspirations, please leave. If you want to accomplish anything, you must dream of reaching the top."

"If you don't dream of being a general in Torah," Harav

"Everyone has to strive to be a general."
Harav Ovadia addressing a Shas-sponsored Torah gathering for yeshiva students in Ashdod

Chapter Twenty-Three: Channeling the Gifts □ 435

Ovadia would conclude, "then you'll never be able to achieve any success."

No Distractions

WHEN HEARING OF HARAV OVADIA'S *AMEILUT*, ONE MIGHT imagine that he enjoyed a blissful life devoid of any pain or difficulty, and was therefore able to apply himself to Torah study.

That was far from the truth. As we have described earlier, he grew up during a time of war and privation. He was persecuted as a rav in Egypt and had to flee for his life. For years, he and his family lived in abject poverty. He lost a daughter in infancy, and he sat *shiva* for his son Rav Yaakov in his old age. Throughout his life, he was under attack from rivals bent on preventing him from disseminating Torah and encouraging others to observe halacha. In the last few decades of his life, he suffered from diabetes, and had to take insulin shots before every meal. He also suffered several

No matter what the circumstances, Harav Ovadia wouldn't be distracted from learning.

heart attacks and endured other painful maladies. Yet none of this deterred him from learning.

"I would watch in wonder," recounts Rav Yitzchak Yosef, "how he sustained all these illnesses and battles, and through it all, he somehow continued to learn, never becoming sidetracked by what was going on in his life."

> *Toward the end of his life, Harav Ovadia would spend upward of 18 hours a day studying Torah, feeling a particularly pressing need to keep learning and writing sefarim.*
>
> *His assistants and family members relate that although he gave generously of his time to the public, if they would allow people in outside his official reception hours, he would say, "Do you want me to remain a complete am ha'aretz (ignoramus)?"*
>
> *When his son-in-law Rav Aron Butbul's son was born, the brit was called for 10 a.m. At exactly 10 o'clock, Harav Ovadia turned to Rav Aron and said, "Nu, let's start."*
>
> *"Harav," his son-in-law protested, "the guests haven't arrived yet. Let's wait a few minutes."*
>
> *"I need to learn," Harav Ovadia replied, "Do you want me to remain a complete am ha'aretz?"*[1]
>
> *From his tone of voice, his family members could tell that this wasn't a jocular statement. Even after becoming one of the greatest halachic arbiters of the past few centuries, he was still concerned about remaining an am ha'aretz, for he measured his level of learning against the whole of the Torah, not against what others had accomplished.*

No Cutting Corners

ONE ASPECT OF MARAN'S *AMEILUT* IN TORAH, RELATES HIS son Rav Yitzchak, was his insistence on studying every *sefer* or essay that he could possibly lay his hands on before ruling or writing a *teshuva* on the topic. His interest in studying every work — no matter how deep or intricate — began when he was a mere child. He related that the first *sefer* he bought as a child was *Sh'eilot V'Teshuvot Torat*

---
1. Rav Moshe Hizkiya, Rav of Kiryat Herzog.

Hessed, in which the author, Rav Shneur Zalman of Lublin, writes long, difficult *pilpulim* before arriving at his halachic conclusions.[2]

Before signing off on a *teshuva*, Harav Ovadia would retrieve every volume that discussed that topic. Rather than rely on his impeccable memory, he actually opened each *sefer* to the relevant pages and reviewed what the author wrote. He could have sufficed with researching the primary sources on the topic — the *Rishonim*, the *Shulhan Aruch*, and the works of the greatest halachic authorities — but he went as far as to draw upon halachic essays written by young *avreichim* or those printed in recent periodicals.

"In his younger years, he never asked us to get him a *sefer*," says Rav Yitzchak. "He would jump up quickly and reach for whichever *sefer* he needed."

At times, his *teshuvot* read like a long list of sources, which prompted some cynics to conclude that he ruled simply by counting how many authorities rule that something is prohibited versus how many permit it, and then siding with the majority opinion.

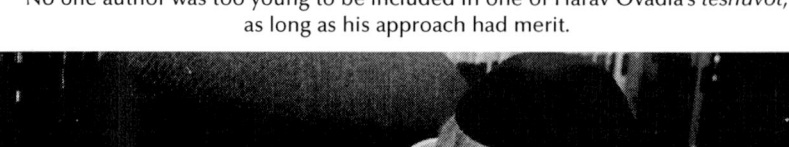
No one author was too young to be included in one of Harav Ovadia's *teshuvot*, as long as his approach had merit.

---
2. Grandson R' Yitzhak Toledano.

Nothing could be further from the truth, however. In his *teshuvot*, he would first explain the ruling he had reached, based on a full understanding of the Talmud and *Rishonim*.

Why did he subsequently cite a lengthy list of *poskim*?

R' Benzion Reich, a neighbor who developed a warm relationship with Harav Ovadia, notes that while some people are quick to dismiss the opinions of modern-day Torah scholars, Harav Ovadia took *every* scholar seriously, and considered the merit of their words even if they weren't known as great Torah leaders. His respect for even very young scholars, suggests R' Benzion, prompted him to quote their opinions and either show that they had reached the truth or explain why they were mistaken.

Harav Ovadia himself once told a confidant that by quoting young authors, he encouraged them to keep writing and publishing Torah works.

Others suggest that he cited every single work available to him because he was concerned that later, people might say, "Had Harav Ovadia seen So-and-so's reasoning, he would have ruled differently." By citing each opinion available to him, and either refuting or bolstering that view, he ensured that his *piskei halacha* would continue to stand for generations to come.

The Ultimate Matmid

HARAV OVADIA'S GENIUS MAY ACTUALLY HAVE BEEN eclipsed by his endless *hatmada* (diligence). This pattern began in his youngest years, when he and Hacham Benzion Abba Shaul would take advantage of times that most people would never have used for learning, such as when they were walking to and from school or preparing *l'chvod Shabbat*.[3]

> Many people wondered why Harav Ovadia's eyesight was so poor, to the extent that he had to protect his eyes with sunglasses for most of his adult life. The mekubal Rav David Batzri recounted that his father, Rav Yosef Batzri, told him that he thought he knew the reason: He remem-

---
3. See p. 310.

As a youngster Harav Ovadia learned by moonlight; later he would have to protect his vision with sunglasses, even indoors.

bered that when Harav Ovadia was a teenager, his parents were so poor that they couldn't afford candles by which to learn at night. Harav Ovadia would sit outside his home and learn by moonlight, and perhaps this affected his vision adversely when he grew older.

A prominent Ashkenazi Rosh Yeshiva once heard someone denigrate Harav Ovadia. He immediately quieted this man, saying, "You don't realize whom you are talking about."

He then related that during the 1960s, he lived near Harav Ovadia's home in Tel Aviv, when the latter served as the city's chief rabbi. One night, there was a blackout in the homes on the Rav's block, but the streetlights were working. "At 11 p.m., I saw Harav Ovadia standing outside, under a lamppost, and learning. The next morning, when I was *leaving for the vatikin minyan, I passed the Rav's home and saw him in the exact same pose, learning by the light of that streetlamp. Don't denigrate someone who is capable of such hatmada."*

Pining for Each Word

AS HE GREW OLDER AND HIS TORAH KNOWLEDGE GREW TO unfathomable proportions, he only seemed to make more time for learning.

Rav Yitzchak Yosef recalls that his father would retell the following *dvar Torah* frequently:

The verse in Tehillim (119:162) states: שָׂשׂ אָנֹכִי עַל אִמְרָתֶךָ כְּמוֹצֵא שָׁלָל רָב, *I rejoice over Your word, like one who finds abundant spoils. The Vilna Gaon differentiates between the terms simha and sasson, explaining that simha refers to unmitigated joy, while sasson refers to joy that is incomplete for some reason. Why, then, do we refer to someone who takes delight in the Torah as being* שָׂשׂ*, rather than* שָׂמֵחַ*? Shouldn't the Torah confer unmitigated joy?*

Harav Ovadia would answer with a parable: A group of troops that was battling another country managed to capture a city and drive out the opposing forces. After ensuring that no enemy troops remained, they started walking around the city and noticed that it contained great riches.

Excitedly, they began to plunder the spoils, grabbing everything they could. At the same time, however, their joy was mitigated because they realized that they must move on before enemy reinforcements arrived; in their haste, they would have to leave much of the riches behind.

Harav Ovadia would explain that the joy of Torah study is mitigated by the knowledge that no matter how much one masters, there will always be some that he will leave behind.

"That was Abba," concludes Rav Yitzchak. "No matter how much he learned, he never considered it enough. Because he loved the Torah so much, anything he would have to 'leave behind' would pain him."

DURING THE YEARS WHEN HIS CHILDREN WERE GROWING UP, Harav Ovadia would regularly make time to learn or converse with them, but the children realized early on how precious their father's time was.

Forcing Him to Eat

Rav Yitzchak shares a recollection from the period of his childhood when Harav Ovadia was writing the third volume of Yabia Omer. He would sit on Rav Waldenburg's beit din in the morning[4] and then come home, withdraw into the bedroom that doubled as his study, and begin to write.

"Ima would go into his room at 2 o'clock to tell him that it's time for lunch," relates Rav Yitzchak. "That would set off a negotiation.

"'Soon,' he would say. She would go back at 3, and then at 4, and each time he would tell her, 'Soon.' Some days she would give up on him coming to lunch of his own volition, and she would turn off the light in his study so that he would finally get up and join us.[5]

"He would come into the kitchen and eat quickly while we, who were in absolute awe of him, sat at the table watching him. The entire time, he would continue thinking about the sugya he was writing about.

"When there were infants and toddlers in the house, he would help Ima by feeding a child — but even then, he would take a sefer and read from it, place a spoonful into the baby's mouth, and then read another few lines. A spoonful, and a couple of lines. Another spoonful, and another couple of lines, until the baby had eaten his fill.

---

4. See p. 291.
5. Rav David Yosef recalls that some days she would say, "If you don't come, I'll be upset at you." As soon as she would say those words, Harav Ovadia would get up quickly and run to the kitchen, not wanting to cause her pain.

> "As soon as the meal was over, he would run back to his room and quickly jot down all that he had learned, either from a sefer or in his mind, during the meal.
>
> "On the days when Ima wanted him to come to the kitchen sooner, after one or two trips to his study she would tell him, 'Ani mat'hila lehakpid — I'm beginning to feel upset.'
>
> "As soon as those words emerged from her mouth, Abba would get up and stride quickly to the kitchen. He respected Ima so much that he didn't want to disappoint her."

The Two-Minute Pictures

GRANDSON RAV YITZHAK TOLEDANO MAKES A SIMPLE CALculation to show just how careful Harav Ovadia was to use every moment for learning: There are hundreds of pictures of him learning in his study wearing his *glima*, the robe worn by the Rishon LeZion. When he sat and learned in his study, however, he didn't wear a *glima*. When were all those pictures taken? Rav Toledano explains that if Harav Ovadia was supposed to go out to an event — to serve as *sandak* at a *brit*, for instance — he would don his *glima*. Sometimes, however, his driver would be held up in traffic. Instead of waiting outside for a minute or two for his car to arrive, Harav Ovadia would sit down with a *sefer* and begin learning again with such intensity that he wouldn't even notice if someone snapped a picture — as they often did.

A "two-minute" photo

Chapter Twenty-Three: Channeling the Gifts □ 443

Torah on the Road

"WHEN IT WAS TIME TO BUY THE RAV A NEW CAR," RELATES R' Tzvi Hakak, Harav Ovadia's personal assistant, "philanthropists from abroad would vie for the privilege of buying him a comfortable car. But to Maran, only one thing mattered: Before we switched cars, we had to ensure that there was a light installed in the back seat by which he could learn from a *sefer* if we were traveling at night."

Those who remembered Harav Ovadia from the 1930s and 1940s were not surprised that he was able to learn during a bus ride or while waiting for a bus; it was his ability to learn out of a *sefer* while *walking to the bus stop* that they found astonishing.

Yet despite his ability to learn on the road, he didn't fool himself; his best learning was done at his desk, and he tried to avoid accepting extraneous obligations upon himself if he could avoid them.

> *In his younger years, Harav Ovadia rarely went to semahot, and when he went, he would attend for a matter of minutes. Someone pointed out to him that perhaps people would be hurt if he didn't stay at their simha for longer. "In the future," he pledged, "I'll give them much more happiness." Indeed, in his later years, when the hatmada of his early years propelled him to become the gadol hador, he was able to make people happy by showing up at their simha for a mere few moments — much more so than if he had stayed at these events for hours early on in life rather than devoting those hours to learning.[6]*

Harav Ovadia's car had to have only one feature: a light in the backseat by which to learn.

---

6. Rav Yitzhak Toledano.

> Later in the Rav's life, R' Benzion Reich invited him to one of his children's weddings. When Harav Ovadia opened the invitation and saw that the wedding was in Bnei Brak, he said, "Reb Benzion, do you feel that my attending the simha warrants the bitul Torah that it will cause?
>
> "Everyone knows that the Rav spends his time in the car learning," R' Benzion replied, "so why should it cause bitul Torah?"
>
> "Learning in the car is not the same," he replied.

Although he did accept invitations to serve as *sandak* at *britot*, he would limit the time he spent in this capacity. The *mohelim* knew that by the time Harav Ovadia arrived, the baby had to be prepared and ready to be placed on his lap.

> A rav made an appointment to discuss an important halachic matter with Harav Ovadia. The Yosef family told him to be there at noon. Knowing that Harav Ovadia's time was precious, the rav made sure to be there at a quarter to

Even when serving as *sandak*, Harav Ovadia wasted no time from learning.

twelve. He parked outside the building and waited in his car until his scheduled appointment. At 11:53, he was shocked to see Harav Ovadia leave the building with his assistant, enter a waiting car, and be driven away.

The rav was baffled. Had Harav Ovadia forgotten about their appointment? Had he been called away for an urgent matter? Before he could contact the Yosef family to find out if he should return a different day, the car reappeared, and the rav reentered his building at 11:59, on time for their appointment.

After speaking to Harav Ovadia, the visiting rav asked his assistant what had transpired before the appointment.

"Someone invited the Rav to serve as sandak at his son's brit mila, which was held in the nearby Yehaveh Daat building. The Rav asked them to be ready for him. He entered the hall, the baby was placed on his lap, and the brit was performed expeditiously so the rav could return on time for your appointment."

Making the Most of Shabbat

IF HIS WEEKDAY SCHEDULE SEEMED DEVOID OF ANY TIME away from learning, his Shabbatot were devoted completely to Torah. His children and others who were privileged to spend Shabbat with him recall that he would be awake literally the entire Shabbat night. He would say that the *sefarim* state that Torah learned on Shabbat has extra *kedusha* and is worth far more than Torah studied during the week, and he didn't want to lose any opportunity to learn on Shabbat.

> Rav David Yosef recounts that a Jew from America once begged him for the opportunity to watch Harav Ovadia make Kiddush on Friday night. Since this person was willing to do a great deal for the Rav's Torah institutions, Rav David acquiesced, but warned him that he would be sorely disappointed. The fellow insisted that he wanted to watch nonetheless, so Rav David allowed him to escort the family home from the beit knesset.

> "The visitor watched in surprise as Abba sang Shalom Aleichem — each stanza only once, except for Tzeitchem LeShalom, which he didn't sing at all because there's a dispute whether one should recite it — and then Eishet Hayil. He filled his Kiddush cup and recited the words of Kiddush without any fanfare. Then he went to wash and handed out the halla.
>
> "When I escorted our guest to the door, he turned to me and said, 'You warned me that I would be let down, but I didn't realize just how much of a letdown it would be.'
>
> "'If you could stick around for another half hour,' I told him, 'your disappointment would be replaced by surprise. You would see how Abba finishes the meal within half an hour or so, and then runs to his study to learn for hours.'"

In his last years, Harav Ovadia would sit at the table for a little more time and sing with his grandchildren, but he still kept the meals short by most people's standards. Afterward, he would retire to his study and begin learning. At some point, he would make a guise of going to sleep, but would then return to his study.

> "I caught him red-handed trying to make believe that he slept," relates Rav Benzion Mutzafi. "I merited to spend a few Shabbatot with him. The seuda was over at, say, 9 p.m., and he would then sit down at his desk and learn until 10:30. I would see him get up and start walking slowly, exhaustedly, down the hall to his bedroom. He looked tired enough to easily sleep for 12 hours.
>
> "Not once, but on two or three occasions, I saw him return to his table by 11:15 and start learning. One Friday night, at around 2 a.m., I asked him a question, and then said, 'Excuse me for asking, but isn't the Rav tired?'
>
> "'Benzion,' he answered, 'Friday night is the only time that I can learn undisturbed, without any public obligations. If I don't take advantage of this time, when will I learn? I'll be an am ha'aretz!'"

Rav Yitzchak Yosef recalls that sometimes, at 2 a.m., the Rav would stand up and begin learning in an upright position. "Abba," his children would ask, "why are you standing?"

"I'm exhausted," he would answer. "If I don't stand up, I'm going to fall asleep."

The obvious move for most people at that point would have been to go to sleep. Harav Ovadia's reaction to exhaustion was to stand on his feet so he could learn until the morning without falling asleep.

"When people would tell him, 'Didn't our sages teach that שַׁבָּת is an acronym for שֵׁינָה בְּשַׁבָּת תַּעֲנוּג, *Sleep on Shabbat is pleasurable*'?[7] he would laugh it off," recalls Rav Mansour Ben Shimon, a student of Harav Ovadia in the 1960s who remained close with the Rav throughout his life and even substituted for Harav Ovadia at some of his *shiurim* when the Rav traveled abroad. "He would say, 'How do you know that it's supposed to be read שֵׁינָה בְּשַׁבָּת תַּעֲנוּג, maybe it should read שִׁינּוּן בְּשַׁבָּת תַּעֲנוּג, *Torah study on Shabbat is pleasurable?*' "

RAV YITZCHAK YOSEF RELATES THAT HE ONCE TRAVELED TO Mexico via New York with his father. The Rabbanit willingly traded her first-class seat[8] with her son (who was supposed to travel in economy class), so that her husband could learn with him. As soon as they boarded the plane, Harav Ovadia asked Rav Yitzchak to take out galleys of one of his *sefarim* that was nearly ready for publication, and they began to review the *teshuvot* to check for mistakes. Harav Ovadia was able to correct errors from memory — even noticing something as minor as a *hei* that was mistakenly entered as a *het*, so that a source that should have read *kaf-hei* (25) read *kaf-het* (28).

"I've Never Seen Anything Like It"

After a few hours, the flight attendants brought Harav Ovadia's meal, and Rav Yitzchak cut his father's main course into pieces

---

7. Figuratively, this means that sleep is a fulfillment of the mitzvah of *oneg Shabbat*, engaging in pleasurable activities on Shabbat.
8. As chief rabbi, Maran Ovadia was entitled to travel first class with the Rabbanit.

If it meant Harav Ovadia could learn with a companion, Rabbanit Margalit would give away her first-class seat.

while he continued to learn. He alerted him that his food was ready, and Harav Ovadia ate quickly and returned to his learning.

When they deplaned in New York, philanthropist R' Moshe Reichmann, who had been on the plane with them, pulled Rav Yitzchak to the side. "I want to tell you something," he said. "I've traveled with many great people, and I have *never* seen such *hatmada* in my life. Not for one second did he notice anything that was going on around him; he was just learning the entire time."

IN ADDITION TO HIS CONSISTENT USE OF EVERY AVAILABLE moment for learning, Harav Ovadia honed the ability to engross himself in learning and tune out anything that was going on around him.

Deeply Engrossed

Harav Ovadia's brother Na'im, who was two years younger than him and predeceased him by two weeks, was filled with simhat hahayim, and he loved to joke and make others laugh. He related that he and Harav Ovadia were once supposed to eat a meal together. They had both been served plates of food, and while Na'im began to eat, Harav Ovadia was busy learning out of a sefer. Na'im ate his food slowly and deliberately, and when he finished his entire portion, he noticed that Harav Ovadia had yet to touch his. Curious to see what would happen, he surreptitiously switched plates, placing the empty one in front of Harav Ovadia and taking the full one for himself.

A few minutes later, Harav Ovadia closed his sefer, looked down at his plate and said, "Oh, we finished eating?"

"Great," he said with a smile, and reopened his sefer. "I can continue learning!"

HIS OBLIVIOUSNESS TO HIS SURROUNDINGS WAS NOT MERELY the stuff of jokes; at times it was downright dangerous.

Rav Elyashiv's Long Visit

During the 1940s, while the Jews in Eretz Yisrael were vying for independence from the British, the Arabs living in the country were trying to prevent them from creating a state. There were sporadic riots in which the Arabs would attack Jews, attempting to instill fear in the hearts of the Jewish residents.

Once, a group of Arabs began to hurl projectiles at the Porat Yosef building in the Old City. All of the yeshiva's students ran down to the bomb shelter, but when Rosh Yeshiva Hacham Ezra Attia surveyed the room, he noticed two people missing.

"Please go up to the beit midrash and find Ovadia and Benzion," he asked one of his students.

Sure enough, when the student crept into the beit midrash, taking care to avoid the windows, he saw the young Ovadia Yosef and Benzion Abba Shaul learning at their seats, entirely unaware of the danger lurking just outside the windows.

Perhaps the most legendary story about Harav Ovadia's absolute immersion in learning occurred when the family lived on Rehov Elkana.

Maran Ovadia was working on a teshuva regarding all the sh'eilot related to using soap on Shabbat.⁹ As usual, although he had already based his ruling on the Gemara, the Rishonim, and the Shulhan Aruch, he still sought the opinions of any other authorities who discussed the matter so he could add these opinions to the teshuva. In the course of this quest, he climbed up a ladder to reach for the sefer Zichru Torat Moshe.¹⁰ When he opened the sefer, he was excited to see that according to the way the author defines some of the melachot of Shabbat, Harav Ovadia's ruling was correct. He ran back to the table to jot down his findings — forgetting that he was still standing at the top of the ladder. He toppled to the ground, sustaining a severe fracture in his arm.

While he was recovering, Rav Yosef Shalom Elyashiv came to visit him and stayed for an hour talking in learning. Rav Yitzchak Zilberstein later asked his father-in-law

"If he can become so engrossed in learning that he'll fall off a ladder, it's worth spending an hour with him."
Rav Yosef Shalom Elyashiv listens to Harav Ovadia's address at a gathering.

---

9. See *Yabia Omer*, Vol. 4, *Orah Haim* 27 and 28.
10. *Zichru Torat Moshe* is a short work written by Rav Avraham Danzig, who is most famous for his halachic work *Chayei Adam*. In *Zichru Torat Moshe* he defines and explains the 39 *melachot* that are forbidden on Shabbat.

Rav Elyashiv, who generally did everything hastily and spoke sparingly, why he stayed so long.

"If someone can become so engrossed in learning that he can forget that he's on top of a ladder," Rav Elyashiv replied, "it's worth spending an hour with him!"[11]

"Stop, Coward"

SOMETIMES HARAV OVADIA WAS SO UNAWARE OF HIS SURroundings that even when others tried to alert him to imminent danger, he just waved it off, assuming that they were exaggerating.

While on a flight from Dallas to New York with his father, Rav Yitzchak Yosef noticed that the plane was flying dangerously low. Neither father nor son understood English, and while Rav Yitzchak noticed that the people around him were talking in frightened voices, he didn't understand that they were saying that the plane's gas tank had developed a hole, and the fuel was quickly leaking out.

The pilot lowered his altitude to try to preserve his fuel and find a spot to land. Upon noticing that the plane was whizzing dangerously close to the rooftops, Rav Yitzchak touched his father on the arm and said, "Abba, we're going to crash!"

Without lifting his eyes from the Gemara that was his constant companion on flights, Harav Ovadia said, "Tafsik, pachdan" (Stop, coward). A couple of seconds later, a Jewish woman who knew some Hebrew stood up and shouted to Rav Yitzchak, "Tell your father that we're in danger. The pilot just announced that he has to make an emergency landing or the plane will crash!"

Rav Yitzchak turned to his father and said, "See, Abba, it's not just me. Now others are saying that the plane is going down. Take a look out the window!" Harav Ovadia finally peeked outside and noticed that the plane was indeed

---

11. Rav Yitzchak Yosef.

flying dangerously low. He closed his Gemara and began to recite Tehillim until the pilot found a military base, circled a couple of times, and landed. The plane was immediately surrounded by emergency vehicles, and the entire area was sprayed with foam to prevent a conflagration.

When the pilot — a gentile — emerged from the cockpit, he saluted Harav Ovadia and motioned to the passengers to allow the Rabbi to descend first, apparently attributing the miracle to his merit.

The Best Anesthetic

BEING ABLE TO DISTRACT HIMSELF COMPLETELY FROM HIS surroundings had many benefits — sometimes even medical benefits.

About seven years before his passing, Harav Ovadia was complaining of terrible stomach pains, and his son Rav David accompanied him to the hospital. The doctors ordered a battery of tests, and they uncovered an issue that required immediate laparoscopic surgery. But at his advanced age, and considering his weak overall medical condition, the doctors felt that it was dangerous to place him under anesthesia. "It will him take several weeks to recover from the anesthesia," they explained. "That's if he'll come out of it."

They told Rav David that they would do the half-hour surgery without anesthesia, but they warned him that the procedure would be extremely painful. "We're going to summon several staff members just to hold him down," they said, "and you must remain outside because you won't be able to handle the sight of him suffering so much. If you want to remain right outside the operating theater, you may, but be prepared for his shrieks of pain."

Rav David asked the doctors to describe to the Rav what the procedure would be like, so that he wouldn't be shocked when the pain began. "B'seder," Harav Ovadia sighed upon hearing the plan. "If this is a pain that I have no choice but to suffer, it should be *kaparat avonot* (an atonement for my sins). But please bring me my Gemara and I'll try to distract myself from the pain as much as possible."

"I brought him his Gemara — he was learning *Bava Batra* at the time — and I left the room," relates Rav David. "A large group of doctors and other hospital staff entered the operating room, but I did not hear a single sound emanating from within. Finally, after about half an hour, the doctors came out and said, 'We were shocked — he didn't utter a peep.'

"I went inside and asked, 'Abba, how are you feeling?' He looked up at me and said, slightly irritated, 'Ask the doctors how long they're going to make me wait. Let them start already!'

"He was so utterly engrossed in his learning that he had not felt them operating."

Four years before his petira, he was learning in the middle of the night, and he stood up to get a sefer. When he returned to his place, he didn't realize that his chair, which was on wheels, had moved backward. When he sat down, he fell onto the floor and broke his pelvis. No one was in the room, and no one heard him calling for help.

To his good fortune, his desk drawers were in reach, and he had handwritten Torah notes in the drawers. He pulled open a drawer, took out some notes, and began to learn. He remained on the floor from 2 a.m. until 6:40 a.m., when one of his assistants arrived to escort him to Shaharit — but ended up driving him straight to the hospital.

Only Torah study could have enabled him to make it through that agonizing night.[12]

After that incident, the family installed a closed-circuit camera in the Rav's study and bedroom, so they could track when he rose

---

12. Rav Benzion Mutzafi.

in the middle of the night to learn and ensure that he was safe. Rav Moshe and Rabbanit Yehudit would awaken when they heard noise coming from the speakers on the monitor. Rav Moshe would run to his father's room and either bring him some *sefarim* so that he could learn there or help him walk to the study and settle him with whatever he needed, before returning to sleep.

IN THE FINAL MONTHS OF HIS LIFE, A WIDELY REPORTED story attesting to Harav Ovadia's complete absorption in learning brought about a great *kiddush Hashem* (sanctification of Hashem's Name) throughout Israel.

The Prime Minister Watches

Israel's prime minister, Binyamin Netanyahu, came to discuss a matter with Harav Ovadia. He was ushered into the Rav's study, along with his entourage and the media crews covering the visit. Harav Ovadia was studying a work on Hilchot Halla.

Each time he reached a source, he would stop for a moment, scour his memory until he was able to recall the exact words of the source, and then continue studying. Prime Minister Netanyahu was awed by the Rav's complete immersion in learning, and shocked that the hullabaloo of the camera crews jockeying for the best positions hadn't caused him to lift his eyes from the sefer.

After a few minutes, MK Eli Yishai, who had arranged the visit, told Mr. Netanyahu that he would inform the Rav that the prime minister had arrived.

"No," Mr. Netanyahu said, waving him off. "I never get to see anything like this." By now, the cameramen had also grown enthralled by the sight, and they started snapping photos of Harav Ovadia engrossed in his sefer. Mr. Netanyahu continued watching in fascination, wondering how long it would take the Rav to notice the dozens of people in the room.

Finally, after a long while, Rav Moshe Yosef explained that if no one interrupted Harav Ovadia, the prime minister

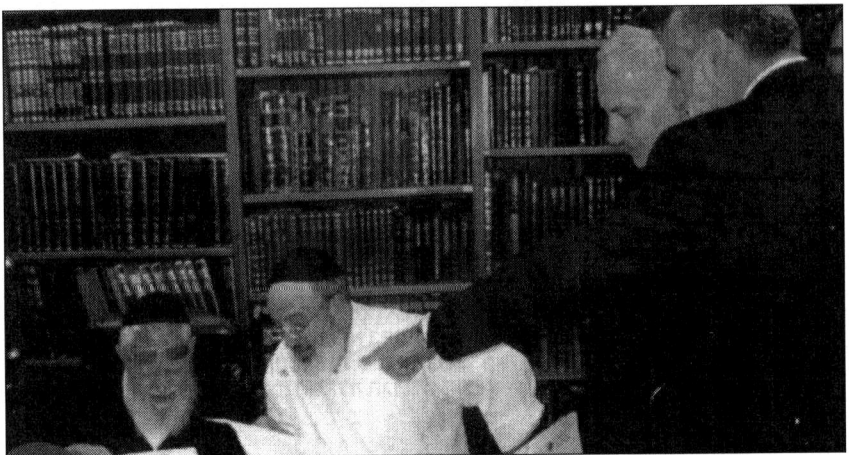

The cameramen jockeyed for position,
the Prime Minister waited, but Harav Ovadia kept learning, oblivious to it all.

would wait all day. Rav Moshe crouched down next to his father and said, "Abba, the Rosh Hamemshala is here."

Harav Ovadia looked up in surprise, and said, "Ah, Baruch Haba, Baruch Haba."[13]

---

13. Rav Yitzchak Yosef.

Chapter Twenty-Four
One for the Books

From a very young age, Harav Ovadia harbored a passion for books. But unlike your typical bibliophile, Harav Ovadia's passion was limited to one type of book: Torah works. Even as a child, he realized that the more access he would have to *sefarim*, the more he would be able to rule properly in halacha. He felt strongly that one must seek as many *sevarot* (logical explanations) as possible each halachic topic, because *sevarot* are the underpinnings of halacha.

Already as a teenager, he went about compiling his library in an extremely organized fashion. He kept prioritized lists of the *sefarim* that he wanted to purchase, and each time he acquired money — be it from his earnings as a 17-year-old *maggid shiur* or from rewards he received from Porat Yosef for excelling on tests — he immediately put it aside for these purchases.

> *Even when Harav Ovadia couldn't afford a particular sefer, he did not allow that to stop him from learning.*
>
> *In his youth, he approached the owner of a sefarim store in Yerushalayim who, he had heard, had just suffered a midnight burglary in his store.*
>
> *"Would you like to have someone guard your store?" Harav Ovadia asked.*

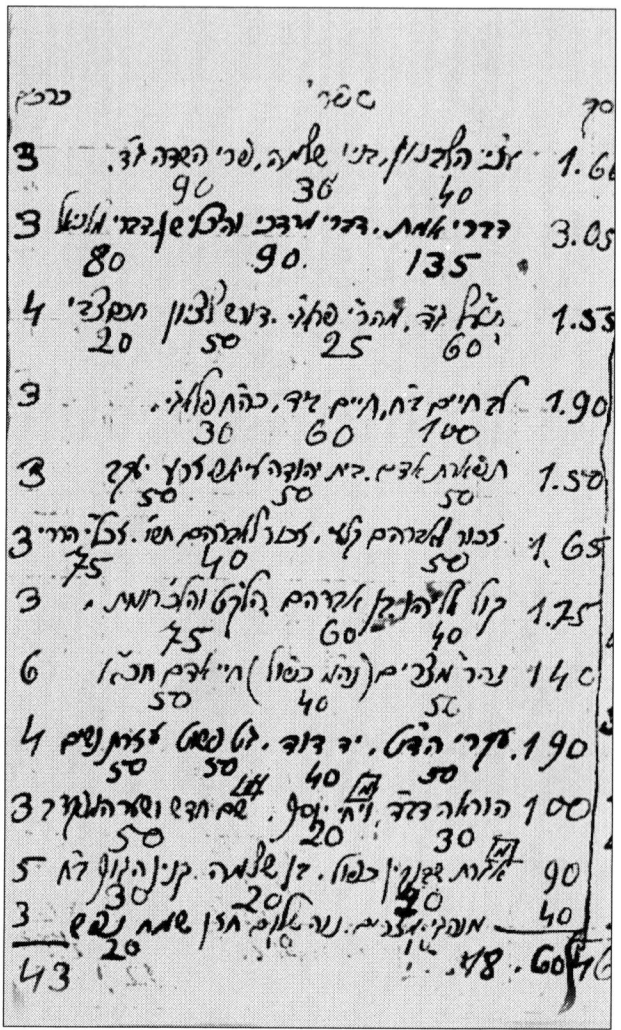

Harav Ovadia's list, written during his teenage years, of the *sefarim* he planned to buy, including the prices and the number of volumes in each set

"I wish I could afford one," the man said wistfully.

"How about we make a deal?" suggested Harav Ovadia. "If you allow me to learn from the sefarim in your store, I'll guard it for you overnight free of charge."

The storeowner gladly agreed, and the arrangement worked for both sides: the storeowner was able to sleep well knowing that no one would burglarize his store, and Harav Ovadia had access to works that would otherwise not have been available to him.

ALTHOUGH HARAV OVADIA CONSIDERED IT HIS MAIN OBJEC-

All Torah, Any Torah
tive in life to study the halachic sections of the Torah and issue rulings for the public, his library was hardly confined to halachic works. He would purchase any *sefer* that could aid his learning or his general knowledge of Torah and Judaism, study it, and then place it on a shelf.

Rabbanit Margalit once told a visitor that no new volume made its way onto a shelf until Harav Ovadia had learned it cover to cover. This feat would have be astounding even if his library had contained a few thousand works — let alone the nearly 40,000 volumes that the family counted shortly before his passing.[1] And it wasn't just about learning the material. He annotated or commented on almost every volume he learned, pointing out where the author had missed some point or noting where else a particular topic was discussed.

Delighting in one of the nearly 40,000 *sefarim* in his library

> *During the last twenty years of his life, Harav Ovadia lived in a large apartment in Har Nof along with his son Rav Moshe, his daughter-in-law Rabbanit Yehudit, and their children.*[2]

---

1. Rishon LeZion Rav Yitzchak Yosef, who notes that this was not akin to a library in a *beit midrash*, in which there are multiple copies of the same work; almost each *sefer* in his library was unique.
2. See Chapter 31.

Aside from covering every wall of the large study and an adjacent room, sefarim also lined the hallways leading to these rooms.

During his early years in that apartment, tefillot were held in his study. At one point, however, he asked his helpers to arrange for a separate beit knesset to be designated for the tefillot. Before long, they were able to rent an apartment below Harav Ovadia's and convert it into a beit knesset.[3]

Logic would have dictated that as he grew older, the Rav should have sought to make things easier for himself, rather than move the beit knesset downstairs. The family wondered why he wanted to move it out of his study, especially since his health was deteriorating.

"First of all," Harav Ovadia explained, "some pages of notes have recently gone missing from my desk during tefillot. Some of the people who join the tefillot apparently don't realize that each page is precious to me, and they help themselves to a 'souvenir.'

"More importantly, however, when I write comments in the margins of sefarim, I do so for myself, not for others to see. Sometimes, those comments can be interpreted as derogatory to the author, even if no offense was intended. Recently, the author of a sefer told me that his friend had prayed with me one day, and had noticed the author's sefer on a shelf. He opened it and saw that I had written a comment that could be interpreted as a criticism of his work. The author was very hurt, and he came to discuss it with me.

"It's worthwhile to me to have to leave my home for every tefilla rather than take a chance of hurting the feelings of an author."

---

3. The *beit knesset* was referred to simply as "*Beit Knesset shel Harav.*" The reason for this simple name was because of Harav Ovadia's sensitivity toward the neighbors, who, when they heard that an apartment was going to be converted into a *beit knesset*, grew concerned that this would make their residential building into a thoroughfare. Harav Ovadia pledged that it would only serve his needs, not turn into a permanent fixture that would remain even after his *petira*, and to highlight its temporary status he never gave the *beit knesset* an official name.

IN SOME INSTANCES, HARAV OVADIA'S *SEFARIM* LIBRARY became one of the most important factors in his decisions.[4]

High Ceilings, Not Location, Location, Location

After his election to the post of Rishon LeZion, Harav Ovadia wanted to move back to Yerushalayim, after having spent several years in Tel Aviv as the city's chief rabbi. He initially wanted to move to the Bucharim neighborhood, near his childhood home, but some politicians insisted that he live in the upscale Rehavia neighborhood where the country's leaders reside.

R' Shlomo Zevihi, who served as Harav Ovadia's driver during those years, relates that a real estate agent who was helping the family with their apartment hunt recounted that each time Harav Ovadia walked into an apartment to check whether it would be suitable, the first thing he would do was

Harav Ovadia entering his building on Rehov Rothschild in Rehavia. When it came to choosing apartments, only the height of the ceilings mattered.

---

4. See p. 178 regarding how much of a factor it played in his plans to flee Egypt and return to Eretz Yisrael.

> stare up at the ceiling. *The real estate agent found this habit extremely strange; some clients check the walls for moisture or mold, but why the ceiling?*
>
> *"I need to see whether the ceilings are high enough for me to fit in all of my sefarim,"* Rav Ovadia explained.

When they actually moved into the new apartment on Rehov Jabotinsky in Rehavia, Harav Ovadia would not allow his family or students to put away his *sefarim* in his new library. "I need to put them away myself so I know where they are," he explained. "This way, I won't have to waste time finding a *sefer* when I need it."

He was always careful to put a *sefer* back in its place so he wouldn't lose even a moment trying to find it again. In his later years, when he had several people working with him on his *teshuvot*, some of them were charged specifically with bringing him the *sefarim* he needed and returning them to their places when he was finished with them.

Once, a cleaning woman straightened his desk and put a *sefer* away in the wrong place. Maran was deeply pained when he couldn't find that *sefer*. Only later, when he was putting away a different volume that was on his desk, did he find the missing *sefer*, in the other *sefer*'s place.[5] To Harav Ovadia, those moments lost were precious, and from then on he asked that only those who knew the exact spot for each *sefer* put the volumes from his desk back on the shelves.

Nothing Too Minor

TO HARAV OVADIA, EVERY PRINTED WORD HAD VALUE, AND nothing escaped his eagle eyes. Shortly before his passing, a team of *talmidei hachamim* were brought in to review his extensive writings and work on publishing them.

Rav Binyamin Huta,[6] a member of that team, relates that they found all sorts of surprises in the margins of the *sefarim* in his library.

---

5. R' Shlomo Zevihi.
6. Rav Binyamin Huta's quotes in this chapter were culled from a radio interview that took place on Harav Ovadia's *sheloshim*.

Harav Ovadia's copy of *Areshet Sefateinu*, a 436-page compendium of *shirim ubakashot*, which are extremely complex poetic compositions, was full of small corrections to the text: a word or two that he realized had been copied incorrectly because they didn't fit into the rhythm of the poem; a word whose *dikduk* (Hebrew grammar) was wrong; a word that didn't fit the overall style.

"Nothing escaped his purview, even poetic *tefillot*," notes Rav Huta.

Most incredible, says Rav Huta, was how he used his encyclopedic memory to correct errors that almost no one else — even a computer program — could have caught.

One author attributed a quote to Sefer Zivhei Tzedek, Siman 100. Harav Ovadia noted on the side, "This is actually in Vayashav Moshe, Siman 100."

An extensive list of *sefarim* purchased in 1951,
a year after the family returned from Egypt

"Someone learning this work who wanted to see the citation inside might have looked in other simanim in *Zivhei Tzedek* when he didn't find it in Siman 100," noted Rav Huta. "But who would have thought of looking for it in the very same siman in a **different** work?

"Only Harav Ovadia, who had both works committed to memory, could discern such a thing."

SOMETIMES THE ANNOTATIONS FOUND IN HIS *SEFARIM* contained a window into Harav Ovadia's wit.

"He Forgot Yosef"

"There were some contemporary authors who would quote Harav Ovadia frequently when his rulings could bolster their own *teshuvot*," relates Rav Huta, "but wouldn't even mention his ruling if it differed from their own.

"In one such instance, Maran wrote in the margin of a *teshuva*: וְלֹא זָכַר אֶת יוֹסֵף וַיִּשְׁכָּחֵהוּ — *and he did not remember Yosef, and he forgot him.*"[7]

DURING THE SHIVA FOR MARAN, THE *SEFARIM* IN HIS library were boarded up to ensure that none of the thousands of people milling through the apartment helped themselves to any of his precious volumes. When the boards were removed and the team of *talmidei hachamim* and family members began to peruse the works, they were shocked to find that many of the *sefarim* contained wads of money in a variety of currencies. Some of the money was old Israeli currency that was now useless, but much of it was current. There were also checks from both Israel and abroad.[8]

Shocking Discoveries

---

7. Harav Ovadia paraphrased the last verse in *Parashat Vayeishev*: וְלֹא זָכַר שַׂר הַמַּשְׁקִים אֶת יוֹסֵף וַיִּשְׁכָּחֵהוּ, *Yet the Chamberlain of the Cupbearers did not remember Joseph, but he forgot him* (*Bereishit* 40:23), to describe the fact that the author had "forgotten" to mention that Harav Ovadia had already written a *teshuva* on the same *sh'eila* but had reached a different conclusion.
8. Rabbanit Yehudit Yosef.

Why was all this money stashed away in his *sefarim*?

Although Harav Ovadia needed money for all the Torah institutions on whose behalf he fundraised — as well as the many *hessed* projects he supported — if he sensed that someone was giving him money to influence a decision, he considered that a bribe, and refused to use it. He would place it into a *sefer*, and then forget about it. Similarly, if he sensed that the person's money was earned in an improper manner, he refused to use it for any purpose.

Apparently, there were also times that he placed money into a *sefer* planning to use it later on, and simply forgot about it. To him, learning was primary, money was secondary — to the extent that he even took solace in the fact that he occasionally forgot about cash left in *sefarim*.

> *Harav Ovadia's havruta, Rav Eliyahu Shitrit, related that he once opened a sefer and a few hundred Israeli lira fell out. Harav Ovadia initially told him to exchange them, but Rav Shitrit replied that they were valueless.*
>
> *"It's good that this happened," Harav Ovadia said, "because sometimes I forget something in learning. This way I'll be able to tell the beit din shel ma'alah that I also forgot about money."*

RAV HUTA RELATES THAT EVEN A BOOK OF STORIES ABOUT *gedolim* didn't escape Harav Ovadia's careful review.

Nothing Escapes a Halachic Worldview

One story in the book stated that the Shach (so named for the acronym of the title of his commentary on Shulhan Aruch, Siftei Kohen) was once involved in a din Torah. Before he entered the beit din, he prepared what he considered winning arguments on his behalf, and he was shocked when the dayanim ruled in favor of his opponent.

"Can you explain why I'm wrong?" the Shach asked.

Apparently unaware of the identity of the man standing before him, the Av Beit Din took out a Shulhan Aruch and pointed to a comment from the Shach, upon which he had based his ruling against the Shach.

"How wondrous are the words of Hazal," exclaimed the Shach. "They said that a person cannot see past his own interests — and because I had a personal interest in this case, I didn't remember my own comment on the Shulhan Aruch!"

In the margin, next to this story, Harav Ovadia wrote, "This cannot be true, because the Shach on Hoshen Mishpat[9] was published posthumously."

He added, however, that this story was true — but about a different person. He cites from a different sefer that tells the same story about the Sma,[10] the other major commentary printed alongside the text of the Shulhan Aruch in Hoshen Mishpat.

More significant than his corrections based on historical accuracy were those in which he noted that a story couldn't be correct because of a halachic issue.

Another story in a book stated that Rav Zusya of Anipoli's wife desperately needed new clothing. Although they were poverty-stricken, Rav Zusya saved up money to buy her a new dress.

One day, he noticed that she looked disappointed. When he asked what was wrong, she replied that when she had gone to pick up her dress, a hattan had come to the tailor at the very same time. He saw the dress and assumed that it was for his kalla. When he saw Rav Zusya's wife picking up the dress, he looked disappointed. "I didn't want to diminish his happiness, so I gave the dress away to the kalla."

"Did you pay for it?" Rav Zusya asked.

"No, the hattan is going to pay for it," his wife replied.

"What will be with bal talin (the prohibition of making a worker wait for his wages)?" said Rav Zusya. "You have to pay the tailor for his work on the day he finishes the work!"

---

9. The section of *Shulhan Aruch* that deals with monetary matters.
10. An acronym for *Sefer Meirat Einayim*.

> *In the margin next to this story, Harav Ovadia commented, "This cannot be true, because in this case, there is no problem of bal talin, which applies only if one actually takes possession of the item he ordered."*

Somehow, in the course of compiling the 40,000 volumes in his library, Harav Ovadia succeeded not only in reading each *sefer* from cover to cover, but also in applying his extensive halachic knowledge to each word on each page.

CHAPTER TWENTY-FIVE
A MEMORABLE MEMORY

PERHAPS HARAV OVADIA'S MOST ASTOUNDING NATural gift was his phenomenal memory. Upon hearing stories about the staggering amount of material at his fingertips and his ability to recall any source seemingly at will, many people were prompted to rationalize, "Well, had I been born with his memory, I could also have mastered the amount of Torah he did."

In truth, however, memory alone could never have made a Maran Harav Ovadia. Only his self-inspired ambition to master all of Torah and his decision to dedicate his prodigious mind to Torah could have resulted in the marvel known as Maran.

> *Those who knew Harav Ovadia from his early years relate that until the age of 31, he did not own a watch. In his teenage years, perhaps he could not afford to purchase one, but by the time he was 27 and served as the av beit din in Egypt, he could easily have found some money for a watch. Why didn't he buy one?*
>
> *"What did he need a watch for?" asks a close student in answer to the question. "He learned every second of the day*

and night, except when he prayed. He didn't need a watch to tell him when to go to sleep, because he went to sleep only when he felt too exhausted to continue learning."

What changed at the age of 31? The story goes that some students who attended his nightly shiurim were faced with a dilemma each night when his shiur went overtime. The shiurim were so fascinating that no one could pull himself away, but some attendees had other obligations and wanted the rav to end on time. They decided to pool their resources and buy him a watch as a gift so he would be aware of the time and end the shiur after the scheduled 1½ hours.

Harav Ovadia's ability to master material wasn't due only to his maximizing his time; it was combined with his single-mindedness in pursuing Torah study.

Later in life, Harav Ovadia mentioned to his family that until the age of 30, he had never read a newspaper. He was not referring only to secular newspapers, clarifies his son Rav Yitzchak; he did not read any newspaper, period.

Until he was 31, Rav Ovadia didn't own a watch until his students — seen here surrounding him at a wedding — bought him one so he would end his *shiur* on time.

"You have to consider the historical context of his first 30 years to fully appreciate this little fact of his life," notes Rav Yitzchak. *"Those three decades included the Holocaust, Israel's declaration of independence, and the establishment of the State — during which time he was in Egypt and might have felt that he had to know what was happening back home, across the border.*

*"But to him, nothing mattered other than Torah. He felt that whatever he **had** to know would somehow reach his ears without him setting aside some of his precious time to read the newspaper."*

Building the Database

THE GIFTED MIND, THE ENDLESS DILIGENCE, AND THE ABILITY to shut out all else don't tell the full story of Maran's memory, however, because his total recall surpassed anything recently known to man.

Eliezer Shmueli, the irreligious director general of the Education Ministry from 1976-1987, recounted in a television broadcast just how far-ranging Harav Ovadia's memory was.

"During those years," related Mr. Shmueli, *"I visited his home to consult with him on an Education Ministry issue. Before we discussed the matter at hand, he told me to choose any volume in his library and tell me the title and the page number."*

Shmueli figured that this would be some sort of test, so he went into a corner and retrieved the dustiest, most forlorn-looking volume he could find. He told Harav Ovadia the title and page number.

"This doesn't sound believable," admits Shmueli, *"but he began to recite word for word what it said on that page."*

Even with all the natural gifts in the world, only one thing enabled Harav Ovadia to build such a vast mental database: review, review, and more review. When asked to explain how his father could know that much Torah, Rav David Yosef answers by way of an example in which his father tried to teach him the "trick":

> *Abba once instructed me to become a ba'al korei, but not to suffice with reviewing the parasha just to be able to read it in shul; I should review it, he said, until I would know the entire Torah by heart.*
>
> *I took his challenge seriously, and spent a couple of years becoming a ba'al korei. I read the parashiyot so many times that at some point I realized that if someone would blindfold me and start reading anywhere in the Torah, I could continue — not by retrieving the words from memory, but by "reading" from the column in the Sefer Torah that had been "burned" into my mind.*
>
> *With me that was true for the Torah; with Abba it was true for much more.*

Rav David and his siblings had the ultimate role model in their midst.

Harav Ovadia challenged his son to know the Written Torah by heart, but Maran's memory extended far beyond that.

During Rav David's teenage years, Harav Ovadia was once testing him at a Shabbat seuda on what he had learned that week in Yeshivat Hevron. He was pleased with David's progress, but disappointed that his son couldn't remember the daf on which each passage appeared. David tried to wave off the issue, telling his father that it wasn't vital to remember the specific location of a passage, but Harav Ovadia insisted that it was important.

"I decided to test my father's proficiency in naming a precise source," recounts Rav David. "I took a kitchen towel, covered the set of Shas in the bookcase so he couldn't see which volume I was removing, and then opened a volume to a page at random. I covered everything on the page with the towel besides one small Tosafot toward the bottom of the page, and brought the volume to him. Abba smiled, glanced at the Tosafot and said, 'Zevahim, daf such-and-such.'"

HARAV OVADIA'S MEMORY WASN'T MERELY A CONVENIENT repository; at some points in his life it was essential to his survival.

From Memory for Months

During the 1970s, Harav Ovadia suffered from serious complications with his eyes. At first he experienced sudden sharp pains in his eyes, and then his vision grew blurry. He was examined by some of the greatest specialists in the country, and they recommended that he undergo surgery. Before going ahead with it, Harav Ovadia consulted with Rav Chaim Greineman, a nephew of the Hazon Ish who had inherited some of his uncle's legendary medical acumen. Rav Greineman told him not to undergo any procedure until he was examined by a specific specialist from London. Some askanim succeeded in bringing this doctor to Eretz Yisrael to examine Harav Ovadia.

"You don't need surgery," the doctor advised upon concluding his examination. "Your eyes are suffering from extreme overuse from continuous learning from books with tiny letters, and they need a break. Don't read for a couple of months, and they'll be as good as new."

Rav Ovadia looked at the doctor in dismay and said, "I don't know if I can accept your recommendation. What would you do if you had a problem with your lungs and a specialist would tell you to stop breathing for a couple of months to give your lungs a break? To me, learning is like breathing."

Nevertheless, realizing that his eyesight was at stake, Harav Ovadia asked his children and others to read the Gemara to him, in order to give his eyes a rest.

Rav David Yosef, who was single at the time, came home from yeshiva early every night to read to his father. He recalls that as soon as he would start reading the Gemara to his father, Harav Ovadia would begin to recite the Gemara from memory. Then David would read the Rashi, and as soon as he would say the first words, Harav Ovadia would take over and recite the rest of the Rashi. The real shock was that even when they began to study long and complicated comments of Tosafot, Harav Ovadia was able to recite entire passages word for word without any errors, as if the page were inscribed on his memory.

Fourteen
Sources at
His Fingertips

DURING THE EARLY 1990S, HARAV OVADIA summoned Rav Shlomo Moshe Amar, who was then the Av Beit Din in Petah Tikva, and asked him to join Badatz Beit Yosef's kashrut department. Rav Amar demurred, explaining that he did not have enough time. Harav Ovadia then asked him if he would be willing to serve on the beit din's division for monetary matters, and Rav Amar consented.

At an inaugural meeting of this beit din, Rav Amar was surprised to hear that Harav Ovadia considered oversight of mikvaot to be within the beit din's purview.

One of the other two dayanim charged with sitting on this special beit din for mikvaot questioned why it was necessary to have three rabbanim overseeing mikvaot;

wouldn't it be enough to have one *rav* rule on halachic issues of this nature?

Harav Ovadia replied that having a *beit din* of three *rabbanim* would ensure that no situation would arise in which a *mikveh* employee's word would clash with that of the *rav* (e.g., if the *rav* would say that he had instructed the *mikveh* employee to fix something and the employee would claim that he or she had never received such an instruction).

In response, Rav Amar noted that there is a *Pit'hei Teshuva*[1] that discusses this issue. The *Pit'hei Teshuva* cites *Sh'eilot V'Teshuvot Shivat Zion*[2] (23), which states that a *rav* would be believed against a layman in such a situation, because the *rav* was accepted as the authority by the people — and more specifically, as the supervisor of the *shohet*.[3]

"As soon as I mentioned the *Pit'hei Teshuva*," said Rav Amar, "*Harav* Ovadia replied, 'You are referring to what he says in the name of the *Shivat Zion*?'

"The *Shivat Zion* is unrelated to *Hilchot Mikvaot*, and is a relatively obscure source that I just happened to have known. *Harav* Ovadia could not have been prepared with the counterarguments to the *Shivat Zion*, because he didn't know that I was going to pose this question. Yet he immediately listed fourteen sources from the breadth and

---

1. To *Shulhan Aruch Yoreh Dei'a*, 1:21.
2. Written by Rav Shmuel Landau, a son of the Noda B'Yehuda, Rav Yechezkel Landau.
3. The *Shivat Zion* was asked to rule on the following matter: A *shohet* fell seriously ill and was on the verge of death. When the rav of the city paid him a visit, the *shohet* asked everyone else to leave the room and started to recite *vidui* (the prayer of atonement), during which he admitted to the rav that he had knowingly allowed *treifot* to be passed off as kosher. Shortly before falling ill, he had found blemishes in his knife after *shehita* on at least five different occasions, and had nonetheless pronounced the animals he had slaughtered kosher — thereby causing others to inadvertently eat nonkosher meat.

The rav immediately instructed the townspeople to throw out any meat in their possession and *kasher* their utensils. Several days later, the *shohet* had a miraculous recovery, and he denied that he had ever made a statement to the rav invalidating his own *shehita*. One of the questions posed to the *Shivat Zion* was whether we can believe the rav over the *shohet*, who would ordinarily be trusted as a fine, upstanding Jew. The *Shivat Zion* ruled that because the townspeople had accepted the rav as the authority in their community — and more specifically, as the supervisor of the *shehita* process in the city — his statement is considered to override that of the *shohet*.

Rav Amar attempted to apply this principle to the case of a *mikveh* employee as well.

depth of Torah that held differently from the Shivat Zion to explain why he chose to appoint a panel of three to rule on mikvaot."

EVEN SEEMINGLY MEANINGLESS DETAILS DID NOT ESCAPE his memory if they were related to Torah.

Minute Details On the night of bedikat hametz, a halachic question arose with regard to the sale of hametz. Harav Ovadia summoned one of his sons and said, "Please go into the inner room of the library, and on the bottom shelves you'll find cardboard boxes. In the third box from the door, there are piles of handwritten notes. Bring me the second pile; I have a teshuva there about this question."

How did the Rav remember exactly where he had placed those handwritten notes, which were decades old? Because every word of Torah was important to him.[4]

OVER THE COURSE OF THE YEARS, HUNDREDS OF DELIGHTFUL stories regarding Harav Ovadia's memory made their way around the world — anecdotes that could certainly fill a few volumes of their own. Though not all were true, a sampling of some confirmed stories provides insight into just how great a man lived among us.

100 Percent Accuracy

> Rav Ovadia was occasionally invited to deliver shiurim in yeshivot both in Israel and abroad. One of the yeshivot he addressed most frequently was Kol Yaakov.[5] In the course of each such shiur, he would cite dozens of sefarim, listing the exact source for each citation — down to the daf, siman, or se'if in which one could find the words he was quoting.
>
> One year, two students decided to "test" Harav Ovadia's memory. They resolved between themselves to carefully record each citation, and then later check it for accuracy.

---

4. Harav Benzion Mutzafi.
5. See pp. 97-98.

Walking up the steps of Yeshivat Kol Yaakov with Rosh Yeshiva Rav Yehuda Ades

> *Rosh Yeshivat Kol Yaakov, Rav Yehuda Ades, related that these two students approached him a few days after the shiur, and said that they had tracked all of the citations in that shiur. Harav Ovadia had cited over 110 sources — and had given the correct citation for every single one!*

During the 1960s, when the third volume of Yabia Omer was ready for publication, Harav Ovadia brought the manuscript to the printer and then realized that there was a page missing. To the printer's surprise, rather than return home to retrieve the page, Harav Ovadia sat down in the print shop, with the heavy-duty printing machines of old roaring in the background, and rewrote the entire page without the benefit of a single sefer.[6]

At the wedding of Hacham Benzion Abba Shaul's only son, Rav Eliyahu, Harav Ovadia was sitting next to Rav Chaim Kreiswirth, waiting for the proceedings to begin. Rav Kreiswirth turned to Harav Ovadia and said, "While we're waiting, why don't we learn something?"

---
6. Rav Benzion Mutzafi.

"I can't compete."
Rav Chaim Kreiswirth (L), Harav Ovadia, and Rav Yekusiel Yehuda Halberstam, the Admor of Sanz-Klausenberg, at the cornerstone-laying ceremony for Laniado Hospital

"What should we learn?" asked Harav Ovadia.

"Since we're sitting at the wedding of the son of Harav Abba Shaul," suggested Rav Kreiswirth, "let's go through the Talmud and recall all of the words of the Tanna Abba Shaul."[7]

The two took turns: Harav Ovadia cited the first statement from Abba Shaul listed in the Talmud, then Rav Kreiswirth said the next one, and so on. At one point, when Harav Ovadia mentioned a source, Rav Kreiswirth said, "I'm sorry, but there's one that you missed, a few dapim earlier."

"Yes," Harav Ovadia replied, "but the Aharonim suggest that the Abba Shaul listed there was a different one from the one we're referring to."

Rav Kreiswirth shook his head in wonderment. "I can't compete!" he conceded.

Rav Aharon Shadmi runs an institution that republishes the sefarim of the Maharit Algazi, a Turkish hacham who passed away in 1727. In the course of his work, Rav Shadmi

---

7. Abba Shaul's name appears over 150 times in the Talmud. That the two would undertake such a challenge is alone a testament to their greatness.

came across an acronym he could not decipher: רש"פ. He asked many learned friends, but nobody could help him. After nearly giving up hope, he decided to speak to Harav Ovadia. Since Harav Ovadia's appointments were scheduled in advance, Rav Shadmi asked Harav Ovadia's assistant to take a copy of that page of Maharit Algazi into the Rav and ask him what the acronym meant.

Seconds later, the assistant was back. "Harav Ovadia said that it stands for רב שמואל פרימו, the author of Imrei Shefer, and you can find the quote Maharit Algazi refers to on such-and-such page in his work," he reported.

Rav Shmuel Primo, from Adrianople, Turkey, passed away in 1708. Armed with this new information, Rav Shadmi quickly found the quote in Imrei Shefer — thanks to Harav Ovadia's incredible range of knowledge.

Rav Shmuel Wosner in a Torah discussion with Harav Ovadia, to whom he sent inscribed copies of *Shevet HaLevi* (inset)

Not Relying on Memory

DESPITE HIS UNFAILINGLY RELIABLE MEMORY, WHEN IT CAME to quoting from *sefarim* in his written works, Harav Ovadia took great care not to rely on his memory alone. Rav Amir Krispal, one of the *havrutot* who worked with Harav Ovadia to produce his last works, relates that even if the Rav had to quote from one of his own *teshuvot* in *Yabia Omer*, he would ask one of his assistants to retrieve the volume, open to the page, and check the exact words before he recorded them.

And this from the person about whom Rav Shmuel Wosner, author of *Shevet HaLevi* and one of the contemporary *poskei hador*, once remarked, "He knows my *sefarim* better than I do!"[8]

"I'm Learning It Anew"

IT IS SAID THAT RAV AKIVA EIGER ONCE GOT STUCK IN A storm while traveling, and had to spend the night at an inn. Since he had planned to return home before night, he did not have any *sefarim* with him, so he asked the Jewish innkeeper if he had any *sefarim*. The innkeeper, an unlearned man, brought the only *sefer* he had in his home: a Rashba on *Masechet Yevamot*.

Rav Akiva Eiger began to learn with enthusiasm, until he reached a page that had fallen out. Rather than skip the page, he pulled out a pen and paper, wrote out the entire text of the Rashba from memory, and placed the page into the *sefer*.

Although many people see this story as a testimony to Rav Akiva Eiger's phenomenal memory, it has been noted that there is a greater lesson to be learned from this story: despite knowing the entire Rashba on *Yevamot* by heart, Rav Akiva Eiger still sat and learned the work with excitement.

The same could be said for Harav Ovadia. No matter how much he knew, he still learned with the same excitement and vigor as when he first began to learn from a *Torah Temimah Humash* as a young child.[9]

---

8. Rav Krispal.
9. See p. 49.

Rav Benzion Reich[10] *relates that during Harav Ovadia's last years, he went to discuss a sh'eila regarding a mikveh with the Rav. When he entered the study, he saw Harav Ovadia studying Tur with Beit Yosef. "He was so engrossed in it," says Rav Reich, "that you might have thought this was the very first time he was learning it."*

Rav Reich added that he once asked Harav Ovadia how he was managing with the new edition of Tur and Beit Yosef, released by Machon Shirat w[11] *— a valid question considering that Harav Ovadia had learned out of the old print for over half a century, and had probably studied these works dozens — if not hundreds — of times.*

"I'm learning it anew," he replied simply.

---

10. See p. 439.
11. Interestingly, this was one of the only *sefarim* for which Harav Ovadia made the switch to a new print, because the newer edition had certain vast improvements over the old one. Otherwise, he generally continued to learn from his old *sefarim*, which contained the extensive marginalia he had written in the course of decades of learning and reviewing.

Chapter Twenty-Six
A Walking Miracle

WHEN DISCUSSING A TORAH SCHOLAR AND righteous man of Harav Ovadia's caliber, people will often focus on the miracles the holy man wrought. And in the case of Harav Ovadia, such stories are plentiful. To quote his assistant R' Tzvi Hakak, "There wasn't a day that the door to his study opened to the public without us seeing miracles."

Harav Ovadia himself, however, was dismissive of such stories. When family members would tell him about a miracle that occurred

"The door didn't open to the public without us seeing miracles."
Rav Tzvi Hakak holds the place for Harav Ovadia at a *selihot* gathering at the Kotel at the end of 5772/2011.

as a result of his *beracha*, he would say, "You see how much Hashem loves Klal Yisrael, that He's willing to make *nissim* for them?"

In general, he was very wary of giving the impression that humans could somehow change nature, because he was extremely opposed to the myriad "Kabbalists" who were taking advantage of people's belief in their "hidden powers." Although Harav Ovadia himself had mastered many Kabbalistic works, when yeshiva students would ask him if they could study Kabbala, he would reply, "Those who love me should study *Shas* and *Poskim*."

ALTHOUGH HE WAVED OFF STORIES OF HIS OWN POWERS, Harav Ovadia differentiated between *talmidei hachamim* who were known to possess special merits and whose prayers or blessings were therefore effective, and many popular "Kabbalists" who were not learned.[1] Applying this principle back to him, one might say that his blessings carried weight because he spent every second either learning or teaching Torah.

In the Merit of Torah

Rosh Yeshivat Kisei Rahamim, Rav Meir Mazuz (R), whose eye disease disappeared after Harav Ovadia's blessing

Rav Meir Mazuz, Rosh Yeshivat Kisei Rahamim, related that doctors diagnosed him with an eye disease that required surgery. The nature of the surgery was such that a wrong move could cause permanent blindness. Rav Mazuz went to Harav Ovadia to receive his blessing, and the latter placed his hands directly over Rav Mazuz's eyes and blessed him.

When Rav Mazuz came to the hospital for the surgery, the doctors did a pre-surgical checkup and found that the eye disease had disappeared completely.[2]

---

1. See p. 105.
2. Rav Ehud Shraga.

Sometimes, the correlation between the Torah he learned and the subsequent salvation was even more direct.

> When daughter-in-law Rabbanit Yehudit Yosef suffered unexplained head pains approximately 15 years before Harav Ovadia passed away, he sensed something was wrong in the home they shared even though the family tried to shield him from the information.
>
> Suspecting an aneurism or other life-threatening condition, the doctors sent her for testing to determine what was causing her headaches, but she was only able to schedule those tests for three days later.
>
> While this was going on, someone in the family noticed that Harav Ovadia, who slept a precious few hours in each 24-hour period as it was, wasn't going to his bedroom at night. They tried to determine why he remained in his study all night, but he wouldn't answer their questions.
>
> Three days later, Rabbanit Yehudit underwent the tests, which showed nothing wrong. When she came home and the family was finally able to relax after three tense days, she saw Harav Ovadia heading to his bedroom for the first time that week. Suddenly, it dawned on her why he hadn't slept during those days. But before she could confirm her suspicion, Harav Ovadia said, "I dedicated my learning in these three days for your recovery."

"It's on My Shoulders"

IN AT LEAST ONE INSTANCE, HARAV OVADIA TOOK RESPONSIbility for a matter that was liable to end in tragedy, apparently aware that he could make certain assurances.

In Shem HaGedolim, Hida writes that he heard from the elderly sages of Yerushalayim that there are two sefarim written by Rishonim that one may not try to rework into a new format: Itur and Rabbeinu Yeruham. Hida explains that these two sefarim are from the "עולם דאסבתיא — the hidden world," and that anyone who *attempts to rework the text or write his own commentary on these sefarim will either die at a young age or lose his manuscript.*

Hida writes that he knew of people who tried, and they either passed away or their manuscripts just disappeared into thin air.

Until recently, therefore, the only extant texts of these two works were copies of ancient prints that were extremely hard to read.

There was a young man by the name of Rav Yair Hazzan learning in Rav Moshe Yosef's kollel who heard that a publishing house abroad was interested in releasing a new edition of Rabbeinu Yeruham, and he was offered the opportunity to work on the project.

He approached several gedolei Yisrael to ask whether he should work on it, and each one said, "Don't try it. You have a wife and children, and in light of the Hida's comment, it's not worth taking a chance."

He then asked Harav Ovadia, who said, "Publish it. Don't be afraid, I'll help you."

When Rav Hazzan brought up the Hida's comment, Harav Ovadia said, "The Hida says that he heard this from elderly sages, but those elders were mistaken. Go ahead and publish it."

Shortly after Rav Hazzan began to work on the Rabbeinu Yeruham, strange things started to happen around his house. First one child was hospitalized, then another.... He returned to Harav Ovadia and said, "Things seem to be going wrong for me. Perhaps I should stop working on Rabbeinu Yeruham?"

This time, Harav Ovadia didn't instruct Rav Hazzan not to be afraid. Rather, he asked him, "Are you afraid?"

Rav Hazzan replied that if he had Harav Ovadia's assurance, then he was not afraid.

"Continue working on it," Harav Ovadia told him. "On my shoulders."

Sure enough, by now Rav Hazzan has published several volumes of Rabbeinu Yeruham in a clear, easy-to-read format, and he and his entire family are alive and well.

Ready for the Brit

MANY STORIES CIRCULATE REGARDING HARAV OVADIA'S *ruah hakodesh*.[3] Although many of these stories are likely apocryphal, some have been confirmed to be accurate.

A grandson who had several daughters and no sons came for a blessing on a Friday for his wife, who was to undergo a Caesarean section that Sunday. Harav Ovadia gave his blessing, and then added, "Ah, so next Sunday we'll have a brit." Sure enough, it was a boy.

This same grandson related that Harav Ovadia once asked him to pray for a certain person in the blessing of Refa'einu.[4]

A few weeks later, he visited Harav Ovadia again, and his grandfather asked, "Why aren't you praying for So-and-so in Refa'einu?"

"I am," the grandson said, stretching the truth to some extent. In all honesty, he now admits, he had forgotten to mention the name during most of his prayers, and had remembered to pray for this person in Refa'einu only once or twice. The rest of the time he had prayed for the person in the blessing of Shema Koleinu.

"It can't be," Harav Ovadia replied. "Please pray for him in Refa'einu."

"But I have prayed for him in Refa'einu," the grandson persisted.

"It can't be," Harav Ovadia repeated. "Had you prayed for him in Refa'einu, he would already have merited a recovery."

---

3. Roughly translated as "Divine inspiration," in this context *ruah hakodesh* refers to the ability to perceive or "see" things that are hidden to ordinary people.
4. There is a prayer that can be inserted into the blessing of *Refa'einu*, the blessing for healing in *Shemoneh Esrei*, in which one can mention the names of specific people in need of a cure.

A student related that when his wife was expecting their first child, she went for an ultrasound, and the doctor told her that her baby would be born with serious defects. Both husband and wife were filled with anxiety over the next few days, and the wife suggested that they visit Harav Ovadia and receive his blessing.

When they went into his room, the student seated himself beside Harav Ovadia and began to explain the reason for their visit.

"If this is about your wife," Harav Ovadia interjected, "why is she seated down there? Let her sit close by."

The wife moved closer, and Harav Ovadia listened to what the doctors had said.

Lifting his hands over the woman's head, he blessed her with an easy and speedy delivery, and then instructed the couple not to worry. "The baby will be born perfectly healthy," he assured them.

"I can't say that I was as strong as my wife," this student admits. "Even after we received Harav Ovadia's beracha, I was still nervous. My wife, on the other hand, was absolutely calm. When I asked her whether she was concerned, she said, "No. Maran told us that the baby will be fine, so what is there to be nervous about?"

Sure enough, not only was the baby born perfectly healthy, but the delivery was so swift and smooth that even the hospital staff were caught off guard.

The Scent of Gan Eden

ONE OF THE MOST REMARKABLE STORIES DEMONSTRATING Harav Ovadia's *ruah hakodesh* unraveled over the better part of a century.

Mr. Moshe Friedman[5] was born in Poland in 1930, and his family survived the war through a series of miracles that brought them to Siberia.

---

5. This story was heard from the daughter of the protagonist, with the proviso that the name be changed in deference to her father's obvious attempts to keep it a secret.

When the war was over, Moshe's father heard that the Nazis ym"sh had made soap out of Jewish bodies, and he decided to return to Poland to buy as many of these bars of soap as he could and give these remains a Jewish burial.

Father and son traveled back to their hometown, and spent days combing the streets and offering to purchase the townspeople's Nazi-supplied soap.

This part of Moshe Friedman's life story was known to the family; the rest was not — until it became revealed through Harav Ovadia.

Mr. Friedman moved to America, married, and had children. When he was getting on in years, one of his sons-in-law, who is of Syrian descent, offered to accompany him to Eretz Yisrael. Mr. Friedman was delighted to visit the Holy Land, and especially to see gedolei Yisrael and receive blessings.

One of the stops they made was at Harav Ovadia's home.

No sooner had Mr. Friedman walked into the study than Harav Ovadia asked, "Why do I detect the scent of Gan Eden on your clothing?"

Mr. Friedman did not know what to answer.

"What special deed have you done in your life?" Harav Ovadia asked.

At first Mr. Friedman would not answer, but when Harav Ovadia kept repeating the question, he said, "Well, I have a several children whom I support so they can devote their lives to studying Torah."

"That's not it," Harav Ovadia said. "Others do that as well and their clothing doesn't have the scent of Gan Eden. What else did you do?"

Harav Ovadia sensed that Mr. Friedman knew the answer, but wasn't willing to say it in front of others. He sent all the people present out of his room, including Mr. Friedman's son-in-law. The only other person who remained was a young man named David, who acted as an interpreter, translating Mr. Friedman's English and Harav Ovadia's Hebrew.

When everyone left, Mr. Friedman told Harav Ovadia a story that had happened on the last day he and his father had attempted to buy and bury human soap in Poland — a tale, he said, he had not shared with anybody.

After spending a few weeks in Poland, they had already bought and buried all the soap they could find, and they decided it was time to rejoin their family in Siberia.

The day they were planning to leave, however, a non-Jewish man approached the 15-year-old Moshe Friedman and asked, "Are you the one who is buying the human soap?"

Moshe confirmed that he was.

"I have a full box of such soap, and I'm willing to sell it to you."

The man named a price, but Moshe did not have enough money on him, and his father was nowhere in sight. "I don't have money here," he said, "but give me the soap, I'll bury it, and I'll bring you money later."

"No, I want the money up-front," insisted the seller.

Moshe thought for a while and then said, "Look, I have this pair of warm, woolen pants, and yours are thin cotton. I'm willing to trade my pants for yours if you'll allow me to buy the soap."

The man quickly agreed to the deal; a pair of warm woolen pants were a premium commodity in the harsh European winters.

After the two traded pants, Moshe buried the box of soap, and then rejoined his family in Siberia, undoubtedly shivering his way through the winter in those cotton pants.

When Harav Ovadia heard this story, he said, "This explains why your clothes have the scent of Gan Eden. The neshamot of all the Jews whose remains you buried were all kedoshim, who died 'al Kiddush Hashem' and are therefore in Gan Eden, and these neshamot have been accompanying you throughout your life."

Visitors spoke of open miracles Harav Ovadia effected, but he attributed it to Hashem loving every Jew.

The humble Mr. Friedman never told his family of this exchange. When they asked about his visit to Harav Ovadia, he just said, "It was very inspiring."

In 2004, Mr. Friedman passed away, and David, the interpreter who had been in the room and now lived in the same community, came to console the mourners. "The story with the pants was so inspiring," he remarked.

"What story? What pants?" the mourners asked, befuddled.

David was shocked that they hadn't heard the story. True, Mr. Friedman had told Harav Ovadia that he hadn't shared the tale with anybody, but David hadn't realized that that included Mr. Friedman's own family. He then retold the entire story, giving the family great comfort as they came to appreciate their father in a new light — all due to the ability of a *gadol hador* to detect the "scent of Gan Eden" on his clothing.

The Walking Miracle

IN THE FINAL ANALYSIS, HOWEVER, HARAV OVADIA'S CLAIRvoyance and the miracles he effected pale in comparison to what we might call the walking miracle that was Harav Ovadia.

In a eulogy, Rav Moshe Hizkiya, rav of Kiryat Herzog, recounted a story that Harav Ovadia himself used to tell.

The son of the Hafetz Haim was once sitting with a group of Hassidim, and the talk turned to the miracles that their respective Admorim had performed. One Hassid told a fantastic tale about his rebbe, a second tried to top that with a miracle story regarding his own rebbe, and so on.

At one point, one of the Hassidim turned to the son of the Hafetz Haim and said, "Your father is known for his tzidkut. What miracles has he performed?"

"Many people like to tout the miracles their spiritual leaders have wrought," the son of the Hafetz Haim replied, "in the spirit of the Sages' teaching, 'Tzaddik gozer veHaKadosh Baruch Hu mekayem — a righteous person decrees, and God fulfills.'

"My father does the opposite: HaKadosh Baruch Hu gozeir, vehatzaddik mekayem. My father fulfills all of Hashem's decrees."

The same held true for Harav Ovadia, concluded Rav Hizkiya. More amazing than any miracles Harav Ovadia effected was his zeal to follow the statutes of Hashem unflinchingly, never veering off the path of piety and diligence he had blazed for himself from the time he was a young child.

CHAPTER TWENTY-SEVEN
THE POWER OF A POSEK

ALTHOUGH HARAV OVADIA'S POLICY THROUGHOUT his life was to rule with *koha d'heteira* — literally, the power of leniency — secular media and even some religious sources would point to certain *piskei halacha* he issued in his later years as a sign that he had somehow become "radicalized." This contention could not have been farther from the truth.

We have discussed Harav Ovadia's approach to halacha sporadically throughout the book, but as Rav David Yosef put it, "No volume about Abba could be complete without a chapter dedicated to his approach to *psak*."

PERHAPS THE CLEAREST MISSION STATEMENT HARAV OVADIA ever delivered was in a media interview he granted less than four months before his passing, on the day his son Rav Yitzchak was elected to the position of Rishon LeZion, Sephardic Chief Rabbi of Israel.[1]

Koha D'Heteira

Channel 10's interviewer, a non-religious Jew, asked, "What does the rav expect from Rav Yitzchak in the capacity of chief rabbi?

---

1. Parts of this interview, especially sections in which Harav Ovadia used long passages from the Torah to express himself, have been paraphrased.

Harav Ovadia reciting *Nishmat* upon hearing of his son Rav Yitzchak's election to the position of Rishon LeZion

What is a chief rabbi expected to do for the people, for the country, for society, for Torah?"

"My friend, what is the job of the chief rabbi?" Harav Ovadia asked rhetorically. "He teaches Torah to the nation. He does not sit in his own house; rather, like Moshe Rabbeinu, he goes to the people, as the verse states: וַיֵּרֶד מֹשֶׁה מִן הָהָר אֶל הָעָם, *Moshe descended from the mountain to the nation* (*Shemos* 19:14).

"The chief rabbi must be full of *ahavat Yisrael*," Harav Ovadia added. "He must love people and draw them close to the Torah. Without love, it is impossible to do anything."

Turning to the newly elected Rav Yitzchak, he said, "You have to have compassion for the oppressed, for the dejected."

Harav Ovadia went on to exhort Rav Yitzchak to help women in difficult marriages, and to be particularly dedicated to freeing *agunot*, as he himself had done.

When the interviewer then mentioned that *koha d'heteira* had always been Harav Ovadia's "motto," the Rav explained that it is easy for a *posek* to rule stringently on all matters, because if he's ever in doubt, it's safer to rule that way.

That easy approach is not the one to use when one must rule for the public, Harav Ovadia explained on many occasions. Rather, a *posek* must use his broad knowledge to try to help as many people as possible follow the Torah.

IN THIS INTERVIEW, HARAV OVADIA SUCCINCTLY EXPRESSED what he had been working to accomplish in the seventy-odd years since he had begun to issue halachic rulings.

Knowledgeable, Not Flippant

Never did a lenient ruling arise out of flippancy or out of disregard for the Torah's prohibitions; on the contrary, he was extremely careful when issuing a lenient ruling. Rather, using the *koha d'heteira* meant that he would go to the greatest lengths to plumb a given topic so that if there was legitimate reason to rule leniently, he could do so.

> *Rishon LeZion Rav Shlomo Moshe Amar relates that on one occasion in which he visited Harav Ovadia to discuss a sh'eila, Rav Moshe Yosef requested a favor of Rav Amar. He handed him a belt and said, "In France, there is a problem with carrying house keys on Shabbat because there is no eruv, and the people have created a belt buckle into which they insert their house key, holding the belt in place. This has been the practice for decades, but recently people started to claim that one may not use this device, because it is considered a form of carrying. They sent a sample of this belt for Abba to examine. Can you show it to him and discuss the matter with him?"*
>
> *Rav Amar gladly agreed.*
>
> *Harav Ovadia took one look at the belt and said, "Maran [the Beit Yosef] rules that one may not use such a belt on Shabbat."*
>
> *Sensing that Rav Amar had some hesitation regarding this ruling, he asked, "Do you feel otherwise?"*
>
> *"Perhaps we can differentiate between the belt Maran was referring to and this one," suggested Rav Amar. "Maran might be referring to a belt that is usable without the key; the key is added to the belt only to allow it to be carried on Shabbat. In this case, however, it seems that the key is an integral part of the belt, which cannot be buckled at all without the key. Perhaps in this case Maran would agree that one may use the belt on Shabbat?"*
>
> *Rav Ovadia did not address Rav Amar directly, but instead turned to his bookcase, lost in thought. "Maran says*

that one may not use a key on a belt, and Rav Shlomo Amar wants to differentiate [between different types of belts]." He repeated this sentence three times, then turned back to Rav Amar and said, "What else did you want to discuss?"

Rav Amar left that day with an answer to the sh'eila he had come to discuss, but he did not receive a conclusive answer regarding the belt.

"I knew," he related, "that Harav Ovadia wanted to think about what I had suggested.

"Two days later, I found out that he had instructed Rav Moshe to notify those who had sent the belt that they could use it; he had accepted my suggestion."

This anecdote, concludes Rav Amar, illustrates Harav Ovadia's approach to *psak*. On one hand, he would not rule on any halachic matter without giving it due diligence — especially if it involved a possible contravention of a ruling by Maran, the Beit Yosef. If there was a sound halachic reason to be lenient, however, then Harav Ovadia would rule that way, even if that was not his initial impression.

That approach did not change at any point in his seven decades as a *posek*. Whether as the newly elected Rishon LeZion — when he would not be bullied into issuing a *heter* for those who were halachically barred from marrying[2] — or as the father of the newly elected Rishon LeZion, who delineated his approach to *psak* to the next generation, his message was the same: A rav's job is to learn the *sugyot* at hand and issue halachic rulings. If there is a valid way to rule leniently, the rav should use the power invested in him to do so. But if not, he cannot depart from the Torah.

No "Rabbinic Will, Rabbinic Way"

IN MODERN TIMES, SOME HAVE ARGUED THAT "WHERE there's a rabbinic will, there's a rabbinic way" — in other words, if rabbanim would decide to "solve problems," they could permit anything the public wants. Harav Ovadia is proof that no such panacea exists. Yes, he was committed to finding

---

2. See p. 366.

solutions to thorny halachic issues, but only within the framework of valid halacha, and only after deep deliberation.

When no *heter* could be found, Harav Ovadia stood firm and refused to fabricate a leniency. Nor did he balk at encouraging stringency when he deemed that the correct halachic approach.

Already in Volume Two of *Yabia Omer*, released when he was still in his 30s, Harav Ovadia embarked on a lifelong quest to encourage people to keep Shabbat until Rabbeinu Tam's later *zman* (time).[3] Similarly, as electricity gained widespread use in Eretz Yisrael, *poskim* grappled with the *sh'eila* of whether electricity could be used on Yom Tov. Harav Ovadia ruled unequivocally that one may not turn on or off an electrical current on Yom Tov.[4]

Clearly, the concept of *koha d'heteira adif* has its limits. Harav Ovadia's lenient rulings during his long "career" as a *posek* were not issued by default, Heaven forbid, or to prove that he could rule leniently on any issue. Arriving at the correct halacha was a rigorous, absolute process that could end in either leniency or stringency — and could be determined only inside a *beit midrash*.

Hawk or Dove?

ONE OF THE AREAS IN WHICH HARAV OVADIA'S STANCE WAS most commonly misconstrued was his approach to Israel's security. Like every other public position the Rav took, his position on security issues could only be understood correctly by those who appreciated him as a man of halacha.

During the late 1970s, while serving as the Sephardic chief rabbi, he issued a series of *piskei halacha* that took the country by storm. In highly publicized *shiurim*, he ruled that Israel should cede territory in order to make peace with its Arab neighbors.[5]

Although Harav Ovadia made it amply clear that his *psak* was based on the halacha that preventing *any* bloodshed took

---
3. *Orah Haim* 21. Rabbeinu Tam ruled that full nightfall occurs long after the sun dips under the horizon, and one must refrain from doing any *melacha* that would be prohibited on Shabbat until that time.
4. Ibid. 26.
5. There was wide consensus among *gedolei Torah* on this issue. Similar rulings were issued over the years by Rav Shach and Rav Yosef Shalom Elyashiv, among others.

precedence over retaining territory in Eretz Yisrael — and not on some hidden peace agenda or on love and compassion for the Arabs — the left-leaning media distorted his views, labeling him a "dove." His counterpart, Ashkenazi Chief Rabbi Goren, countered with a ruling that not one inch of territory captured during Israel's wars could be ceded for peace.

Within fifteen years of his first rulings on these matters, Harav Ovadia would make even greater waves by joining Israeli coalitions led by "peaceniks" such as Yitzhak Rabin and Shimon Peres — both of whom were great admirers of Harav Ovadia. These alliances were outgrowths of his position that forging peace agreements with Arab neighbors would reduce Jewish bloodshed.

Right-wing groups took to protesting outside Harav Ovadia's house each time he issued such a ruling, but he would not back down. This was a question of halacha, not a decision that should be influenced by nationalistic stirrings. If Israel was halachically required to give human life precedence over land, he would not be deterred from ruling that way.

In the last decade of his life, when Harav Ovadia instructed Shas's Knesset members to vote against peace initiatives — and even threatened to pull these MKs out of coalition agreements that

Discussing security matters with Yitzhak Rabin before releasing his ruling that Israel should cede land if that would help achieve peace with the Arabs

leaned toward signing peace agreements — the media once again misunderstood the basis for his stance. They either interpreted his new positions as a reversal of his previous rulings, or, more cynically, as a way of placating voters who would have voted Likud rather than Shas had he maintained his "dovish" position.

In truth, as Harav Ovadia explained publicly on numerous occasions, nothing had changed in his position; it was the facts on the ground that had changed. When he had issued his first rulings on security matters, it had seemed that diplomatic initiatives would reduce Jewish deaths — and, in fact, the peace agreements signed in 1979 with Egypt and in 1994 with Jordan did lead to a reduction in hostilities and bloodshed. Harav Ovadia continued to maintain throughout his life that the Israeli government should try to sign a peace accord with Syria to further secure Israel's borders.

The only diplomatic initiatives upon which Harav Ovadia had soured were the on-again, off-again negotiations with the Palestinians, whose leaders would consistently torpedo any peace agreement and resort to terrorism at any opportunity. Even after the "peace process" began, with the signing of the Oslo Accords in

Viewing a map of the Golan with Ariel Sharon.
Though many thought he was a dove-turned-hawk, Harav Ovadia's worldview was informed only by halacha, not nationalistic ambitions.

1993, hundreds of Israelis were killed in terror attacks. Although Harav Ovadia had instructed Shas to back the Rabin-led government on that initiative, when he saw that the resulting agreement had not succeeded in reducing Jewish bloodshed, he realized that the time was not ripe for peace with the Palestinians. If the peace process was not reducing bloodshed, there was no longer any halachic justification for handing over territory to the Palestinians.

To those unwilling to listen to Harav Ovadia's own explanations of his positions, he might have seemed like a dove-turned-hawk. But his own unequivocal statements on security matters prove that as in every other realm, Harav Ovadia's position on security issues was determined by only one standard: that of the Torah, as spelled out in halacha.

The "Minor" Matters

BECAUSE HARAV OVADIA'S WORLDVIEW WAS SHAPED SOLELY by halacha, he did not limit his attention to major decisions such as those related to Israel's security. No matter how hectic his life became, he continued to tend to matters that others might have considered insignificant, for halacha does not differentiate between "major" and "minor."

> On 5 Iyar 5497/1737, the Torah leaders of Yerushalayim signed on a statute that no bachelor over the age of 20 could reside in Yerushalayim.[6] They did not invent this statute; it had existed for centuries. In their times, however, it had become increasingly common for young men to claim that they could not afford to marry before the age of 20, and they would continue to live in Yerushalayim beyond their 20th birthday.
>
> These 18th-century Torah leaders reaffirmed the earlier statute, writing that any bachelor who did not marry before Rosh Hodesh Elul of that year would be required to leave the city, and that the lay leaders of Yerushalayim would be

---

6. Though the reason for this is not spelled out in the statute, it appears to be due to a dissonance between bachelorhood and the holiness of Yerushalayim; see the periodical *Beit Hillel*, Iyar 5762, p. 33.

Harav Ovadia formed a *beit din* with Rav Yehuda Tzadka (C) and Hacham Benzion Abba Shaul (R) to annul an old statute.

charged with the task of banishing these bachelors from the city if they did not leave of their own accord.

Harav Ovadia wrote[7] that when he learned of this ordinance, he immediately conferred with his two lifelong friends, Rav Yehuda Tzadka and Rav Benzion Abba Shaul, the two heads of Yeshivat Porat Yosef, and noted that many young men learning in their yeshiva — and in many other yeshivot — were residing in Yerushalayim despite each having passed his 20th birthday.

Although no one was attempting to enforce this ordinance, Harav Ovadia ruled that it was necessary for a beit din to annul the statute, rather than allowing bachelors over the age of 20 to live in the city in violation of an ordinance enacted by earlier Torah leaders.

After explaining the halachic basis for annulling a statute passed by an earlier beit din, Harav Ovadia writes that he and his two colleagues indeed formed an official beit din to void the statute, thus ensuring that bachelors could live in Yerushalayim without violating a city ordinance.

This issue may have seemed inconsequential or irrelevant. But when it came to halacha, any issue — no matter how weighty, or how trivial — warranted Harav Ovadia's involvement.

---

7. *Yabia Omer*, Vol. 7, *Yoreh Dei'a* 14.

Kulot for Others, Humrot for Himself

A FINAL MISUNDERSTANDING REGARDING HARAV OVADIA'S embrace of the concept of *koha d'heteira adif* was that he was trying to "make life easier" for everyone — as though the Torah made life difficult, Heaven forbid, and he was trying to mitigate that difficulty.

Many areas of Torah have room for stringency as well as for leniency. Those who are extremely committed to Torah and filled with *yirat Shamayim* may *choose* to be stringent in such matters; however, writes Harav Ovadia, a *posek* may not rule that one is *required* to be stringent. He cites proof from the Talmud that if someone brings a chicken to a rav to determine whether it is kosher, and the rav rules stringently even though there is room for leniency, the rav may be halachically liable for the resulting financial loss incurred by the owner of the chicken.

A rav's objective, explains Harav Ovadia, should be to make basic observance of halacha possible for *all*, even those who are not on the level to keep halachic stringencies, and to allow devout Jews to decide for themselves whether to be more stringent.[8]

Accordingly, Harav Ovadia's lenient rulings were for the public, while he himself kept many *humrot* — even on matters on which he had ruled leniently.

> One Shabbat when he was already at an advanced age, Harav Ovadia was visiting a multistory building in Yerushalayim, and he began to walk up the steps to reach his destination. Someone saw him struggling and said, "There's a Shabbat elevator here. Didn't the rav himself rule that it's permissible to use a Shabbat elevator?"
>
> Harav Ovadia would not hear of taking the Shabbat elevator, however. True, he had ruled that people could use Shabbat elevators, but for himself he was stringent.

---

8. He felt that this policy was extremely important in Eretz Yisrael after the establishment of the State of Israel, because many Jews were willing to extend themselves somewhat in order to keep basic halachot, but would not observe halacha if they viewed it as too taxing. For the sake of these people, Harav Ovadia sought leniencies whenever halacha allowed it. Yet he would also indicate when there was room for stringency, for the sake of those who were interested in going beyond the minimal halachic requirements.

His level of devotion went beyond humrot — sometimes he wouldn't even do something that was absolutely halachically permissible. Rabbanit Margalit passed away during Av, one of the hottest months of the year in Eretz Yisrael. Halacha states that prior to the burial of a deceased person, the immediate relatives of the deceased may not recite any berachot, including those recited over food or drink. Rather, they are to eat without a beracha. At the Rabbanit's funeral, family members urged the 74-year-old Rav to drink, but he just could not bring himself to have something pass his lips without a beracha.

ONE STORY MIGHT JUST CAPTURE HARAV OVADIA'S DEVOTION to the halachic process better than any analysis:

No Visitors Allowed *On Taanit Esther, 13 years before his passing, Harav Ovadia was feeling ill, but he fasted nonetheless. Right before Arvit, three people paid him an emergency visit — Rav Shimon Bitton, the Sephardic Chief Rabbi of Beit Shemesh; the owner of a matza factory in that city; and the head of the workers' union at that factory.*

It seems that an employee at the factory had decided to add some salt to the matzot to make them tastier. There is a dispute in halacha, however, whether matzot with salt may be eaten on Pesah, and whether one may use them at the Seder to fulfill the obligation of eating matza.

"We have eighty workers in this factory," the visitors explained, "and if we can't market these matzot, these eighty workers can't be paid. We might even have to fire all of them because of the financial loss."

After hearing this quandary, the diabetic Harav Ovadia asked for a cup of tea and a cookie, and then instructed his family members, "Please don't let anyone in to see me now. Even if Kissinger comes, tell him I can't see him. I need to look into this sh'eila with peace of mind, and they need an answer by tomorrow morning."

> In a eulogy for the Rav, Rav Benzion Mutzafi could only marvel at this devotion:
>
> "At the age of 80, without having ingested more than a cookie and some tea after a fast, he went into his study, and by 3 o'clock in the morning he had written a teshuva permitting the use of these matzot b'diavad (ex post facto).[9]

No shortcuts, no easy way out. Just an elderly, ailing rav, alone in his study with mountains of *sefarim*, trekking through the halachic process that has sustained the Jewish people for millennia, in order to explore whether there was a valid basis to keep a factory and its eighty workers afloat.

---

9. The *teshuva* is printed in *Yabia Omer*, Vol. 9, *Orah Haim* 43.

Chapter Twenty-Eight
A Visit With Maran

MANY PEOPLE STRUGGLE TO FIND SPACE FOR Torah learning in a schedule packed with business and family obligations. For Harav Ovadia, the challenge was exactly the opposite: Because studying Torah was his default state, he had to struggle to find time for all his other obligations.

> *Harav Ovadia also grappled with the question of how to allocate time for his various methods of disseminating Torah. He writes[1] that at one point, he was unsure whether he should continue to invest a significant amount of time into delivering shiurim, or whether he should focus primarily on writing sefarim. The former might have a more marked effect in the short term, but the latter have a "shelf life" — generations down the line, people would still be able to benefit from his sefarim.*
>
> *One night, writes Harav Ovadia, he dreamt that the Ben Ish Hai visited his home, his face shining like the sun, and*

---
1. Introduction to *Taharat Habayit*, Vol. 2.

entered his room and sat down by the desk, where one of Harav Ovadia's sefarim lay open. The Ben Ish Hai flipped through the sefer — "I think it was a volume of Yabia Omer," Harav Ovadia writes — and when he finished, he said, "Very good."

Then he asked Harav Ovadia whether he was still giving shiurim to the public. Harav Ovadia answered that he indeed was, often in tandem with Rav Yehuda Tzadka (who was related to the Ben Ish Hai). He added, however, that his shiurim were interfering with his ability to publish his writings.

In response, the Ben Ish Hai uttered the verse: טוֹב אֲשֶׁר תֶּאֱחֹז בָּזֶה וְגַם מִזֶּה אַל תַּנַּח אֶת יָדֶךָ, *It is best to grasp the one and not let go of the other (Kohelet 7:18). In this verse, King Shlomo advises a person not to limit his efforts to one endeavor, but rather to invest in many endeavors simultaneously. The Ben Ish Hai explained that Hashem has great pleasure when the masses hear words of Torah and are spurred to teshuva; each individual who does teshuva is, in fact, an entire universe.*

Harav Ovadia would spend hours with yeshiva students to encourage them to grow in Torah. Here he is seen blessing Daniel Weiss, son of Mr. Joe Weiss.

> *Harav Ovadia understood this dream to mean that he should continue delivering shiurim while writing his sefarim.*

Aspects of Harav Ovadia's life that to others may have seemed of paramount importance — such as making decisions for the Shas party — were actually less significant in his eyes, and were therefore confined to a specific time. For 10 minutes after Shaharit, he would sit with Shas leaders, most of whom prayed with him every day. During that short window, he would hear their reports and answer their questions. Immediately afterward, he would return to his learning, not to be disturbed again that day with political issues unless it was an emergency.

Yet despite his use of every second to study Torah, Harav Ovadia loved receiving visitors, because he loved the everyman. Even secular reporters seeking to do an exposé on Harav Ovadia couldn't help but note his love for his fellow Jews.[2]

As Rav David Yosef explains, Harav Ovadia's affection for other Jews was not the fluffy, campaign-slogan *"ahavat Yisrael,"* but rather a deep-seated concern that spanned all segments of society. Whether it was a recent Yemenite immigrant who needed help with a halachic matter or a Hassidic Jew who needed a salvation; a soccer team seeking a blessing for success or a young yeshiva student coming for his first audience with Maran, every Jew was welcomed and cherished. But while all Jews were welcome, the latter were the ones to whom Harav Ovadia was willing to devote an inordinate amount of time.

On Friday afternoons, young yeshiva students would stream into his home. One would request that Harav Ovadia sign the *sefarim* he had authored and the young man was starting to learn; another would ask for a *beracha* for *hatzlaha* in his studies; a third would want to have his picture taken with Maran; and a fourth would have a Torah question. Harav Ovadia received them all patiently — perhaps because he knew the experience could prompt these youths to strive for greater heights in Torah.[3]

---

2. A reporter for *Panim Amitiyot*, a television program produced and hosted by secular, often anti-Torah reporters (see p. 71, fn. 16), couldn't help but exclaim, "You can see how this elderly Rav just craves the company of every Jew."
3. The younger generation's reverence toward the Rav took on whimsical proportions around

A young man receives a trademark playful slap from Harav Ovadia.

A typical visit would end with what would be become known as "the Rav's chap'hot." For some unknown reason, as he blessed each person before he left, Harav Ovadia would give playful slaps on the cheek, often reciting the words: "אֹרֶךְ יָמִים בִּימִינָהּ, Length of days is at its right," as he slapped the right cheek, and the end of the verse:"בִּשְׂמֹאולָהּ עֹשֶׁר וְכָבוֹד, at its left, wealth and honor,"[4] while slapping the left.

No one escaped these slaps — there are videos of him slapping such notables as Prime Minister Binyamin Netanyahu and longtime friend and Israel's president, Shimon Peres — and people considered them a great honor. Many eulogizers actually bemoaned the fact that they would no longer be able to receive them.[5]

The slaps were so ubiquitous, in fact, that when former Defense Minister Binyamin Ben-Eliezer, a prominent government official, was asked by an interviewer the day after

---

Purim time each year, when stores throughout Israel would sell an extremely popular costume called *tahposet Harav Ovadia* (the Harav Ovadia costume), complete with a *glima* (robe), special hat, beard, and... sunglasses.

4. *Mishlei* 3:16.
5. The story is told of a visitor who apparently did not know about the slaps he would receive at the end of his visit, and when the Rav slapped him, he looked up indignantly and said, "Why is the rabbi slapping me? How would the rabbi feel if I would slap him?" Those surrounding Harav Ovadia gasped, shocked that someone would challenge him so insolently. Harav Ovadia, on the other hand, delighted in the man's question, for he was thrilled that someone felt comfortable addressing him so directly and openly.

Harav Ovadia's passing, "What did you get from Harav Ovadia?" his response was, "First of all, in the course of decades, I received hundreds of slaps on my cheek!"

HARAV OVADIA DID NOT LIMIT HIS ATTENTION TO ADULTS and teenagers; he would try to build the confidence of younger children as well.

Never Too Young

Rav Moshe Hizkiya, Rav of Kiryat Herzog, related that when he was a child of about nine, his family moved into the Tel Arza neighborhood of Yerushalayim, near Harav Ovadia's home. The first day that he prayed in the same beit knesset as the Rav, the latter approached him while removing his tallit and tefillin and asked this young child what his name was, who his father was, and all sorts of other questions. When he finished, he said, "Please come to pray with us every day."

Over half a century later, Rav Hizkiya still recounts that warm greeting from a then-much-younger Harav Ovadia and how important it made him feel.

Even in public forums, where some might have perceived it as a lack of honor for the Rav to spend his time answering questions from children, Harav Ovadia had endless patience for his young admirers. On one occasion, he even found a way to publicly console a child when the answer to his question was not what he wanted to hear.

As chief rabbi, Harav Ovadia held public question-and-answer sessions at which anyone could ask a sh'eila and receive an answer on the spot. During one such session, a nine-year-old approached the microphone. In the recording of this event, the moderator can be heard trying to control his laughter as he asks, with no small hint of sarcasm, "Only nine and you already have a sh'eila?"

Harav Ovadia, on the other hand, took the questioner extremely seriously.

The child asked, "I feel that at nine, I'm already physically capable of fasting the entire Yom Kippur. My father feels that it is unnecessary, and he will not allow it. Am I required to listen to my father?"

Rav Ovadia first explained that according to Shulhan Aruch, a child his age is not allowed to fast a full day. Before concluding his answer, however, Harav Ovadia added, "If one desires to perform a mitzva and is unable to follow through in action, he is credited as if he did it."

Although the child would ultimately have to eat on Yom Kippur against his own wishes, he would still have the feeling that he had done something special to honor the day.

Investing in the Future

HARAV OVADIA APPARENTLY FELT THAT AS THE NEXT GENERATION of Torah Jews, the youth of today deserve the attention of the *gadol hador* no less than the adults.

Renowned lecturer R' Menachem Nissel, who lives in the Har Nof neighborhood where Harav Ovadia resided during the last twenty years of his life, relates that he once spoke at his Shabbat table about the importance of having respect for all Torah leaders, not only those of one's own sector.

After hearing his father's dvar Torah, one of the Nissel boys felt that he and his friend should really ask Harav Ovadia for forgiveness, because they had repeated a baseless claim against him. One day, on the way home from school, they walked up to the door at HaKablan 45 and told the attendant who opened the door why they had come. The attendant felt that Harav Ovadia would want to meet them, so he asked them to wait. He went inside, and was quickly joined at the door by Harav Ovadia himself. The elderly Rav welcomed the two children inside, waving off their apology but inviting them in for some cake, some berachot, and his characteristic pinches on the cheek — making them feel, as R' Menachem puts it, like a million dollars.

THE LIFE OF A *GADOL* IS NOT ONLY ABOUT SMILING FACES posing for pictures; it is often filled with a great deal of pain.

Feeling the Pain
Myriads would come to Harav Ovadia for *berachot*, unburdening their hearts of the *tzarot* they were suffering. What they didn't realize was that while they left his presence feeling encouraged and uplifted, Harav Ovadia himself was pained by their stories long afterward. In fact, at times when he was ill, his family could not allow visitors to meet him, because his emotional involvement in their *tzara* might be too taxing on him.

> *A rav of a large South American community suffered a horrific tragedy: his three-year-old daughter was hit by a car and killed in front of her mother's eyes. The mother was so shattered by the loss that she could no longer live in that community, and the couple decided to move back to their native Israel to try to piece their lives back together.*
>
> *They lived in Bnei Brak for several years, until finally they felt ready to move back to South America. But before they could make the move, another daughter caught a rogue bacterial infection and died several days later.*
>
> *When Harav Ovadia heard about this second tragedy, he decided to console the mourners, even though he did not know them personally.*
>
> *When he entered the shiva home, the mother began to wail uncontrollably. Harav Ovadia managed to offer the mourners consolation, but for the next two days, each time he thought about the tragedy he began to cry.*

ALTHOUGH CLOSING HIS GEMARA WAS ONE OF THE HARDEST things for Harav Ovadia to do, when another Jew was in need, he

One Life Leads to Another
would drop everything and run. Once, his willingness to help one Jew enabled him to save the life of one of his closest friends.

> *Approximately thirteen years before Harav Ovadia passed away, his close friend Hacham Baruch Ben-Haim[6] sustained*

---
6. See p. 106.

a serious heart attack and lay unconscious in the hospital for several months.

A medical referral specialist in New York spoke to his doctors at length and then informed the family that the main problem was not with Hacham Baruch's heart, but with his lungs. There was only one doctor in the New York area who could treat this problem, and he worked far from the hospital in which Hacham Baruch lay. The family called this doctor and asked whether he would be willing to examine Hacham Baruch, but he demurred, explaining that he had no time. Even when they offered a large sum of money for his services, he could not be swayed. His patient roster was simply too full to make time to examine someone in a faraway hospital.

The family was wondering what to do next, when Rav David Yosef, who happened to be in New York at the time and was privy to their conversation, asked whether he could perhaps speak to the doctor, who, he had heard, was a nonreligious Jew. "Perhaps I can speak to his Jewish heart," Rav David suggested.

He called the doctor and asked, "Have you heard of Harav Ovadia Yosef?"

"Certainly," replied the doctor.

"Well, his childhood friend is lying the hospital, unconscious, and I'm certain that Rabbi Yosef would greatly appreciate if you could examine his friend."

"Oh, he's Rabbi Yosef's friend?" the doctor asked in surprise. "I'm coming right down."

Thankfully, the doctor was able to diagnose Hacham Baruch correctly. Within a few weeks he had returned to full function, and he lived for another two years.

When the family called the doctor's office to settle payment, they were astonished to hear that the doctor did not want money. "I didn't do this for pay," he explained. "I owed this to Rabbi Yosef."

He then shared a fascinating tale.

Several years earlier, this doctor's son had visited Israel, and wound up in the wrong place at the wrong time: While he was in Yerushalayim, a terrorist detonated a suicide bomb right beside him.

The doctor got a call that his son had been rushed to Hadassah Hospital in critical condition. He booked the next flight to Israel and ran to his son's bedside, but despite his medical knowledge, there was little he could do for his son.

Having heard about great rabbis and their power of blessing, he asked someone to arrange for him to visit some of these rabbis. Each rabbi whose house he visited empathized with his plight and promised to pray for his son. When he reached Harav Ovadia's home, the Rav listened to him, and then closed his Gemara and told his driver, "Come, we're going to Hadassah."

When they reached this young man's room, Harav Ovadia began to recite chapter after chapter of Tehillim, with tears streaming down his face. After 15 minutes of crying the words of Tehillim, he blessed the young man to have a refua sheleima, and left.

"My son had a miraculous recovery," the doctor related. "And if Rabbi Yosef, who was thoroughly engrossed in his books when I walked in, was willing to drop everything and run to my son's bedside, didn't I owe him the same in return when his friend's life was on the line?"

"When I told my father what had transpired, he was overwhelmed with emotion," concludes Rav David Yosef. "He said, 'Who would have thought that my visit to that boy's bedside would lead to Hacham Baruch's recovery?'"

Family Time

INTERESTINGLY, GRANDSONS WHO DELIVERED *HESPEDIM* on Harav Ovadia presented what seemed to be conflicting views of their grandfather. Some highlighted the fact that he devoted time to all members of Klal Yisrael, not merely to his own family, while others spoke about the particularly loving bond he maintained with his family. Perhaps with great men, both are true: they are able to give to the public without their family feeling left out.

> *A grandson recounted that when his wife was expecting, she was not feeling well, and he went to ask Harav Ovadia whether she should fast on Yom Kippur.*
>
> *Harav Ovadia replied that it was the grandson's job to ensure that it would be possible for her to fast, even if he had to remain at home all day to enable her to stay in bed.*
>
> *As the grandson was about to leave, Harav Ovadia summoned him back, and launched into a long pep talk about how important it was to take care of his wife in general, not just on Yom Kippur, giving him specific instructions how to ease her burden during those difficult months.*

With his grandsons, Harav Ovadia could develop the type of bond that came most naturally to him: Torah study. But he made a point of devoting time to his granddaughters as well.

> *Rabbanit Yehudit Yosef relates that when he lived with her family during the last twenty years of his life, he was the one who signed all the children's report cards — reveling in the accomplishments of the girls and praising them as much as he did the boys.*

Harav Ovadia converses with a granddaughter.

When he was ailing in his last months, he was extremely concerned about his granddaughter's shidduchim, and would frequently ask how things were going. In the end, he was able to celebrate the engagement of that granddaughter together with the family, but he passed away a day before her scheduled wedding date.

Throughout the years he spent in the home of Rav Moshe and Rabbanit Yehudit, he educated their boys in the mitzva of zimun for Birkat Hamazon. The family's youngest children were twins, a boy named Aharon and a girl named Efrat. When they grew old enough to answer to zimun, he would call both of them to zimun so as not to make Efrat feel left out.

A Package From Home

HARAV OVADIA KEPT TRACK OF GRANDCHILDREN WHO WERE away from home as well, and even made an effort to send one a care package.

An American boy learning in a yeshiva in Yerushalayim wanted to receive Harav Ovadia's blessing before returning to the United States for Pesah. He signed up for an appointment and took his friend along with him for the visit. Harav Ovadia seated them right beside him and asked, "Which one of you is going to America?"

When the fellow indicated that he was the one traveling, Harav Ovadia asked, "Are you going to Brooklyn?"

"Yes," the boy answered.

"Do you know of the Ateret Torah yeshiva?" he asked.

"Certainly," the boy replied. "I learned there last year."

"Do you know my grandson who goes by the same name as I do, Ovadia Yosef?"

"I don't," replied the boy, "but I'm sure I can track him down easily."

"Would you be able to bring him something from me?"

"Certainly."

The two boys wondered what the gadol hador might want to send to his grandson. A recently published sefer? Perhaps a personal letter?

To their surprise, Harav Ovadia pulled out a kosher-for-Pesah chocolate bar. "Please tell my grandson that this is from his grandfather," he said.

So great, yet so simple.

Trips Abroad

HARAV OVADIA DIDN'T LIMIT HIS CONTACT TO PEOPLE WHO came to him; he traveled throughout Eretz Yisrael — and beyond — to encourage his fellow Jews toward growth in Torah and mitzvot.

During the course of his years as chief rabbi and in the decade that followed, he made trips to all major North American Sephardic communities, including annual visits to Brooklyn, New York; Deal, New Jersey; and Los Angeles, California.[7] He also traveled to Mexico, Argentina, England, France, and Spain, in addition to official state visits he paid to Arab countries such as Iran (in 1979) and Egypt (in 1989).

The purpose of these trips was not only to bring *hizzuk* to the local communities, but also to lobby foreign governments to support the interests of Israel and world Jewry.

Beginning in the 1970s, when Syrian Jews were being mistreated by both the regular citizenry and the government, he pleaded with any government official he met to see to the humanitarian needs of the Jews remaining in Syria.

In Egypt, he met with President Hosni Mubarak and beseeched him to divert a highway whose planned construction would have uprooted a Jewish cemetery. Although Mr. Mubarak originally raised a sad comparison, noting that in Israel, too, the government sometimes uproots cemeteries to build roads — Harav Ovadia eventually succeeded in convincing him to change the highway's route. He blessed him with success, and Mr. Mubarak was clearly moved by the blessing.[8]

---

7. See Chapter 29.
8. After Mubarak was overthrown in early 2011, the sickly former president was ordered to stand trial for a host of charges, both financial and criminal. During the trial, in appreciation

Harav Ovadia visits a Jewish cemetery in Cairo, while on a trip during which he lobbied Egyptian president Hosni Mubarak not to move the cemetery so a highway could run through it.

On trips abroad during the 1970s and 1980s, when Soviet Jews were still barred from practicing Judaism or leaving Russia, Harav Ovadia met with any government officials he could and urged them to use their influence to free Soviet Jewry. He also addressed a massive protest rally in New York held on behalf of Jews trapped behind the Iron Curtain.

BUT THE MOST MARKED IMPRESSION HARAV OVADIA MADE during his trips abroad was not on the politicians, or even, *l'havdil*, the *gedolei Torah*, who welcomed him warmly and were invariably astounded by his Torah knowledge. It was, rather, on the regular man, woman, and child of the communities he visited. Entire communities would be swept up in excitement as he visited their *batei knesset* and schools,

Sweeping Success

---

for what Mubarak had done in the past to protect Jewish interests, Harav Ovadia prayed for his acquittal and his health. Although Mubarak was originally found guilty on many charges, his appeals were eventually accepted, and he was released in August 2013, to Harav Ovadia's relief.

Chapter Twenty-Eight: A Visit With Maran ☐ 517

A postcard Harav Ovadia and Rabbanit Margalit sent to their children in Eretz Yisrael during one of their trips abroad. The Rabbanit wrote, "Learn well, and don't go outside without a sweater."

Harav Ovadia greets a member of the Syrian community in a Jerusalem hotel.

becoming a role model for many children in those communities and undoubtedly contributing to their subsequent growth in Torah.

"He developed a personal relationship with Sephardim in America," explains Rav Yitzhak Dwek, who was the rav of the Deal,

New Jersey community during the years Harav Ovadia visited America, and hosted him each year. "He wasn't just a leader from a distance. Many American Jews of Syrian descent would go to Eretz Yisrael for midwinter vacation, and he wanted to see all of them. He even rented the hall of a Jerusalem hotel so he could speak to them.

"But he didn't confine his relationship to public appearances. He was a leader of individuals, and kept up a personal relationship with anyone who sought one."

> *David, one of the children awed by Harav Ovadia during his visits to America, eventually achieved his dream: after learning in yeshivot in America and then in Eretz Yisrael, he joined one of the Rav's kollelim. Eventually Harav Ovadia felt that it was time for David to return to America and teach Torah.*
>
> *There was one problem, though: David had a phobia of public speaking. So intense was this fear that as a child, he could barely deliver a dvar Torah in his own home. When he returned to America to deliver a model lesson, he walked into a classroom full of children and immediately froze. He ran out of the room and straight to the school office, where he frantically dialed Eretz Yisrael. Although it was generally extremely difficult to reach Harav Ovadia by phone, when Harav Ovadia heard who it was, he came to the phone quickly.*
>
> *"Don't worry," Harav Ovadia soothed him. "I had the same problem as a young man. Walk back into the room, and make believe that there are pillows on each chair in the room instead of children."*
>
> *Harav Ovadia spent long minutes on the phone calming him and urging him to return to the classroom.*
>
> *"When I got back to Eretz Yisrael," continues David, "he made me serve as the hazzan in his minyan and lead the Pirkei Avot, to ease me out of my phobia."*
>
> *Today, David is a successful rabbi, having been coached by the gadol hador out his fear of public speaking.*

Most remarkable, notes David, is that this story happened when Harav Ovadia was over 80, learning countless hours each day, while running many other important endeavors in 10-minute slots he created for them. Yet he had all the time in the world to ensure that a beloved student would succeed in his subsequent career as a rebbi.

CHAPTER TWENTY-NINE
HARAV OVADIA GOES ABROAD

WHEN HARAV OVADIA BECAME RISHON LeZion, he accepted a responsibility to serve not only the Jews of Israel, but also Sephardic Jews everywhere. From 1974-1994 — until overseas travel became very difficult for him — he traveled to the United States almost every year. Less often he visited communities in Mexico, Panama, Brazil, and Argentina. Wherever he went, his presence was electric. His scholarship, charisma, love for every Jew, and ability to relate to all people on their own level captivated audiences and individuals alike. As one person put it, "He made all of us feel that he was our personal rabbi."

The First Visit to America

ON HIS FIRST VISIT TO AMERICA, HE WAS MET AT KENNEDY Airport by a reverent and enthusiastic entourage of over one hundred people, with several police officers on hand to control the crowd and ensure his safety. When he left the plane, resplendent in his ceremonial garb, he was greeted with song and people pushing to kiss his hand.

The author thanks Rabbi Nosson Scherman, who wrote this chapter, since he had direct access to information about the Sephardic-Syrian community in America.

Rav Ovadia greeted at JFK Airport (Top)

Article in *The New York Times* (Left)

In his public addresses, he spoke in Hebrew and, when necessary, one of the local rabbis would do a simultaneous translation. Many remember the theme from *Tehillim* (20:8) that was repeated at many of the podiums: *Some with chariots and some with horses but we call out with the Name of Hashem, our God.* Actually, this was his message throughout his long career. The mission of the Jewish people is to be strong in our faith that Hashem and Hashem alone is the purpose of our existence, and everything else is secondary. With this message he had invigorated the Sephardic communities of Israel, and now he was setting out to do the same in America and beyond.

(L-R) Rabbi David Ozeirey, Rav Ovadia, and Hacham Baruch Ben-Haim in Cong. Shaare Zion

According to the Audience

FOR GENERAL NON-SCHOLARLY AUDIENCES, THE RAV PEPpered his speeches with stories and humor. When the audience laughed, he smilingly said he knew that the translator had done his job well. He could deliver a complex *shiur* on *Masechet Hullin*, a speech for lay adults, and a talk for schoolchildren, one after another on the same day, and tailor his lectures for the level of each audience, without notes and seemingly without preparation. Especially in farflung communities where observant Jews were relatively few and Torah education was sparse, such visits injected people with pride in their Torah heritage and inspired them to intensify it in their own lives and especially in the education of their children.

During one of his visits to America, he wished to meet President Ronald Reagan to request his assistance on a matter of importance to Sephardic Jews. Mr. Raymond Cohen made the arrangements and escorted him to the Oval Office. Their discussion completed, the Rav blessed the president and Reagan rose and kissed his hand. Even the most powerful man in the world was not immune to the Rav's greatness and charm.

With President Reagan

The Rav speaking at Yeshiva Mikdash Melech in Flatbush

Rav Ovadia with Ellis Safdeye, a prominent supporter of Torah causes, and Hacham Ben-Haim

The Rav Renders Honor

WHEN HE WAS IN THE SEPHARDIC COMMUNITY IN BROOKLYN, which was almost every year, he would visit every yeshiva and speak to the students. In those years, the only Sephardic schools in New York were Ahiezer, Ateret Torah, Magen David, and Mikdash Melech. Today there are many more — and their number and enrollment grow every year. Surely his exhortations about the overriding importance of Torah education, and his affectionate urgings, inspired many parents to choose such schools for their children, and moved many people of means to build and support more Torah institutions.

On Shabbat he would walk to every synagogue in the community and visit the senior rabbis in their homes. He especially relished his time with Hacham Baruch Ben-Haim, rav of Shaare Zion. He was honored like a visiting chief of state and was frequently provided with a police escort. We can imagine the impact he made as he walked through the streets of Flatbush in his *glima* and *mitznefet*, surrounded by adoring congregants, and escorted by New York's Finest.

The Rav with Hacham Ben-Haim and Hacham Yaakob Kassin, Chief Rabbi of the Flatbush Syrian community

Shabbat in a Closet

WHEN HE WAS IN FLATBUSH, HIS HOST WAS RABBI DAVID Ozeirey. As much as people knew about the Rav's extraordinary love of learning and how every minute was precious to him, Rabbi Ozeirey learned that whatever we thought we knew was but a fragment of the truth.

The first Friday the Rav arrived at the Ozeirey home, he asked to see his bedroom. His host took him to the master bedroom, which had been set aside for him and the

Rav Ovadia with his host, Rabbi David Ozeirey, rav of the Yad Yosef Torah Center

Chapter Twenty-Nine: Harav Ovadia Goes Abroad ☐ 525

Rav Ovadia blesses Rabbi Ozeirey with his trademark slap.

Rabbanit. The Rav asked if there was a place for a lamp, so that he could learn without disturbing the Rabbanit's sleep. Rabbi Ozeirey was quiet. The bedroom was not large and there was no room for such a lamp.

But there was a small walk-in closet with a light. Rabbi Ozeirey opened the door and the Rav said the closet would suit his need. Was there a chair? The closet was not big enough for a regular chair, but a folding chair would fit. Excellent. The chair was opened and the Rav took a bag of sefarim into the closet. No table, just a small, not very comfortable chair. Then they went back downstairs to prepare for Shabbat.

Rabbi Ozeirey assumed that Harav Ovadia would learn for a an hour or two before retiring for the night. He was wrong. The Rav was up learning all night — sitting on a narrow folding chair in a tight closet with no ventilation, with his lap as a "table," and the door closed to avoid disturbing the Rabbanit's sleep. The next morning she told the Ozeireys that the Rav never slept on Shabbat; Torah study on the holy day was too precious to be lost to slumber.

Members of the Yad Yosef Torah Center visiting the Rav in Jerusalem. Rabbi David Sutton is second from the left.

In later years Rabbi Ozeirey founded the Yad Yosef Torah Center in Flatbush, where he serves as rav, together with Rabbi David Sutton.

The Rav blesses Yosef Sutton, from the Yad Yosef Torah Center

Visits to Deal

WHENEVER THE RAV WAS IN NEW YORK, HE WOULD VISIT the Sephardic community of Deal, New Jersey. Although it is best known as the summer home of the Flatbush Syrian-Sephardic Jews, Deal and nearby Long Branch are year-round communities, with synagogues, the Hillel Day School, and the thriving Long Branch Kollel, led by Rabbi Shlomo Diamond. The Rav was very proud of the kollel, and regularly delivered a *shiur* to its members.

The Rav with Rabbi Shlomo Diamond, head of the Long Branch Kollel

Funding in Israel

ANOTHER REASON FOR HIS REGULAR VISITS WAS TO RAISE funds for Torah institutions in Israel. As we have seen, much as he avoided losing even a minute from his personal study and writing, he felt equally responsible to give priority to building Torah allegiance and yeshivot in the Land. Wealthy members of the community knew that they would be solicited, but the Rav made them proud to be his partner in his avowed mission of "restoring the crown."

The Rav delivering a *shiur* to the kollel

מכתב ברכה ממרן הרב הראשי ראשון לציון
הגאון ר' עובדיה יוסף שליט"א

עובדיה יוסף
ראשון לציון הרב הראשי לישראל

OVADIA YOSSEF
RISHON LEZION CHIEF RABBI OF ISRAEL

ב"ה, ירושלים ___ כ"ז טבת תשל"ט

לכבוד
המחונך הדגול הרה"ג ר' נחן שידפאן שליט"א.

שלום וישע רב,

שמחתי לשמוע שכבודו עומד להוציא לאור ספר זמירות ופזמונים
לשבת, אשר נהוגים לזמרם בקהלות הספרדים והאשכנזים, כולל תרגום
בלועזית, וליקוט נפלא של ביאורים המקרבים את ישראל לצור מחצבתם.
צוף דבש אמרי נועם מתוק לנפש ומרפא לעצם, אישר חילי' לאורייתא.
והנני מברכו שחפץ ה' בידו יצלח להגדיל תורה ולהאדירה, באורך
ימים ושנות חיים ברוב אושר וכבוד והצלחה.
וברכה לראש משביר, יושב ראש המערכת הרה"ג ר' מאיר יעקב
זלאטרוביץ שליט"א, וליתר חברי המערכת אשר אדרך חיל להפיץ תורה
ויראה בלשון המדוברת לזכות את הרבים, ישלם ה' פעלם ותהי משכורתם
שלמה מעם ה' אלקי ישראל, ויזכר לבני סמיכי חיי אריכי ומזוני
רויחי שובע שמחות וכל טוב.

בכבוד רב,
עובדיה יוסף
ראשון לציון הרב הראשי לישראל.

Harav Ovadia's sense of responsibility to support Torah projects extended not only to Sephardic communities, but to any project that could enhance the glory of Torah. Harav Ovadia encouraged ArtScroll since its inception. Shown is a *Michtav Beracha* dated Tevet 5739/1979, for one of its earliest works, *Zemiros*.

Chapter Twenty-Nine: Harav Ovadia Goes Abroad

It is common in the community that when there is illness or some other crisis, family members will contribute substantial sums as a *z'chut*. Sometimes they will travel to Israel to personally distribute the funds and seek blessings. This, too, is in great measure thanks to the Rav's contagious love of Torah and his teaching that it is not only an obligation, but a privilege to be a partner in the growth of Torah life and learning among their Sephardic brethren.

CHAPTER THIRTY
A LEGACY FOR THE AGES

After Harav Ovadia's passing, many applied to him the accolade: מִיוֹסֵף עַד יוֹסֵף לֹא קָם כְּיוֹסֵף, *From [Rav] Yosef [Karo, the Beit Yosef] to [Harav Ovadia] Yosef, no Yosef arose like this Yosef.*[1]

It is quite possible that no other individual in recent Jewish history caused as much of a sea change among his people as did Harav Ovadia. He was single-handedly responsible for the incredible transformation of Sephardic Jewry from a community that was practically "left for dead" — with most of its members abandoning religion entirely or holding onto a mere modicum of observance — to a burgeoning force in Eretz Yisrael and throughout the world.

In a particularly moving eulogy, after describing the sorry state of Sephardic Jewry in the 1940s and 1950s, Harav Benzion Mutzafi summarized Harav Ovadia's achievements as follows:

> *Who uplifted the status of a ben Torah? Maran.*
> *Who built Talmudei Torah? Maran.*

---

1. This was a variation of the famous tribute to the Rambam: מִמֹּשֶׁה עַד מֹשֶׁה לֹא קָם כְּמֹשֶׁה, *from Moshe [Rabbeinu] until Moshe [ben Maimon, the Rambam], no Moshe has arisen like this Moshe.*

> *Who taught halacha to Klal Yisrael? Maran.*
>
> *Who drew people to the Torah with the sweetness of his words? Maran.*
>
> *Who allowed himself to be humiliated for the sake of the Torah? Maran.*
>
> *Who remained silent while the secular media tried to embarrass him and say vile things about him? Maran.*
>
> *He watched people betray him and engage in all sorts of mudslinging, trying to tarnish his reputation, but he just kept on building Torah, without paying any heed to their efforts.*
>
> *Don't think this came at no cost to his own Torah. He couldn't learn as much as he wanted to, and that was the greatest source of anguish in his life. Just a month before he passed away, when he was in intense pain, he asked me to pray for him and encourage others to pray so he would merit a full recovery.*
>
> *Why? Because he couldn't learn Torah.*
>
> *Learning Torah was the only thing that was important to him, and yet he gave up his own learning time to restore the Torah tradition to Sephardic Jewry.*

No doubt, Harav Ovadia's impact on his generation and generations to come cannot be fully measured today; only the ensuing decades — perhaps even centuries — will reveal the full scope of his influence. Nevertheless, we can already shine the spotlight on several of Harav Ovadia's primary accomplishments, the fruits of which ripened during his lifetime.

Teeming With Torah

AS DOCUMENTED EARLIER, WHEN HARAV OVADIA FIRST started teaching Torah to the public, few were interested in attending his *shiurim*. In order to draw a crowd, he had to devise all sorts of creative methods.[2]

Over the years, his *shiurim* drew ever-larger crowds, which peaked with his signature Motza'ei Shabbat *shiur*. Initially hosted by Beit Knesset Olei Mashhad in Bnei Brak when

---

2. See pp. 234-235.

Harav Ovadia delivering his Motza'ei Shabbat *shiur* at Yazdim that was heard live via satellite feed throughout the world — even in Islamist-controlled Iran

Harav Ovadia was the chief rabbi of Tel Aviv, the *shiur* moved to Beit Knesset HaYazdim when Harav Ovadia moved back to Yerushalayim after being elected Rishon LeZion in 1973.

In 1993, *batei knesset* throughout Eretz Yisrael began to carry a satellite feed of the *shiur*, and it was also broadcast on the radio.[3] The satellite feed was also accessible from other countries; there were reports that Jews in Iran were able to listen to Harav Ovadia's shiur on Motza'ei Shabbat!

Each week, hundreds of listeners filled every nook and cranny of Beit Knesset HaYazdim, while tens of thousands tuned in to listen to the *shiur* live. Yet even after Harav Ovadia's passing, his words

---

3. For many years, there was a battle between "*arutzei hakodesh*" and the Israeli government. *Arutzei hakodesh* (lit., *holy stations*) were radio stations – the most famous of which was "Radio Kol Ha'emet" – that broadcast over pirated radio frequencies. The reason they did so was because the government refused to grant a radio license to a station that would broadcast Torah to the public. The government's frequent attempts to shut down these stations by locating their broadcasting equipment and antennas were met with increasingly cunning ways of evading the authorities, including moving the broadcasting equipment onto ships in the Mediterranean Sea.

Eventually the government relented and issued a license for a religious station, which resulted in the launch of Kol Berama, a Sephardi-run station that broadcasts many Torah programs.

Initially, Rav Ovadia's *shiur* was often broadcast over the *arutzei hakodesh*, but from the inception of Kol Berama in 2009, the *shiur* was broadcast on that station.

at the *shiur* live on, in the form of a treasure trove of recordings that will endure for posterity. In addition, a written transcript of those *shiurim* was published by one of the listeners under the title *MiShiurei HaRashal (HaRishon LeZion)*. The *shiur* itself continues under his son, the Rishon LeZion Rav Yitzchak Yosef.

Taking Responsibility

ALTHOUGH THE MOTZA'EI SHABBAT *SHIURIM* CONTAINED almost exclusively *divrei Torah*, occasionally Harav Ovadia would use the platform to discuss other matters that were weighing on his heart. When the Israeli government passed laws to reduce funding to Torah schools or to impose their own curriculum onto these schools, Harav Ovadia spoke out strongly against the officials responsible for those laws.

At some point, the secular media took to listening to his *shiurim* and pouncing on any quotation that they knew would cause a public uproar.

Though Harav Ovadia generally did not react to their incendiary methods, there was one situation in which he felt that his words had been misunderstood, causing many people to be hurt. Like the true giant he was in every regard, rather than evade the issue, he did something extremely out of character in order to soothe those he had hurt.

> During one Motza'ei Shabbat shiur, Harav Ovadia was talking about gilgulei neshamot, the concept of reincarnation. He mentioned in passing that many of those murdered during the Holocaust had been gilgulim from other neshamot.
>
> The mainstream media in Israel took to the airwaves to protest, claiming that he had profaned the memory of the six million who had perished by asserting that they were somehow "bad" people who deserved to die young. Harav Ovadia was aghast that his statement had been misconstrued, and he told some of his assistants, "I want to stop broadcasting via satellite. The people I speak to in Yazdim

understand me; the media do not. I'm trying to cause a kiddush Hashem, and instead this has brought about a hillul Hashem."

Since so many people were benefiting from the broadcasts, however, Harav Ovadia's assistants succeeded in convincing him to continue the satellite feed, and he decided to repair the damage a different way. Harav Ovadia, who had always shied away from television cameras, even as chief rabbi, invited a television crew into his home — the only time he did so in his life — so that he could explain to the nation what he had meant.

He began by apologizing to anyone who had been hurt by his words, and then clarified the intent behind his statement. "The neshamot who perished were not sinners at all," he said. "On the contrary, they were pure souls that needed to be rectified just a bit more before ascending to the highest levels of Gan Eden, and they had to enter this world for a short time in order to achieve that level."

Though the media continued their search for any statement that would "incriminate" Harav Ovadia in the public's eyes, he had already demonstrated to the Israeli public that he took responsibility for his words, even if they were misconstrued and should never have been reported as incendiary in the first place.

ANOTHER OUTSTANDING PART OF HARAV OVADIA'S LEGACY is his treasure trove of published works — and although he published more than fifty volumes in his lifetime, family members estimate that he left behind notes that could fill an equal number of *sefarim*.

The Written Word

Rav Yisrael Pinhasi, Rosh Kollel Ha'Ari in Bnei Brak and a student of Harav Ovadia during the 1960s, notes that from a logistical standpoint, it should have been impossible to publish the amount of material Harav Ovadia did in a lifetime. "Take out a volume of *Yabia Omer*," says Rav Pinhasi to illustrate his point, "and learn one *teshuva* — just one *teshuva* — but from beginning to end. Just to open all the *sefarim* he quotes can take a full day. Then learn each Gemara, *Rishon*, and *Aharon* he quotes until you understand them clearly — it will take days upon days. And that's **one** *teshuva*. He published ten volumes of such *teshuvot* in *Yabia Omer* alone, besides his numerous other sets of *sefarim*."

While he did publish works on the Pesah Haggada and *Pirkei Avot*, as well as on other topics, Harav Ovadia's primary focus was halacha. Toward the end of his life, he was working as fast as he could to publish more volumes of *Hazon Ovadia*, the first volume of which he had published more than six decades earlier, on *Hilchot Pesah*. He also left behind a partial manuscript for another volume of *Yabia Omer*.

But Harav Ovadia's contribution to Torah publishing wasn't limited to the fruit of his own pen; he was responsible — directly or indirectly — for many, many more *sefarim*. Two of his sons, Rishon LeZion Rav Yitzchak Yosef and Rav David Yosef, rav of Har Nof, have released over fifty volumes between them, all based on their father's *piskei halacha*. Rav Yitzchak's *Yalkut Yosef* and Rav David's *Halacha Berura* are written in different styles, but they both codify Harav Ovadia's *piskei halacha* as well as provide background for those rulings.

In addition to these strictly halachic works, Harav Ovadia continues to influence the *tefillot* of tens of thousands every day, through the many different *siddurim* that incorporate his *nussah* and his rulings.

Harav Ovadia was indirectly responsible for hundreds of other *sefarim*, too. Some of his original students from the 1950s, who began learning with him as simple laymen and could barely sit through the *shiur*, developed into accomplished *talmidei hachamim* and eventually published works of their own.

And aside from his students, there are others who owe their written works to Harav Ovadia, either because his scholarship encouraged them to grow in Torah, or because his overarching knowledge served as an incredible resource for them.

> "Avraham," a fellow from Bnei Brak, received a phone call one day. The caller, "Moshe," said that he was writing a sefer

on Shir HaShirim, and he needed a certain rare handwritten manuscript. "Do you have this manuscript?" Moshe asked.

"I do," Avraham replied. "But very few people know that I have it. How did you know to contact me?"

"Harav Ovadia Yosef told me to call you."

"Harav Ovadia Yosef?" exclaimed a shocked Avraham. "How could he have told you to contact me? I've never met him!"

Was this ruah hakodesh?

Not exactly. Moshe went back to Harav Ovadia and asked him how he had known that Avraham had the manuscript if the latter had never even visited the Rav, let alone mentioned the manuscript to him.

"I don't know him," replied Harav Ovadia. "But a while ago I was reading a Torah periodical that publishes letters from readers, and Avraham wrote a letter that indicated that he had access to this manuscript."

Through this connection, forged as a result of Harav Ovadia connecting two men who were unlikely to have met otherwise, Moshe was able to publish yet another *sefer*. This, too, is part of Harav Ovadia's contribution to Torah publishing.

Halacha and Kashrut

WHEN HARAV OVADIA BEGAN TEACHING TORAH AT THE AGE of 17, even well-meaning religious laypeople would frequently violate halacha out of sheer ignorance or because distorted customs that contravened halacha had been transmitted from one generation to another.

By emphasizing repeatedly just how important it is to study halacha, and by going to the far ends of the country to deliver *shiurim* on halachic topics, he created a renaissance among his Sephardic brethren.

Perhaps the area of halacha in which Harav Ovadia's influence was most significant was the observance of *kashrut*. Although he toiled during his years as chief rabbi — first of Tel Aviv and then

The *kashrut* symbol of Badatz Beit Yosef

of Israel — to ensure that *every* Jew in Israel had access to food that met basic standards of *kashrut*, in his later years he focused on creating a *hechser* that would run on higher standards.

Named Badatz Beit Yosef — apparently because it would follow all of the Beit Yosef's rulings, as one would expect of Harav Ovadia — this *hechsher* became one of the most popular private *hashgahot*.

Harav Ovadia originally appointed non-family members to run Badatz Beit Yosef, but when it faltered during its first few years, he asked his son Rav Avraham to run it. Rav Avraham, who is a very organized and dynamic person, managed to restructure the *hechsher* and turn it into a viable entity.

When Avraham was elected chief rabbi of Holon in 2000, Harav Ovadia asked his youngest son Rav Moshe to take the reins. Badatz Beit Yosef has continued to thrive under Rav Moshe's directorship — earning the trust of its venerable founder.

> *For years, related Rav Moshe,[4] Abba wouldn't eat canned tuna, because it's sold without scales. Unless there is a mashgiah who sees scales on each fish before it is skinned — a costly standard not required by many hashgahot — there's no way to know with certainty that the fish one is eating is actually kosher.*
>
> *One day, I decided to serve tuna manufactured under the Badatz Beit Yosef and see whether Abba would eat it.*
>
> *Abba asked me which mashgiah had traveled abroad to supervise the production of the tuna and what kashrut guidelines I had given him. I answered him in detail, and then something happened that made me very happy: Abba*

---

[4]. In an interview with the Hebrew *Mishpacha* shortly after *shiva* for Harav Ovadia (issue 1127, 13 Heshvan).

began eating the fish — apparently satisfied with the level we had reached on the Badatz.

The existence of Badatz Beit Yosef also enabled Harav Ovadia to implement certain guidelines that he felt everyone should keep, but that he had not been able to enforce in the Rabbanut because doing so would have raised consumer costs and caused some people to purchase nonkosher products. He held, for instance, based on the Beit Yosef, that all Sephardim must eat *halak* (*glatt*).[5] While he could not force the Rabbanut to invalidate meat that was not *halak*, in Badatz Beit Yosef he could insist on it.

Similarly, the Beit Yosef rules that on wine or grape juice produced using certain types of processing, one should recite the blessing of *Shehakol*, not *Borei Pri Hagafen*.

At times, Harav Ovadia's blessing under a huppa would stun the wedding guests. If, while serving as mesader

Harav Ovadia checks the knife of a Badatz Beit Yosef *shohet*, as son Rav Moshe Yosef, the head of the Badatz, looks on.

---

5. *Halak* refers to meat from animals that were found to be free of blemishes called סִירְכוֹת (*sirchot*). Although some authorities maintain that *sirchot* do not render an animal *treif*, the Beit Yosef rules that they do. See *Yabia Omer*, Vol. 5, *Yoreh Dei'a* 3 for insight into just how stringently Harav Ovadia viewed this issue.

kiddushin, he determined that the wine poured into the cup did not require a Hagafen, he would recite Shehakol, true to the ruling of the Beit Yosef.

Today, thanks to Harav Ovadia, many wines produced in Israel — even those produced under different *hashgahot* — carry the words, "Birkato Borei Pri Hagafen af lefi shitat haBeit Yosef — the blessing is *Borei Pri Hagafen* even according to the opinion of the Beit Yosef."

A Living Torah

YET ANOTHER ASPECT OF HARAV OVADIA'S LEGACY WAS HIS boundless love and passion for Torah. Harav Ovadia didn't just learn Torah and teach Torah — Torah was a living entity to him, one that evoked deep feeling. Family members tell astounding stories about how episodes in the Torah could bring forth such strong emotions; it almost seemed as though he were himself experiencing those events.

> One Purim, the family heard Harav Ovadia crying bitterly. Crying? On Purim? What could possibly cause him to cry on this joyous day?
> They ran into the other room and saw that he was reading Megillat Esther and had reached the part of the narrative where Haman's decree is sealed and the Jews of Shushan are sent into mourning.
> To Harav Ovadia, this wasn't a story that occurred in ancient Persia; it was a tragedy he himself was living.

> One night, after Harav Ovadia had slept enough and was getting dressed to start learning, a grandson heard him weeping. He waited until his grandfather was dressed and then asked, "Saba, what happened to you?"
> Harav Ovadia looked at him quizzically, not comprehending his question.
> "Were you crying because you are in pain?" the grandson pressed.

> "No," replied Harav Ovadia, now understanding his grandson's question. "While I was getting dressed, I was thinking about the story of the prophet Ovadia's wife. After he passed away, she was left penniless, and her husband's debtors were hounding her for payment. I was thinking about how painful that must have been for her, and I began to cry."

Emotions weren't reserved only for stories that occurred millennia ago, however. Copious tears also came when he contemplated what he perceived as his shortcomings.

> *People fortunate enough to have prayed with Harav Ovadia on Yom Kippur will never forget the sight of Harav Ovadia reciting vidui, and adding the words "batalti Torah."[6] He would then collapse into a fit of tears, unable to continue for a long time. And this from the man who learned with such hatmada that had anyone else been keeping an accounting of his time, they would undoubtedly have found nary a single squandered moment.*

Although the public was not privy to these displays of intense feeling, an intuitive observer could discern the emotional undercurrent in many of the Rav's statements that caused uproars in Israel's secular media. When Harav Ovadia would speak out in strong terms against politicians who sought to diminish Torah study and mitzva observance in Israel, the media generally interpreted it as a lack of respect for other people's lifestyle choices. More honest observers could listen to those very same statements and perceive the truth: Just as a person who sees someone attack his child or parent would certainly launch a counteroffensive and not watch passively as his loved one is hurt, Harav Ovadia could not bear to see Hashem and His Torah be degraded. To Harav Ovadia, the Torah was alive — as alive as one's own kin[7] — and those seeking to destroy it were enemies that had to be exposed and castigated in the strongest terms.

---

6. Roughly: I have wasted time that could have been spent studying Torah.
7. See Chapter 1 for the incident when Harav Ovadia told Prime Minister Netanyahu that the State's undermining of Torah study was more painful to him than the loss of his son Rav Yaakov.

Exulting in Torah

HARAV OVADIA'S PASSION FOR TORAH DIDN'T CAUSE HIM TO emote only in a melancholy or combative manner; he reacted with equal or greater passion when Torah brought him joy.

Family members recall how, when reciting "Kama maalot tovot," the section of the Pesah Haggada in which we thank Hashem for the miracles He performed for Klal Yisrael from the Exodus through the building of the Beit HaMikdash, Harav Ovadia would get stuck on the words "Venatan lanu et haTorah."

He would hug his Haggada (the closest Torah volume) to his heart and sing, over and over, "Venatan lanu et haTorah, Venatan lanu et haTorah...."

Harav Ovadia's legacy is perhaps most eloquently expressed in a grandson's single most powerful memory of his grandfather. This grandson relates that he once heard Harav Ovadia joyously humming words to himself. At first he couldn't quite comprehend the words, until he realized what had just transpired.

Harav Ovadia had seen one of his young grandchildren learning Torah in another room, and the words he was singing reflected not only his hopes for his own grandchildren, but his vision for every member of Klal Yisrael — all of whom he considered his own kin:

"אֵיזֶה כֵּיף לִי שֶׁיֵּשׁ לִי נֶכֶד שֶׁלּוֹמֵד תּוֹרָה," he sang. "How delightful it is for me that I have a grandchild who learns Torah."

CHAPTER THIRTY-ONE
SUNSET

The last two decades of Harav Ovadia's life were extremely fulfilling: He published more *sefarim* in those years than in his years in the Rabbanut, and he was able to reap the *nahat* of watching both his own family and the broader Sephardic community that he had nurtured grow into beautiful trees that bore delectable fruit.

On a personal level, however, the joy of those years was mitigated by the loss of Rabbanit Margalit, a blow from which he never really recovered.

> *David, a member of New York's Syrian community, merited to have a particularly close relationship with Harav Ovadia. He relates that one Friday night, he was fortunate enough to eat with the Yosefs. As the family sang Eishet Hayil, he noticed tears at the corner of Harav Ovadia's eyes as he thought of his own eishet hayil — and this was fifteen years after she had passed away.*

From the day of her passing, 19 Menahem Av 5754/1994, Harav Ovadia dedicated his every achievement to her memory. Each Torah volume he published from that time on carries words of dedication in her name, Margalit bat Zakiya, and he credits her with his Torah accomplishments, noting how she selflessly and single-handedly tended to the home and the children so he could be free to study Torah.

He had promised her that she would be an equal partner in the merits of the Torah he learned and taught,[1] and now he was fulfilling that promise.

Their marriage, devoted as it was to Hashem's Torah, was exemplary on every level. The two loved and respected each other so much that they could not bear to see the other in the slightest pain. During the periods when Harav Ovadia was under attack for his *piskei halacha* or for defending Torah, she would rise up like a lioness against those who sought to malign her husband. If someone whom she perceived to be undermining Harav Ovadia ever called the house or tried to gain an audience with him, that person was certain to receive an earful from the feisty Rabbanit.

Harav Ovadia was no less defensive of her. When right-wingers began to protest outside his home after he ruled that Israel would be halachically required to cede land for lasting peace,[2] he voiced his objections to these demonstrations at a *shiur* on Motza'ei Shabbat. "If they want to protest against me, that's fine," he said. "But they yell at Rabbanit Margalit when she leaves or enters my home. Why are they bothering her? What did she do wrong?"

Having traversed more than fifty years with the Rabbanit — half a century throughout which they struggled through every challenge together and celebrated every triumph together — Harav Ovadia was understandably crushed by her final illness and passing. At the end of the *shiva*, his children gathered to discuss what they could do to help their father now that the Rabbanit was gone.

Some felt that at a relatively youthful 73, he should remarry. Others felt that a rotation should be established, in which each child would take a turn living with him in his Har Nof apartment, where he had moved from Rehavia a few months before the Rabbanit fell ill.

Rav Moshe Yosef recounted how Harav Ovadia ended the debate.

"During Ima's hospitalization, my family had stayed with Abba, tending to all his needs. But we thought that was a temporary

---
1. See p. 117.
2. See p. 497.

Harav Ovadia was crushed by the loss of his life's partner, with whom he had promised to share the merits of his Torah.

measure, that Ima would recover and we would go back to our own home.

"One evening after Ima's *shiva*, Abba called me into his study. 'I heard what you're discussing,' he said. 'I don't want to remarry. Are you prepared to care for me? Are you willing to come live here?'

"I said to him, 'Of course I want to live here. It's a *z'chut* for me!'

"But then he said, 'It's not your decision to make, it's your wife's, because the burden will fall on her, not on you. Call her.'"

Rabbanit Yehudit[3] filled in the rest of the story.

"When I entered Harav's study, he asked, 'Are you willing to come live here?'

"I started to cry. 'As a descendant of the Abuhatzeira family,' I said, 'serving *talmidei hachamim* comes naturally to me. It will be a *z'chut* for me; I will see this as the crowning achievement of my life.'"

---

3. In an interview.

Harav Ovadia was very pleased with her reply. On the spot, he telephoned his oldest child, Rabbanit Adina Bar-Shalom, and said, "Rav Moshe and Rabbanit Yehudit are staying here to live with me. Please stop planning anything else, and don't look for a *shidduch* for me. This is what I want."

The Home of a Gadol

TENDING TO THE RAV'S NEEDS WAS ONE THING, BUT THE young couple could hardly have been prepared for what living in a *gadol*'s home would entail.

On the one hand, it was extremely difficult for Rav Moshe and Rabbanit Yehudit. The public wanted unfettered access to Harav Ovadia, and their home was often bustling until 2 a.m. with visitors who clamored for an audience with him. But it was the couple's responsibility to care for his health and well-being. Over the years, people who felt slighted when they were told that there were no appointments available hurled all manner of insult on the younger Yosefs. Once, the rhetoric against them became so heated that Harav Ovadia himself summoned Rav Moshe and told him, "Don't worry about people's grievances against you; even after I pass away, I'll be a *meilitz yosher* to defend you."

In the Rav's later years, as his medical condition deteriorated, the couple slept little at night, because they were constantly monitoring his activities to ensure that he wouldn't fall after going into his study to get a *sefer*, as he had in the past.

But no difficulty could overshadow the benefits of living with this Torah giant, even if it took some adjustment.

Harav Ovadia with his son Rav Moshe.

"On the first Shabbat, we sent the children to others," says Rav Moshe Yosef.[4] "We thought that their noise would disturb him. When we were about to start *Kiddush*,

---

4. In an interview with the Hebrew *Mishpacha* shortly after *shiva* for Harav Ovadia (issue 1127, 13 Heshvan).

Abba asked, 'Where is everyone?' We told him that we had divided the children among our relatives.

"'I need the children!' he said. 'I'm not planning to sit here with just a couple.'

"We told him then that we'd keep the children home every Shabbat from then on. In the twenty years that followed, we knew not to send them away for Shabbat unless Saba agreed."

Harav Ovadia was very involved in the *hinuch* of his grandchildren. "Who signed their report cards?" recounts Rabbanit Yehudit. "Saba! We never signed them. He would give them a candy, a kiss on the cheek — and, of course, one of his playful slaps — and praise them for their achievements.

"We have a son who had trouble with reading. When he was supposed to advance to second grade, the principal told us that he had to repeat first grade.

"When Saba heard about this, he was visibly disturbed. One day, I came home and found a tutor, Rav Gadanian, sitting with my son and reviewing *aleph-beit*. 'Who told you to learn with him?' I asked.

"'Forgive me, Rabbanit,' he replied. 'Maran saw me in the *beit knesset* and asked me to help your son with reading so he can advance to second grade.'

"But he didn't suffice with hiring someone else to do the work. One day, we saw Maran himself bent over beside our son, patiently reviewing the *aleph-beit* with him.

"Sure enough, a month later, our son was placed in the second grade, with his peers. What joy Maran had when he heard that he had advanced after all!"

An Exhausting Schedule

EVEN INTO HIS 90S, HARAV OVADIA DIDN'T SHOW ANY SIGNS of slowing down in terms of studying or publishing *sefarim*; if anything, he seemed to be filled with an even greater sense of urgency. He would learn with his librarian, Rav Shealtiel, and with Rav Shitrit. He would write the drafts of his *sefarim* by hand, and Rav Shitrit would type these pages quickly and bring them back to Harav Ovadia for review. "Maran instructed me to be there at 10 a.m. each day," recalls Rav Shitrit. "But by the time I would arrive, he would already be absorbed in a *sefer*. We would learn until 2 p.m., then pray Minha."

Family members recall a constant battle to get the Rav to eat after Minha. Unless someone led him to the dinette, he would simply forget that it was dinnertime and go back to his desk to resume learning. Once he sat down there, it was hard to shake him out of his concentration and get him to eat.

"His best rest each 24-hour period happened between 4 and 7 p.m.," says Rabbanit Yehudit. "After that he would go pray Arvit, receive the public, and then begin learning again."

"We began learning again at 10 p.m.," says Rav Shitrit, "and we were officially supposed to stop at 2 a.m. If Maran noticed that it was 2 o'clock, he would say: 'וּבִשְׁתַּיִם יְעוֹפֵף' — at two, you fly.'[5]

"He learned much later than that, but he felt uncomfortable keeping me so late, so he would send me home. Sometimes, however, he simply wouldn't notice the passage of time, and we would continue learning until 3 or 4 in the morning. When he would suddenly take note of the time, he would apologize profusely for keeping me late."

Rabbanit Yehudit relates that sometimes, if Rav Shitrit offered to stay later, Harav Ovadia would demur, claiming he was tired — even going as far as to head to his bedroom. As soon as his *havruta* left, however, Harav Ovadia would double back to his study and resume learning.

Rav Shitrit relates that Harav Ovadia used this expression regarding sleep: "לֹא בָּא לִי שֵׁנָה — Sleep didn't come to me."

"I never quite understood that expression, until the *shiva*," says Rav Shitrit. "Suddenly it hit me: most people finish their day's work, and *go* to sleep. They bring sleep upon themselves. Maran didn't *go* to sleep; he waited until sleep came to him. Sometimes, it simply didn't come — *lo ba li sheina* — so he didn't sleep that night, but instead continued learning."

Even when he retired to his bedroom, Harav Ovadia wasn't finished learning for the night. He had a small library there, and

---

5. These words appear in the prophet Yeshaya's description (6:2) of the heavenly angels moving. Literally translated, these words speak of the angels using two of their wings to fly. Harav Ovadia, who often used words of *Tanach* or *Hazal* to express himself, used this phrase to convey that at 2 a.m., his *havruta* was free to leave.

he would continue to learn. In his later years, when he was prone to falling and hurting himself, the family installed cameras in his bedroom so that they could see when he rose and run to help him.[6] Rabbanit Yehudit reports that many nights, after learning in his bedroom for a while, he would lie down in bed, but a half-hour later he would awaken and start learning again.

DESPITE THE FRENETIC SCHEDULE HE SET FOR HIMSELF, Harav Ovadia was a very gracious person. Despite being a public figure, he was actually shy by nature, and did not feel comfortable having outsiders at his *seudot*. Rabbanit Yehudit says that she rarely invited guests around whom he might feel uncomfortable. When he realized that she was avoiding inviting her own parents, concerned that he wouldn't be relaxed in their company, he encouraged her to invite them.

Always Gracious

At the Shabbat meals, he would talk about a variety of topics. "I wish I could have recorded some of those conversations," says Rabbanit Yehudit wistfully, "especially the ones in which he told stories of his own life.

"His *divrei Torah* invariably contained *mussar*. But he wouldn't deliver his *mussar* directly; rather, he would tell a story or a *dvar Torah* that related to something that had happened that week. Although he didn't reprove anyone explicitly, the person to whom the message was directed generally understood that he was addressing him or her."

And no meal — weekday or Shabbat — would end without Harav Ovadia thanking his daughter-in-law for the food she prepared, using an expression in Arabic that means, "May your hands be blessed."

LIKE MUCH OF HARAV OVADIA'S LIFE, HIS FINAL FEW MONTHS were a roller-coaster of tragedy and triumph.

Losing a Son

On 2 Iyar 5774, almost exactly half a year before Harav Ovadia's *petira*, his son, Rav Yaakov Hai, passed away after a yearlong battle with cancer. Shortly before his passing, the two met in a very tearful and highly publicized

---
6. See p. 454.

farewell. During the *shiva*, nearly every Torah leader in Eretz Yisrael — even those who had disputed Harav Ovadia's rulings vociferously — came to console him.

But the Rav suffered even greater heartache from the latest round of secular-religious tensions in Eretz Yisrael. During the 2013 Knesset election, the Yesh Atid and Bayit Yehudi parties garnered a combined total of 31 seats and joined the coalition led by Binyamin Netanyahu of Likud. The leaders of these two parties set a precondition for their joining the government: they would compel nearly all yeshiva students to join the IDF in some capacity. Although Harav Ovadia was not averse to military service — many of his sons and sons-in-law are IDF

Rav Yaakov Yosef with Harav Ovadia

Harav Ovadia and his four surviving sons recite the *hashkava* for his son, Rav Yaakov Hai Yosef. R-L: Rav Yitzchak, Rav David, Rav Moshe, and Rav Avraham.

veterans — he was strongly opposed to forcing yeshiva students into the army.

Yesh Atid also had several other anti-Torah items on their agenda, such as wresting control of marriage-related issues from the Rabbanut and finding a way to convert people who had no plans to keep Torah and mitzvot. For Harav Ovadia, this was a tragic déjà vu, as he had fought similar battles for decades, with tensions reaching a peak during his years as chief rabbi.

Elections for the two chief rabbi positions were also scheduled for 2013, with some candidates talking openly about finding ways to "solve" the halachic problems related to conversion and marriage. This rhetoric harked back to Harav Ovadia's own days at the helm of the Rabbanut.[7] Harav Ovadia watched the election campaign unfold with no small measure of fear and concern.

Not long before the elections, his son Rav Yitzchak, author of over 30 volumes of *Yalkut Yosef*, announced his candidacy, as did Rav David Lau, a son of Harav Ovadia's close friend Rav Yisrael Meir Lau, who had served as Ashkenazi chief rabbi from 1993-2003.

The election results were far from a foregone conclusion. Riding on a wave of anti-religious sentiment, those seeking to challenge Torah and halacha united in support of the candidates for chief rabbi who had promised to compromise on halachic issues.

Nevertheless, on 17 Av 5773, Rav Yitzchak Yosef and Rav David Lau were elected Sephardic and Ashkenazic chief rabbis, respectively, allaying some of Harav Ovadia's fears for the future.

Uniting Klal Yisrael Once More

IN HIS FINAL MONTHS, HARAV OVADIA STRUGGLED WITH SEVeral illnesses. As his condition deteriorated, Jews throughout Eretz Yisrael — Sephardi and Ashkenazi, religious and secular — rallied to pray for him and accept specific mitzva resolutions upon themselves as a merit for his full recovery.

At times, his prospects for recovery looked promising, but after each of these upturns his condition would deteriorate yet again.

---

7. See Chapter 18.

Rav Benzion Mutzafi had a chilling observation regarding those final months. "The *Zohar* (*Parashat Pinhas*) states that when Klal Yisrael is supposed to undergo a calamity, HaKadosh Baruch Hu will allow the Satan to cause a *tzaddik* pain, for the pain of a *tzaddik* can prevent tragedy from befalling the entire generation.

"At one point during his illness," recalled Rav Mutzafi, "well-meaning people were asking others to 'donate' some time from their lives to Harav Ovadia. I told them that it wouldn't work, because the time of ordinary people is not equivalent to the time of a *tzaddik*."

Rav Mutzafi then noted that we might have witnessed with our own eyes the result of the Satan's attention being "diverted" to Harav Ovadia. "Before Rosh Hashana (5774), there was speculation that Syria would soon invade Israel with unprecedented force — a threat that didn't materialize in the end. Who knows if the danger wasn't forestalled because in his final months, when he was in such intense pain and could not learn, Harav Ovadia was actually protecting us from catastrophe?"

Rav Ovadia had the unique *nahat* of watching his son being coronated as Rishon LeZion.

Last Rays

THOUGH HIS BODY WAS RACKED WITH PAIN DURING HIS LAST weeks, there were two high points during that time. On 12 Tishrei 5774, Harav Ovadia's doctors cleared him to take part in the coronation of his son Rav Yitzchak as Rishon LeZion, some four decades after his own coronation ceremony in the very same Beit Knesset Rabbi Yohanan ben Zakkai in the Old City. He was able to enjoy the unique *nahat* of placing the *mitznefet* on his own son's head, seeing the next generation carry forth his legacy in the public arena.

Last Shabbat at Home

HIS LAST SHABBAT AT 45 HAKABLAN WILL FOREVER BE engraved on the minds of the family of Rav Moshe and Rabbanit Yehudit Yosef. It was Shabbat Hol HaMoed Succot, and already on Friday, there were signs that Harav Ovadia's kidneys weren't functioning properly. Yet he was fully conscious, and the pain that had gripped his body for weeks had somehow subsided. That Shabbat, for the first time in months, he was able to sit at the table, and he even summoned his grandchildren Aharon and Efrat for *zimun* — something that had not happened in several months because he had been too weak.

Though he *looked* better than he had in weeks, several times during that Shabbat, Harav Ovadia alluded to the family that he realized that his life was ebbing away. At one point on Shabbat, he called out to his grandson Avraham. When Rabbanit Yehudit heard him calling, she hurried over to tell him that Avraham wasn't home.

"Actually," Harav Ovadia replied, "I wanted to speak to you." In his modesty, Harav Ovadia never called his daughter-in-law's name aloud, even though he lived in her home for close to 20 years; he had summoned Avraham to ask him to call his mother.

"I wanted to thank you for all the years you cared for me," he began. "I know it wasn't easy to have me around, and I apologize for the burden."

Rabbanit Yehudit relates that tears immediately sprang to her eyes as she tried to allay his fears. "We'll continue to care for you," she told him.

"But I could see that he didn't accept what I said," she continued. "He waved with his hands, as if to say, 'I know that my days are numbered.'"

There was another goodbye during that Shabbat. A nurse who lived in far-off Gilo had always been devoted to Harav Ovadia, dropping everything at a moment's notice to come give him an injection or take blood samples. Earlier on Shabbat, when the family noticed Harav Ovadia's condition deteriorating, they sent a non-Jew to summon the nurse to do a blood test. When she finished taking blood, Harav Ovadia thanked her for her devotion over the years and complimented her on her professionalism. She, too, tried to convince him that she would yet have the opportunity to serve him, but it was clear that he was sure that Harav Ovadia wouldn't recover.

On Motza'ei Shabbat, Maran Ovadia summoned his grandson Avraham, who, as a strapping 16-year-old, was the one most able to help him during the last months of his life, from the time his condition began to deteriorate. Harav Ovadia thanked him profusely for all the time and energy he had expended in helping him, and Avraham walked out of the room visibly confused, until his mother explained in a few words that Harav Ovadia was obviously saying his goodbyes.

At that point, his doctors arrived and determined that he had to be hospitalized; the blood test the nurse had taken showed that his kidneys were in near-complete failure. Harav Ovadia begged his family not to hospitalize him. He apparently sensed that he would not survive, and he wanted to die at home. But his medical condition necessitated that he be taken to the hospital.

Before being wheeled into a waiting ambulance, Harav Ovadia — ever scrupulous about halacha — insisted on eating *Seuda Revi'it* (*Melaveh Malka*). Since he had no appetite, he asked for a minimal amount of bread to fulfill his obligation, but Rabbanit Yehudit offered to prepare one of his favorite foods. This improved his appetite slightly, and he thanked her profusely once again for her help.

After two uneventful days in the hospital, Harav Ovadia's lung collapsed, and he was unconscious for ten days, sending world Jewry into prayer on his behalf. In those last weeks, yeshivot throughout Eretz Yisrael — both Sephardi and Ashkenazi — interrupted their learning several times to pray for Harav Ovadia when news came from the hospital that his condition had worsened. A radio station hosted a program during which callers could take some mitzva upon themselves as a merit for his recovery. Callers kept the phones busy throughout the duration of the program, resolving to improve in Shabbat observance, *tzniut*, *lashon hara*, and many other areas.

It wasn't only religious Jews who were concerned for him; myriads of secular Jews united on his behalf as well. Nearly every newscast — even on secular stations — began with an update on his condition. It was as though the entire country was on hold, waiting to hear of his miraculous recovery.

More importantly, many non-religious Jews were willing to take on a concrete action in his merit, each person on his or her level. At a *sheloshim* gathering, Rav Erez Elharar related that he has a friend who lives in Ashkelon, not far from the Mediterranean Sea. On Motza'ei Shabbat Hol HaMoed Succot, he was attempting to fall asleep in his *succa*, but his sleep was disturbed by a raucous party on a nearby beach. The revelers had set up a loudspeaker system, and the "music" was deafening.

Suddenly, when it was already past midnight, the music stopped, and the DJ announced, "Ladies and gentlemen, we just received news that Harav Ovadia Yosef is gravely ill. We are going to stop and recite *Tehillim* on his behalf."

The *Tehillim* was followed by *Kabbalat Ol Malchut Shamayim*. "Even Jews so far removed from Torah sensed that Maran was their leader," noted Rav Elharar, "and they realized that they should stop their festivities to pray for him."

Huge billboards went up on buildings and buses all over the country, with a picture of Harav Ovadia and the caption, "*Ohavim Otecha Maran* — We love you, Maran," reminding everyone to pray for his recovery.

One Final Hope

LESS THAN A WEEK BEFORE HIS PASSING, HARAV OVADIA came out of his coma, and Jews around the globe began to hope for a full recovery.

When he awoke, his vocal chords had been damaged as a result of intubation, and he could only motion. The first things he motioned for were a lulav and etrog. When family members informed him that he had been in a coma for ten days, and Succot had ended, he immediately motioned that he wanted his tefillin. His assistant R' Tzvi Hakak helped him don his tefillin, and he recited the beracha.

Notwithstanding the hopes and dreams of Jews around the world, Harav Ovadia seemed to know that it was only a matter of time. In his last words on earth, Harav Ovadia expressed a wish to be in Olam Haba already, where the pain that made it impossible to learn Torah would be gone. "If I can't learn," he told Rav Moshe, "then what is the purpose of my life?"

Petira

ON MONDAY MORNING, 3 HESHVAN 5774, ISRAEL WOKE UP TO the news that Harav Ovadia was in critical condition. Friends and relatives streamed to Hadassah Hospital, while the rest of the country continued to pray. In the early afternoon, hospital officials conveyed the sad news that Harav Ovadia had passed away, throwing the entire country — and countless others around the world — into mourning.

The funeral was scheduled for 6 p.m. that evening, mere hours after Harav Ovadia's passing. Yerushalayim had seen many massive *levayot* over the years, but nothing could have prepared the police for this turnout.

An estimated 850,000 people, running the gamut of Israeli society, came to pay their last respects to Harav Ovadia — and that figure does not include the multitudes who could not make it into Yerushalayim in time. Taking into account all those in Israel who wanted to participate, the figure rises to well over a million. The streets were so crammed that it took several hours for the bier

Harav Ovadia's *kever* in Sanhedria Cemetery

to make its way from Yeshivat Porat Yosef in Geula to Sanhedria Cemetery — a walk that ordinarily takes 15 minutes.

The mourning did not end with the funeral; each night during the *shiva*, public *hespedim* were held in yeshivot and *batei knesset*

throughout the world, with hundreds of thousands turning out to hear words of inspiration. At the end of the *shiva*, tens of thousands attended an event held near Sanhedria Cemetery where Harav Ovadia was buried. Jews the world over — even those far removed from Judaism — were disconsolate.

As Rav Benzion Mutzafi so poignantly expressed it:

> *Even people distant from Torah found themselves crying after his petira, because even if externally they didn't realize what his presence in this world did for them, their neshamot did recognize it.*

Sign covering several floors of a building at the entrance to Yerushalayim expressed the public's sense of loss.

> *The morning after the levaya, I took a cab ride in Yerushalayim. The driver was obviously not religious, and certainly hadn't prayed that morning. He didn't know who I was or that I had some kesher to Maran, but he turned to me and said,* "אֵין לִי חֵשֶׁק לַעֲבוֹד הַיוֹם — *I have no interest in working today."*
>
> *"Why?" I asked him.*
>
> *"Maran is gone," he replied. "What do we have to live for?"*

Maran's life had been replete with valiant efforts to bring his brethren — every Jew he could reach — closer to Judaism. And in the final analysis, even those who had not yet returned to mitzva observance expressed — with their presence at the *levaya* and the tears they shed upon the loss of the giant who to them represented Hashem and his Torah — a desire to eventually find their way back.

That desire found expression in three words posted throughout the country in the weeks before his passing:

Ohavim Otecha, Maran.

EPILOGUE
IF SEFARIM COULD SPEAK

IT HAS BEEN NINETY-odd years since we first met. Your reaction upon meeting us, even as a tiny child, was to embrace us with all your heart. At just 6 years old, you were driven to take us in hand and slowly, with great effort, decipher the millennia-old secrets hidden within us.

Things moved quickly after that. By 10 you had mastered whole sections by heart; by 17 you were placing us upon a lectern and beginning to teach others.

We traveled together far and wide. First we were in Egypt, where a policeman instructed you to reveal your weapons — and you pointed to us.

And weapons we would be, when you brought us back to Eretz Yisrael and used us to begin a revolution. It was you who turned the few in your community who delighted in our words into the hundreds of thousands who now study us each day.

We would wait with great anticipation, soldiers each of us, waiting to be called to milhamta shel Torah, the "war" of Torah. How our authors – many of them long since forgotten – must have rejoiced when you pulled us from your shelves, unveiling their pure and holy expressions to a world that would otherwise never have known that they existed.

And then you added to our numbers, growing increasingly prolific as you grew older, until your soul gave out in the midst of several new volumes.

Maran, on that last Motza'ei Shabbat at home, when your body ceased to function but your spirit still burned strong, we watched you being wheeled out to the hospital. You had said your goodbyes that day, to your family and to those who had assisted you. You knew that you weren't coming back.

As you were wheeled past us, tears appeared at the corner of your eyes. And then slowly, they trickled down your face as you said your last goodbye to us – your most beloved treasure of all. And though human eyes may not have seen it, we shed our own copious tears that night, realizing that our general would never return.

We miss you, Maran. We miss being held in your reverent grasp, your holy eyes pressed into our pages. But we are sure that your lips continue to murmur in the grave – שִׂפְתוֹתֶיךָ דּוֹבְבוֹת בַּקֶּבֶר – as you delight in the reward of a lifetime spent in pursuit of the ultimate Truth.

GLOSSARY

Note: We have provided Ashkenazic transliteration in parentheses following the Sephardic transliteration.

admor (pl. *admorim*) — leader of a Hassidic community.

Aggada — homiletical, non-halachic teaching of the Sages.

aguna (pl. *agunot*) — lit., *chained*; a woman who cannot remarry because she has not received a halachic divorce or because her husband is missing.

Aharon (*Acharon*) (pl. *Aharonim*) — authoritative commentators on the Talmud, late-14th century to the present.

ahavat Hashem (*ahavas Hashem*) — love of Hashem.

ahavat haTorah (*ahavas haTorah*) — love of the Torah.

ahdut (*achdus*) — unity.

ahuz hahasima (*achuz hachasimah*) — the minimum number of votes necessary to receive a Knesset seat.

aliya (pl. *aliyot*) — lit., *going up*; immigration to Israel.

am ha'aretz — ignoramus.

ameilut — toil, esp. in Torah study.

Amora'im — Sages cited in the Gemara.

aron kodesh — holy ark.

Arvit — the evening prayer service; Maariv.

askan (pl. *askanim*) — community activist.

atzeret teshuva (pl. *atzarot teshuva*) — repentance gathering.

Av Beit Din — the head of a religious court.

avreich — a young married man.

b'diavad — after the fact.

b'iyun — in-depth study.

baalebatim — lit., *householders*; laymen.

baal teshuva — a penitent; one who returns to mitzvah observance.

bakashot — requests; here, requests made during prayer.

bal talin — the prohibition of making a worker wait for his wages.

batei din — rabbinical courts.

battim — *tefillin* boxes containing verses of Scripture.

bedikat hametz (*bedikas chametz*) — the search for *hametz* carried out on the night before the Pesah Seder.

Beit HaMikdash (*Beis HaMikdash*) — the Holy Temple in Jerusalem.

beit knesset (pl. *batei knesset*) — synagogues, houses of worship.

bekiut (*bekius*) — breadth of Torah knowledge.

ben Torah (pl. *bnei Torah*) — one who studies and observes the teachings of the Torah.

ben zekunim — lit., *the child of one's old age*; a child born when his/her parents are elderly; one's youngest child.

Birkat Hamazon (Bircas Hamazon) — Grace After Meals; the series of four blessings recited after eating bread.

bishul — cooking.

bitul Torah — idle use of time that could be used for Torah study.

bodek — a ritual inspector; one who checks the animal after it is slaughtered to determine whether it had any blemishes that would render it nonkosher.

brit, brit mila (bris, bris milah) (pl. *britot*) — circumcision.

chinuch — see *hinuch*.

Chinuch Atzmai — lit., *independent education*; the organization in charge of religious schools in Israel.

daf — lit., *page*; one folio of the Gemara.

dayan (pl. *dayanim*) — halachic decisor or judge.

derasha (pl. *derashot*) — a Torah lecture; sermon or Torah discourse.

dibbuk (pl. *dibbukim*) — a spirit that enters into a living person.

dikduk — Hebrew grammar.

din Torah — 1. case brought to a halachic court. 2. decision rendered by a halachic court.

diskit — a soldier's metal ID tag; a dog tag.

dvar Torah (pl. *divrei Torah*) — a lesson from the Torah; a Torah thought

eirusin — engagement.

eruv — lit., *mixture*; refers to several halachic procedures or devices, most commonly used to refer to a string surrounding the perimeter of an area to allow people to carry within that place on Shabbat.

Eishet Hayil (Eishes Chayil) — (u.c.) Mishlei 31:10-31, traditionally recited before the Friday night Shabbat meal. (l.c.) a woman of valor; a worthy wife.

eishet ish — lit., *the wife of a man*; refers to the prohibition of a married woman remarrying while her first husband is still alive.

emuna — faith; belief in G-d; faithfulness.

erva — illicit relationships.

etrog (esrog) — a citron, one of the Four Species taken in hand during the Succot Festival.

ezrat nashim (ezras nashim) — women's section in a synagogue.

gabbai (pl. *gabbaim*) — person responsible for the proper functioning of a synagogue or other communal body; sexton.

gadol (pl. *gedolim*) — lit., *great*; a great Torah scholar; a term referring to a person of great stature; a saintly individual.

gan (pl. *ganim*) — preschool.

gaon (pl. *geonim*) — brilliant Torah scholar.

gedolei Yisrael — outstanding Torah scholars.

get (pl. *gittin*) — halachic bill of divorce.

gezeira (pl. *gezeirot*) — a decree.

gilgul, gilgulei neshamot (gilgulei neshamos) (pl. *gilgulim*) — reincarnation of the soul into another living being.

giyus banot (giyus banos) — mandatory conscription of women into the Israeli Army.

glima — traditional robe worn by Sephardic rabbis.

guf haboher (guf habocher) — the committee formed to elect the chief rabbi.

hacham (chacham) (pl. *hachamim*) — lit., *a wise person*; here, a rabbinic leader.

hachtara — coronation.

hag (chag) (pl. *hagim*) — the Festivals.

halacha — a Torah Law.

halak — glatt kosher; meat from animals that were found to be free of blemishes called *sirchot*.

haluka (chalukah) — lit., *sharing*; the system through which Jews in Europe shared the merit of living in Eretz Yisrael by providing support to its religious Jewish residents.

halutz (chalutz) (pl. *halutzim*) — pioneer.

hametz (chametz) — leavened foods prohibited during the Passover festival.

hamin (chamin) — lit., *something hot*; here, cholent, a stew prepared before the Sabbath and kept hot overnight.

hareidi (chareidi) — strictly religiously observant.

Hashem — G-d.
hashgaha (hashgachah) (pl. *hashgahot*) — (u.c.) Divine intervention; Hashem's involvement in every aspect of existence; (l.c.) rabbinic supervision on food; supervision.
hashkafa (pl. *hashkafot*) — outlook; ideology; worldview; a concept of *emuna*; perspective.
haskama (pl. *haskamot*) — approbation.
hashkava — lit., *laid to rest*; Sephardic memorial service.
has veshalom (chas veshalom) — G-d forbid.
hatmana — insulating.
hatmada (hasmadah) — diligence.
hattan (chassan) — a bridegroom.
hatzlaha (hatzlachah) — success.
hatzuf (chatzuf) — insolent one.
havruta (chavrusa) (pl. *havrutot*) — a study partner.
hazzan (chazzan) (pl. *hazzanim*) — a cantor; one who leads the prayer service in the synagogue.
hesped — a eulogy.
hessed (chessed) — lovingkindness; acts of beneficence; charitable giving.
heter — permission; something permitted.
heter agunot — finding a halachic basis to free women whose husbands' whereabouts are unknown.
hiddush (chiddush) (pl. *hiddushim*) — Talmudic or halachic novella.
hilchot Shabbat (hilchos Shabbos) — the laws pertaining to Shabbat observance.
hillul Hashem (chillul Hashem) — desecration of Hashem's Name.
hillul Shabbat (chillul Shabbos) — desecration of the Sabbath.
hilula — anniversary of a person's death.
hinuch (chinuch) — Jewish education; Torah education (of minors).
hinuch ahid (chinuch achid) — unified education.
hizzuk (chizzuk) — emotional support; encouragement.
Hol HaMoed (Chol HaMoed) — the intermediate days between the first and last days of Pesah and Succot.
huppa (chuppah) — 1. a wedding canopy. 2. the marriage ceremony.

issur v'heter — lit., *prohibited and permitted*; the laws that related to *kashrut*.
k'vatikin (k'vasikin) — at sunrise.
Kabbala — (u.c.) the body of Jewish mystical teachings. (l.c.) lit., *acceptance*; the act of taking on a specific action to elevate oneself spiritually; an obligation taken upon oneself.
Kabbalat Ol Malchut Shamayim (Kabbalas Ol Malchus Shamayim) — reciting a series of verses including *Shema Yisrael* and other acknowledgments of G-d as Sovereign and Master over the Universe.
kalla (pl. *kallot*) — a bride.
kamei'ot (kamios) — amulets.
kapparat avonot (kapparas avonos) — an atonement for sins.
kasher — to make fit for use according to Torah law; purified; to purge (a utensil) of absorbed nonkosher taste.
kavas — an honor guard who accompanies key government figures.
kaytanot (katanos) — day camps.
kedusha — holiness; sanctity.
kesher — connection.
ketuba (kesubah) (pl. *kesubos*) — marriage contracts.
kibbutz (pl. *kibbutzim*) — a communal farm.
Kiddush — the prayer said over wine, before the Friday evening or Saturday lunch Sabbath meal.
kiddush Hashem — sanctification of G-d's holy Name.
kippa (pl. *kippot*) — a yarmulke; a skullcap.
kiruv — outreach; outreach movement drawing people to Torah observance.
klalei haShas — the rules of how specific words and phrases are used in the Talmud.
Klal Yisrael — Jewish people in general; the Jewish nation.
koha d'heteira adif (kocha d'heteira adif) — lit., *the power of permitting is preferable*; a halachic approach that seeks to establish valid halachic grounds — if they exist — to permit certain actions.
kol b'isha erva — the prohibition against a man hearing a woman sing.

kollel (pl. *kollelim*) — an academy of higher Jewish study, usually for married men.

Kotel (Kosel), Kotel HaMaaravi — the Western Wall.

Kriat HaTorah (Krias HaTorah) — the reading of the Torah in the synagogue.

Kriat Shema (Krias Shema) — three paragraphs of the Torah recited twice daily, beginning with the words "*Shema Yisrael,* Hear, O Israel."

ktav rabbanut (ksav rabbanus) — a rabbinic installation letter.

kuntres (pl. *kuntreisim*) — a pamphlet; here, a section of a larger written work; a chapter.

l'hayim (l'chaim) — a toast over a drink of wine or whiskey.

l'chatchilah — initially; in the preferred manner.

lashon hara — lit., *evil speech*; forbidden speech, including gossip and slander.

lehumra — stringently.

lehavdil — lit., *to separate*; used when making a point of comparison between something sacred and something mundane.

lomdus (lomdut) — the approach to learning developed in the Lithuanian yeshivot. It requires the learner to study the subject he is learning in depth, presenting as many possible *sevarot* in each direction in order to come to a valid approach to a *sugya*.

luhot habrit (luchos habris) — the Tablets of the Ten Commandments.

lulav — a palm branch, one of the Four Species taken in hand on Succot.

maamad hachtara — a coronation ceremony.

maasrot — tithes.

mahloket (machloket) — an argument; a dispute.

makolet — a grocery store.

mamlachti — national educational system.

mamlachti-dati — lit., *national-religious*; educational system run by the government for religious students.

mamzeirut (mamzeirus) — illegitimacy.

mamzer (pl. *mamzerim*) — child born from a forbidden union.

mara d'atra (mara d'asra) — lit., *the owner of the land*; the uncontested rav of a city.

mashgiah (mashgiach) (pl. *mashgihim*) — 1. (cap.) dean of students in a yeshiva who oversees students' spiritual and ethical development. 2. *kashrut* supervisor.

matmid (masmid) (pl. *matmidim*) — 1. an exceptionally dedicated Torah scholar who spends much time immersed in Torah study. 2. exceptionally diligent student.

mekadesh — to sanctify.

mekarev — to bring closer to religious observance.

mekubal (pl. *mekubalim*) — a Kabbalist.

melachot (melachos) — the 39 labors forbidden to be performed on the Sabbath.

melamed tinokot (melamed tinokos) — teacher of young children.

melechet Shamayim (meleches Shamayim) — the work of Heaven.

melicha — salting during the koshering process.

menahel ruhani — dean in charge of spiritual development.

menahem avel (menachem avel) — to comfort a mourner; to pay a condolence call.

mesader kiddushin — the person who performs the marriage ceremony.

mesora — Jewish heritage.

mezonot (mezonos) — lit., *food*; (n.) support.

Mi Shebeirach — a prayer invoking Heavenly blessings.

mide'oraita (mide'oraisa) — [based on] Torah law.

mide'rabbanan — [based on] Rabbinic law.

midrash (pl. *midrashim*) — homiletic teachings of the Sages.

mikveh (pl. *mikvaot*) — a ritual bath; a ritual pool made under specific halachic specifications used for both purification and conversion.

milkamta shel Torah — lit., *war of Torah*; the struggle to maintain a Torah-true life.

minyan (pl. *minyanim*) — quorum of ten men necessary for conducting a prayer service.

mitznefet — the turban-like hat worn by Sephardic rabbis.

mo'adon (pl. *mo'adonim*) — club.
mohel (pl. *mohelim*) — one who performs a circumcision.
moreh derech — a mentor who guides one through life.
moshav (pl. *moshavim*) — a settlement in which the land is owned communally.
moshava — a settlement in which each parcel of land is owned by an individual.
mukar she'einu rishmi — recognized but unofficial (school).
mussar — ethical teachings geared toward self-refinement; reproof.
nahat (*nachas*) — satisfaction; pleasure, usually from one's children; spiritual or emotional pleasure.
nekudot (*nekudos*) — Hebrew vowels.
neshama (pl. *neshamot*) — the soul.
neveila (pl. *neveilot*) — carrion; the carcass of an animal that died without benefit of *shehita*.
niftar — (n.) a person who has died. (v.) died.
nussah, nussah hatefilla — the text of the prayer service.
oleh (pl. *olim*) — 1. one who immigrates to Israel. 2. one called to the Torah during prayer services.
olei — immigrants from ....
oneg Shabbat — lit., *joy of Sabbath*; engaging in pleasurable activities on the Sabbath.
parasha (pl. *parashiyot*) — the weekly Torah portion; parchment inscribed with Torah paragraphs and inserted into *tefillin*.
parashat hashavua (*parashas hashavuah*) — the weekly Torah portion.
parochet (*paroches*) — the curtain covering the Torah ark in a synagogue.
pattur — exempt.
perek (pl. *perakim*) — a chapter.
petira — lit., *departure*; death; .
pidyon shevuyim — the mitzva to redeem prisoners.
pikuah nefesh (*pikuach nefesh*) — mortal danger; a life-and-death situation.
pilpul (pl. *pilpulim*) — vigorous analysis of Talmudic topics.

Pirkei Avot (*Pirkei Avos*) — Ethics of the Fathers.
piyut (pl. *piyutim*) — liturgical poem.
posek (pl. *poskim*) — halachic authority; authoritative Rabbinic decisor.
posek aharon (*posek acharon*) — the final judge; the judge who has the final word when delivering a verdict.
prozbol — a mechanism in which the lender "hands over" his loan to *beit din*, and may then collect the loan after *Shemitta*.
psak — a halachic ruling.
psak halacha (pl. *piskei halacha*) — a rabbinical decision made on a halachic issue.
Raavad — acronym for Rav Av Beit Din.
rabbotai (*rabbosai*) — lit., *gentlemen*, a polite term of address.
rebbi (pl. *rebbeim*) — a male Torah teacher.
refua sheleima — lit., *a full/complete recovery*; a blessing for a complete/speedy recovery extended to an ailing person.
remez (pl. *remazim*) — allusion.
Rishon (pl. *Rishonim*) — early commentators on the Talmud, 11th-15th centuries.
Rosh Hamemshala — head of state; prime minister.
rosh yeshiva (pl. *roshei yeshiva*) — the dean of a yeshiva; senior lecturer in a yeshiva.
rosh keves — the head of a sheep; here, the head of a sheep used to commemorate the Binding of Yitzhak, eaten on Rosh Hashana Eve as a omen for a good year.
rov — majority.
ruah hakodesh (*ruach hakodesh*) — Divine inspiration; Divine Spirit.
safrut (*safrus*) — the writing of holy texts on parchment.
sakanot nefashot (*sakanos nefashos*) — risk to life.
sandak — person who holds the baby while the *brit* is performed.
sefer (pl. *sefarim*) — a book, specifically a book on Torah subjects.
Sefer HaZikaron — memorial book written to commemorate an event or the anniversary of a death.
Selihot (*Selichos*) — prayers said during the Ten Days of Repentance.
semiha (*semichah*) — Rabbinical ordination.
seuda — meal.

seuda hamafseket (*seudah hamafsekes*) — the final meal eaten before the fasts of Yom Kippur and Tisha B'Av.

Seuda Revi'it (*Seuda Revi'is*) — lit., *the fourth meal;* Melaveh Malka, a meal eaten after the Sabbath ends to "escort" the Sabbath Queen.

seudat mitzva (*seudas mitzvah*) — a festive meal, characterized by speeches of *divrei Torah,* celebrating completion of a volume of the Talmud or other significant event.

seudat preida (*seudas preida*) — a farewell banquet.

seudat Shabbat (*seudas Shabbos*) — the festive meal(s) served on the Sabbath.

sevarot (*sevaros*) — logical reasoning.

Shabbat (*Shabbos*) (pl. *Shabbotot*) — the Sabbath.

Shaharit (*Shacharis*) — the morning prayer service.

Shalom Aleichem — lit., *peace be with you;* Friday evening song of welcome to the ministering angels.

she'eila (pl. *she'eilot*) — a question asked of a rabbinical authority regarding a halachic issue.

shehita — ritual slaughter.

shekia — sunset.

sheloshim — the 30-day period of mourning observed for a close relative.

shemirat Shabbat (*shemiras Shabbos*) — Sabbath observance.

Shemitta — the Sabbatical year, occurring every seventh year, during which the land is not worked. This law pertains only to the Land of Israel.

shidduch (pl. *shidduchim*) — 1. match, esp. a marriage match. 2. proposed marriage match. 3. one's betrothed.

shikul hadaat (*shikul hadaas*) — one's own judgment.

shirei habakashot (*shirei habakashot*) — complex poetic *tefilla* compositions.

shiur (pl. *shiurim*) — a Torah lecture.

shiva — lit., *seven;* the seven-day mourning period immediately following the death of a close relative.

shlita — acronym for (Hebrew) "May he live a long and good life."

shohet (*shochet*) (pl. *shohtim*) — one who slaughters an animal in accordance with Torah law.

shtiebel (pl. *shtieblach*) — (Yiddish) lit., *room;* small synagogue, often situated in a house, used mainly by Hassidim.

siman (pl. *simanim*) — lit., *symbol;* foods traditionally eaten on Rosh Hashana because of their symbolic implications.

simha (*simchah*) (pl. *semahot*) — happiness, joy; a joyous occasion. 2. a celebration, esp. a celebration of a family milestone such as a wedding, a bar mitzva, or a birth.

simhat hahayim (*simchas hachaim*) — joie de vivre; a positive attitude toward life.

siyata d'Shmaya — Heavenly assistance; Divine Providence.

sofer (pl. *sofrim*) — a scribe who writes religious materials such as a Torah Scroll, a *mezuza, tefillin,* etc.

sugya (pl. *sugyot*) — topic.

ta'amim — cantillation notes for the Torah reading.

taharat hamishpaha (*taharas hamishpachah*) — the laws of family purity.

tallit (*tallis*) — four-cornered prayer shawl with *tzitzit,* worn during morning prayers.

talmid muvhak — lit., *primary student;* a devoted student.

Tannaim — the Sages who are quoted in the Mishna.

tefilla (pl. *tefillot*) — prayer.

tefillat haderech (*tefillas haderech*) — the wayfarer's prayer.

tefillin — phylacteries, small black leather boxes containing parchment scrolls inscribed with Biblical passages, bound to the arm and forehead of adult Jewish males during the weekday morning prayer service.

teivah — a coffin.

tereifot (*tereisfos*) — nonkosher foods.

teruma (pl. *terumot*) — the first portion of the crop separated and given to a Kohen.

teshuva (pl. *teshuvot*) — 1. answer. 2. repentance. 3. rediscovery of Torah Judaism. 4. an answer to a halachic query.

tikkun — rectification.

Tikkun Hatzot (*Tikkun Chatzos*) — prayer mourning the destruction of the Holy Temple, recited at midnight.

treif — colloquial term for nonkosher.

treifa (pl. *treifot*) — lit., *torn*; an animal that is mortally injured, therefore not kosher.

tzara (pl. *tzarot*) — difficult, painful situation.

tzidkut (tzidkus) — righteousness.

tzniut (tznius) — modesty.

vaad hakehilla — community council.

vatikin minyan (*vasikin minyan*) — the Shacharit service performed at the earliest possible time.

vidui — confession of sins recited on Yom Kippur and before death.

Yamim Nora'im — High Holidays.

yibbum — levirate marriage.

yirat Shamayim (*yiras Shamayim*) — fear of Heaven.

z'chut (*z'chus*) (pl. *zechuyot*) — merit.

zimun — lit., *invitation*; the brief introductory prayer to Grace After Meals.

zman (pl. *zmanim*) — lit., *time*; 1. the time the Sabbath or a holiday begins. 2. a school semester.

This volume is part of
THE ARTSCROLL SERIES®
an ongoing project of
translations, commentaries and expositions on
Scripture, Mishnah, Talmud, Midrash, Halachah,
liturgy, history, the classic Rabbinic writings,
biographies and thought.

For a brochure of current publications
visit your local Hebrew bookseller
or contact the publisher:

Mesorah Publications, ltd

4401 Second Avenue
Brooklyn, New York 11232
(718) 921-9000
www.artscroll.com